PHILOSOPHY: A SELECT, CLASSIFIED BIBLIOGRAPHY
OF ETHICS, ECONOMICS, LAW, POLITICS, SOCIOLOGY

PHILOSOPHICAL QUESTIONS SERIES

Editor in Chief

Sebastian A. Matczak, Ph. D., Th. D.
Professor of Philosophy
St. John's University
New York

No. 1. *Le Problème de Dieu dans la pensée de Karl Barth.* Louvain, Editions Nauwelaerts, 1968.

No. 2. *Research and Composition in Philosophy.* Louvain, Editions Nauwelaerts, 1968.

No. 3. *Philosophy: A Select, Classified Bibliography of Ethics, Economics, Law, Politics, Sociology.* Louvain, Editions Nauwelaerts, 1970.

No. 4. *Philosophy: Its Nature, Methods and Basic Sources.* In press.

No. 5. *Philosophy: Its Histories, Systems and Specific Settings.* To be published.

No. 6. M. R. Barral, Ph. D., *Progressive Neutralism: A Philosophical Aspect of American Education.* Louvain, Editions Nauwelaerts, 1970.

No. 7. W. Smith, Ph. D., *Giovanni Gentile on God.* Louvain, Editions Nauwelaerts, 1970.

Others will follow.

Library of Congress Catalog Card Number: 72-80678
LEARNED PUBLICATIONS, INC.
83-53 Manton St., Jamaica
New York

PHILOSOPHICAL QUESTIONS SERIES
3

SEBASTIAN A. MATCZAK

DOCTOR IN PHILOSOPHY, DOCTOR IN THEOLOGY,
PROFESSOR AT ST. JOHN'S UNIVERSITY, NEW YORK.

PHILOSOPHY

A Select, Classified Bibliography of Ethics, Economics, Law, Politics, Sociology

EDITIONS NAUWELAERTS

Muntstraat, 10, B 3000 — Louvain
rue de Fleurus, 4, 75006 — Paris

1970

BY THE SAME AUTHOR

Karl Barth on God: The Knowledge of the Divine Existence. New York: St. Paul's Publications (Alba House), 1962.

Le problème de Dieu dans la pensée de Karl Barth. Louvain: E. Nauwelaerts, 1968.

Fideism, Traditionalism. New York: The Catholic Encyclopedia (McGraw-Hill), 1967.

Stanislaus Cardinal Hosius on the Sacraments. Paris: Libella, 1951.

Stanislaus Cardinal Hosius: Present State of Research — Results and Postulates. New York: The Polish Review, 1961.

An Archiepiscopal Election in the Middle Ages: Jacob II Swinka. New York: The Polish Review, 1963.

A Select and Classified Bibliography of David Hume. Saint Louis, Mo.: The Modern Schoolman (Saint Louis University), 1964.

Research and Composition in Philosophy. Louvain: E. Nauwelaerts, 1968.

Philosophy: Its Nature, Methods and Basic Sources. In press.

Philosophy: Its Histories, Systems and Specific Settings. To be published.

ABOUT THE AUTHOR

Contemporary Authors (Detroit, Michigan: Gale Research Co.), Vol. IX-X, p. 322.

Directory of American Scholars (New York: R. R. Bowker), Vol. IV, p. 129; also Vol. V, 1968-1969.

Who's Who in American Education. 22nd ed. (Nashville, Tennessee: Who's Who in American Education), p. 988. In the Collection Vol. XXII (1965-66).

Who's Who in American Education. 23d ed. (3 vols. Hattiesburg, Mississippi: Who's Who in American Education), Vol. I, p. 553. In the Collection Vol. XXIII (1967-68).

Who's Who in the East (Chicago: Marquis — Who's Who, 1967), Vol. XI, p. 689; Vol XII, in press.

Directory of the Catholic Theological Society of America (Yonkers, New York: CTSA Editorial Office, 1965), p. 80.

Community Leaders of America. Raleigh, North Carolina: News Publishing Co., 1969.

Directory of International Biography. 6th. ed. London, S. W. 1: Artillery Mansions - Victoria Street, 1969-1970.

Reviews of his writings in various scholarly magazines.

PREFACE

The present work deals with selected and classified biblio-graphies in the fields of ethics, economics, law, politics, and sociology from the point of view of their relevance to philoso-phy. It is a part of a broader study embracing the whole of phi-losophy with its main branches and affiliated sciences. By chance, the treatment of ethics and its main related disci-plines is being published prior to the other studies on philoso-phy, which we hope, will appear in the near future as *Philo-sophical Questions Series*, No. 4.

At this time I would like to express my sincere gratitude to Mrs. Mabel A. Perham, for her retypings of the manuscript of the present study. My grateful thanks are also directed to John J. McDonnell and J. Angus Wilkinson, both F.M.S., for their help.

S. A. M.

New York

TABLE OF CONTENTS

Chapter I.   ETHICS

Chapter II. ECONOMICS

Chapter III.   LAW

Chapter IV. POLITICS

Chapter V. SOCIOLOGY

ABBREVIATIONS

PQS — *Philosophical Questions Series.* Louvain: Éditions Nauwelaerts, 1968—.
The number of the book in the *Series* is indicated with each abbreviation.

Above ⎰— they refer to this book, even to the same chapter
below ⎱ of this book, if not indicated otherwise.

Index — it refers to the Index at the end of this book.

S.l. — the place of publication not indicated.

S.d. — the date of publication not indicated.

S.p. — the same place of publication.

Other abbreviations are easily understandable.

———————

For quick reference to particular authors see the Index of Authors at the end of this book.

For the addresses of the Publishers see, *Publishers' International Year Book: World Directory of Book Publishers.* 5th ed. London W.C. 2: 18 Charing Cross Road 1968. Pp. 610.

INTRODUCTION

The bibliography which is offered here has the main purpose of calling the attention of the student of philosophy to various fields in which his studies have been and may continue to be conducted. Consequently, this bibliography is not and even cannot be completed, for that is the task of a researcher working on a specific topic. However, the present work offers selected writings which may lead to other treatises, according to the personal interest of each individual; it may also suggest new fields for enquiry and research.

The bibliography listings can be completed relatively easily. The main sources to use for that purpose, particularly in the field of our own interest, are general bibliographies of philosophy and those of affiliated sciences. A prominent place among them belongs to these works:

Bibliographie de la philosophie. Paris: J. Vrin, 1935 —.
Répertoire bibliographique de la philosophie. Louvain: Éditions de l'Institut Supérieur de Philosophie, 1949 —.

The printed catalogues of large libraries are also of great importance. Particularly useful are the following:

British Museum General Catalogue of Printed Books. 263 vols. London: The Trustees of the British Museum, 1964-1966.
   Additions: 1963-1965. 6 vols. London: The Tustees of the British Museum, 1964-1966.
A Catalogue of Books Represented by Library of Congress Printed Cards. 2nd series. 167 vols. Through July 31, 1942. Ann Arbor, Michigan: Edwards, 1942-1946.
   Supplement. 42 vols. August 1942 - December 1947. Paterson, New Jersey: Rowman and Littlefield, 1963.
The Library of Congress: Author Catalog 1948-1952. 24 vols. New York: Rowman and Littlefield, 1964.
The National Union Catalog. A Cumulative Author List Representing Library of Congress Printed Cards and Titles Reported by Other American Libraries, 1953-1957. 28 vols. Paterson, New Jersey: Rowan and Littlefield, 1961. Also 1958-1962. 54 vols., 1963.
Library of Congress Catalog: A Cumulative List of Works Represented by Library of Congress Printed Cards. Books: Subjects, 1950-1954. 20 vols. Ann Arbor, Michigan: J. W. Edwards, 1955. Also 1955-1959, 22 vols. Totowa, New Jersey: Rowan and Littlefield, 1966. Also 1960-1964, 25 vols. Ann Arbor: J. W. Edwards, 1965. Also 1965. Washington, D.C.: The Library of Congress, 1966—.

Catalogue général des livres imprimés de la Bibliothèque Nationale.
192 vols. Paris: Paul Catin, 1905-1965.
Catalogue général des livres imprimés: Auteurs, 1960-1964. 8 vols. Paris:
Bibliothèque Nationale, 1965-1967.

We have divided the bibliography on ethics and its related
sciences into five main classes: (1) general ethics, simply
called ethics, (2) economics, (3) law, (4) politics, and (5) sociology.

General ethics is a science in itself. It constitutes a basis for
man's behavior, private as well as social. Economics and other
sciences offered here are considered, at least by some thinkers,
as related to ethics since their specific subject matter evokes
ethical questions.

Each of these branches is subdivided into (a) general studies,
(b) special studies, and (c) special questions. General studies
embrace histories of individual branches, systematic presen-
tations, and their philosophical studies, including ethics. Special studies are usually subdivided into particular historical
periods and countries. Special questions include specific problems characteristic of each of the branches. Further subdivi-
sions of these classes sometimes occur dictated by need or
usefulness.

In these divisions we also include studies of the subject
matter of a particular science, like histories of economics, politics, and so on. The reason for the listing these non-philoso-
phical works is that the scholar cannot develop his knowledge
of the philosophy and ethics inherent in the disciplines without
an awareness of their subject matter.

The bibliography is directed mainly to Englisch-speaking
students. Hence, the English studies are particularly empha-
sized, and placed before studies in other languages.

Some overlapping in the listings is unavoidable. We have
tried to place each work in the category where it basically belongs or where it can be consulted most profitably. For refe-
rences the Index of Authors at the end of this book may prove
particularly useful.

Chapter I

ETHICS

The term *ethics* is derived from ἦϑος, ἔϑος meaning custom, way of acting, character, behavior. Ethics is traditionally considered as one of the basic branches of philosophy. In this sense it is a science which deals with human actions and inquires into their characteristics, like good, right, evil, wrong, freedom, obligations and punishability. Ethics is taken also in a broader sense, namely, as a science of various customs, rules of behavior, and moral codes. Understood in both senses ethics is also a practice or art, an application of moral principles and rules in daily life.

The main ethical problems center around the meaning and nature of good, right, obligation, and sanction. More specific questions concern the existence of intrinsically good or evil actions, of an absolute standard of right and wrong, and the concept of freedom. There is also the warmly debated problem of the nature and task of ethics itself. The variety of answers to these problems is considerable, as may be seen from the classification listed below in the Bibliography.

From this variety of answers has emerged the science of meta-ethics, which analyzes them and tries to find the meaning or uses of the main ethical concepts. It must be added that ethical theories sometimes overlap. Meta-ethics may also be viewed as the philosophy of various ethical theories and an investigation of background and causes of their development. It also inquires into the consistency of the systematic presentation of the theories.

We have classified the answers to the ethical problems by indicating particular schools in the main periods of man's thought, and by emphasizing particular moral questions, like evil, freedom, medecine, value, and war. Modern and contemporary philosophers diverge from each other more significantly than did their predecessors. Consequently, their opinions require more detailed division than do those from earlier periods.

Bibliography

1. GENERAL STUDIES

See Bibliographies, above, p. XX, also Chs. II - V, 1; Encyclopedias, below, a, and in *PQS*, No. 4.

(a) Histories

In English

ABELSON, Raziel and NIELSEN, Kai, «History of Ethics», *The Encyclopedia of Philosophy* (8 vols. New York: The Macmillan Co., 1967), III, 81-117.
BRINTON, Crane C., *A History of Western Morals*. New York: Harcourt, Brace and World, Inc., 1959. Pp. 502.
BROAD, C. D., *Five Types of Ethical Theory*. New York: Harcourt, Brace and Company, 1930, Pp. XXV, 288.
BRUCE, A. B., *The Moral Order of the World in Ancient and Modern Thought*. London: Hodder and Stoughton, 1899. Pp. VIII, 431.
FERM, Vergilius, *Encyclopedia of Morals*. New York: Philosophical Library, 1956. Pp. 682.
HASTINGS, James, *Encyclopedia of Religion and Ethics*. 13 vols. New York: Charles Scribner's Sons, 1951. First published in 1928.
HOBHOUSE, L. T., *Morals in Evolution: A Study in Comparative Ethics*. London: Chapman and Hall, 1951. Pp. LIV, 648. First published in 1915.
HUDSON, W. D. (ed.), *New Studies in Ethics*. New York: St. Martin's Press, 1967. The series of studies on the main ethical theories.
JONES, W. T.; BECKNER, Morton; FOGELIN, Robert; SONTAG, Frederick (eds.), *Approaches to Ethics*. New York: McGraw-Hill Co., 1962. Pp. 592.
MACINTYRE, Alasdair Chalmers, *A Short History of Ethics*. New York: The Macmillan Co., 1966. Pp. 280.
MARITAIN, Jacques, *La philosophie morale: examen historique et critique des grandes systèmes*. Paris: Gallimard, 1960. English translation by Marshall SUTHER *et al.*, *Moral Philosophy: An Historical and Critical Survey of the Great Systems*. New York: Charles Scribner's Sons, 1964. Pp. XII, 468. See also Scholastic Philosophy, in *PQS*, No. 5.
MARTINEAU, James, *Types of Ethical Theory*. 2 vols. 3rd ed. Oxford: Clarendon Press, 1889. First published in 1866.
MATHEWS, Shailer and SMITH, Gerald B., *A Dictionary of Religion and Ethics*. New York: The Macmillan Co., 1921. Pp. 513.
RAND, Benjamin, *The Classical Moralists*. Boston, Massachusetts: Houghton Mifflin, 1909. Pp. XIX, 797.

ROBERTSON, John Mackinnow, *A Short History of Morals*. London: Watts and Co., 1920. Pp. 475.

ROGERS, Reginald Arthur Percy, *A Short History of Ethics, Greek and Modern*. London: Macmillan and Co., 1911. Pp. 325.

SIDGWICK, Henry, *Outlines of the History of Ethics for English Readers*. 6th ed. London: Macmillan and Co., 1931. Pp. 350. First published in 1886.

WESTERMARCK, Edward Alexander, *The Origin and Development of the Moral Ideas*. 2 vols. London: Macmillan and Co., 1924-1926. First published in 1908.

In Other Languages

BILLICSICH, Friedrich, *Das Problem des Übels in de Philosophie des Abendlandes*. 2 vols. Vienna: Verlag Sexl, 1936-1952. See Evil, below, 3, p. 59.

Dictionnaires des passions, des vertus et des vices. 2 vols. Paris: Chez Vincent, 1769.

Dictionnaire de spiritualité: ascétique et mystique, doctrine et histoire. Ed. by M. Viller, S. J. *et al.* 19 fasc. Paris: Beauchesne et ses fils, 1932-1955 —.

DITTRICH, Ottmar, *Geschichte des Ethik. Die Systeme der Moral vom Altertum bis zur Gegenwart*. 4 vols. Leipzig: F. Meiner, 1926-1932.

EUCKEN, Rudolf, *Die Lebensanschauungen der grossen Denker. Eine Entwicklungsgeschichte des Lebensproblems der Menschheit von Plato bis zu Gegenwart*. 18th ed. Berlin: W. de Gruyter und Co., 1922. Pp. 564.

—— and CHANG, Carsun, *Das Lebensproblem in China und Europa*. Leipzig: Quelle und Meyer, 1922. Pp. VIII, 200.

JANET, Paul Alexandre René, *Histoire de la science politique dans ses rapports avec la morale*. 2 vols. Paris: F. Alcan, 1925. See Politics, below, Ch. IV, p. 176.

JODL, Friedrich, *Geschichte der Ethik als philosophischer Wissenschaft*. 2 vols. Stuttgart and Berlin: J. G. Gottasche Bundhandlung Nachfolger, 1912-1920.

LOTTIN, Odon, *Études de morale; histoire de doctrine*. Gembloux: J. Duculot, 1961. Pp. 365.

PADOVANI, Umberto A., *Storia della filosofia con particulare riguardo ai problemi morali*. 2 vols. 3rd ed. Como: Marzorati, 1950. Pp. VIII, 391. Vol. I: Il pensiero indiano. Vol. II: Il pensiero classico.

WENTSCHER, Max, *Geschichte der Ethik*. Berlin: Junker und Dunnhaupt, 1931. Pp. VI, 113.

(b) Systematic Studies

See also Special Studies, below, 2.

In English

ABELSON, Raziel (ed.), *Ethics and Metaphysics*. New York: St. Martin's Press, 1963. Pp. 592.

BOURKE, Vernon J., *Ethics: A Textbook in Moral Philosophy*. New York: The Macmillan Co., 1967. Pp. 497.

CRONIN, Michael, *The Science of Ethics*. 2 vols. 2nd impression. New York: Benzinger Brothers, 1920-1922. Also later impressions.

EDEL, Abraham, *Method in Ethical Theory*. New York: Bobbs-Merrill, 1963. Pp. 380.

EDWARDS, Paul, *The Logic of Moral Discourse*. New York: The Free Press (Macmillan Co.), 1965. Pp. 248.

EWING, A. C., *Ethics*. New York: The Macmillan Co., The Free Press, 1965. Pp. 160.

FAGOTHEY, Austin, S. J., *Right and Reason: Ethics in Theory and Practice*. St. Louis, Missouri: The C. V. Mosby Co., 1957. Pp. 583.

GARNER, Richard and ROSEN, Bernard, *Moral Philosophy: A Systematic Introduction to Normative Ethics and Meta-ethics*. New York: The Macmillan Co., 1967. Pp. 367.

HART, Samuel L., *Ethics: The Quest for the Good Life*. New York: Philosophical Library, 1963. Pp. 127.

HARTMANN VON, Nicolai, *Ethics*. 3 vols. Translated from the German by Stanton Coit. New York: The Macmillan Co., 1932. See Phenomenology, in *PQS*, No. 5.

HIGGINS, Thomas J., *Ethical Theories in Conflict*. Milwaukee, Wisconsin: The Bruce Publishing Co., 1967.

——, *Man as Man*. Milwaukee, Wisconsin: The Bruce Publishing Co., 1958.

HILDEBRAND VON, Erich and JOURDAIN, Alice, *True Morality and Counterfeits*. New York: McKay Co., 1955. Pp. 179.

HOSPERS, John, *Human Conduct: An Introduction to the Problems of Ethics*. New York: Harcourt, Brace and World, Inc., 1961. Pp. 600.

LAIRD, John, *An Enquiry into Moral Notions*. London: G. Allen and Unwin, 1935. Pp. 318.

MENCKEN, Henry Louis, *Treatise on Right and Wrong*. New York: Alfred A. Knopf, 1934. Pp. VIII, 331.

NIELSEN, Kai, «Problems of Ethics», *The Encyclopedia of Philosophy* (8 vols. New York: The Macmillan Co., 1967), Vol. III, pp. 117-134, see also pp. 69-81.

PEPPER, Stephen C., *Ethics*. New York: Appleton-Century-Crofts, 1960. Pp. 351.

RAPHAEL, David Daiches, *Moral Judgment*. London: George Allen and Unwin, 1955. Pp. 224.

SELSAM, Howard, *Ethics and Progress: New Values in a Revolutionary World*. New York: International Publishers, 1965. Pp. 126.

SIDGWICK, Henry, *The Methods of Ethics*. 6th ed. London: Macmillan, 1901. Pp. XXXVIII, 526. First published in 1875. See also Histories, above, a.

URBAN, Wilbur Marshall, *The Fundamentals of Ethics*. New York: Holt, Rinehart and Winston, Inc., 1930. Pp. 486.

WHEELWRIGHT, Philip, *A Critical Introduction to Ethics*. 3rd ed. New York: The Odyssey Press, 1959. First published in 1949. Pp. 401.

WILD, John, *Introduction to Realistic Philosophy*. New York: Harper and Row, 1948. Pp. 517.

WUNDT, Wilhelm Max, *Ethik. Eine Untersuchung der Thatsachen und Gesätze des sittlichen Lebens*. Stuttgart: Enke, 1886. Pp. XI, 577. English translation (from the 2nd ed. 1892) by E. B. Titschener *et al.*, *Ethics:*

An Investigation of the Facts and Laws of the Moral Life. London: Swan Sonnenschein and Co., and New York: The Macmillan Co., 1897-1901.

ZINK, Sidney, *The Concepts of Ethics.* New York: St. Martin's Press, 1962. Pp. 310.

In Other Languages.

CAPOGRASSI, Giuseppe, *Introduzione alla vita etica.* Turin: Edizioni di Filosofia, 1952. Pp. VI, 114.

EUCKEN, Rudolf, *Prolegomena und Epilog zu einer Philosophie des Geisteslebens.* Berlin: W. de Gruyter und Co., 1922. Pp. VIII, 156. See Histories, above, a.

GURVICH, Georges D., *Morale théorique et science des mœurs, leurs possibilité, leurs conditions.* Paris: F. Alcan, 1937. Pp. 208.

GUYAU, Jean Marie, *Esquisse d'une morale sans obligation ni sanction.* Paris F. Alcan, 1885. Pp. 254.

GUZZO, Augusto, *La moralità.* Turin: Edizioni di Filosofia, 1950. Pp. XXXIX, 530.

LECLERCQ, Jacques, *Les grandes lignes de la philosophie morale.* New edition. Louvain: E. Nauwelaerts, 1964.

LE SENNE, R., *Traité de morale générale.* Paris: Presses Universitaires de France, 1949. Pp. 763.

LOTTIN, Odon, *Morale fondamentale.* Tournai: Desclée et Cie, 1954. Pp. VII, 546.

NABERT, Jean, *Eléments pour une éthique.* Paris: Presses Universitaires de France, 1943. Pp. 240.

RAUH, Frédéric, *Essai sur le fondement métaphysique de la morale.* 3rd ed. Paris: F. Alcan, 1926. First published in 1890. Pp. 259.

(c) Excerpts from Selected Writings

ABELSON, Raziel (ed.), *Ethics and Metaphysics.* New York: St. Martin's Press, 1963, Pp. 587.

ALBERT, Ethel M., DENISE, Theodore C. and PETERFRUEND, Sheldon P. (eds.), *Great Traditions in Ethics.* New York: American Book Company, 1953. Pp. 362.

BRANDT, Richard (ed.), *Value and Obligation: Systematic Readings in Ethics.* New York: Harcourt, Brace and World, 1961. Pp. 715.

CASTANEDA, Calderon; HECTOR, Neri and NAKHNIKIAN, George (eds.), *Morality and the Language of Conduct.* Detroit: Wayne State University Press, 1963. Pp. 367.

CLARK, Gordon H. and SMITH, T. V. (eds.), *Readings in Ethics.* New York: Crofts, 1935; paper, 1963. Pp. 435.

DEWEY, Robert E.; GRAMLICH, Francis W. and LOFTSGORDON, Donald (eds.), *Problems of Ethics.* New York: Macmillan Co., 1961. Pp. 495.

EKMAN, Rosalind, *Readings in the Problems of Ethics.* New York: Charles Scribner's Sons, 1965. Pp. X, 369.

FOOT, Philippa (ed.), *Theories of Ethics.* New York: Oxford University Press, 1968. Pp. 190.

JOAD, C. E. M. (ed.), *Philosophy and Ethics: A Course of Selected Readings by Authorities*. Nottingham: International University Society, 1958. Pp. XXVI, 313. Reading guide.

JOHNSON, Oliver A. (ed.), *Ethics: Selections from Classical and Contemporary Writers*. New York: Holt, Rinehart and Winston, Inc., 1965. Pp. 496.

JONES, W. T., SONTAG, Frederick; BECKNER, Morton O. and FOGELIN, Robert J. (eds.), *Approaches to Ethics: Representative Selections from Classical Times to the Present*. New York: McGraw-Hill Book Company, 1965. Pp. 592.

KATZ, Joseph, MOCHLIN Philip and STOVER, Robert (eds.), *Writers on Ethics: Classic and Contemporary*. Princeton, New Jersey: D. van Nostrand Company, Inc., 1962. Pp. 673.

LEIBELL, J. F., *Readings in Ethics*. Chicago: Loyola University Press, 1926. Pp. XIV, 1098.

MANN, Jesse A., KREYCHE, Gerald F. *et al.* (eds.), *Approaches to Morality: Readings in Ethics from Classical Philosophy to Existentialism*. New York: Harcourt, Brace and World, 1966. Pp. 697. This is Vol. III of *The Harbrace Series in Philosophy*.

MELDEN, A. I., *Ethical Theories: A Book of Readings*. 2nd ed. New York: Prentice Hall, 1955. Pp. 496.

—— (ed.), *Essays in Moral Philosophy*. Seattle, Washington: University of Washington Press, 1958. Pp. 216.

MOTHERSILL, Mary (ed.), *Ethics*. New York: The Macmillan Co., 1965. Pp. 122.

MUNITZ, Milton Karl (ed.), *A Modern Introduction to Ethics: Readings from Classical and Contemporary Sources*. Glencoe, Illinois: The Free Press, 1958. Pp. 667.

RAMSEY, Ian Thomas (ed.), *Christian Ethics and Contemporary Philosophy*. London: Macmillan Co., 1966.

SELLARS, Wilfrid and HOSPERS, John (eds.), *Readings in Ethical Theories*. New York: Appleton-Century-Crofts, 1952. Pp. 707.

WARD, Leo R., *Ethics: A College Text*. New York: Harper and Row, 1965. Pp. 390.

2. PARTICULAR PERIODS

ANTIQUITY

(a) Comprehensive Studies

In English

FERGUSON, John, *Moral Values in the Ancient World*. London: Methuen, 1958. Pp. 256. Bibliography.

HARKNESS, Georgia Elma, *The Sources of Western Morality from Primitive Society through the Beginnings of Christianity*. New York: Charles Scribner's Sons, 1954. Pp. 257.

HUBY, Pamela, *Greek Ethics*. New York: St. Martin's Press, 1967. Pp. 104.

LECKY, William Edward Hartpole, *History of European Morals from Augustus to Charlemagne*. 2 vols. New York: D. Appleton and Co., 1929. First published in 1919.

ZELLER, Edward, *The Stoics, Epicureans and Sceptics.* English translation by Oswald J. REICHEL. New edition. New York: Russell and Russell, 1962. Pp. XV, 585. First translation published in 1870. See Late Ancient Philosophy, in *PQS,* No. 5.

In Other Languages

DENIS, Jacques, *Histoires des théories et des idées morales dans l'antiquité.* 2 vols. Paris: A. Durand, 1856.

GRANDE DEL, C., «La Grecia antichissima, i moniti ei concetti etici», in *Filologia minore* (Milan: R. Ricciardi, 1956), pp. 1-40.

HOWALD, Ernst, *Ethik des Altertums,* Munich, Berlin: R. Oldenbourg, 1925. Pp. 64.

MONDOLFO. Rodolfo, *Moralisti greci: la coscienza morale da Omero à Epicuro.* Milan, Naples: R. Ricciardi, 1960. Pp. 154.

WUNDT, Max, *Geschichte der griechischen Ethik.* 2 vols. Leipzig: W. Englemann, 1908-1911.

(b) Specific Studies

The Sophists: no objectively valid knowledge, including moral knowledge; there exist practical persuasions.
See History of Ancient Philosophy. Pre-Socratics, in *PQS,* No. 5. Plato's Dialogues, *ibid.,* and below.

CREMONA, Antonino, «La norma giuridica nella filosofia morale e nella dottrina politica dei Sofisti», *Rivista internazionale di filosofia del diritto* (Milan), 1960, pp. 139-142.

PLATO (429-348): good is conformity to the ideal reality; virtue is knowledge.
See History of Ancient Philosophy, in *PQS,* No. 5; Idealism, *ibid.;* Politics, below, Ch. IV, p. 181.

——, *Laches.* What is courage ?
——, *Charmides.* Same.
——, *Euthyphro.* What is piety ?
——, *Republic.* What is justice ?
——, *Phaedo.* Immortality of the soul, death of Socrates.
——, *Laws.*
——, *Timaeus,* Cosmology, Forms.
——, *The Republic.* Translated and edited by F. M. Cornford. New York: Oxford University Press, 1945. Pp. 365.
Platonis dialogi, graece et latine. Ed. by Immanuel BEKKER. 10 vols. Berlin: G. Reimerus, 1816-1823.
Plato. Ed. by the Loeb Classical Library. 12 vols. Cambridge, Massachusetts: Harvard University Press, 1914-1930.

CROSS, R. C. and WOOZLEY, A. D., *Plato's Republic. A Philosophical Commentary.* New York: St. Martin's Press, 1964. Pp. 310.

GOULD, John, *The Development of Plato's Ethics.* Cambridge: Cambridge University Press, 1955. Pp. 240.

LODGE, Rupert Clendon, *Plato's Theory of Ethics.* New York: Humanities Press, 1953. Pp. 558. Reprint. First published in 1928.

NETTLESHIP, Richard Lewis, *Lectures on the Republic of Plato.* 2nd ed. New York: St. Martin's Press, 1962. Pp. 364.

TENKU, J., *The Evaluation of Pleasure in Plato's Ethics.* Helsinki: Societas Philosophica, 1956. Pp. 234.

LACHIEZE-REY, Pierre, *Les idées morales, sociales et politiques de Platon.* Paris: J. Vrin, 1951. Pp. 224.

ROBIN, L., *La théorie platonicienne de l'amour.* Paris: F. Alcan, 1908. Pp. 229.

ARISTOTLE (384-322): good is that toward which the things aim; the highest good for man is happiness or good life, which consists in a harmonious fulfillment of man's natural faculties; the practice of virtue is a mean between extremes.

See History of Ancient Philosophy, in *PQS*, No. 5; Realism, *ibid.*; Politics, below, Ch. IV, p. 181.

——, *Aristotelis quae feruntur Magna Moralia.* 2 bks. Ed. F. SUSEMIHL. Leipzig: Teubner, 1883. Pp. XIX, 126.

——, *Ethica Eudemia.* New York: Oxford University Press, 1925.

——, *Ethica Aristotelis ad Eudemium.* Translated into Latin by Leonard ARETIN. Louvain: For J. de Westphalia, 1475.

——, *The Nicomachean Ethics.* English translation by H. RACKHAM. New edition. Cambridge, Massachusetts: Harvard University Press, 1947. Pp. XXIX, 649. Other translation by Martin OSTWALD, *Nicomachian Ethics.* New York: The Bobbs-Merrill Co., 1962. Pp. XXVII, 316. Also translation by James Alexander THOMSON, *The Ethics of Aristotle.* London: Macmillan, 1953, Pp. 289; also by Sir W. David Ross, *The Nicomechean Ethics of Aristotle.* New York: Oxford University Press, 1954. Pp. 332.

——, *Aristotle's Ethics and Politics Comprising the Practical Philosophy.* Translated from the Greek by John GILLES. 2 vols .London: A. Strahan, 1797.

——, *Morale et politique.* Textes choisis par Florence et Claude KHODOSS. Paris: Presses Universitaires de France, 1961. Pp. 204.

HAMBURGER, Max E., *Morals and Law: The Growth of Aristotle's Legal Theory.* New York: Oxford University Press, 1952. First published in 1951. Pp. XXII, 191.

GRENE, Majorie, *A Portrait of Aristotle.* Chicago: University of Chicago Press, 1963. Pp. 271.

JAFFA, Harry V., *Thomism and Aristotelianism: A Study of the Commentary by Thomas Aquinas on the Nicomachean Ethics.* Chicago: University of Chicago Press, 1952. Pp. VIII, 230.

JAEGER, Werner, *Aristotle: Fundamentals of the History of His Development.* 2nd ed. New York: Oxford University Press, 1962. Pp. 475.

MARSHALL, Thomas, *Aristotle's Theory of Conduct.* London: T. F. Unwin, 1906. Pp. 578.

OATES, W. J., *Aristotle and the Problem of Value.* Princeton, New Jersey: Princeton University Press, 1963. Pp. X, 387.

ROSS, William David, *Aristotle.* 5th ed. London: Methuen, 1956. Pp. VII, 300.

——, *Foundations of Ethics.* The Gifford Lectures in the University of Aberdeen, 1935-1936. Oxford: The Clarendon Press, 1939. Pp. XVI, 328.

THOMAS ST., AQUINAS, *Commentaries,* — see Writings of St. Thomas Aquinas, in *PQS,* No. 5; below, p. 15.

VEATCH, Henry Babcock, *Rational Man: A Modern Interpretation of Aristotelian Ethics.* Bloomington, Indiana: Indiana University Press, 1962. Pp. 226.

WALSH, James Jerome, *Aristotle's Conception of Moral Weakness.* New York: Columbia University Press, 1963. Pp. 199.

ARIM VON, Hans, *Die drei aristotelischen Ethiken.* Vienna: Holder-Pichler-Tempsky, A. G., 1924. Pp. 142.

——, «Nochmals die aristotelischen Ethiken», in *Akademie der Wissenschaften in Wien. Phil.-hist. Klasse, Sitzungsberichte,* Vol. CCIX, Abh. 2, pp. 1-57. 1929. Against W. W. Jaeger's position.

FILKUKA, Lambert, *Die metaphysischen Grundlagen in Ethik bei Aristoteles.* Vienna: C. Konegen, 1895. Pp. IV, 138.

GAUTHIER, René A., «Trois commentaires averroistes sur l'Ethique à Nicomaque», *Archives d'histoire doctrinale et littéraire du Moyen âge* (Paris), 1948, pp. 187-336.

——, *La morale d'Aristote.* Paris: Presses Universitaires de France, 1958. Pp. 136.

GILLET, M., *Du fondement intellectuel de la morale d'après Aristote.* Paris: J. Vrin, 1928. Pp. 180.

LÉONARD, Jean, *Le bonheur chez Aristote.* Brussels: Palais des Académies, 1948. Pp. 224.

LIBRIZZI, Carmelo, *La morale di Aristotele.* Padua: Cedam, 1960. Pp. 104.

MANSION, Augustin, *Autour des éthiques attribués à Aristote.* Louvain: Publications Universitaires, 1931.

MARTHA, Benjamin Constant, *Les moralistes sous l'Empire Romain, philosophes et poètes.* 8th ed. Paris: Librairie Hachette, 1907. Pp. VIII, 479.

OLLÉ-LAPRUNE, Léon, *Essai sur la morale d'Aristote.* Paris: E. Belin et fils, 1881. Pp. 315.

WALZER, Richard, *Magna moralia und Aristotelische Ethik.* Berlin: Weidmansche Buchhandlung, 1929. Pp. IX, 300.

WITTMANN, M., *Die Ethik des Aristoteles.* Regensburg: G. J. Manz, 1920. Pp. XIX, 335.

ZUCCANTE, Giuseppe, *Aristotele e la morale.* Florence: Vallecchi, 1926. Pp. 209.

Epicureanism (Hedonism): pleasure is the standard of good.
See History of Late Ancient Philosophy, in *PQS*, No. 5.

EPICURUS (342/1-270), *De rerum natura*. English translation by Cyril BAILEY,
On the Nature of Things. 3 vols. Oxford: Clarendon Press, 1947.
——, *Morals*. English translation by Mr. JOHNSON. London: S. Briscoe,
1712. Pp. XXXIII, 224.
——, *The Life and Morals of Epicurus*. Translated from the Greek by
John DIGBY. Ed. by Joseph TELA (pseudonym). London: J. Souter,
1818. Pp. XV, 233.
——, *Ethica Epicurea*. Ed. by Wolfgang SCHMID. Leipzig: O. Harrassowitz,
1939. Pp. 93.
——, «Letter to Menoceus», in *Epicurus, the Extant Remains*. Translated
and edited by Cyril BAILEY. Oxford: At the Clarendon Press, 1926.
——, *Etica: opere e frammenti*. Ed. by Ruggero SAMMARTANO. Bologne:
Cappelli, 1959: Pp. 124.
Epicurea, Ed. by H. USENER. Leipzig: Teubner, 1887. Pp. LXXXIV, 445.
Reprint in New York: Um. C. Brown, 1967.

DEWITT, Norman Wentworth, *Epicurus and His Philosophy*. Minneapolis: University of Minnesota Press, 1954. Pp. 362.

——, *St. Paul and Epicurus*. Minneapolis: University of Minnesota
Press, 1954. Pp. 201.

MERLAN, Philip, *Studies in Epicurus and Aristotle*. Wiesbaden: Ha-
rassowitz, 1960. Pp. 112.

BIGNONE, Ettore, *Nuove richerche sull' Etica di Epicuro*. Florence:
Le Monnier, 1936.

GUYAU, Jean Marie, *La morale d'Épicure et ses rapports avec les
doctrines contemporaines*. Paris: G. Baillière, 1878. Pp. 291.

MONDOLFO, Rodolfo, «Il superamento dell' utilitarismo e la conscienza
morale nella dottrina epicurea», *Problemi del pensiero antico*. Bologna: Zanichelli, 1936.

SCHILDHAUER, Hans, *Seneca und Epikur. Ethik und Weltanschauung*.
Greifswald: Adler, 1932.

LUCRETIUS, Carus Titus (c. 98-54), — see History of Late Ancient Philoso-
phy, in *PQS*, No 5.
——, *Discourses*. 2 vols. Translated by T. W. GIGGINSON. Boston, Mas-
sachusetts: Little Brown, 1891.
——, *De rerum natura*. Translated by R. C. TREVELYAN. Cambridge: The
University Press, 1937. Pp. XV, 295.

GORDON, Cosmo, Alexandre, *A Bibliography of Lucretius*, New York:
Oxford University Press, 1964. Pp. 319.

HADZSITS, George Depue, *Lucretius and His Influence*. New York:
Longmans, Green and Company, 1935. Pp. VIII, 372.

BIGNONE, Ettore, «Lucrezio come interprete della filosofia di Epicuro»,
in *Italia e Grecia*. Florence: Le Monnier, 1939.

MARTHA, J., *Le poème de Lucrèce, morale, religion, science.* 5ème éd. Paris: Hachette, 1896. Pp. XIX, 398.

Stoicism: calculated discipline, or man's behavior in harmony with the determining law of nature (κοινὸς λόγος).

See Stoics, History of Late Ancient Philosophy, in *PQS*, No. 5.

ARNOLD, Edward Vernon, *Roman Stoicism.* Oxford: Oxford University Press, 1911. Pp. IX, 468.

BRUSSELL, F. W., *Marcus Aurelius and the Later Stoics.* New York: Charles Scribner's Sons, 1910. Pp. 212.

Du VAIR, Guillaume, *Moral Philosophy of the Stoics.* Translated from the French by Thomas JAMES, edited by Rudolf KIRK. New Brunswick, New Jersey: Rutgers University Press, 1952. Pp. IX, 134.

HICKS, R. D., *Stoic and Epicurean.* New York: Russell and Russell, 1962. Pp. 412.

MURRAY, Gilbert, *Stoic, Christian and Humanist.* 2nd ed. London: George Allen and Unwin, 1950. Pp. 191.

WENLEY, Robert Mark, *Stoicism and Its Influence.* New York: Longmans, Green and Co., 1925. Pp. 188.

ZELLER, Eduard, *Stoics, Epicureans and Sceptics.* Translated by Oswald J. REICHEL. New edition. New York: Russell and Russell 1962. Pp. XV, 585. First translation published in 1870. See above, p. 7.

Stoicorum Veterum Fragmenta. Ed. by J. VON ARNIM. 4 vols. Leipzig: Teubner, 1903-1924.

EPICTETUS (c. 60-110), «Complete Extant Writings», in Whitney J. Oates (ed.), *Stoic and Epicurean Philosophers.* New York: Random House, 1940.

MARCUS AURELIUS (121-180), *The Meditations.* Translated by G. M. A. GRUBE. Indianapolis, Indiana: Bobbs-Merrill, 1963. Pp. XXVII, 143.

SENECA, L. Annaeus (4 B. C. - 65 A. D.), *De constantia sapientis.* Leiden, Netherlands: E. J. Brill, 1964. Pp. VI, 41.

——, *Oedipus.* Ed. by T. H. SLUITER. Leiden, Netherlands: E. J. Brill, 1941. Pp. 126.

SEVENSTER, J. N., *Paul and Seneca.* Leiden, Netherlands: E. J. Brill, 1961. Pp VIII, 251.

BRÉHIER, Émile, *Chrysippe et l'ancien stoïcisme.* Paris: Presses Universitaires de France, 1951. Pp. 295.

GENTILE, Marino, «Etica e metafisica nel pensiero di Seneca», *Rivista di filosofia neoscolastica* (Milan), 1931, No. 6.

——, *I fondamenti metafisici della morale di Seneca.* Milan: Vita e Pensiero, 1932. Pp. 92.

NOTHDURFT, K. D., *Studien zum Einfluss Senecas auf die Philosophie des zwölften Jahrhunderts.* Leiden, Holland: E. J. Brill, 1963. Pp. XII, 218.

PROOSDIJ VON, B. A. (ed.), *Seneca als Moralist.* 2 vols. Leiden. Holland: E. J. Brill, 1961. Pp. XVI, 585.

Neoplatonism: man's happiness consists in return to God and it is accomplished through progressive improvement of man's superior faculties.

ELSEE, Charles, *Neoplatonism in Relation to Christianity: An Essay.* Cambridge: University Press, 1908. Pp. XII, 144.

FEIBLEMAN, James Kern, *Religious Platonism: The Influence of Religion on Plato and the Influence of Plato on Religion.* New York: The Macmillan Co., 1960. Pp. 236.

WHITTAKER, Thomas, *The Neoplationists: A Study in the History of Hellenism.* 2nd ed. Cambridge: University Press, 1918. Pp. XV, 318.

PHILO OF ALEXANDRIA (c. 10 B. C. - 50 A. D.), forerunner and mystic.

Philonis Judaei Opera Omnia. 8 vols. Leipzig: E. B. Schwickerti, 1828-1830.

——, *On the Contemplative Life.* Translated with notes and essay on Philo's religious ideas by Frank W. TILDEN. Bloomington, Indiana: Indiana University Studies, 1922. Pp. 37.

——, *Philosophical Writings.* Selections edited by Hans LEWY. Oxford: Phaidon Press, 1946. Pp. 112.

BELKIN, Samuel, *Philo and the Oral Law.* Cambridge, Massachusetts: Harvard Semitic Series (Vol. XI), 1940.

GOODENOUGH, Erwin Ramsdell, *By Light, Light: The Mystic Gospel of Hellenistic Judaism.* New Haven, Connecticut: Yale University Press, 1935. Pp. XV, 436.

——, and GOODHART, Howard, *The Politics of Philo Judaeus: Practice and Theory.* New Haven, Connecticut: Yale University Press, 1938. Pp. XII, 348. Bibliography.

WOLFSON, Harry Austryan, *Philo: Foundation of Religious Philosophy in Judaism, Christianity and Islam.* 2 vols. 4 th impression. Cambridge, Massachusetts: Harvard University Press, 1968. First published in 1947.

KNUTH, Werner, *Der Begriff der Sünde bei Philon von Alexandria.* Würzburg: K. Triltsch, 1934. Pp. VI, 85

NEUMARK, Hermann, *Die Verwendung griechischer und jüdischer Motive in den Gedanken Philons über die Stellung Gottes zu seinen Freuden.* Inaugural Dissertation. Würzburg: K. Triltsch, 1937. Pp. X, 66.

PASCHER, J., «Η βασιλίχὴ ὁδός. *Der Konigsweg zu Wiedergeburt und Vergottung bei Philon von Alexandreia.* Paderborn: Schöningh, 1931. Pp. 280.

STAEHLE, Karl, *Die Zahlenmystik bei Philon von Alexandreia.* Leipzig: Teubner, 1931. Pp. 92.

Gnosticism, — see below.

PLOTINUS (205-270), the founder.

Plotini Opera. Ed. by Paul Henry and Hans R. SCHWYZER. Paris: Gembloux, 1951.

Plotinus. Translated by Stephen MACKENNA. 5 vols. London: P. L. Warner, 1917-1930.

Plotin, The Philosophy of Plotinus. Representative books from the Enneads edited by Joseph KATZ. New York: Appleton-Century-Crofts, 1950. Pp. XXXIII, 158.

Five Books of Plotinus. Translated from the Greek by T. TAYLOR. London: Printed for E. Jeffrey, 1794. Pp. 288. On Felicity; On the Nature and Origin of Evil; On Providence; On Nature, Contemplation and the One; On the Descent of the Soul.

Plotinus, *On Suicide.* Translated and edited by T. TAYLOR. London: Printed for the translator, 1834. Pp. 131.

——, *Our Birth is but a Sleep and a Forgetting.* Translated from the Greek by T. H. JOHNSON. Osceola, Missouri: The Sun Printing Office, 1880. Pp. IV, 18.

ARMSTRONG, Arthur H., *Aristotle, Plotinus and St. Thomas.* Oxford: Blackfriars, 1946. Pp. 11.

——, *The Architecture of the Intelligible Universe in the Philosophy of Plotinus: An Analytical and Historical Study.* Cambridge: University Press, 1940. Pp. XII, 126.

FOLKEL, Charles, *Human Life in Plotinus and Judaism.* Newport, Montmouthshire: R. H. Johns, 1954. Pp. VII, 46.

FULLER, Benjamin A. G., *The Problem of Evil in Plotinus.* Cambridge: University Press, 1912. Pp. XX, 336.

KATZ, Joseph, *Plotinus' Search for the Good.* New York: King's Crown Press, 1950. Pp. IX, 106.

PISTORIUS, Philippus Villiers, *Plotinus and Neoplatonism.* Cambridge: Bowes and Bowes Publishers, 1952. Pp. 175.

ARNOU, René, *Le désir de Dieu dans la philosophie de Plotin.* Paris: F. Alcan, 1921. Pp. XIX, 324.

GUYOT, H., *Les réminiscences de Philon le Juif chez Plotin: étude critique.* Paris: F. Alcan, 1906. Pp. 92.

HENRY, Paul, S. J., *Bulletin critique des études plotiniennes, 1929-1931.* Extrait de la *Nouvelle revue théologique* (Tournai), 1932. Pp. 68.

——, *Études plotiniennes.* 2 vols. Paris: Gembloux, 1938-1941.

Skepticism: certitude can never be obtained about what is morally good or evil, right or wrong.

See History of Late Ancient Philosophy, in *PQS*, No. 5.

MacCOLL, Norman, *The Greek Sceptics from Pyrrho to Sextus.* Cambridge: Cambridge University Press, 1869.

ZELLER, Edward, *Stoics, Epicureans and Sceptics.* Translated by O. J. REICHEL. London: Longmans, Green and Co., 1880. Pp. XVI, 585. See above, Stoics.

RENSI, G. *Introduzione alla scepsi etica.* Florence: Perrella, 1921. Pp. 310.

The Sophists, — see above, p. 7.

Gnosticism: more profound experience of religious and ethical principles by the electes.
See *PQS*, No. 5.

Doresse, Jean (ed.), *The Secret Books of the Egyptians Gnostics*. New York: The Viking Press, 1960. Pp. 445. The gospel according to Thomas.

Grobel, K. (ed.), *The Gospel of Truth*. New York: Abingdon Press, 1960. Pp. 206. Translated *Evangelium veritatis*; a Valentinian meditation on the Gospel.

Scott, W. and Ferguson, A. S. (eds.), *Hermetica*. 4 vols. New York: Oxford University Press, 1924-1936.

Hennecke, E. and Schneemelcher, W. (eds.), *Neutestamentliche Apokryphen*. Tübingen: Mohr, 1959-1964.

Voelker, Walter (ed.), *Quellen zur Geschichte der christlichen Gnosis*. Tübingen: Mohr, 1932. Pp. 147.

Groningen van, G., *First Century Gnosticism: Its Origins and Motifs*. Leiden, Holland: E. J. Brill, 1967. Pp. XII, 204.

Jonas, Hans, *Gnosis und spätantiker Geist*. 2 vols. Göttingen: Vandenhoeck & Ruprecht, 1933-1954. 3 rd ed. 1964.
——, «Gnosticism», The Encyclopedia of Philosophy (8 vols. New York: The Macmillan Co., 1967), Vol. III, pp. 336-342.

Bianchi, Ugo, *Le origini dello gnosticismo*. Leiden, Holland: E. J. Brill, 1967. Pp. XXXII, 801. Text and discussions, Manicheism included.

Festugière, A. J., *La révélation d'Hermès Trismégiste*. 4 vols. Paris: Gabalda. 1944-1954.

Quispel, Gilles, *Gnosis als Weltreligion*. Zurich: Origo-Verlag, 1951. Pp. 94.

Rudolph, Kurt, *Die Mandäer*. 2 vols. Göttingen: Vandenhoeck & Ruprecht, 1960-1961.

Patristic philosophy: good is obedience to divine authority, or else it is satisfaction of natural faculties subordinated to eternal salvation.
See *PQS*, No. 5.

Migne, J. P. (ed.), *Patrologiae cursus completus*. Series I, *Ecclesiae Graecae*. 161 vols. Paris: J. P. Migne, 1857-1866. Series II, *Ecclesiae Latinae*. 221 vols. Paris: J. P. Migne, 1844-1855. Reprint, 1863-1866.
The Fathers of the Church. A new translation. Founded by Ludwig Schopp. 132 vols. — New York: Cima Publishing Co.; Fathers of the Church 1947.

St. Augustine (354-430) *Augustine: Earlier Writings*. London: 1943. De libero Arbitrio, 388-389; De vera religione, 391; De natura boni, 399.

——, *The Confessions*. Translated by John K. RYAN. Garden City, New York: Doubleday, 1960. Pp. 423. Written in 397-401.

——, *The City of God*. Translated by John HEALEY. London: J. M. Dent, 1931. Pp. 267. Written in 413-426.

——, *De libero arbitrio*. English translation by M. PONTIFEX, *The Problem of Free Choice*. Westminster, Maryland: Newman Press, 1955.

BURTON, M. L., *The Problem of Evil: A Criticism of the Augustinian Point of View*. Chicago: The Open Court Publishing Co., 1909. Pp. 234.

SWITALSKI, Bruno, *Neoplatonism and the Ethics of St. Augustine*. New York: Polish Institute of Arts and Sciences in America, 1946. Pp. XXXII, 113.

JOLIVET, Regis, *Le problème du mal d'après saint Augustin*. Paris: Beauchesne et ses fils, 1936.

MIDDLE AGES

See Scholastic Philosophy, Ethics, in *PQS*, No. 5.
History of Medieval Philosophy, *ibid*.

(a) Comprehensive Studies

In English

See the Studies in History, above p. 2.

BOURKE, Vernon J., *Ethics*. New York: The Macmillan Co., 1967. Pp. 497.

GILSON, Étienne, *Reason and Revelation in the Middle Ages*. New York: Sheed and Ward 1938. Pp. *114*.

LECKY, William Edward Hartpole, *History of European Morals, from Augustus to Charlemagne*. New York: Braziller, 1955. Pp. 407.

MARITAIN, Jacques, *La philosophie morale: examen historique et critique des grandes systemes*. Paris: Gallimard, 1960. English translation, *Moral Philosophy: An Historical and Critical Survey of the Great Systems*. New York: Charles Scribner's Sons, 1964. Pp. XII, 468.

In Other Languages

DEUMPF, Alois, *Ethik des Mittelalters*. Munich: R. Oldenbourg, 1927. Pp. 111.

LUTHARD, C. E., *Geschichte der christlichen Ethik*. 2 vols. Berlin, 1886-1887.

(b) Specific Studies

St. AUGUSTINE, — see Patristic Philosophy, above, p. 14.

AQUINAS, THOMAS SAINT (1224/5-1274): human reason as a derivation of God's reason is the norm of morality.

S. Thomae Aquinatis Opera Omnia. 25 vols. Ed. by Giovanni Maria AL-LODI, Parma: Typis P. Fiaccadori, 1852-1873. Philmographic reproduction in New York: Musurgia Publishers, 1948-1950. See also Middle Ages, below, Ch. II-V.

——, *Summa theologiae*. Rome: Marietti, 1952. English translation by the Fathers of the English Dominican Province, *The Summa Theologica*. 2nd ed. New York: Benzinger Brothers, 1947-1948. Also in New York: McGraw-Hill Co., 1964.

——, *Summa de veritate Catholicae Fidei contra gentiles*. English translation by Anton Pegis *et al.*, *On the Truth of the Catholic Faith*. 5 vols. New York: Image Books, 1955-1957. See *Opera Omnia*, above.

——, *In X Libros Ethicorum ad Nicomachum Expositio*. Turin: Marietti, 1934. English translation by C. I. Litzinger, O. P., *Commentary on the Ethics of Aristotle*. Chicago: H. Regnery, 1964. Other Translation: *Ethics*, Bk. VIII - IX, by Pierre Conway, *On Aristotle's Love and Friendship*. Providence, Rhode Island: Providence College Press, 1951.

——, *A Treatise on the Virtues*. Translated by John A. Oesterle of *Summa Theologiae*, I-II, qq. 49-67. Englewood Cliffs, New Jersey: Prentice-Hall, 1966. Pp. 194.

——, *De virtutibus in communi*. Translated by John Patrick Reid, *On the Virtues in General*. Providence, Rhode Island: Providence College Press, 1951. Pp. XXIX, 185.

——, *On Charity*. Translated by Lottie H. Kendzierski. Milwaukee, Michigan: Marquette University Press, 1960.

Fagothey, Austin, S. J., *Right and Reason: Ethics in Theory and Practice*. St. Louis, Missouri: The C. V. Mosby Co., 1953. Pp. 583.

Farrell, Walter, *The Natural Moral Law according to St. Thomas and Suarez*. Boston, Massachusetts: Bruce Humphries, 1930. Pp. X 162.

Maritain, Jacques, *St. Thomas and the Problem of Evil*. Milwaukee, Wisconsin: Marquette University Press, 1942.

Sertillanges, Antonin Dalmace, *La philosophie morale de Saint Thomas d'Aquin*. Paris: F. Alcan, 1916. Pp. 592.

Scotus, John Duns (1266/74-1308): good acts must be in accordance with right reason; the norm of such a reason is the divine will; there exist indifferent elicited acts.

——, *Opera Omnia*. 2nd ed. 26 vols. Paris: Vivès, 1891-1895

Gilson, Étienne, *Jean Duns Scot: introduction à ses positions fondamentales*. Paris: J. Vrin, 1952. Pp. 698. English translation by B. M. Bonasea, O. F. M., *Duns Scotus: The Basic Principles of His Philosophy*. Washington, D. C.: The Catholic University of America Press, 1961. Pp. 220.

Watson, S. Y., «Duns Scotus' Voluntarism» in John K. Ryan and Bernardine M. Bonasea (eds.), *John Duns Scotus, 1265-1965* (Washington, D. C.: The Catholic University of America Press, 1965), Ch. V.

OCKHAM, William (c. 1285-1349): the divine will is the norm of morality.

——, *Dyalogus.* 2 vols. Paris, 1476.
——, *Super Quatuor Libros Sententiarum subtilissimae quaestiones.* Lyons, 1495.
——, *The Tractatus de praedestinatione et de praescientia Dei et de futuris contingentibus.* Ed. by Ph. BOEHNER, O. F. M. St. Bonaventure, New York: St. Bonaventure College, 1945. Pp. XI, 139.
——, *Selected Philosophical Writings.* Ed. by Philotheus BOEHNER, O. F. M. London: Nelson, 1952.
——, *The De imperatcrum et pontificum potestate.* Ed. by C. K. BRAMPTON. Oxford. The Clarendon Press, 1927. Pp. XXXVIII, 108.
Gulielmi de Occam Breviloquium de potestate papae. Ed. by L. BAUDRY. Paris: J. Vrin, 1937. Pp. XX, 179.
Gulielmi de Ockham Opera Politica. Ed. by J. O. SIKES. Manchester: Typis Universitatis, 1940.

BAUDRY, Léon,*Guillaume d'Occam: sa vie, ses œuvres, ses idées sociales et politiques.* Paris: J. Vrin, 1949. Vol. I: L'homme et ses œuvres. Pp. 317.
GIACION, Carlo, *Guglielmo di Occam.* 2 vols. Milan: Vita e Pensiero, 1941.
HAMMANN, Adalbert, O. F. M., *La doctrine de l'église et de l'état chez Occam.* Paris: Éditions franciscaines, 1942. Pp. 212.
GUELLUY, R., *Philosophie et théologie chez Guillaume d'Ockham.* Louvain: Editions Nauwelaerts, 1947. Pp. XXIV, 383.
LAGARDE DE, G., *Naissance de l'esprit laïque au déclin du Moyen âge.* Louvain: E. Nauwelaerts, 1956—.

SUAREZ, Francis (1548-1617): human nature completely taken is the proximate norm of morality; the ultimate norm is God.

See Law, below, Chapter III, p. 129.

——, *Opera Omnia.* 28 vols. Paris: Vivès, 1856-1878.
——, *Selection from Three Works of Francisco Suarez, S. J.: De Legibus, Defensio Fidei Catholicae, De Triplici virtute theologica.* 2 vols. Oxford: Clarendon Press, 1944.

DUMONT, P., *Liberté humaine et concours divin d'après Suarez.* Paris: G. Beauchesne et ses Fils, 1936. Pp. VI, 382.
ELORDUY, E., «La moral suareciana», in *Annuario de la Association Francisco de Vitoria»* 1946, Vol. VI, pp. 97-189.
MAHIEU, L., *François Suarez: sa philosophie et les rapports qu'elle al avec la théologie.* Paris:: Mescleée De Brouwer, 1921. Pp. XVII, 532.

VITORIA, Francis, — see below, pp. 67, 129.

——, *Relectiones morales duobus tomis comprehensae.* Cologne: Sumptibus A. Boetii, 1696.

MODERN

See History of Modern Philosophy, in *PQS*, No. 5.
General Studies, above, 1.

(a) Comprehensive Studies

In English

BROAD, Charlie, Dunbar, *Five Types of Ethical Theory.* New York: Harcourt,
Brace and Co., 1930. Pp. XXV, 288. Spinoza, Butler, Hume, Kant and
Sidgwick.

HODANN, Max, *History of Modern Morals.* Translated by Stella BROWNE.
London: W. Heinemann, 1937. Pp. XV, 338.

MACKINNON, Donald M, *A Study in Ethical Theory.* New York: The Macmillan and Co., 1957. Pp. 280.

MOTHERSHEAD, John L., *Ethics: Modern Conceptions of the Principles of
Right.* New York: Holt, Rinehart and Winston, Inc., 1955. Pp. 329.

MUNITZ, Milton K. (ed), *A Modern Introduction to Ethics: Readings from
Classical and Contemporary Sources.* New York: The Free Press
(Macmillan), 1958. Pp. 667. See above, p. 6.

RAMSEY, P. (ed.), *Nine Modern Moralists.* Englewood Cliffs, New Jersey:
Prentice-Hall, 1962.

SWABEY, W. C., *Ethical Thought from Hobbes to Kant.* New York: Philosophical Library, 1961. Pp. 284.

WERKMEISTER, W. H., *Theories of Ethics: A Study in Moral Obligation.*
Lincoln, Nebraska: Johnsen Publishing Co., 1961. Pp. 445.

In Other Languages.

VINET, A., *Moralistes des seizième et dix-septième siècles.* 2nd ed. Paris:
Librairie Fischbacher, 1904. Pp. VIII, 449. First published in 1859.

(b) Specific Studies

(aa) RATIONALISM: reason provides true moral principles from
which the morality of particular cases can be deduced.
See Rationalism, in *PQS*, No. 5; above, Ch. III, p. 131.

France-Holland

DESCARTES, René (1596-1656), *A Discours on Method.* Translated from the
French by John VEITCH. New York: E. P. Dutton and Co., 1953. Pp.
XXVI, 254.

——, *Œuvres de Descartes.* 10 vols. Ed. by Charles ADAM and Paul TAN-
NERY. Paris: J. Vrin, 1956-1957. First published in 12 vols. vith Index, 1897-1913.

——, *Correspondance.* 5 vols. in the *Œuvres*, 1956; see above.

ESPINAS, Alfred, *Descartes et la morale.* 2 vols. Paris: Bossard, 1925.
Pp. 252.

GILSON, E., *La liberté chez Descartes et la théologie.* Paris: F. Alcan, 1913. Pp. 452.

MATTEI, André, *L'homme de Descartes.* Paris: Montaigne, 1945. Pp. 264.

MESNARD, Pierre, *Essai sur la morale de Descartes.* Paris: Bowin et Cie., 1936.

SPINOZA, Baruch (1632-1677), *Ethica more geometrico demonstrata,* 1677; posthumously published. English translation by William Hale WHITE, revised by Amelia Hutchinson STIRLING, edited by James GUTMANN, *Ethics* preceded by *On the Improvement of the Understanding.* New York: Hafner, 1957. Pp. XXXIV, 294.
——, *Tractatus de Deo et homine ejusque felicitate.* Ed. by E. BOEHMER. Halle: Lippert, 1852. Pp. 63. English translation by A. WOLF, *Spinoza's Short Treatise on God, Man and Human Welfare.* London: Adam and Charles Black, 1910. Pp. CXXVIII, 246.
——, *Tractatus theologico-politicus.* Hamburg: H. Kunraht, 1670. Anonymously published. Pp. 234.

BIDNEY D., *The Psychology and Ethics of Spinoza.* New Haven, Connecticut: Yale University Press, 1940. Pp. XV, 454.

DUFF, R. A., *Spinoza's Ethical and Political Philosophy.* Glasgow: Maclehose, 1903. Pp. XII, 516.

JOACHIM, H. H., *A Study of the Ethics of Spinoza.* Oxford: At the Clarendon Press, 1901. Pp. XIV, 316.

SHANKS, Alexander, *Introduction to Spinoza's Ethics.* London: Macmillan Co., 1938. Pp. 103.

BIAGINI, L., *L'ascetismo di Spinoza.* S. Maria degli Angeli (Assisi): Porziuncola, 1935. Pp. 14.

DELBOS, V., *Le problème moral dans la philosophie de Spinoza et dans l'histoire du Spinozisme.* F. Alcan, 1893. Pp. XII, 569.

ROBINSON, Lewis, *Kommentar zu Spinozas Ethik.* Leipzig: F. Meiner, 1928. Pp. 379.

England

Cambridge Platonists: insist on spiritualist and religious interpretation of reality and on moral life as the essence of Christianity. See Moral Sense Philosophers, below, p. 23.

CASSIRER, Ernst, *Die platonische Renaissance in England und die Schule von Cambridge.* Leipzig: Studien der Bibliothek Warburg, 1932. English translation by J. P. PETTEGROVE, *The Platonic Renaissance in England.* Edinburgh: Nelson, 1953. Pp. VII, 207.
POWICKE, Frederick James, *The Cambridge Platonists.* London: J. M. Dent and Sons, 1926. Pp. X, 219.

Selby-Bigge Sir, Lewis Amherst (ed.), *British Moralists.* 2nd ed. 2 vols. Oxford: Oxford University Press, 1897.

Representatives

Cudworth, Ralph (1617-1688), *The True Intellectual System of the Universe, wherein all the Reason and Philosophy of Atheism is Confuted, and it Impossibility Demonstrated.* New Edition: London: R. Priestley, 1820.

——, *The True Intellectual System of the Universe. A Treatise on Immutable Morality.* First American edition. 2 vols. New York: Gould and Newman, 1837-1838. See also Law below, Ch. III, p. 122.

More, Henry (1614-1687). *Enchiridion ethicum, praecipua moralis philosophiae rudimenta complectens.* London: J. Fisher, 1668. Pp. 230. English translation. New York: The Facsimile Text Society, 1930.

Germany

Leibniz, Gottfried W. (1646-1716), — see below, pp. 131, 191.

——, *Essais de théodicée sur la bonté de Dieu, la liberté de l'homme et l'origine du mal.* 2 vols. in one. Amsterdam: I. Troyel, 1710. English translation by E. M. Huggard, *Theodicy: Essays on the Goodness of God, the Freedom of Man and the Origin of Evil.* London: Routledge and Kegan Paul, 1951. Pp. 448. Psychological determinism.

——, *Systema theologicum inscriptum.* Paris: A. Le Clere, 1845. Pp. viii, 148. Posthumously published.

Barth, Karl, *Die kirchliche Dogmatik* (4 vol. Zollikon-Zürich: Evangelischer Verlag, 1932-1955), Vol. III/I, 843. English translation by T. F. Torrance and G. W. Bromiley, *Church Dogmatics.* 4 vols. Edinburgh: T. and T. Clark, 1959-1960.

Hildebrandt, Curt, *Leibniz und das Reich der Gnade.* The Hague: M. Nijhoff, 1953. Pp. VIII, 504.

Pufendorf, Samuel (1632-1694), *De officio hominis et civis juxta legem natuarlem libri duo.* 2 vols. New York: Oxford University Press, 1927. First published in 1715. English translation by Basil Kennet, *The Law of Nature and Nations, or a General System of the Most Important Principles of Morality, Jurisprudence and Politics.* London: J. and J. Bonwicke, 1749.

Wolff, Christian (1679-1754), — see Rationalism, in *PQS*, No 5.

——, *Philosophia practica universalis, methodo scientifio pertractata.* New edition. 2 vols. Halle: Renger, 1744-1750. See Law, below, p. 133.

The Nineteenth Century Rationalism

Kant, — see Autonomous Ethics, below, p. 27.

Hegel, — see Dialectical Idealism, below, p. 32.

(bb) EMPIRICISM: Morality and its rules are discovered by studying man's experiences expressed in customs and feelings. See Empiricism, in *PQS*, No. 5.

SELBY-BIGGE, L. A. (ed.), *British Moralists*. 2nd ed. 2 vols. Oxford: Oxford University Press, 1897. See England, above.

Transitional Stage: empiricism and scholasticism.

BACON, Francis (1561-1626): good is that which is useful for mankind; however, the divine revelation gives complete idea of human destiny.

——, *Of the Proficience and Advancement of Learning, divine and humane.* 2 parts. London: For Henric Tomes, 1605.
——, *De divinitate et argumentis scientiarum.* London: J. Haviland, 1623. Pp. XVIII, 494.
——, *Essays, Moral, Economical and Political.* New edition. London: F. C. and J. Rivington, 1813. Pp. XIX, 387.
Francisci Baconi operum moralium et civilium tomus. London: R. Whitaker, 1638. See below, p. 133.

Interest Theories: profit is a criterion of goodness.

HOBBES, Thomas (1588-1679): self-interest or egotism. See Modern Histories of Philosophy, in *PQS*, No. 5; Politics, below, Ch. IV, p. 190; Index.

——, *Leviathan or The Matter, Form and Power of a Common-Wealth Ecclesiastical and Civil.* London: Andrew Crooke, 1651. Pp. 396. See Law, below, Ch. III, p. 131.
——, *The Elements of Law, natural and politic.* Ed. by Ferdinand TONNIES with critical notes. London: Simpkin Marshall and Co., 1889. Reprint at Cambridge: University Press, 1928. Pp. XVII, 195. First published as *De Corpore Politico or the Elements of Law, Moral and Politick* (sic). London: Ram-Alley, 1650.
——, *Elementa philosophiae.* 2 vols. London: A. Crook, 1642-1658. Vol. I: De corpore. Vol. II: De homine, de cive.

GOOCH, George P., *Hobbes.* London: Humphrey, Milford, 1940.

JAMES, David G., *Life of Reason: Hobbes, Locke, Bolinbroke.* New York: Longmans, 1949. Pp. XII, 272.

MCNEILLY, F. S., *The Anatomy of Leviathan.* New York: St. Martin's Press, 1968, Pp. 288.

STEPHEN Sir, Leslie, *Hobbes.* Ann Arbor, Michigan: University of Michigan Press, 1961. Pp. 243.

LUBIENSKI, Zbigniew, *Die Grundlagen des etisch-politischen Systems von Hobbes*. München: Reinhardt, 1932. Pp. 302.

MONDOLFO, Rodolfo, *Saggi per la storia della morale utilitaria*. 2 vols Verona, Padua: Drucker, 1903-1904. Vol. I: La morale di T. Hobbes; Vol. II: le teorie morali e politiche di C. A. Helvetius.

——, «Il concetto del bene e la psicologia dei sentimenti in Hobbes», *Rivista di filosofia e scienze affini*, Vol. I, No. 1-2 (1903).

POLIN, R., *Politique et philosophie chez Thomas Hobbes*. Paris: Presses Universitaires de France, 1952. See Politics, below, p. 191.

TARANTINO, G., *Saggio sulle idee morali e politiche di Tommas Hobbes*. Naples: Gianni, 1900. Pp. 144.

——, *Le idee morali e politiche di Tommaso Hobbes*. Naples: Gianni, 1901.

——, *Saggio sulle idee morali e politiche di Tommaso Hobbes*. Naples: Giamnini, 1900. Pp. 144.

LOCKE, John (1632-1704): man's innate desire to experience pleasure and escape pain compel him to form a moral code which agrees with God's will.
See below, pp. 135, 192.

——, *The Works of John Locke*. 9 vols. 12th ed. London: Printed for C. and J. Rivington, 1824.
——, *The Works of John Locke*. New Edition. New York: Ward, Lock and Co., 1899. An Essay on the Human Understanding. Four letters on toleration. Some thoughts on Education, and an essay on the value of money.

BYRNE, James W., «The Notion of Obligation in Lockes Philosophy», *The Personalist* (Los Angeles, California), Winter 1963.
——, «The Basis of the Natural Law in Locke's Philosophy», *The Catholic Lawyer* (New York), Winter 1964.
——, «John Locke's Philosophy of Religious Toleration», *The Personalist* (Los Angles, California), spring 1965.
—, «The Meaning of Natural Law in Locke's Philosophy», *The Personalist* (Los Angles, California), Winter 1968.

LAMPRECHT, Sterling Power, *The Moral and Political Philosophy of John Locke*. New York: Columbia University Press, 1918. Pp. VIII, 168.

Sympathy Theories: good is that which provides for the welfare of community life.

BACON, Francis, — see above, p. 21.

HUME, David (1711-1776), ,— see Economics, below, p. 93; Politics, below, p. 193; Index.

——, *A Treatise of Human Nature: Being an Attempt to Introduce the Experimental Method of Reasoning into Moral Subjects*. 3 bks. Ed. by L. A. SELBY-BIGGE. Oxford: At the Clarendon Press, 1958. First published in London: John Noon, 1739.

——, *An Inquiry concerning the Principles of Morals*. Ed. by Charles HENDEL. New York: Bobbs-Merrill, 1955. Pp. 222. First published in London: A. Millar, 1751.

——, *Essays, Moral, Political and Literary*. London: Longmans, Green and Co., 1875. First published in 1752.

MATCZAK, S. A., «A Select and Classified Bibliography of David Hume», *The Modern Schoolman* (St. Louis, Illinois), 1964, pp. 70-82.

ANDERSON, Robert Fendel, *Hume's First Principles*. Lincoln, Nebraska (68508): University of Nebraska Press, 1966. Pp. XV, 189.

BROILES, R. David, *The Moral Philosophy of David Hume*. The Hague: Martinus Nijhoff, 1964. Pp. VI, 97.

KYDD, Rachael Mari, *Reasons and Conduct in Hume's Treatise*. Oxford University Press, 1946. Pp. IX, 196.

McNABB, Donald G., *David Hume: His Theory of Knowledge and Morality*. New York: Longmans, Green and Co., 1951. Pp. 208.

STEWART, John B., *The Moral and Political Philosophy of David Hume*. New York: Columbia University Press, 1963. Pp. VIII, 422.

CORSI, Mario, *Natura e società in David Hume*. Florence: La Nuova Italia, 1954. Pp. XII, 75.

HUTCHESON, Francis, — see Moral Sense Philosophies, below.
SMITH, Adam, — see *loc. cit.*

Moral Sense Philosophers: moral good is a quality immediately grasped by specific moral feeling. See Cambridge Platonist, above, p. 19.

BONAR, James, *Moral Sense*. New York: The Macmillan Co., 1930. Pp. 304.
RAPHAEL, David Daiches, *The Moral Sense*. Oxford: Oxford University Press, 1947. Pp. 201.

England

BUTLER, Joseph (1692-1752), *Fifteen Sermons upon Human Nature*. London, 1726.

——, *Sermons*. New York: Robert Carter & Brothers, 1873.

——, *Five Sermons*. New York: Little Library of Liberal Arts (Liberal Arts Press). 1950. Pp. 100.

DUNCAN-JONES, A. E., *Butler's Moral Philosophy*. New York and Harmondsworth: Penguin Books Inc., 1952. Pp. 191.

MOSSNER, E. C. *Bishop Butler and the Age of Reason*. New York: The Macmillan Company, 1936. Pp. XV. 271.

FERGUSON, Adam (1724-1816), *Institutes of Moral Philosophy*. Edinburgh: Kincaird and Bell, 1769. Pp. XVI, 319.

HUTCHESON, Francis (1694-1747), *An Inquiry into the Original of Our Ideas of Beauty and Virtue*. 2nd ed. London. J. Darby, 1726. Pp. XXVI, 304. First published in 1725.

——, *A System of Moral Philosophy*. Ed. by his son, Francis HUTCHESON. 2 vols. Glasgow: R. and A. Foulis, 1755.

SCOTT, William Robert, *Francis Hutcheson*. Cambridge: University Press, 1900. Pp. XX, 296. Reprint in New York: Augustus M. Kelley, 1966.

MANDEVILLE DE, Bernard (1670-1733), *The Faible of the Bees, or Private Vice, Public Benefits, with an Essay on Charity and Charity — Schools, and an Search into the Nature of Society*. 5th ed. 2 vols. London: J. Tonson, 1728-1729. First published in 1714.

——, *Free Thought on Religion, the Church, and National Happiness*. 2nd ed. London: J. Brotherton, 1729. Pp. XIX, 364. First published in 1720.

——, *An Inquiry into the Origin of Honour*. London, 1732.

——, *The Virgin Unmasked*. 4th ed. London: T. Cooper, 1742. Pp. X, 239.

PALEY, William, *The Principles of Moral and Political Philosophy*. 17th ed. 2 vols. London: J. Faulder; 1809. First published in 1785.

REID, Thomas (1710-1796), *Essays on the Powers of the Human Mind*. 3 vols. Edinburgh: J. Bell, 1803.

——, *The Works of Thomas Reid*. Ed. by Sir W. HAMILTON. 2 vols. Edinburgh: J. Bell, 1846-1863.

——, *An Inquiry into the Human Mind, on the Principles of Common Sense*. Dublin: printed for A. Ewing, 1764. Pp. XII, 316.

JOHNS, Olin M., *Empiricism and Intuitionism in Reid's Common Sense Philosophy*. Princeton, New Jersey: Princeton University Press, 1927.

SHAFTESBURY, Anthony A. C. (1671-1713), *Characteristics of Men, Manners, Opinions and Times*. 3 vols. s. c. 1723.

GREAN, Stanley, *Shaftesbury's Philosophy of Religion and Ethics: A Study of Enthusiasm*. Athens, Ohio: Ohio University Press, 1967, Pp. 316.

BANDINI, Luigi, *Shaftesbury: etica e religione, la morale del sentimento*. Bari: Laterza, 1930. Pp. XXXII, 232.

SMITH, Adam (1723-1790), — see Economics, below, Ch. II, p. 80; Index.

——, *The Theory of Moral Sentiments*. 2nd ed. London: A. Millar, 1761. Pp. VIII, 436. First published in 1759.

BONAR, J., *Moral Sense*. New York: The Macmillan Co., 1930. See above, general.

MORROW, Glenn R., *The Ethical and Economic Theories of Adam Smith*. Ithaca, New York: Cornell Studies in Philosophy, 1923.

BAGOLINI, L., *La simpatia nella morale e nel diritto: aspetti del pensiero di A. Smith*. Bologne: C. Zuffi, 1952. Pp. 119.

LIMENTANI, L., *La morale della simpatia: saggio sopra l'etica di A. Smith nella storia del pensiero inglese.* Geneva: Formiggini, 1914. Pp. XVI, 260.

France

BECKER, Carl Lotus, *The Heavenly City of the Eighteenth Century Philosophers.* New Haven, Connecticut: Yale University Press, 1932. Pp. 168.

BUFFIER, Claude, S. J., *Traité des premières vérités.* 2 parts in one vol. Paris: V. Monge, 1724.

HALÉVY, Élie, *La formation du radicalisme philosophique.* 3 vols. Paris: F. Alcan, 1901-1904. English translation by Mary MORRIS, *The Growth of Philosophic Radicalism.* New York: The Macmillan Co., 1928. Pp. XVII, 554.

ROUSTAN, Marius, *The Pioneers of the French Revolution.* Translated from the French by Frederick WHYTHE. Boston, Massachusetts: Little Brown and Co., 1926. Pp. 302.

ROUSSEAU, Jean Jacques (1712-1778), *Émile, on de L'Éducation.* 4 vols. La Haye: J. Néaulme, 1762. English translation by Barbara FOXLEY, *Emile.* London: .J M. Dent and Sons, 1933. Pp. X, 444.

——, *La Nouvelle Héloïse, ou Lettres de deux amans, habitans d'une petite ville au pied des Alpes.* New edition. 4 vols. Avignon: Guichard aîné, 1816. First published in 1780. English translation from the French, *Julia or The New Eloisa.* 3 vols. Edinburgh: J. Bell, 1773.

——, *The Minor Educational Writings of Jean Jacques Rousseau.* Selected by William BOYD. London: Blackie and Son, 1911. Pp. 159.

——, *The Social Contract.* Translated by Henry J. TOZER. London: G. Allen and Unwin, 1924. Pp. 246.

——, *Œuvres de J. J. Rousseau.* New edition. 11 vols. Amsterdam: M. M. Rey, 1769.

HENDEL, Charles W., *Jean-Jacques Rousseau: Moralist.* 2nd ed. Indianapolis, Indiana: Bobbs-Merrill and Co., 1963. Pp. 348.

Contemporary Empiricism, — see Contemporary Theories, below, pp. 36-58.

Germany

FREUD, Sigmund, — see Psychoanalysis, below, p. 41.

Utilitarianism: what is useful is good.

ALBEE, Ernest, *A History of English Utilitarianism.* London: Swan Sonnenschein and Co., 1902. Reprint in New York: The Macmillan Co., 1962.

HALÉVY, Élie, — see France, above.

MELDEN, Abraham Irving, «Two Comments on Utilitarianism», *Philosophical Review,* 1951.
——, *Rights and Right Conduct.* Oxford: Blackwell, 1959. Pp. 87.
NARVESON, Jan, *Morality and Utility.* Baltimore, Maryland: The Johns Hopkins Press, 1967. Pp. 320.
STEPHEN Sir, Leslie F., *The English Utilitarians.* 3 vols. London: Duckworth, 1900. Reprint, Gloucester, Massachusetts: Peter Smith, 1950.

GUYAU, Jean Marie, *La morale anglaise contemporaine, morale de l'utilité et de l'évolution.* Paris: G. Baillière, 1879. Pp. XII, 420.
MONDOLFO, R., *Saggi per la storia della morale utilitaria.* 2 vols. Verona, Padua: Drucker, 1903-1904. See HOBBES, below.

Representatives

BENTHAM, Jeremy (1748-1832): it is the greatest happiness of the greatest number that is the measure of right and wrong.

——, *A Fragment on Governement.* London: T. Payne, 1776. Pp. 208.
——, *An Introduction to the Principles of Morals and Legislation.* London: T. Payne and Son, 1789. Also ed. by Laurence J. LAFLEUR, New York: Hafner, 1948.
——, *Deontology, or the Science of Morality.* In which the harmony and coincidence of duty and self-interest, virtue and felicity, prudence and benevolence are explained. Ed. by John BOWRING. 2 vols. London: Longman and Co., 1834.

ATKINSON, Charles Milner, *Jeremy Bentham: His Life and Work.* London: Methuen and Co., 1905. Pp. XII, 247.

BAUMGARDT, D., *Bentham and the Ethics of Today.* Princeton, New Jersey: Princeton University Press, 1962. First published in 1951.

SORLEY, W. R., «Bentham and the Early Utilitarians», in the *Cambridge History of English Literature* (15 vols. Cambridge: University Press, 1907-1927), Vol. XI (1914).

WALLAS, Graham, *Jeremy Bentham.* London: University College, 1922. Pp. 15.

MILL, John Stuart (1806-1873), — see Positivism, in *PQS,* No. 5; below, Index.

——, *On Liberty.* Ed. by Currin V. SHIELDS. New York: The Bobbs-Merrill, 1956. Pp. XXVIII, 141. First published in London, 1859.
——, *Utilitarianism.* Ed. by Oskar PIEST. New York: The Liberal Arts Press, 1957. Pp. VIII, 79. First published in London, 1861.
Mill's Ethical Writings. Ed. by J. B. SCHNEEWIND. New York; The Macmillan Co., 1965. Pp. 346.

COWLING, Maurice, *Mill and Liberalism.* Cambridge: Cambridge University Press, 1963. Pp. 161.

Douglas, Charles M. (ed), *The Ethics of John Stuart Mill*. Edinburgh: Blackwood and Sons, 1897. Pp. CXXVI, 233.

Mabbott, J. D., «Interpretations of Mill's Utilitarianism», *Philosophical Quarterly* (Dundee, Scotland), 1956, Pp. 115-120.

Neff, Emery E., *Carlyle and Mill, Mystic and Utilitarian*. New York: Columbia University Press, 1924. Pp. VII, 334.

——, *Carlyle and Mill: An Introduction to Victorian Thought*. 2nd ed. New York: Columbia University Press, 1926. Pp. IX, 435.

Plamenatz, J. (ed.), *Mill's Utilitarianism*. Reprinted with a study of *The English Utilitarians*. Oxford: Basil Blackwell and Mott Ltd., 1949

Raphael, D. D., «Fallacies in and about Mill's 'Utilitarianism'», *Philosophy*, 1955, Pp. 344 ff.

Urmson, J. O., «The Interpretation of Moral Philosophy of John Stuart Mill», *Philosophical Quarterly* (Dundee, Scotland), 1953. Pp. 33 ff.

Zuccante, Giuseppe, *La Morale utilitaristica dello Stuart Mill: esposizione della dottrina*. Milan: Hoepli, 1899. Pp. 113.

——, *Giovanni Stuart Mill e l'utilitarismo*. Florence. Vallecchi, 1922. Pp. 455.

Positivism, — see below, p. 35.

Dialectical Materialism, — see Contemporary, below, p. 38.

Pragmatism, — see Contemporary, below, p. 38.

(cc) Theological Theories: God's commandment is the ultimate criterion of moral good.

Cambridge Platonist, — see Modern Rationalism, England, above, p. 19. Moral Sense Philosophers (particularly J. Butler and William Paley), above, p. 23.

Clarke, Samuel (1675-1729), *The Works of Samuel Clarke*. 4 vols. London: J. and P. Knapton, 1738-1742.

Le Rossignol, J. E., *The Ethical Philosophy of Samuel Clarke*. Leipzig, 1892.

Contemporary Theological Ethics, see below, p. 49.

Tradionalism, see below, p. 207.

(dd) Autonomous Ethics: insists on man's own authority in matters of his behavior.

Critical Idealism or Ethics of Pure Duty: what ought to be done remains good regardless of human experience. Hence, good is a fulfillment of duty or a pursuit of the categorical imperative.

KANT, Immanuel (1724-1804), — see Idealism, in *PQS*, No. 5;
below, Index.

——, *Kritik der praktischen Vernunft*. Riga: J. F. Hartknoch, 1788. English
translation by L. W. BECK, *Critique of Practical Reason and Other
Writings in Moral Philosophy*. Chicago: University of Chicago Press,
1949.

——, *Grundlegung zur Metaphysik der Sitten*. 2nd ed. Riga: J. F. Hart-
knoch, 1786. First published in 1785. English translation by Thomas
K. ABBOTT, *Fundamental Principles of the Metaphysics of Morals*.
New York: The Liberal Arts Press, 1949. Also by H. J. PATON, *The
Moral Law or Kant's Groundwork of the Metaphysics of Morals*.
3rd ed. New York: Barnes and Noble, 1956.

——, *Eine Vorlesung Kants über Ethik*. English translation by Louis IN-
FIELD, *Kant's Lectures on Ethics*. London: Methuen, 1930. Pp. XIII,
253.

——, *Metaphysik der Sitten*. 2 parts. Königsberg: F. Nicolovius, 1797. English translation by J. W. SEMPLE, *The Metaphysics of Ethics*. 3rd ed.
Edinburgh: Clark, 1836.

——, *Metaphysische Anfangsgründe der Rechtslehre*. Königsberg: F. Nicolovius, 1797. Pp. XII, 236. See below, p. 136.

BECK, Lewis White, *A Commentary on Kant's Critique of Practical
Reason*. Chicago: University of Chicago Press, 1960. Pp. 308.

JONES, W. T., *Morality and Freedom in the Philosophy of Immanuel
Kant*. New York: Oxford, 1940. Pp. VII, 178.

PATON, H. J., *The Categorical Imperative*. Chicago: University of
Chicago Press, 1948. Pp. 283.

——, *The Moral Law, or Kant's Groundwork of the Metaphysics of
Morals*. New York and London: Hutchinsons University Library, 1948.

SCHILPP, P., *Kant's Pre-Critical Ethics*. Revised edition. Evanston
and Chicago: Northwestern University Press, 1960. Pp. 119. First
published in 1938.

SCOTT, J. W., *Kant on the Moral Life*. New York: The Macmillan Co.,
1924.

TEALE, Alfred E., *Kantian Ethics*. Oxford: Oxford University Press,
1951. Pp. X, 328.

DELBOS, Victor, *Essai sur la formation de la philosophie pratique
de Kant*. 2nd ed. Paris: F. Alcan, 1926. First published in 1903. Pp. X,
312.

RUVO DE, Vincenzo, «Il problematicismo de Kant», *Il Saggiatore*,
1954, pp. 226-241.

——, *L'etica kantiana*. Trani: Vecchi 1955. Pp. 52.

DRAGO DEL BOCA, Susanna, *Kant e i moralisti tedeschi: Wolff, Baum-
garten, Crusius*. Naples: Loffredo, 1937.

KLAUSEN, Sverre, *Kants Ethik und ihre Kritiker*. Oslo: Det norske vi-
denskapsakademi, 1954. Pp. 64.

Superman Ethics: Good is that which contributes to the emergence of a superman.

NIETZSCHE, Friedrich Wilhelm (1844-1900), — see Histories of Modern Philosophy, in *PQS,* No. 5.

——, *Also sprach Zarathustra. Ein Buch für Alle und Keiner.* 4 parts. Chemnitz: Schmeitzner, 1883-1891. English translation by Alexander TILLE and M. M. BOZMAN, *Thus Spake Zarathustra.* London, Toronto: J. M. Dent and Sons, 1933. Pp. XXIII, 288.

——, *Morgenröthe. Gedanken über die moralischen Vorurtheile.* Chemnitz: Schmeitzner, 1881. Pp. 363.

——, *Jenseits von Gut und Böse. Vorspiel einer Philosophie der Zukunft.* Leipzig: G. G. Neumann, 1886. Pp. VII, 271. English translation by Helen ZIMMERN, *Beyond Good and Evil: Prelud to a Philosophy of the Future.* New York: The Macmillan Co., 1907.

——, *Zur Genealogie der Moral, Eine Streitschrift.* Leipzig: G. C. Naumann, 1887. Pp. XIV, 192. English translation by H. SAMUEL, *The Geneology of Morals.* Edinburgh: T. N. Foulis, 1913.

——, *Die Geburt der Tragödie aus dem Geiste der Musik.* Leipzig: Fritzsch, 1872. Pp. IV, 143. English translation by Francis GOLFFING, *The Birth of Tragedy and the Genealogy of Morals.* Garden City, New York: Doubleday Anchor, 1956.

——, *Ecce Homo.* Edited posthumously by Raoul RICHTER. Leipzig: Insel-Verlag, 1908. Pp. 155.

Portable Nietzsche. Selections and translation by Walter KAUFMANN. New York: Viking Press, 1954. Pp. 687.

BARKER, Ernest, *Nietzsche and Treitschke: the Worship of Power in Modern Germany.* New York: Oxford University Press, 1914. Pp. 28.

BENTLEY, Eric Russell, *Century of Hero-Worship: A Study of the Idea of Heroism in Carlyle and Nietzsche with Notes on Other Hero-Worshipers of Modern Times.* New York: Longmans, 1944. Pp. 337.

COPLESTON, Frederick Charles, *Friedrich Nietzsche. Philosopher of Culture.* London: Burns, Oates and Washbourne, 1942. Pp. XII, 217.

——, *St. Thomas and Nietzsche.* Oxford: Blackfriars Publications, 1955. Pp. 24.

HELLER, Peter, *Dialectics and Nihilism: Essays in Lessing, Nietzsche, Mann and Kafka.* Amherst, Massachusetts: The University of Massachusetts Press, 1967. Pp. 344.

JASPERS, Karl, «Zu Nietzsches Bedeutung in der Geschichte der Philosophie», *Die Neue Rundschau* (Frankfurt A. M.), 1950, No. 3, pp. 346-358. English translation by Stanley GODMAN, «The Importance of Nietzsche, Marx and Kierkegaard in the History of Philosophy», *Hibbert Journal,* 1951, pp. 226-234.

——, *Nietzsche und das Christentum.* 2nd ed. Munich: R. Piper und Co., 1952. Pp. 71. First published in 1947.

KNIGHT, George Wilson, *Christ and Nietzsche.* London: Staples Press, 1949. Pp. 244.

LICHTENBERGER, Henri, *Gospel of Superman: The Philosophy of Frie-drich Nietzsche*. Translated from the French by J. M. Kennedy. New York: The Macmillan Co., 1926. Pp. XXXIII, 219.

MORGAN, George Allen, *What Nietzsche Means*. Cambridge, Massachusetts: Harvard University Press, 1941. Pp. XVIII, 408.

NICOLAS, Marius Paul, *From Nietzsche Down to Hitler*. Translated from the French by E. G. ECHLIN. London: W. Hodge and Co., 1939. Pp. XXII, 149.

THOMPSON, R. Motson, *Nietzsche and Christian Ethics*. London: Epworth Press, 1950. Pp. 104.

WRIGHT, W. H., *What Nietzsche Taught*. New York: Huebsch, 1915.

ANDLER, Charles, *Nietzsche: sa vie et sa pensée*. 3 vols. Paris: Librairie Gallimard, 1958.

BARTH, Hans, *Wahrheit und Ideologie*. Zürich: Manesse Verlag, 1945. Pp. 350.

BERTINI, Giovanni, *Un asceta e un superuomo: Schopenhauer e Nietzsche*. Pistoia. Tipografia Pistoiese, 1947.

CARDONE, Domenico Antonio, *Il problema del sovraumano*. Florence: La Nuova Italia, 1936. Pp. 78.

FLEMMING, Siegbert, «Nietzsches Metaphysik und ihr Verhältnis zu Erkenntnistheorie und Ethik», in *Bibliothek für Philosophie* (11 vols. Berlin: L. Simon, 1911-1914), Vol. X, 1914. Pp. 118.

HEIMSOETH, Heinz, *Metaphysische Voraussetzungen und Antriebe in Nietzsches «Immoralismus»*. Wiesbaden: Steiner, 1955. Pp. 67.

KESSELRING, Max, *Nietzsche und sein Zarathustra in psychiatrischer Beleuchtung*. Affoltern a. A: Aehren-Verlag, 1954. Pp. T53.

MESS, F., *Nietzsche der Gesetzgeber*. Leipzig; F. Mezner, 1930. Pp. XX, 408.

MOLINA, E., *Nietzsche dionisiaco y asceta*. Santiago, Chile: Nascimento, 1944. Pp. 231.

REININGER, Robert, *Friedrich Nietzsches Kampf um den Sinn des Lebens. Der Ertrag seiner Philosophie für die Ethik*. Vienna: W. Braunmüller, 1922. Pp. X, 187.

VIDARI, Giovanni, *L'individualismo nelle dottrine morali del sec. XIX*. Milan: Hoepli, 1909. Pp. XX, 400.

Hitlerism: good is that which contributes to the national supremacy of the German race. See Politics, below Ch. IV, p. 211.

Racism: there exists a privileged race (the Aryan) which alone possesses the ideal of human value, and therefore should dominate other races.

HIRSCHFELD, Magnus, *Racism*. Translated from the German by E. and C. PAUL. London: V. Gollancz, 1938. Pp. 320.

ROYCE, Josiah, *Race Questions, Provincialism, and Other American Problems.* New York: The Macmillan Co., 1908. Pp. XIII, 287.

SOPER, E. D., *Racism, A World Issue.* New York; Nashville, Tennessee: Abingdon, 1947. Pp. 304.

SOROKIN, Pitirim A., «Anthropo-Racial, Selectionist, and Hereditarist School», in his *Contemporary Sociological Theories* (New York: Harper and Brothers, 1928), pp. 218-308.

AMMON, Otto, *Anthropologische Untersuchungen der Wehrpflichtigen in Baden.* Hamburg: Aktien-Geselschaft, 1890. Pp. 36.

——, *Die natürliche Auslese beim Menschen.* Jena: G. Fischer, 1893. Pp. X, 326.

——, *Die Geselschaftsordnung und ihre natürlichen Grundlagen.* 3rd ed. Jena: G. Fischer, 1900. Pp. VI, 303. First published in 1895.

BRESSOLES, Adrien, *Racisme et christianisme.* Paris: Flammarion, 1939. Pp. XIII, 210.

Representatives

CHAMBERLAIN, Houston Stewart (1855-1926), *Die Grundlagen des neuzehnten Jahrhunderts.* 28th ed. Munich: Bruckmann, 1942. Pp. XV, 632. First published in 1899.

——, *Arische Weltanschauung.* 9th ed. Munich: Bruckmann, 1943. Pp. 94.

——, *Goethe.* 9th ed. Munich: Bruckmann, 1938. Pp. XI, 800.

——, *Deutsches Wesen.* 3rd ed. Munich: Bruckmann, 1942.

——, *Lebenswege meines Denkens.* 3rd ed. Munich: Bruckmann, 1942. Pp. 414.

MEYER, Hugo, *Houston Stewart Chamberlain als völkischer Denker.* Munich: Bruckmann, 1939. Pp. 235.

SELLIÈRE, E., *Houston Stewart Chamberlain, le plus récent philosophie du pangermanisme mystique.* Paris: La Renaissance du Livre, 1917. Pp. 182.

GOBINEAU de, Arthur (1816-1882), *Essai sur l'inégalité des races humaines.* 4 vols. Paris: Firmin-Didot frères, 1853-1855. English translation of the first volume by A. COLLINS, *The Inequality of Human Races.* New York: G. P. Putman's Sons, 1915. P. XIV, 217.

——, *Histoire des Perses d'après les auteurs orientaux, grecs et latins.* 2 vols. Paris: H. Plon. 1869.

HONE, J. M., «Arthur, Count of Gobineau, Race Mystic», *Contemporary* Revue (London), 1913, pp. 94-103.

SPRING, Gerald Max, *Vitalism of Count de Gobineau.* New York: Columbia University Press, 1932. Pp. 303.

DREYFUS, R., *La vie et les prophéties du Comte de Gobineau.* Paris: C. Lévy, 1905. Pp. 344.

KRETZER. Eugen, *Joseph Arthur Graf von Gobineau, sein Leben und sein Werk.* Leipzig: H. Seemann Nachfolger, 1902. Pp. 265.

LANGE, Maurice, *Le comte Arthur de Gobineau.* Strassburgh: Librairie Istra, 1924. Pp. 293.

SCHEMANN, L., *Gobineau. Eine Biographie.* 2 vols. Strassburgh, Berlin: Vereinigte wissenschaftliche Verlagen, 1913-1916.

LAPOUGE DE, Georges V. (Georges Vacher de Lapouge), *Les sélections sociales*. Paris: A. Fontemoing, 1896. Pp. XII, 503.
——, *L'Aryen, son rôle social*. Paris: A. Fontemoing, 1899. Pp. XX, 569.
——, *Race et milieu social*. Paris: A. Fontemoing, 1909.

(ee) DIALECTICAL IDEALISM: morality is evolving with social processes.

See History of Modern Philosophy, in *PQS*, No. 5; Idealism, *ibid.;* below, Index.

Germany

FICHTE, Johann G. (1762-1814): Good is what well organized society considers as such.

——, *Die Bestimmung des Menschen*. Berlin: Voss, 1800. Pp. VI, 338. English translation by William SMITH, *The Vocation of Man*. La Salle, Illinois: The Open Court, 1940.
——, *Grundlage des Naturechts nach Principien der Wissenschaftslehre*. 2 parts. Jena Leipzig: C. E. Gabler, 1796-1797.
——, *Das System der Sittenlehre nach den Principien der Wissenschaftslehre*. Jena, Leipzig: C. E. Gabler, 1798. Pp. XVIII, 494. English translation by A. E. KROEGER, *The Science of Ethics as Based on the Science of Knowledge*. New edition. London: Kegan Paul, Trench, Trubner, 1907.
——, *Über das Wesen des Gelehrten und seine Erscheinung im Gebiete der Freiheit*. Berlin: In der Hamburgischen Buchhandlung, 1806. Pp. VI, 215. English translation by William Smith, *On the Nature of the Scholar and Its Manifestations*. 2nd ed. London: J. Chapman, 1848. Pp. VII, 131.

HEGEL, Georg W. F. (1770-1831): Morality consists in being a person and respecting others as persons.

——, *System der Sittlichkeit*. Aus dem handschriftlichen Nachlasse des Verfassers. Ed. by G. MOLLAT. Harz: Osterwieck, 1893. Pp. IV, 71.
——, *Grundlinien der Philosophie des Rechts*. Berlin: Nicolai, 1820. English translation by T. M. KNOX, *Philosophy of Right*. Oxford: Clarendon Press, 1942. See Law. below, Chapter III, p. 138.
——, *The Ethics of Hegel*. Translated selections from his *Rechtsphilosophie* with an introduction by J. M. STERRETT. Boston, Massachusetts: Ginn and Co., 1893. Pp. XII, 216.

CHANG, Wyszie Shionyu, *The Development, Significance, and Some Limitations of Hegel's Ethical Teaching*. Shanghai, China: The Commercial Press, 1926. Pp. 137.

REYBURN, H. A., *The Ethical Theory of Hegel: A Study of the Philosophy of Right*. Oxford: Clarendon Press, 1921.

DELLA VOLPE, Galvano, *Hegel, romantico e mistico, 1793-1800.* Florence: Le Monnier, 1929. Pp. VIII, 224.

PELZER, Roland, «Studien über Hegels ethische Theoreme», *Archiv für Philosophie* (Stuttgart), Vol. XIII, No 1-3. pp. 3-49.

PEPERZAK, Adrien T. B., *Le jeune Hegel et la vision morale du monde.* The Hague. Martinus Nijhoff, 1960. Pp. XV, 264.

SCHOPENHAUER, Arthur (1788-1860); we attain the supreme happiness by destroying our will to live and by vanishing into the Nirvana of the Buddhists.

——, *Parerga und Paralipomena.* 2 vols. Berlin: A. W. Hahn, 1862. English translation of some passages by T. B. SAUNDERS, «On the Suffering of the World», in *Studies in Pessimism.* London: Eckler, 1890.

——, *On the Basis of Morality.* Translated by E. F. J. Payne. Indianopolis, Indiana — Merrill, 1965. Pp. 252.

COPLESTON, F. C., *Arthur Schopenhauer, Philosopher of Pessimism.* London: Burns, Oates and Washburn, 1947. Pp. 216.

McGILL, V. J., *Schopenhauer, Pessimist and Pagan.* New York: Brentano's 1931. Pp. 312.

MANN, Thomas, *Schopenhauer.* Stockholm: Bermann-Fischer, 1938. Pp. 83.

England and America
These schools emphasize the moral and religious tradition against naturalism.

POCHMANN, Henry August, *New England Transcendentalism and St. Louis Hegelianism.* Philadelphia: 420 Chestnut St., 1948. Pp. 144.

SANTAYANA, George, *Character and Opinion in the United States.* New York: Charles Scribner's Sons, 1920. Pp. IX, 233.

SCHNEIDER, Herbert Wallace, *A History of American Philosophy.* New York: Columbia University Press, 1946. Pp. XIV, 646.

BOSANQUET, Bernard (1848-1923, — see State, below, Ch. IV, 5; below, Index.

——, *The Civilization of Christendom and Other Studies.* London: Swan Sonnenschein and Co., 1893. Pp. VII, 383.

——, *Psychology of the Moral Self.* London: Macmillan and Co., 1897. Pp. VIII, 132.

——, *The Principle of Individuality and Value.* The Gifford Lectures, 1911. London: Macmillan and Co., 1912. Pp. XXXVII, 409.

——, *The Value and Destiny of the Individual.* The Gifford Lectures, 1912. London: Macmillan and Co., 1913. Pp. XXXII, 331.

——, *Some Suggestions in Ethics.* London: Macmillan and Co., 1918. Pp. VIII, 248.

HOUANG, François, *Le néo-hégélianisme en Angleterre: la philosophie de B. Bosanquet.* Paris: J. Vrin, 1954. Pp. 232.

——, *De l'humanisme à l'absolutisme: l'évolution de la pensée religieuse du néo-hégélien anglais Bernard Bosanquet.* Paris: J. Vrin, 1954. Pp. 138.

BRADLEY, Francis Herbert (1846-1924), *Ethical Studies.* London: H. S. King and Co., 1876. Pp. VIII, 307. With an introduction by Richard WOLL-HEIM, 2nd ed. at Oxford: Oxford University Press, 1962. Pp. 344.

——, *Mr. Sidgwick's Hedonism: An Examination of the Main Argument of «The Methods of Ethics».* London: H. S. King and Son, 1877. Pp. 64.

ROSS, Ralph G., *Scepticism and Dogma: A Study in the Philosophy of F. H. Bradley.* New York: The Author, 515 W. 116th St., 1940. Pp. 159.

SEGERSTEDT, Torgny T., *Value and Reality in Bradley's Philosophy.* Lund, Sweden: C. W. K. Gleerup, 1934. Pp. 264.

WOLLHEIM, Richard, *F. H. Bradley.* Harmondsworth, England: Penguin Books, 1959.

GREEN, Thomas Hill (1836-1882), *Liberal Legislation and Freedom of Contract. A Lecture.* Oxford: Slatter and Rose, 1881. Pp. 22.

——, *Prolegomena to Ethics.* Oxford: Clarendon Press, 1883. Pp. XXXV, 427.

——, *The Witness of God and Faith.* London: Longmans and Co., 1883. Pp. VII, 105.

——, *Lectures on the Principles of Political Obligation.* London: Longmans and Co., 1895. Pp. XXIV, 252.

JAMES, George Francis, *Thomas Hill Green und der Utilitarismus.* Halle: M. Niemeyer, 1894. Pp. 37.

LAMONT, William D., *Introduction to Green's Moral Philosophy.* London: Longmans, Green and Co., 1935. Pp. 224.

SIDGWICK, Henry, *Lectures on the Ethics of T. H. Green, Mr. Herbert Spencer and J. Martineau.* London: Macmillan and Co., 1902. Pp. XII, 374.

MONTAGNÉ, Paul, *Bibliographie relative à un radical religieux en Angleterre au XIXe siècle, ou la Philosophie de Thomas Hill Green.* Toulouse: Imprimerie ouvrière, 1927. Pp. 67.

ROYCE, Josiah (1855-1916), *The Religious Aspect of Philosophy: A Critique of the Bases of Conduct and of Faith.* Boston: Houghton, Mifflin and Co., 1885. Pp. XIX, 484.

——, *Studies of Good and Evil: A Series of Essays upon Problems of Philosophy and of Life.* New York: D. Appleton and Co., 1898. Pp. XVII, 384.

——, *The Spirit of Modern Philosophy.* Boston: Houghton, Mifflin and Co., 1899. Pp. XV, 519.

——, *The World and the Individual.* Gifford Lectures. 2 series. New York: The Macmillan Co., 1900-1901.

——, *Race Questions,. Provincialism, and Other American Problems.* New York: The Macmillan Co., 1908. Pp. XIII, 287.

——, *The Philosophy of Loyalty.* New York: The Macmillan Co., 1908. Pp. XIII, 409.

——, *The Sources of Religious Insight.* Lectures. New York: Charles Scribner's Sons, 1912. Pp. XVI, 297.

——, *The Problem of Christianity*. 2 vols. New York: The Macmillan Co., 1913.

Cotton, James Harry, *Royce on the Human Self*. Cambridge, Massachusetts: Harvard University Press, 1954. Pp. 347.

Fuss, Peter, *The Moral Philosophy of Josiah Royce*. Cambridge, Massachusetts: Harvard University Press, 1965.

Sears, Annie L., *The Drama of the Spiritual Life*. Introduction by J. Royce. New York: Macmillan Co., 1915. Pp. XXIV, 495.

Smith, John Edwin, *Royce's Social Infinite: The Community of Interpretation*. New York: Liberal Arts, 1950. Pp. XIII, 176.

Smith, Thomas Vernor, *The Philosophic Way of Life*. Chicago: University of Chicago Press, 1929. Pp. XVII, 376.

Aronson, Moses Judah, *La philosophie morale de J. Royce*. Paris: F. Alcan, 1927. Pp. XV, 185.

Yakovenko, Boris V., *L'idealismo costruttivo ed assoluto di Josiah Royce*. Praga: Biblioteca internazionale di filosofia, 1937. Pp. VII, 52.

(ff) Positivism: moral rules must be based on experience, and they attain probable validity only.

See *PQS*, No. 4, Ch. XIII, 5; Sociology, below, Ch. V, 5, Method, p. 263.

Auguste Comte (1798-1857): Humanity or love for others.

Comte, Auguste, *The Positive Philosophy of Auguste Comte*. English edition by Harriet Martineau. Chicago: Belford, Clarke and Co., 1853. Pp. 838.
——, *The Catechism of Positive Religion*. Translated by R. Congreve. London: Reeves and Turner, 1858.

Barzellotti, G., *La morale nella filosofia positiva: Studio critico*. Florence: Cellini, 1871. Pp. XII, 164.

Mill, John Stuart, *Auguste Comte et Positivism*. London: George Routledge and Sons, 1908. Pp. 203.

Moshetti, A. M., *A Comte e la pedagogia positiva*. Milan: C. Marzorati, 1953. Pp. 87.

Mill, John Stuart (1806-1873), — see Utilitarianism, above, p. 25.

Spencer, Herbert (1820-1903), — see Evolutionary Ethics, below, Contemporary, p. 37.

Watson, John, *Comte, Mill and Spencer: An Outline of Philosophy*. Glasgow: J. Maclehose and Sons, 1895. Pp. 302.

CONTEMPORARY

(a) Comprehensive Studies

In English

EKMAN, Rosalind (ed.), *Readings in the Problems of Ethics*. New York: Charles Scribner's Sons, 1965. Pp. 369.

HILL, Thomas English, *Contemporary Ethical Theories*. New York: The Macmillan Company, 1957. Pp. XII, 367.

In Quest of Value: Readings in Philosophy and Personal Values. Ed. by the Associates of Philosophy in San Jose State College. Chicago: Science Research Associates, 1963. Pp. 514.

JOHNSON, Oliver A., *Rightness and Goodness: A Study in Contemporary Ethics*. The Hague: Martinus Nijhoff, 1959. Pp. VI, 163.

KERNER, George C. (ed.), *The Revolution in Ethical Theory*. New York: Oxford University Press, 1966. Pp. 272. Excerpts from G. E. MOORE, Ch. L. STEVENSON, S. TOULIMIN, R. M. HARE, and the Editors suggestions.

KRESGE, Elijah Everett, *The Search for the Way of Life: A Review of the Major Classical and Contemporary Ethical Systems of the Western World*. New York: Exposition Press, 1950. Pp. 434.

McGLYNN, James V., S. J. and TONER, Jules J., S. J., *Modern Ethical Theories*. Milwaukee: The Bruce Publishing Company, 1962. Pp. 167.

MARGOLIS, Joseph (ed.), *Contemporary Ethical Theories*. New York: Random House, 1966. Pp. 544.

MONTEFIORE, Alan, *A Modern Introduction to Moral Philosophy*. New York: Praeger, 1959. Pp. 213.

PRICE, Richard, *A Review of the Principal Questions in Morals*. Ed. by D. Daiches RAPHAEL. New York: Oxford University Press, 1949. Pp. XLVII, 301.

> CUA, Antonio So, *Reason and Virtue: A Study in the Ethics of Richard Price*. Athens, Ohio: Ohio University Press, 1958. Pp. 189.

RAMSEY, Paul (ed), *Nine Modern Moralists: Paul Tillich, Karl Marx, H. Richard Niebuhr, Fyodor Dostoevski, Reinhold Niebuhr, Jacques Maritain, Jean-Paul Sartre, Emil Brunner, Edmund Cahn*. Englewood Cliffs, New Jersey: Prentice-Hall, Inc., 1962.

TAYLOR, Paul W. (ed.), *The Moral Judgment: Readings in Contemporary Meta-Ethics*. Englewood Cliffs, New Jersey: Prentice-Hall, Inc., 1964. Pp. XVII, 296. See also Methods, in *PQS*, No. 4, Ch. II.

THOMSON, Judith Jarvis and Dworkin, Gerald (eds.), *Ethics*. New York: Harper and Row, 1968. Pp. 536.

WARNOCK, G. J., *Contemporary Moral Philosophy*. New York: St. Martin's Press, 1967. Pp. 96.

WARNOCK, Mary, *Ethics Since 1900*. New York: Oxford University Press, 1960. Pp. 212. Includes bibliography. See also Existentialism, below, p. 44; in *PQS*, No. 5.

——, *Contemporary Moral Philosophy*. New York: St. Martin's Press, 1967. Pp. 81.

Wilson, John, *Reason and Morals*. Cambridge: University Press, 1961. Pp. 187.

In Other Languages

Litt, T., *Ethik der Neuzeit*. Berlin: R. Oldenbourg, 1927. Pp. 184.

(b) Specific Studies

(aa) Evolutionary or Process Theories in Ethics: Good is relatively more evolved conduct; evil is relatively less evolved conduct.

Flew, A. G. N., *Evolutionary Ethics*. New York: St. Martin's Press, 1968. Pp. 96.

Huxley, J. S., *Evolutionary Ethics*. London: Oxford: University Press, 1943. Pp. 83.

Broad, C. D., «Review of Julian S. Huxley's Evolutionary Ethics», *Mind*, 1944.

Huxley, Thomas H., *Evolution and Ethics*. New York, London: D. Appleton and Company, 1929. Pp. 334. First published in 1893.

Spencer, Herbert, *First Principles*. 2nd printing. London: Williams and Norgate, 1863. First printed in 1862.

——, *The Data of Ethics*. London: Williams and Norgate, 1879-1880.

——, *The Principles of Ethics*. 2 vols. New York: D. Appleton and Company, 1895. First published in London: Williams and Norgate, 1892. See Sociology, below, p. 242.

MacCosh, James, *Herbert Spencer's Philosophy as Culminated in his Ethics*. New York: C. Scribner's Sons, 1885. Pp. IV, 71.

Cathrein, Victor, *Die Sittenlehre des Darwinismus. Eine Kritik der Ethik Herbert Spencers*. Freiburg i. B.: Stimmen aus Maria-Laach, 1885. Pp. X, 146.

Compayré, G., *Herbert Spencer et l'éducation scientifique*. Paris, n. d. English translation by Maria E. Findlay, *Herbert Spencer and Scientific Education*. New York: Crowell and Co., 1907. Pp. 119.

Halleux, Jean, *L'évolutionisme en morale: étude sur la philosophie de Herbert Spencer*. Paris: F. Alcan, 1901. Pp. 228.

Salvadore, Guglielmo, *L'etica evoluzionista: studio sulla filosofia morale di Herbert Spencer*. Turin: Bocca, 1903. Pp. XV, 476.

Stadler, August, *Herbert Spencer. Spencers Ethik*. Ed. by J. Platter. Leipzig: R. Voigtländer, 1913. Pp. 211.

Waddington, C. H., *Science and Ethics*. London: George Allen and Unwin, 1942.

Williams, C. M., *A Review of the Systems of Ethics founded on the Theory of Evolution*. London: Macmillan and Co., 1893. Pp. XV, 581.

Dialectical Materialism, — see below.

Pragmatism, — see below.

(bb) Dialectical Materialism: Ideas are instruments through which the interest of the proletariat in its class-struggle is to be carried out.

See Economics, below, Ch. II, p. 95; Materialism, in *PQS*, No. 5.

Jordan, Z. A., *The Evolution of Dialectical Materialism*. New York: St. Martin's Press, 1967. Pp. 512.

Kropotkin, P. A., *Ethics, Origin and Development*. Translated by L. S. Friedland and J. R. Piroshnikoff. New York: 1924.

Kautsky, Carl Johann, *Ethik und materialistische Geschichtsauffassung. Ein Versuch*. Berlin: J. H. W. Dietz, 1922. Pp. VII, 144. English translation by J. B. Agnew, *Ethics and the Materialist Concept of History*. Chicago, 1907.

Marx, Karl, *Das Kapital*. 3 vols. Hamburg: O. Meissner, 1867-1894. English translation by Samuel Moore, Edward Aveling and Ernest Utermann, *Capital*. Chicago: Charles H. Kerr and Co., 1915.

——, and Engels, F., *The Communist Manifesto*. New York: International Publischers, 1930. Pp. XI, 365. See below, p. 95.

Kamenka, Eugene, *The Ethical Foundation of Marxism*. London: Praeger, 1962. Pp. 208.

——, *Marxist Ethics*. New York. St. Martin's Press, 1969 (?). In preparation.

Koren, Henry J., *Marx and the Authentic Man*. Pittsburgh, Pennsylvania: Duquesne University Press, 1968.

Ling, Trevor, *Buddha, Marx and God*. New York: St. Martin's Press, 1967. Pp. 240.

Somerville, John, *The Philosophy of Marxism*. New York: Random House, 1967. Pp. 224.

Problemy etiki. Moscow: Nauka, 1964. Pp. 265.

Szvarcman, K. A., *Etika ... bez morali i Kritika sowremennych burzuaznych eticzeskich teorij*. Moscow: Mysl, 1964. Pp. 263.

Mao, Tse-tung, — see below, p. 206.

(cc) Pragmatism: the morality of man's actions is indicated by the workableness or good consequences of his ideas.

See *PQS*, No. 5.

Abel, Reuben (ed.), *Humanistic Pragmatism: The Philosophy of F. C. S. Schiller*. New York: The Macmillan Co., 1966.

Kennedy, G., *Pragmatic Ethics*. New York: St. Martin's Press, 1969 (?). In preparation.

Thayer, H. S., *Meaning and Action: A Critical History of Pragmatism*. Indianopolis, Indiana: Bobbs-Merrill, 1968. Pp. 650.

Representatives

DEWEY, John, «Ethics and Physical Science», *Andover Review* (Boston, New York), June 1887, pp. 573-591.

——, *Outlines of a Critical Theory of Ethics*. Ann Arbor, Michigan: Register Publishing Co., 1891. Pp. viii, 253.

——, «Moral Theory and Practice», *International Journal of Ethics* (Philadelphia), January 1891, pp. 186-203.

——, *The Study of Ethics: A Syllabus*. Ann Arbor, Michigan: Register Publishing Co., 1894. Pp. iv, 151.

——, «The Metaphysical Method in Ethics», *Psychological Review* (Washington, D. C.), March 1896, pp. 181-188.

——, «Evolution and Ethics», *Monist* (La Salle, Illinois), April, 1898, pp. 321-341.

——, «The Evolutionary Method as Applied to Morality», *Philosophical Review* (Ithaca, N. Y.), March 1902, pp. 107-124; June 1902, pp. 353-371.

——, *Logical Conditions of a Scientific Treatment of Morality*. Chicago: The University of Chicago Press, 1903. Pp. 23.

——, «Psychological Method of Ethics», *Psychological Review*, March 1903, pp. 158-160.

——, *Ethics*. New York: The Columbia University Press, 1908. Pp. 26. Lecture at Columbia University, March 25, 1908.

——, «Ethics», in the *Encyclopedia Americana* (30 vols. New York, Americana Corporation, 1967), Vol. X, pp. 535-542.

——, *Human Nature and Conduct*. New York: Henry Holt and Co., 1922.

——, «Ethics of Animal Experimentation», *Hygeia*, February, 1931, Pp. 118-120.

——, *The Theory of Valuation*. Chicago: The University of Chicago Press, 1939. Pp. 67.

——, and TUFTS, James H., *Ethics*. Revised edition. New York: Henry Holt and Co., 1932. Pp. XIII, 528. First published in 1908.

——, «Intimations of Morality: Review of Corliss Lamont, The Illusion of Immorality», *New Republic* (Washington, D. C.), April 24, 1935.

——, «Ambiguity of Intrinsic Good», *Journal of Philosophy* (New York), June 4, 1942, pp. 328-330. Reprinted in *The Problems of Men*. New York: Philosophical Library, 1946. Pp. 424.

——, «Ethical Subject Matter and Language», *Journal of Philosophy* (New York), December 20, 1945, Pp. 701-712.

EZORSKY, Gertrude, «Inquiry as Appraisal: The Singularity of John Dewey's Theory of Valuation», *Journal of Philosophy* (New York), 1958.

KENNEDY, Gail, «Science and the Transformation of Common Sense: The Basic Problem of Dewey's Philosophy», *Journal of Philosophy* (New York), 1954.

STUART, Henry W., «Dewey's Ethical Theory», in Paul A. SCHILPP (ed.), *The Philosophy of John Dewey* (New York: Tudor, 1951), Chapter X.

WHITE Morton, «Value and Obligation in Dewey and Lewis», *Philosophical Review*, 1949.

Bausola, Andriano, *L'etica di John Dewey*. Milan: Vita e Pensiero, 1960. Pp. 225.

James, William (1842-1910), *Is Life Worth Living ?* Philadelphia: S. Burns Weston, 1896. Pp. 63.
——, *Philosophical Conceptions and Practical Results*. Berkeley, California: California University Chronical, 1898.
——, *The Will to Believe and Other Essays in Popular Philosophy*. New York: Longmans and Co., 1897. Pp. XVII, 332.
——, *The Varieties of Religious Experience: A Study in Human Nature*. London: Longmans and Co., 1902. Pp. XII, 534.
——, *The Moral Equivalent of War*. London: Peace Pledge Union, 1943. Pp. 12. Reprint from *Memories and Studies*, — see below. First published in New York by American Association for International Conciliation, 1910.
——, *Memories and Studies*. Ed. by Henry James. London: Longmans and Co., 1911. Pp. 411.
——, *Essays in Radical Empiricism*. New York: Longmans, Green and Co., 1912. Pp. XII, 282.
——, *Essays on Faith and Morals*. Selected by Ralph Barton Perry. New York: Longmans and Co., 1943. Pp. IX, 341.

Perry, Ralph Barton, *The Thought and Character of William James*. 2 vols. Boston, Massachusetts: Little, Brown and Co., 1936.
——, *In the Spirit of William James*. Bloomington, Indiana: Indiana University Press, 1958. Pp. 211.

Mead, G. H., «The Philosophical Basis of Ethics», *International Journal of Ethics* (Philadelphia), VIII (1907-1908).
——, «Scientific Method and the Moral Sciences», *International Journal of Ethics*. XXXIII (1922-1923).
——, *The Philosophy of the Present*. Chicago: The Open Court Publishing Company, 1932.
——, *The Philosophy of the Act*. Chicago: The University of Chicago Press, 1938.
Otto, M. C., *Things and Ideals*. New York: Henry Holt and Company, 1924.
——, *The Human Enterprise*. New York: F. . Crofts, 1940.
Peirce, Charles S. (1839-1914), *Chance, Love and Logic: Philosophical Essays*. Ed. by Morris R. Cohen. London: Kegan Paul and Co., 1923. Pp. XXXIII, 318.

Feibleman, James K., «Ethics», in his *Introduction to Peirce's Philosophy*. New Orleans, Louisiana: The Hauser Press, 1960. Chapter IX.

Tufts, James Hayden (1862-1942), «The Moral Life and the Construction of Values and Standards», in *Creative Intelligence*. New York: Henry Holt and Company, 1917.
——, *The Ethics of Cooperation*. Boston, Massachusetts: Houghton Mifflin Co., 1918. Pp. 73.
——, *Recent Ethics in Its Broader Relations*. Berkeley: University of California Press (Publication in Philosophy), 1930. Pp. 20.

(dd) HUMANIST THEORIES: personal experience rather than social and natural progress are rules of man's behavior.
See Humanism (Contemporary History of Philosophy), in *PQS*, No. 5. Naturalistic Ethics, below, p. 52.

BABBITT, Irving, «The Breakdown of Internationalism», *The Nation* (New York), Vol. C. (June, 1915), pp. 677-680.
——, *On Being Creative*. Boston: Houghton Mifflin Company, 1932. Pp. XIV, 265.
COATES, Wilson H., WHITE, Hayden V., and SCHAPIRO, J. Salwyn, *The Emergence of Liberal Humanism: An Intellectual History of Western Europe*. 2 vols. New York: McGraw-Hill, 1965-1967.
FITE, W., *An Introductory Study of Ethics*. New York: Longmans, Green and Co., 1903. Pp. VI, 383.
——, *Individualism*. New York: Longmans, Green and Co., 1911. Pp. XIX, 301.
——, *Moral Philosophy*. New York: Lincoln MacVeagh, The Dial Press, 1925. Pp. IX, 320.
GARNETT, C. B., *Wisdom in Conduct*. New York: Harcourt, Brace and Company, 1940. Pp. XV, 458.
LEVINE, Israel, *Reason and Morals*. Glasgow: Maclehose, Jackson and Co., 1924. Pp. XI, 176.

Religious Humanism, — see Periodicals, below, p. 71.

Psychoanalysis: good is that which leads man to the formation of his character, and thus morality is reduced to the super-rational level of genuinely psychic life.

BEIER, Ernst G., *The Silent Language of Psychohrapy: Social Reinforcement of Unconscious Processes*. Chicago: Aldine Publishing Co., 1966. Pp. 329.
COLE, William Graham, *Sex in Christianity and Psychoanalysis*. New York: Oxford University Press, 1955. Pp. 229.
DAVIS, James A., *Education for Positive Mental Health: A Critique of Existing Research and Recommendations for Future Studies*. Chicago: Aldine Publishing Co., 1966. Pp. 280.
ERON, Leonard D., *The Classification of Behavior Disorder*. Chicago: Aldine Publishing Co., 1967. Pp. 192.
GRINSTEIN, Alexander, *The Index of Psychoanalytic Writings*. 5 vols. New York: International Universities Press, 1956-1960.
GROVES, Ernest Rutherford, *Moral Sanitation*. New York: Association Press, 1916.
HARTMANN, Heinz, *Psychoanalysis and Moral Values*. New York: International Universities Press, 1960. Pp. 121.
HOOP VAN DER, J. H., *Character and the Unconscious: A Critical Exposition of the Psychology of Freud and Jung*. Translated by Elizabeth TREVELYAN. New York: Harcourt, Brace and Co., 1923.

Hospers, John, «Free Will and Psychoanalysis», in Paul Edwards and Arthur Pap (eds.), *A Modern Introduction to Philosophy: Readings from Classical and Contemporary Sources* (2nd ed. New York: The Free Press-Macmillan, 1965), pp. 75-85.

Munroe, Ruth, *Learned Schools of Psychoanalytic Thought: An Exposition, Critique, and Attempt on Integration.* New York: Dryden, 1955. Pp. 670.

Nuttin, Joseph, *Psychoanalysis and Personality: A Dynamic Theory of Normal Personality.* Translated by George Lamb. New York: Sheed and Ward, 1954. Pp. 310.

Peters, Richard Stanley, *The Concept of Motivation.* New York: Humanities Press, 1958. **Pp. 166.**

Truax, Charles B. and Carkhuff, Robert R., *Toward Effective Counselling and Psychotherapy.* Chicago: Aldine Publishing Co., 1967. Pp. 416.

Zweig, Stefan, *Mental Healers: Franz Anton Mesmer, Mary Baker Eddy, Sigmund Freud.* New York: Frederick Ungar, 1962. Pp. XXVI, 363.

Dictionnaire de psychanalyse et de psychotechnique. Ed. by Maryse Choisy et al. Paris: 19 rue Monsieur, 1946—.

Corvez, M., O. P., «Psychotherapie et psychologie: problèmes de morale», *Revue thomiste* (Toulouse), 1963, pp. 246-258.

Representatives

Freud, Sigmund (1856-1939), *The Interpretation of Dreams.* Translated by A. A. Brill. New York: Modern Library, 1950. Pp. 477. First published in 1900.

——, *The Psychopathology of Everyday Life.* Translated by A. A. Brill. New York: The Macmillan Co., 1917. First published in 1901.

——, *Three Essays on the Theory of Sexuality.* Translated by James Strachey. New York: Anglobooks, 1951. Pp. 133. First published in 1905.

——, *Leonardo da Vinci: A Study in Psychosexuality.* Translated by A. A. Brill. New York: Modern Library, 1955. Pp. 122. First published in 1910.

——, *Three Contributions to the Theory of Sex.* Translated by A. A. Brill. 4th ed. New York: Dutton Press, 1962. Pp. XXVI, 98. First published in 1910.

——, *On Creativity and the Unconscious: Papers on the Psychology of Art, Lit, Love, Religion.* Ed. by Benjamin Nelson. New York: Harper and Row, 1958. Pp. 310.

——, *Totem and Taboo: Some Points of Agreement between the Mental Lives of Savages and Neurotics.* Translated by James Strachey. New York: Northon, 1952. Pp. X, 172. First published in 1913.

——, *Introductory Lectures on Psychoanalysis.* Translated by James Strachey. New York: Northon, 1965. Pp. 202. First published in 1916-1917.

——, *A General Introduction to Psychoanalysis.* Translated by Joan Rivière. New York: Garden City Books, 1949. Pp. 412. First published in 1917.

——, *Beyond the Pleasure Principle.* Translated by James Strachey. London: Hogarth Press, 1950. Pp. 97. First published in 1920.

——, *The Ego and the Id.* Translated by Joan Rivière. New impression. London: Hogarth Press, 1952. Pp. 88. First published in 1923.

——, *Problem of Anxiety.* Translated by Henry A. Bunker. New York: Norton, 1936. Pp. 165. Translated by Alix Strachey, *Inhibitions, Symptoms and Anxiety.* Toronto: Longmans, 1936. Pp. 179. First published in 1926.

——, *The Future of an Illusion.* Translated by W. D. Robson-Scott. London: Hogarth Press, 1950. Pp. 97. First published in 1927.

——, *Civilization and Its Discontents.* Translated by Joan Rivière. New York: Doubleday Anchor Books, 1958. Pp. 105. First published in 1930.

——, *New Introductory Lectures on Psychoanalysis.* Translated by W. J. H. Sprott. London: Hogarth Press, 1933. Pp. VIII, 239.

——, *Moses and Monotheism.* Translated by Katherine Jones. London: Hogarth Press, 1951. Pp. 223. First published in 1939.

——, *Standard Edition of the Complete Psychological Works.* Translated under editorship of James Strachey. 18 vols. London: Hogarth Press, 1953-1957.

Bakan, David, *Sigmund Freud and the Jewish Mystical Tradition.* Toronto: Van Nostrand, 1958. Pp. 326.

Dempsey, Peter James Rory, *Freud, Psychoanalysis, Catholicism.* Chicago: Henry Regnery and Co., 1957. Pp. 209.

Fine, Reuben, *Freud: A Critical Re-evaluation of His Theories.* New York: David McKay, 1962. Pp. 307.

Guirdham, A., *Christ and Freud: A Study of Religious Experience and Observance.* New York: Collier Books, 1962. Pp. 224.

Hartman, Heinz, «Comments on the Psychoanalytic Theory of the Ego», *The Psychoanalytic Study of the Child.* (New York: 1950). Vol. V.

——, «The Mutual Influences in the Development of the Ego and Id», *The Psychoanalytic Study of the Child* (New York: 1952), Vol. VII.

Holt, Edwin Bissell, *Freudian Wish and Its Place in Ethics.* New York: Henry Holt and Co., 1915.

Lee, Roy Stuart, *Freud and Christianity.* London: James Clarke, 1949. Pp. 204.

Philp, Howard Littleton, *Freud and Religious Belief.* New York: Pitman, 1956. Pp. 140.

Rieff, Philip, *Freud: The Mind of the Moralist.* Garden City, New York: Doubleday, 1961.

Sanders, Benjamin Gilbert, *Christianity after Freud: An Interpretation of the Christian Experience in the Light of Psycho-analytic Theory.* New York: The Macmillan Co., 1949. Pp. 157.

Zilboorg, Gregory, *Sigmund Freud, His Exploration of the Mind of Man.* New York: Charles Scribner's, 1951. Pp. 132.

——, *Freud and Religion: A Restatement of an Old Controversy.* Westminster, Maryland: Newman Press, 1958. Pp. 65.

Plé, A., *Freud et la religion*. Paris: Editions de Cerf, 1968. Pp. 144.

Freud, Anna, *The Ego and the Mechanism of Defence*. Translated by Cecil Baines. London: Stechert 1937. Pp. X, 196.

Fromm, Erich, *Man for Himself: An Inquiry into the Psychology of Ethics*. London: Routledge and Kegan Paul,. 1949. Pp. XIV, 254.

——, *Psychoanalysis and Religion*. New Haven, Connecticut: Yale University Press, 1950. Pp. VI, 119.

——, *Forgotten Language: An Introduction to the Understanding of Dreams, Fairy Tales and Myth*. New York: Grove Press, 1957. Pp. 263.

Existentialism: we are free in any situation, responsible only before ourselves and humanity. See Existentialism, in *PQS*, No. 5.

Barnes, Hazel E., *Humanistic Existentialism: The Literature of Possibility*. 18th printing. Lincoln, Nebraska: University of Nebraska Press, 1959. Pp. 418. First published in 1938 as *The Literature of Possibility: Studies in Humanistic Existentialism*.

Novack, George E. (ed.), *Existentialism versus Marxism*. New York: Dell Publishing Co., 1966. Pp. 344. Contribution by F. Nietzsche, Marx and Engels, J. P. Sartre, A. Camus, G. Lukacs and others.

Salmon, Elizabeth G., *The Good in Existential Metaphysics*. Milwaukee, Wisconsin: Marquette University Press, 1953. Pp. 93. Aquinas Lecture.

Warnock, Mary, *Existentialist Ethics*. New York: St. Martin's Press, 1967. Pp. 57.

Wollheim, Richard, «The Political Philosophy of Existentialism», *Cambridge Journal*, 1953.

Battaglia, Felice, *Il problema morale nell' esistenzialismo*. 2nd ed. Bologne: U.P.E.B., 1949.

Representatives

Barth, Karl, — see below, p. 49.

Beauvoir de, Simone, *The Ethics of Ambiguity*. Translation by B. Frechtman. New York: Philosophical Library, 1948. Pp. 163.

——, *Les Mandarins*. Paris: Gallimard, 1956. English translation by Leonard M. Friedman, *The Mandarins, A Novel*. 3rd printing. Cleveland and New York: The World Publishing Co., 1961. Pp. 610.

Buber, Martin, *Die Frage an den Einzelnen*. Berlin: Schrocken, 1936. Pp. 123. English translation by Ronald Gregor Smith, *Between Man and Man*. New York: The Macmillan Co., 1948. Pp. VIII, 210. Included translations of the *Zwiesprache; Rede über das Erzieherische; Über Charactererziehung; Was ist der Mensch ?*

——, *Bilder von Gut und Böse*. Köln: Hegner, 1952. Pp. 114. English translation by Michael Bullock, *Images of Good and Evil*. London: Routledge, and Kegan Paul, 1952. Pp. 84.

——, *Der Weg der Menschen.* Nach der chasidischen Lehre. 3rd ed. Amsterdam: Albert de Lange, 1953. Pp. 44.

PJUETZE, Paul E., *The Social Self.* New York: Bookman Associates, 1954. Pp. 392. Particularly the theories of H. Mead and M. Buber.

SCHILPP, Arthur Paul (ed.), *The Philosophy of Martin Buber.* Evanston, Illinois: The Library of Living Philosophers, 1965.

BULTMANN, Rudolf, — see below, p. 49.

——, *Existence and Faith: Shorter Writings of Rudolf Bultmann.* Selected and translated by Schubert M. Ogden. New York: Meridian Books, 1960. Pp. 320.

MACQUARRIE, John, *The Scope of Demythologizing: Bultmann and His Critics.* New York: Harper and Brothers, 1960. Pp. 255.

CAMUS, Albert, *Le malentendu, suivi de Caligula.* Paris: Gallimard, 1947. English translation by Stuart GILBERT, *Caligula and the three other Plays.* New York: Alfred A. Knopf, 1958.

——, *La peste.* Paris: Gallimard, 1947. English translation by Stuart GILBERT, *The Plague.* New York: Alfred A. Knopf, 1952.

——, *La chute.* Paris: Gallimard, 1956. English translation by Justin O'BRIEN, *The Fall.* New York: Alfred A. Knopf, 1957.

AYER, A. J. «Albert Camus, Novelist-Philosopher», *Horizon,* 1946.

CRUICKSHANK, John, *Albert Camus and the Literature of Revolt.* Oxford: Oxford University Press, 1960.

HANNA, Thomas, «Albert Camus and the Christian Faith», *The Journal of Religion,* October 1956, pp. 224-233.

——, *The Thought and Art in Albert Camus.* Chicago: Henry Regnery Company, 1958. Pp. 264. Bibliography.

HOCHBERG, Herbert, «Albert Camus and the Ethics of Absurdity», *Ethics,* 1965.

MOHRT, Michel, «Ethics and Poetry in the Work of Camus», *Yale French Studies* (New Haven, Connecticut), Spring-Summer, 1948, pp. 113-118.

THODY, Philip, *Albert Camus: A Study of His Work.* London: Hamish Hamilton, 1957.

KIERKEGAARD, Søren A., *Training in Christianity.* Translated by Walter LOWRIE. New York: Oxford University Press, 1941. Pp. XXVII, 275. With *Edifying Discourse.*

——, *Stages on Life's Way.* Translated by Walter LOWRIE. London: Oxford University Press, 1940. Pp. 472.

——, *The Concept of Dread.* Translated by Walter LOWRIE. London: Oxford University Press, 1944. Pp.

MARCEL, Gabriel, *Un homme de Dieu.* Paris: B. Grasset, 1925. Pp. 199.

——, *Être et avoir.* Paris: Éditions Montaigne, 1935. Pp. 357.

——, *Du refus à l'invocation.* Paris: Gallimard, 1940. Pp. 326.

PARAIN Vial, J., «L'être dans la philosophie de Gabriel Marcel et le fondement du droit», *Archives de philosophie du droit.* 1965, Pp. 1-16.

Niebuhr, H. R., — see below, p. 49.

Sartre, J. P., *Existentialism and Human Emotion*. Translated by Bernard
Frechman and Hazel E. Barnes. New York: Philosophical Library,
1957. Pp. 96.   See Index, below.

Ayer, A. J., «Novelist-philosophers: Jean Paul Sartre», *Horizon*,
1946.

Salvan, Jacques L., *The Scandalous Ghost: Sartre's Existentialism as
Related to Vitalism, Humanism, Mysticism, Marxism*. Detroit, Michigan: Wayne State University Press, 1968. Pp. 217.

——, *To Be and not to Be*. Detroit, Michigan: Wayne State University Press, 1962.

Warnock, Mary, *The Philosophy of Sartre*. New York: Hillary House,
1965. Pp. 186.

Situational Ethics: moral value is only determinable by the relationship of the act to its circumstances.

Bonhoeffer, Dietrich, *Creation and Temptation*. London: Student Christian
Movement, 1966. Pp. 128.
——, *The Way to Friedom*. Translated by Edwin H. Robertson and John
Bowden. New York: Harper and Row, 1967. Pp. 272. «In action is
friedom», — the reference to an active participation in the resisten-
ce to Hitler.
Bultman, Rudolf, — see Existentialism, in *PQS*, No. 5; above, p. 45.
Dunphy, William B. (ed.), *The New Morality, Continuity and Discontinuity*.
New York: Herder and Herder, 1967. Pp. 192.
Fletcher, Joseph Francis, *Situation Ethics: The New Morality*. Philadel-
phia: Westminster, Press, 1966. Pp. 176.
——, *Morals and Medicine: The Moral Problems of the Patient's Right to
Know the Truth*. Princeton, New Jersey: Princeton University Press,
1954. Pp. 253.
——, *Moral Responsibility: Situation Ethics at Work*. Philadelphia: The
Westminster Press, 1697.
Lehmann, Paul Louis, *Ethics in a Christian Context*. New York: Harper,
1963. Pp. 384.
McCabe, Herbert, O. P., *The People of God: The Fullness of Life in the
Church*. London: Sheed and Ward, 1964. Pp. 172.
——, *The New Creation: Studies on Living in the Church*. London: Sheed
and Ward, 1964. Pp. 216.
Pike, James A., *You and the New Morality, 74 Cases*. New York: Harper and
Row, 1967.
Ramsey, Paul, *Basic Christian Ethics*. New York: Charles Scribner's Sons,
1965. Pp. 404. Critical.
——, *Deeds and Rules in Christian Ethics*. Edinburgh: Oliver and Boyd,
1965. Pp. 110.
——, (ed.), *Faith and Ethics: The Theology of H. Richard Niebuhr*. New
York: Harper, 1965. Pp. 306.

Objectivism: Man has reason by which he ought to work out his moral code; his individual rights are of absolute supremacy, even higher than those of society, state or church. Thus, man is his objective.

BRANDEN, Nathaniel, *Who is Ayn Rand?* New York: Random House, 1962. Pp. 239.

RAND, Ayn, *The Fountainhead.* New York: Bobbs-Merrill Co., 1943.

RAND, Ayn (Mrs. Frank O'CONNOR), *Atlas Shrugged.* New York: Random House, 1957. Pp. 1168.

HAMBLIN, Dora Jane, «Followers of the Fountainhead philosophy of selfishness are out to lead us back to a 19th Century paradise», *Life,* April 7, 1967, pp. 92-102.

(ee) SOCIAL THEORIES: morality depends on the approval or disapproval by society.

See Sociology, below, Ch. V. 3 Contemporary, ff, p. 251.

ABERLE, D. F. *et al.,* «The Functional Prerequisites of a Society», *Ethics,* 1950, pp. 100-111.

ANSHEN, Ruth Nanda (ed.), *Moral Principles of Action: Man's Ethical Imperative.* New York: Harper and Brothers. 1952. Pp. XII, 720.

DURKHEIM, E., *The Elementary Forms of the Religious Life.* Translated by J. W. SWAIN. New York: The Macmillan Company ,1915. Pp. XI, 456.

——, *On the Division of Labor in Society.* Translation by G. SIMPSON. 2nd ed. Glencoe, Illinois: Free Press, 1960. Pp. 439.

LÉVY-BRUHL, Lucien, *Ethics and Moral Science.* Translated by Elizabeth LEE. London: Archebald Constable and Co., 1905. Pp. XII, 233.

FIRTH, Raymond William, *Elements of Social Organization.* London: Franklin Watts, 1951. Pp. VII, 257.

GINSBERG, Morris, *Essays in Sociology and Social Philosophy.* 2 vols. New York: The Macmillan and Co., 1957. Vol. I: On the Diversity of Morals. Vol. II: Reason and Unreason in Society.

——, *On the Diversity of Morals.* New York: The Macmillan and Co., 1957. Pp. 329.

——, *On Justice in Society.* Ithaca, New York: Cornell University Press, 1965. Pp. 248.

HERSKOVITS, Melville, *Man and His Works: The Science of Cultural Anthropology.* New York: Alfred Knopf, 1948. Pp. XVIII, 678.

WESTERMARCK, Edward Alexander, *The Origin and Development of the Moral Ideas.* 2 vols. New York: The Macmillan Co., 1906-1908.

——, *Ethical Relativity.* New York: Harcourt, Brace and Co., 1932. Pp. XVIII, 301.

WHITE, Morton Gabriel, *Social Thought in America: The Revolt against Formalism.* New York. Viking, 1949. Pp. VIII, 260.

REINER, Hans, *Das Prinzip von Gut und Böse.* Freiburg: Alber, 1949. Pp. 35.

——, *Pflicht und Neigung. Die Grundlagen der Sittlichkeit.* Meisenheim/ Glan: Westkulturverlag, 1951. Pp. XI, 316.

Fascism, — see Politics, below, Ch. IV, 5, p. 217.

Hitlerism, — see Politics, below, Ch. IV, p. 211.

Racism, — see Autonomous Ethics, above, p. 30.

(ff) IDEALISTIC THEORIES: perfection of the self.

See also Idealism, above, p. 32.

Idealistic Theory of Value: good is the preference of higher to lower value. See Value, below, p. 64.

GARNETT, A. Cambell, *Reality and Value*. London: G. Allen and Unwin, 1937. Pp. 320.

OSBORNE, H., *Foundations of the Philosophy of Value*. Cambridge: At the University Press, 1933. Pp. XXII, 132.

URBAN, W. M., *Valuation, Its Nature and Laws*. London: Swan Sonnenschein and Co. New York: The Macmillan Co., 1909. Pp. XVIII, 433.

——, «Value and Existence», *Journal of Philosophy, Psychology, and Scientific Method* (New York), XIII (1916), pp. 452.

——, «Knowledge of Value and the Value Judgment», *Journal of Philosophy, Psychology, and Scientific Method* (New York), XIII (1916).

——, *Fundamentals of Ethics*. New York: Henry Holt and Co., 1930. Pp. 476.

BRADLEY, F. H., *Ethical Studies*. 2nd ed., a reissue. Oxford. Clarendon Press, 1952. Pp. XII, 344. First published in 1876.

CROCE, B., «Frumenti di etica», *Critica* (Bari), Nos. 1-2, 5, 1915; 2, 5, 1916; No. 1, 5, 1917; 2, 1918; 2, 1920; 1, 1921; 4, 1924; 4, 1925; 2, 1930.

——, *Considerazioni sul problema morale del tempo nostro*. Bari: Laterza, 1945. Pp. 23.

Theistic Idealism: good is grounded in God.

BOWNE, Borden P., *Principles of Ethics*. New York: Harper and Brothers, 1892. Pp. XV, 309.

HOWISON, G. H., *The Conception of God*. New York: The Macmillan Company, 1897.

——, *The Limits of Evolution and Other Essays Illustrating the Metaphysical Theory of Personal Idealism*. New York: The Macmillan Company, 1905. Pp. 450.

KNUDSON, A. C., *Philosophy of Personalism*. Boston: Boston University Press, 1927; reprinted 1949. Pp. 438.

SORLEY, W. R., *The Moral Life and Moral Worth*. Cambridge: University Press, 1911. Pp. VII, 147.

——, *Moral Values and the Idea of God*. Cambridge: University Press, 1918. Pp. XIX, 534.

TAYLOR, A. E., *The Problem of Conduct*. New York: The Macmillan Company, 1901. Pp. VIII, 501.

——, *The Faith of a Moralist*. 2 vols. London: Macmillan and Co., Ltd., 1930.

Scholastic Philosophy: Natural Law is imparted by God.
See Scholastic Philosophy (Ethics), in *PQS*, No. 5; Theological
Etihcs, below.

FAGOTHEY, Austin, *Right and Reason: Ethics in Theory and Practice*. St.
Louis, Missouri: The C. V. Mosby Company, 1953. Pp. 583.
OESTERLE, John A., *Ethics: An Introduction to Moral Science*. Englewood
Cliffs, New Jersey: Prentice Hall, 1956. Pp. 269.

LUTHARDT, Christian Ernst, *Die antike Ethik in ihrer geschichtlichen Entwicklung als Einleitung in die Geschichte der christlichen Moral dargestellt*. Leipzig: Dörffling und Franke, 1887. Pp. VIII, 187.
——, *Geschichte der christlichen Ethik*. Vor der Reformation. Leipzig:
Dörffling und Franke, 1888. Pp. XII, 335.

Theological Ethics: Good is known from revelation.
See Theological Theories, above, p. 27; Scholasticism, above.

BARTH, Karl, — see above, p. 44.

——, *The Word of God and the Word of Man*. Translated by Douglas Hor-
ton. Chicago. The Pilgrim Press, 1928.
——, *The Church and the Political Problem of Our Day*. London: Hodder
and Stoughton, 1939. Pp. 87.
——, *The Church and the War*. Translated by Antonia H. FROENDT. New
York: The Macmillan Co., 1944. Pp. XI, 49.
——, *Die Deutschen und Wir*. Zollikon-Zurich: Evangelischer Verlag, 1945.
Pp. 47. Authorized translation by R. G. SMITH, *The Germans and Our-
selves*. London: Nisbet. 1945. Pp. 61.
——, *How to Serve God in a Marxist Land*. New York: Association Press,
1959. Pp. 126.
——, *The German Church Conflict*. Translated by P.T.A. PARKER. London:
Lutterworth Press, 1965. Pp. 77.
——, *Mensch und Mitmensch. Die Grundform der Menschlichkeit*. Göt-
tingen: Vandenhoeck und Ruprecht, 1962. Pp. 85.

BUBER, Martin, — see above, p. 44.
BULTMANN, Rudolf, — see above, p. 45.
MARCEL, Gabriel, — *ibid*.

NIEBUHR, H. Reinhold, *Moral Man and Immoral Society: A Study in Ethics
and Politics*. New York: Charles Scribner's Sons, 1932.
——, *An Interpretation of Christian Ethics*. New York: Harper and Bro-
thers, 1935.
——, *The Nature and Destiny of Man: A Christian Interpretation*. 2 vols.
New York: Charles Scribner's Sons, 1941-1943.

KEGLEY, Charles W. and Bretall, Robert W. (eds.), *Reinhold Niebuhr: His Religious, Social and Political Thought*. New York: The
Macmillan Co., 1961. Pp. XIV, 486.

RAMSAY, Paul, — see above, p. 46.

Religious Humanism, — see Periodicals, below, p. 71.

(gg) PHENOMENOLOGICAL TTHEORIES: good and right are intuitively and directly perceived.

See Intuitive Theories, particularly F. BRENTANO, M. SCHELER, N. HARTMAN, below.

MANDELBAUM, Maurice, *The Phenomenology of Moral Experience*. New York: The Free Press (Macmillan), 1955. Pp. 338.

(hh) Intuitive Theories: good and right are objective qualities, directly perceived, without any consideration of the value of their consequences.

HUDSON, W. D., *Ethical Intuitionism*. New York: St. Martin's Press, 1967. Pp. 96.

Realistic approach: Good, right and duty are intuitively perceived and related to good.

BUTLER, Joseph, — Moral Sense Philosophers in England, above, p. 23.
BRENTANO, Franz, *Vom Ursprung sittlicher Erkenntnis*. Leipzig: Dunker und Humblot, 1889. Pp. XII, 122.
——, *Grundlegung und Aufbau der Ethik*. Ed. by Franziska MAYER-HILLE-BRAND. Bern: A. Francke, 1952. Pp. XXIV, 424. ·
HARTMANN, Nicolai, *Ethics*. Translated by S. COIT. New York: The Macmillan Co., 1932. See Phenomenology, in *PQS*, No. 5.

JENSEN, O. C., «Nicolai Hartmann's Theory of Virtue», *Ethics*, 1942.

MOHANTY, J. N., *Nicolai Hartmann and Alfred North Whitehead*. Calcutta: Progressive Publishers, 1957.

WALKER, Merle, «Perry and Hartmann, Antithetical or Complementary», *International Journal of Ethics*, 1939.

MOORE, G. E., *Principia Ethica*. Cambridge: University Press, 1960. Pp. XXVII, 232. First published in 1903. See Realism, in *PQS*, No. 5.
——, *Ethics*. New York: H. Holt and Co., 1912. Pp. 256.

FRANKENA, W. K., «The Naturalistic Fallacy», *Mind* XLVIII (October 1939), pp. 464-467.

METTRICK, E. F., «G. E. Moore and Intrinsic Goodness», *International Journal of Ethics*, XXXVIII (July 1928), pp. 389-400.

SCHELER, Max F., *Zur Phänomenologie und Theorie der Sympathiegefühl und von Liebe und Hass*. Halle. M. Niemeyer, 1913. Pp. VI, 154.

——, *Wesen und Formen der Sympathie.* 2nd ed. Bonn: F. Cohen, 1923. Pp. XVI, 314. English translation by Peter HEATH, *The Nature of Sympathy.* London: Routledge and Kegan Paul, 1954. Pp. LIV, 274. See Value, below, 3, also p. 67.

——, *Schriften zur Soziologie und Weltanschauungslehre.* 3 vols. Leipzig: Der Neue Geist Verlag, 1923-1924.

ALPHÉUS, Carl, *Kant und Scheler. Phänomenologische Untersuchungen zur Ethik zwecks Entscheidung des Streites zwischen der formalen Ethik Kants und der materialen Wertethik Schelers.* Freiburg im Br.: 1936. Pp. 112.

LAUER, Q., «The Phenomenological Ethics of Max Scheler», *International Philosophical Quarterly* (New York), May 1961, pp. 273-300.

SIDGWICK, Henry, *The Methods of Ethics.* 6th ed. London: Macmillan, 1901. Pp. 564. First published in 1874-1878.

——, *Practical Ethics: A Collection of Addresses and Essays.* Ed. by James WARD. Bloomsburg, West Carolina: Sonnenschein, 1903. Pp. 268. See also Politics, below, Ch. IV, p. 184.

WRIGHT, H. W., «The Objectivity of Moral Values», *Philosophical Review.* Vol. XXXII (July 1923), pp. 385-400.

Deontological Theories: Good, right and duty are intuitively perceived, but right and duty are ontologically not reduceable to good.

BROAD, Charlie Dunbar, *Five Types of Ethical Theory.* London: Kegan Paul, Trench, Trubner and Co., 1930. Pp. XXV, 288.

——, «Some of the Main Problems of Ethics», *Philosophy,* 1946.

——, *Ethics and the History of Philosophy.* London: Routledge and Kegan Paul, 1952. Pp. XIII, 274.

SCHILPP, Paul A. (ed), *The Philosophy of C. D. Broad.* New York: The Library of Living Philosophers, 1939. Pp.

CARRITT, E. F., *The Theory of Morals.* London: Oxford University Press, 1928. Pp. XII, 144.

——, *An Ambiguity of the Word Good.* London: Oxford University Press, 1937.

——, «Moral Positivism and Moral Aestheticism», *Philosophy,* Vol. XIII (1935).

EWING, Alfred Cyril, *The Definition of Good.* New York: The Macmillan and Co., 1947. Pp. 215.

——, *Ethics.* London: English Universities Press, 1953. Pp. VII, 183.

——, *Second Thoughts in Moral Philosophy.* New York: The Macmillan Co., 1959. Pp. 190.

HALL, E. W., — see Value, below, p. 65.

PRICHARD, Harold A., «Does Moral Philosophy Rest on a Mistake», *Mind* (Hants, England), New Series, Vol. XXI (1912).

——, *Duty and Interest.* Oxford: At the Clarendon Press, 1928. Pp. 44.

——, «Duty and Ignorance of Fact», *Proceedings of the British Academy* (London: Humphrey Milford), Vol. XVIII (1932), pp. 28.

——, *Moral Obligation*. Oxford: Oxford University Press, 1949. Pp. 208. Good collection of essays on deontological point of view.

Ross, W. D., *The Right and the Good*. Oxford: At the Clarendon Press, 1930. Pp. 176.

——, *The Foundations of Ethics*. Oxford: At the Clarendon Press, 1939. Pp. XVI, 328.

(ii) Metaethics: philosophy of ethical theories, or else an analysis of the meanings or uses of moral terms concerning moral concepts.

Abelson, Raziel, *Ethics and Meta-ethics*. New York: St. Martin's Press, 1967. Pp. 550.

Garner, Richard and Rosen, Bernard, *Moral Philosophy: A Systematic Introduction to Normative Ethics and Meta-ethics*. New York: The Macmillan Co., 1967. Pp. 367. See Systematic Studies, above, p. 4.

Nielsen, Kai, «Metaethical Theories», *The Encyclopedia of Philosophy* (8 vols. New York: The Macmillan, 196F), III, p. 127-130. See also pp. 75-76, 125-130.

Nowell-Smith, Patrick Horace, *Ethics*. New York: Philosophical library. 1958. Pp. 283.

Taylor, Paul W. (ed), *The Moral Judgement: Readings in Contemporary Meta-Ethics*. Englewood Clifts, New Jersey: Prentice-Hall, 1964. Pp. XVIII, 296. See also above, p. 36.

Deontological Theories, — see above, p. 51.
Naturalistic Theories, — see below.

(jj) Naturalistic ethics: include all sorts of ethical theories built on natural principles with exclusion of any supernatural interference. Among those theories more typical are the hedonistic theories, ethics of affection, logical positivistic, behavioristic, good-reason, and Marxist theories.

Adams, Elie Maynard, *Ethical Naturalism and the Modern World View*. Chapel Hill, North Carolina; University of North Carolina Press, 1960. Pp. 229.

Deshumbert, M., *An Ethical System Based on the Laws of Nature*. Translated from the French by Lionel Giles. Chicago: Open Court Publishing Company, 1917. Pp. 231.

Edel, Abraham, *Ethical Judgment*. New York: City College, 1964. Pp. 348.

Holt, E. B., *The Freudian Wish and Its Place in Ethics*. New York: Henry Holt and Company, 1915. Pp. VII, 212.

Hume, David, — see Modern (Sympathy Theories), p. 22.

Kemp, J., *Ethical Naturalism*. New York: St. Martin's Press, 1969 (?). In preparation.

Nielsen, Kai, «Ethical Naturalism Once Again», *Australasian Journal of Philosophy*. 1962.

——, «On Human Needs and Moral Appraisals», *Inquiry*, 1963.

PERRY, Ralph Barton, *Realms of Value: A Critique of Human Civilization.* Cambridge, Massachusetts: Harvard University Press, 1954. Pp. 497. Classic in Ethical Naturalism. See also Value, below, 3.

——, *Present Philosophical Tendencies: A Critical Survey of Naturalism, Idealism, Pragmatism and Realism.* New York: George Braziller, 1955. Pp. 383.

PRIOR, A. N., «The Autonomy XXXVIII of Ethics», *Australasian Journal of Philosophy*, Vol. XXXVII (1960). See Logical Posltivism, below, p. 54.

RICE, Philip Blair, *On the Knowledge of Good and Evil.* New York: Random House, 1955. Pp. 299.

STAPLEDON, Olaf, *A Modern Theory of Ethics.* London: Methuen and Co., 1929. Pp. IX, 277.

WOODBRIDGE, F. J. E., «Natural Theology», in *Nature and Mind.* New York: Columbia University Press, 1937. Pp. X, 509.

Hedonism, — see Ancient Hedonism (Epicureanism), above, Ch. I, p. 10; Ethics of Affection, below.

BLAKE, R. M.: Good is pleasure or pleasureable consciousness.

——, *Hedonism in the Light of Recent Value Theory.* Oxford, Massachusetts: Harvard University Press, 1915.

——, «Why not Hedonism? A Protest», *International Journal of Ethics.* Vol. XXXVII (1926-1927).

——, «The Ground of Moral Obligation», *International Journal of Ethics,* Vol. XXXVIII (1927-1928).

DRAKE, Durant: Good or bad is equivalent to a feeling of good or bad.

——, *Problems of Conduct.* 2nd revised edition, Boston: Houghton Mifflin Co., 1935. Pp. 520. First published in 1914.

MACKAY, J., *The Logic of Conduct.* New York: Boni and Liverright Publishers, 1924.

SCHILCK, M.,: Morally good is believed to bring the greatest happiness.

——, *Fragen der Ethik,* 1930. English translation by David RYNIN, *Problem of Ethics.* New York: Prentice-Hall, 1939. Paperbound in New York: Dover Publications, 1962. Pp. 217.

STACE, W. T.: Happiness is agreeable feeling.

——, *Concept of Morals.* New York: The Macmillan Company, 1937. Pp. XI, 307.

Ethics of Affection: good is subjectively satisfactory feeling or it depends on subjective affection. — See also skepticism in Ethics, below.

PRALL, David W., — see Value, below, p. 66.

REID, John R., — see Value, *ibid.*

RUSSELL, B., *Religion and Science.* New York: Oxford University Press, 1935.

——, *Human Society in Ethics and Politics.* New York: Simon and Schuster, 1955. Pp. 227. First published in 1954.

SANTAYANA, George (1863-1952), *The Life of Reason or the Phases of Human Progress*. 5 vols. New York: Charles Scribner's Sons, 1905-1906.
——, *The Life of Reason; Reason is Science*. New York: Charles Scribner's Sons, 1906.
——, *The Life of Reason: Reason in Common Sense*. New York: Charles Scribner's Sons, 1906.
——, *Winds of Doctrine*. New York: Charles Scribner's Sons, 1926. Pp. 215.
——, *Skepticism and Animal Faith*. New York: Charles Scribner's Sons, 1923. Pp. XII, 314.

SCHILPP, Paul A. (ed.), *The Philosophy of George Santayana*. Evanson, Chicago: Northwestern University, 1940. Pp. XVI, 698.

Contemporary skepticism, — see Skepticism in Antiquity, above, p. 13; Ethics of Affection, above, p. 53; Hedonism, above. p. 53.

Self-Interest Theories: profit is the criterion of good. — See Modern, p. 21.

OLSON, Robert G., *The Morality of Self-Interest*. New York: Harcourt, Brace and World, 1965. Pp. 182.

Logical Postitivism: ethical sentences are meaningless; good is emotive expression.

AYER, A. J., *Language, Truth, and Logic*. New York: Oxford University Press, 1936. Pp. 254.
——, «On the Analysis of Moral Judgments», *Horizon* (New York), XX (September 1949), pp. 171-184.
CARNAP, R., *Philosophy and Logical Syntax*. London: Kegan Paul, French, Trubner and Co., Ltd., 1935. Pp. 100.

SCHILPP, P. A. (ed.), *The Philosophy of Rudolf Carnap*. La Salle, Illinois: The Open Court Publishers, 1964.

EDWARDS, Paul, *The Logic of Moral Discourse*. New York: The Macmillan Co., 1965. Pp. 248.
EWING, Alfred Cyril, *The Definition of Good*. New York: The Macmillan Co., 1947. See also Systematic, above, p. 4.
FANN, K. T. (ed.), *Ludwig Wittgenstein: The Man and His Philosophy*. New York: Dell Publishing Co., 1967. Pp. 416.
FEIGL, H., «Logical Empiricism», in *Twentieth Century Philosophy*. New York: Philosophical Library, 1943.
HARE, Richard Mervyn, *The Language of Morals*. New York: Oxford University Press, 1952. Pp. 202.
——, *Freedom and Reason*. Oxford: Oxford University Press, 1963. Pp. 228.
HEDENIUS, Ingemar, «Values and Duties», *Theoria*, 1949.

Mayo, Bernard, *Ethics and the Moral Life.* New York: The Macmillan Co., 1958. Pp. 238.

Ogden, C. K. and Richards, I. A., *The Meaning of Meaning.* London: Kegan Paul, Trench, Trubner and Co., Ltd. New York: Harcourt, Brace and Co., Inc., 1936. Pp. XXII, 363.

Prior, A. N., *Logic and the Basis of Ethics.* Oxford: Oxford University Press, 1949. Pp. XI, 111.

Reichenbach, Hans, *The Rise of Scientific Philosophy.* Berkeley, California: University of California Press, 1951. Pp. XI, 333.

Richards, I. A., *The Meaning of Meaning.* London: Routledge and Kegan Paul, 1933.

——, *Speculative Instruments.* Chicago: University of Chicago Press, 1955.

Robinson, Richard, *An Atheist Value.* Oxford: The Clarendon Press, 1964. Pp. 256.

Ross, Alf, «On Moral Reasoning», *Danish Yearbook of Philosophy,* 1964.

Searle, J. R., «How to Derive 'Ought' from 'Is'», *Philosophical Review,* 1964, pp. 43.

Singer, Marcus George, *Generalization in Ethics.* New York: Random House, 1961. Pp. 379.

Stevenson, C. L., *Ethics and Language.* New Haven: Yale University Press, 1944. Pp. XI, 338.

——, «The Nature of Ethical Disagreement», *Sigma,* Vols. I, II, Nos. 8-9 (1947-48).

——, «The Emotive Meaning of Ethical Terms», *Mind,* XLVI (January, 1937), pp. 14-31.

——, «Ethical Judgments and Avoidability», *Mind,* XLVII (January, 1938), pp. 45-57.

——, «Meaning: Descriptive and Emotive», *Philosophical Review* (Ithaca, New York), LVII (April 1938), pp. 127-144.

Zimmerman, M., «The 'Is — Ought': An Unnecessary Dualism,» *Mind,* 1962, pp. 53.

Hägerströme, Axel, *Till Frägen om den Gällande Rättens Begrepp.* Upsala, 1917.

Behaviorism: moral actions are ultimately behaviors reduced to muscular and visceral responses.

See Experimental Psychology (Behaviorism, especially J. B. Watson), in *PQS,* No. 5.

Albert, Ethel M. and Kluckhohn, Clyde, *A Selected Bibliography on Values, Ethics, and Esthetics in the Behavioral Sciences and Philosophy, 1920-1958.* New York: The Free Press (Macmillan), 1960. Pp. 360.

Berta, Frank, *The Moral Theory of Behavior.* Springfield, Illinois: Charles C. Thomas, 1953.

Gerard, R. W., «A Biological Basis for Ethics», *The Philosophy of Science* (East Lansing, Michigan), IX (1942).

Hull, Clark L., *Essentials of Behavior.* New Haven, Connecticut: Yale University Press 1951. Pp. VIII 145.

KAPLAN, Abraham, *The Conduct of Inquiry: Methodology for Behavioral Science*. San Francisco, California: Chandler Publishing Co., 1964. Pp. XIX, 428.

MORRIS, C. W., *Signs, Language, and Behavior*. Englewood Cliffs, New Jersey: Prentice-Hall, 1946. Pp. XII, 365.

SKINNER, B. F., *Science and Human Behavior*. New York: Macmillan, 1953. Pp. 461.

TURNER, Merle B., *Philosophy and the Science of Behavior*. New York: St. Martin's Press, 1967. Pp. 528.

(kk) THE GOOD-REASON APPROACH: moral statements are mainly for practical purposes and not only theoretical and emotive result.

AIKEN, Henry David, *Reason and Conduct: New Bearings in Moral Philosophy*. New York: Alfred A. Knopf, 1962. Pp. 375.

BAIER, Kurt, *Moral Point of View: A Rational Basis of Ethics*. Ithaca, New York: Cornell University Press, 1958. Pp. 326.

FALK, W. D., «Morals without Faith», *Philosophy*, 1944.

——, «Morality and Nature», *Australasian Journal of Philosophy*, 1950.

——, «Action-guiding Reason», *Journal of Philosophy*, 1963.

GAUTHIER, David Peter, *Practical Reasoning: The Structure and Foundations of Prudential and Moral Arguments and Their Exemplification in Discourse*. Oxford: Oxford University Press, 1963. Pp. 210.

LADD, John, *The Structure of a Moral Code: A Philosophical Analysis of Ethical Discourse Applied to the Ethics of the Navaho Indians*. Cambridge, Massachusetts: Harvard University Press, 1957. Pp. 474.

MURPHY, Arthur Edward, *Reason and Common Good*. Ed. by William HAY and Marcus SINGER. Englewood Cliffs, New Jersey: Prentice-Hall, 1963. Pp. 413.

NIELSEN, Kai, «Justification and Moral Reasoning», *Methodos*, 1957.

——, «Is 'Why Should I Be Moral?' an Absurdity», *Australasian Journal of Philosophy*. 1958.

——, The 'Good Reason Approach' and 'Ontological Justification of Morality'», *Philosophical Quarterly*, 1959.

——, «Can a Way of Life Be Justified?», *Indian Journal of Philosophy*, 1960.

——, «Conventionalism in Morals and the Appeal to Human Nature», *Philosophy and Phenomenological Research*, 1962.

——, «Why Should I Be Moral?», *Methodos*, 1963.

——, «The Good Reason Approach Revisited», *Archiv für Rechts-und Sozialphilosophie*, 1965.

RAWLS, John, «Outline of a Decision Procedure for Ethics», *Philosophical Review*, 1951.

——, «The Sense of Justice», *Philosophical Review*, 1963.

SINGER, Marcus George, *Generalization in Ethics*. New York: Alfred A. Knopf, 1961. Pp. 351.

——, «The Golden Rule», *Philosophy*, 1963.

TAYLOR, Paul, «On Justifying a Way of Life», *Indian Journal of Philosophy*, 1961.

——, «The Ethnocentric Fallacy», The Monist, 1963.
TOULMIN, Stephen Edelston, An Examination of the Place of Reason in Ethics. Cambridge: Cambridge University Press, 1950. Pp. XIV, 228.
——, «Principles of Morality», Philosophy, 1956.
WILD, John David (ed.), The Return to Reason. Chicago: Regnery, 1953. Pp. 373.
WRIGHT VON, Georg Henrik, The Logic of Preference. Edinburgh: University Press, 1963. Pp. 67.
——, Norm and Action: A Logical Inquiry. New York: Humanities Press, 1963. Pp. 214.
——, The Varieties of Goodness. New York: Humanities Press, 1963. Pp. 222.

Psychoanalysis, — see above, p. 41.

(ll) COGNITIVE THEORIES: the statements of moral facts and values are true or false.

Naturalism, — see, above, p. 52.
Pragmatism, — see, above, p. 38.
Phenomenologists (intuitionists, realists, particularly G. E. MOORE, and deontologists), see above, pp.50-51.

(mm) NONCOGNITIVE THEORIES: moral statements cannot be considered as true or false since moral facts or values are cognizable neither empirically nor intuitively.

Logical Positivists, particularly A. J. AVER, R. CARNAP, I. HEDENIUS, H. REICHENBACH, Ch. STEVENSON, R. ROBINSON, A. ROSS, see above, pp. 54-55.

Existentialists, particularly, A. CAMUS, J. P. SARTRE, see pp. 45-46.

NIELSEN, Kai, «Noncognitivism», The Encyclopedia of Philosophy (8 vols. New York: The Macmillan Co., 1967), Vol. III, pp. 129-130, cf. 106-109.

Subjectivism, — see below, p. 58.
Relativism, — ibid.

(nn) ETHICAL PLURALISM: there are different kinds of good or value, and not only one, i.e. pleasure; thus there are not only quantitative differences of good (degrees of pleasure), but also qualitative differences (knowledge, freedom, consciousness, etc.).

MOORE, G. E., — see above, p. 50.
NIELSEN, Kai, «Ethical Pluralism», *The Encyclopedia of Philosophy* (8 vols. New York: The Macmillan Co., 1967), Vol. III, pp. 123-125.

(oo) ETHICAL SUBJECTIVISM: moral statements are personal attitudes (and not objectively true or false utterances) of those who make such statements, and they intend to evoke a similar attitude in others.

See Hedonism, — see above, pp. 10, 53.
Ethics of affection, — see above, p. 53.

NIELSEN, Kai, «Subjectivism», *The Encyclopedia of Philosophy* (8 vols. New York: The Macmillan Co., 1967), Vol. III, pp. 125-126.

(pp) ETHICAL RELATIVISM: there is no objective criterion justifying what is morally good and right.
　　　See Pragmatism, above, p. 38.
Utilitarianism, above, p. 25.
Evolutionism, above, p. 37, cf. 150.

NIELSEN, Kai, «Relativism», *The Encyclopedia of Philosophy* (8 vols. New York: The Macmillan Co., 1967), Vol. III pp. 125-126.
WESTERMARCK, Edward, *Ethical Relativity*. Paterson, New Jersey: Littlefield Adams, 1960. Pp. 301. First published in 1932.

3. SPECIAL QUESTIONS

See Economics, Law, Politics, Sociology, below, Ch. II - V.

ART

CRUICKSHANK, John (ed.), *The Novelist as Philosopher: Studies in French Fiction*, 1935-1960. Oxford: Oxford University Press, 1962. Pp. 257. See also Existentialism, above, p. 44.
POLE, David, «Morality and the Assessment of Literature», *Philosophy*, 1962, pp. 193-207.

EVIL — SIN

AIKEN, H. D., «God and Evil», *Ethics*, 1958, pp. 77-97.

DE COURSEY Sr., Mary Edwin, S.C.L., *The Theory of Evil in the Metaphysics of St. Thomas*. Washington, D.C.: The Catholic University of America Press, 1948. Pp. 178.

FARRER, Austin, *Love Almighty and Ills Unlimited*. New York: Doubleday, 1961. Pp. 168. Containing lectures of N. Taylor.

FERRÉ, Nels F. S., *Evil and the Christian Faith*. New York: Harper, 1947. Pp. XI, 173.

HICK, John H., *Evil and the God of Love*. New York: Harper, 1966. Pp. 404.

——, «The Problem of Evil», *The Encyclopedia of Philosophy* (8 vols. New York: The Macmillan Co., 1967), Vol. III, pp. 136-141. Bibliography.

JOURNET, Charles, *Le mal*. Paris: Desclée De Brouwer, 1961. Pp. 330. English translation by Michael BARRY, *The Meaning of Evil*. New York: P. J. Kenedy and Son, 1963. Pp. 293.

LEWIS, Clive Staples, *The Problem of Pain*. London: Geoffrey Bles, 1940. Pp. IX, 148.

McCLOSKEY, H. J., «The State and Evil», *Ethics* (Chicago) 1959, pp. 182-195.

MARITAIN, Jacques, *St. Thomas and the Problem of Evil*. Milwaukee, Wisconsin: Marquette University Press, 1942. Pp. 46. See Middle Ages, above, p. 16.

——, *God and the Permission of Evil*. Chicago: Ideal Book Store, 1965.

MÜLLER, Julius, *Die Christliche Lehre von der Sünde*. 6th ed. 2 vols. Stuttgart: A. Heitz, 1877. English translation by William URWICK, *The Christian Doctrine of Sin*. 2 vols Edinburgh: Hamilton, 1868.

PETIT, François, *Le problème du mal*. Paris, 1958. English translation by Christopher WILLIAMS, *The Problem of Evil*. New York: Hawthorn Books, 1959. Pp. 141.

RICE, Philip Blair, *On the Knowledge of Good and Evil*. New York: Random House, 1955. Pp. 299.

RICOEUR, Paul, *The Symbolism of Evil*. Translated from the French by EMERSON BUCANNON. New York: Harper and Row, 1967. Pp. 357.

SIWEK, P., S.J., *The Philosophy of Evil*. New York: Ronald, 1951. Pp. IX, 226.

TSANOFF, Radoslav Andrea, *The Nature of Evil*. New York: The Macmillan and Co., 1931. Pp. XVI, 447.

WHALE, John Seldon, *The Christian Answer to the Problem of Evil*. London: Student Christian Movement Press, 1939. Pp. 96.

WILLIAMS, Norman Powell, *The Ideas of the Fall and of Original Sin*. London: Longmans, Green and Co., 1927. Pp. XXXV, 571.

WISDOM, John, «God and Evil», *Mind*, 1935, pp. 1-20.

BILLICSICH, Friedrich, *Das Problems des Übels in der Philosophie des Abendlandes*. 3 vols. 2nd ed. Vienna: Verlag Sexl, 1936-1959. See Histories above, 1.

FAZIO ALLMAYER, Vito, *Moralità dell' arte: rievocazione estetica e rivocazione suggestiva*. Florence: Sansoni, 1953. Pp. 158.

Lüthi, Kurt, *Gott und das Böse.* Zürich: Zwingli Verlag, 1961. Pp. 296. Schelling — Karl Barth.

Paris, C., «El mal en el mondo fisico», *Theoria,* Vol. V-VI (1953), pp. 125-132.

Sertillanges, A. D., *Le problème du mal: l'histoire.* Paris: Aubier, 1949. Pp. 414.

Werner, Charles, *Le problème du mal dans la pensée humaine.* Lausanne: Payot, 1944. Pp. 126.

FAMILY

See Population, below, p. 62; Sex, below, p. 64; Social Ethics, below, p. 266.

FREEDOM

See Psychology, in *PQS,* No. 6; Internationalism, below, p. 221; Responsibility, below, p. 167; Slavery, cf. Colonies, below, p. 214: Christianity, *ibid.*

Academic Freedom in the United States. Ed. by Gustav Auzenne. Washington, D. C.: Haward University Press, 1953. Pp. 153.

Allen, Alexander, *Freedom in the Church, or the Doctrine of Christ.* New York: The Macmillan Co., 1907. Pp. XIV, 223.

Augustin, St., *On Free Choice of the Will.* Translated by Anna Shaw Benjamin. New York: Bobbs-Merrill, 1964. Pp. 194.

Berofsky, Bernard (ed.), *Free Will and Determinism.* New York: Harper and Row, 1966. Pp. 376.

Berger, M., Abel, T. and Page, C. H. (eds.), *Freedom and Control in Modern Society.* Princeton, New Jersey: D. Van Nostrand, 1954. Pp. XII, 326.

Carlyle, Alexander James, *Political Liberty: A History of the Conception in the Middle Ages and Modern Times.* Oxford: The Clarendon Press, 1941. Pp. XIII, 220.

Dewey, John, «State or City Control of Schools», *New Republic* (Washington, D. C.), March 20, 1915, Pp. 178-180.

——, «Professorial Freedom», *New York Times,* October 22, 1915. Reprinted in *School and Society* (Chicago: University of Chicago Press), November 6, 1915, under the title, «The Control of Universities».

——, «Philosophies of Freedom», in *Freedom in the Modern World* (ed. by Horace M. Kallen. New York: Coward McCann, 1928), pp. 236-271.

——, *Freedom and Culture.* New York: G. P. Putnam's Sons, 1939. Pp. 176.

Edwards, Jonathan, *A Careful and Strict Enquiry into the Modern Prevailing Notion of that Freedom of Will which is supposed to be Essential to Moral Agency, Virtue and Vice, Reward and Punishment, Praise and Blame.* Boston, New England, 1754.

——, *Remarks on the Essays, On the Principles of Morality and Natural Religion*. Wilmington, Delaware, 1790. First published in Edinburgh, 1758.

FARRER, Austin, *The Freedom of the Will*. London: A. and C. Black, 1958. Pp. 330.

FRANK, Jerome, *Fate and Freedom*. New York: Simon and Schuster, 1945. Pp. VIII, 375.

FRIEDRICH, Carl, J. (ed.), *Liberty*. New York: Atherton Press, 1962. Pp. 333.

GRINDEL, Carl, C. M. (ed.), *Concept of Freedom*. Chicago: Henry Regneny, 1955. Pp. 512.

HOOK, Sidney (ed.), *Determinism and Freedom*. New York: New York University Press, 1958. Pp. 237.

HUNOLD, Albert (ed.), *Freedom and Serfdom: An Anthology of Western Thought*. Translated by R. H. STEVENS. Dordrecht: D. Reidel, 1961. Pp. 288.

LOCKE, John, *Locke and Liberty: Selections from the Works of John Locke*. Ed. by Massimo SALVADORI. London: Pall Mall Press, 1960. Pp. XL, 196.

MacIVER, Robert Morrison, *Academic Freedom in Our Time*. New York: Columbia University Press, 1955. Pp. XIV, 329.

MILL, John Stuart, *On Liberty* 2nd ed. London: J. W. Parker and Son, 1859. Pp. 208.

——, *On Social Freedom*. New York: Columbia University Press, 1941. Pp. 69. Reprint from the *Oxford and Cambridge Review*, June, 1907.

MORGENBESSER, Sidney and WALSH, James (ed.), *Free Will*. Englewood Cliffs, New Jersey: Prentice-Hall, 1962. Pp. 171.

MULLER, Herbert J., *Freedom in the Modern World: The 19th and 20th Centuries*. New York: Harper Colophon Books, 1967. Pp. 576.

OFSTAD, Harald, *Freedom of Decision*. Oslo, 1960.

O'NEILL, James, *Catholicism and American Freedom*. New York: Harper, 1952. Pp. 287.

OPPENHEIM, Felix E., *Dimensions of Freedom: An Analysis*. New York: St. Martin's Press, 1961. Pp. 250.

ORTEGA Y GASSET, J., *Concord and Liberty*. Translated from the Spanish by Helene WEYL. New York: W. W. Norton and Co., 1946. Pp. 182.

PEARS, D. F., *Freedom and the Will*. New York: St. Martin's Press, 1963. Pp. 142.

RICOEUR, P., *Freedom and Nature: The Voluntary and the Involuntary*. Evanston: Ideal Book Store, 1966.

RUSSELL, Bertrand, *Freedom versus Organization, 1814-1914*. Philadelphia: William H. Allen, Bookseller, 1934.

SCHRAG, Calvin O., *Existence and Freedom*. Evanston. Illinois: Northwestern University Press, 1961. Pp. 250.

SPAKOVSKI VON, Anatol, *Freedom, Determinism, Indeterminism*. The Hague: Martinus Nijhoff, 1963. Pp. VII, 117.

STREET, Harry, *Freedom, the Individual and the Law*. Harmondsworth, Middlesex: Penguin Books, 1963. Pp. 316.

BATTAGLIA, Felice, «La libertà della scuola e la chiesa», *Cultura*, No. 7, 1929.

BRINKMAN, Karl, *Freiheit und Verfassung. Das Wesen der Freiheit und Un-freiheit und ihre Berücksichtigung in einer Verfassung.* Bonn: Bou-vier, 1963. Pp. XVIII, 426.
FAUCONNET, P., *La responsabilité.* Paris: F. Alcan, 1920. Pp. 400.
GURVITCH, Georges, *Déterminismes sociaux et liberté.* 2nd ed. Paris: Presses Universitaires de France, 1963. Pp. VIII, 328.
KILE, Frederick O., Jr., *Die theologischen Grundlagen von Schellings Phi-losophie der Freiheit.* Leiden, Holland: E. J. Brill, 1965. Pp. X, 113.
LE SENNE, René, *Le devoir.* Paris: F. Alcan, 1930. Pp. 604.
LÉVY-BRUHL, Lucien, *L'idée de responsabilité.* Paris: Hachette, 1884. Pp. VI. 253.
——, *La morale et la science des mœurs.* Paris: F. Alcan, 1903. Pp. 300.
MARTINETTI, Piero, *La libertà.* Milan: Lombarda, 1928. Pp. 499.
NAVILLE, Ernest, *Le libre arbitre.* Paris: Fischbacher, 1890. Pp. 339.
VIRGA, Pietro, *Libertà giuridica e diritti fondamentali.* Milan: Giuffrè, 1947.

MEDICINE

See Sociology and Medicine, below, Ch. V, 5, p. 274.

FINNEY, Patrick, *Moral Problems in Hospital Practice.* St. Louis Missouri: Herder, 1922.
LAROCHELLE-FINK, *Handbook of Medical Ethics.* Westminster, Maryland: Newman Bookshop, 1943.
MARSHALL, John, *Medicine and Morals.* Twentieth Century Encyclopedia of Catholicism, No. 129. New York: Hawthorn Books, 1960. Pp. 140.

POLITICS

See below, Ch. IV.

POPULATION — BIRTH CONTROL

See Social Ethics, below, p. 266.

BONAR, James, *Theories of Population from Raleigh to Arthur Young.* Lon-don: G. Allen and Unwin, 1931. Pp. 253. Reprint in New York: Au-gustus M. Kelley, 1966.
BRUEHL, Charles Paul, *Birth Control and Eugenics in the Light of Funda-mental Ethical Principles.* New York: J. F. Wagner, 1928. Pp. 256.
CARR-SAUNDERS, A. M., *The Population Problem.* Oxford: The Clarendon Press, 1922. Pp. 516.
«Contraceptive Birth Control», *Insight* (Quincy, Illinois), 1967 a spe-cial issue.
COX, Harold, *Problem of Population.* London: G.P. Putnam, 1923. Pp. 312.

EGNER, G., *Birth Regulation and Catholic Belief: A Study in Problems and Possibilities.* New York: Sheed and Ward, 1966. Pp. 283.

——, *Contraception vs. Tradition: A Catholic Critique.* New York: Herder and Herder, 1967. Pp. 205.

EVERETT, Alexander H., *New Ideas on Population.* Boston: Cummings, Hilliard and Co., 1826. Pp. XXII, 125. Reprint in New York: Augustus M. Kelley, 1966.

FELKNOR, Rhea, «The Current Status on Birth Control: A. U. S. Catholic Special Report», *U. S. Catholic* (Kansas City, Missouri: National Catholic Reporter), 1968, pp. 21-34.

GREEP, Roy O. (ed.), *Human Fertility and Population Problems.* Cambridge, Massachusetts: Schenkman Publishing Company, 1964. Pp. 278.

HAUSER, Philip M., *Population and World Politics.* New York: The Macmillan Co., 1958.

——, (ed.), *Population Dilemma.* Englewood, New Jersey: Prentice-Hall, 1963. Pp. 188.

HIMES, Norman E., «The Place of John Stuart Mill and of Robert Owen in The History of English Neo-Malthusianism», *Quarterly Journal of Economics,* 1927-1928, pp. 627-641.

MALTHUS, Thomas R., *An Essay on the Principle of Population.* London: Printed for J. Johnson, 1798. Pp. 396. Reprint in New York: Augustus M. Kelly, 1965.

BONAR, James, *Malthus and His Work.* 2nd ed. New York: The Macmillan Co., 1924. Pp. VI, 428. Reprint in New York: Augustus M. Kelley, 1966.

NOONAN, John T., Jr., *Contraception: A History of Its Treatment by the Catholic Theologians and Canonists.* Harvard, Mussachusetts: Belknap Press, 1965. Pp. 561.

PAUL VI, «Humanae vitae», *Acta Apostolicae Sedis* (Typis Polyglottis Vaticanis), 1968. English translation, «Human Life» *The Catholic News* (New York), August I, 1968.

RAINWATER, Lee and Weinstein, K. K., *And the Poor Get Children: Sex, Contraception and Family Planning in the Working Class.* Chicago: Aldine Publishing Co., 1967. Pp. 202.

SHAW, Russell, *Abortion and Public Policy.* Washington, D. C.,: Family Life Bureau, National Catholic Welfare Conference, 1966.

STOPES, Marie Ch., *Contraception: Its Theory, History and Practice.* New edition. London: G. P. Putnam, 1931. Pp. XXVII, 487.

The Mysore Population Study. Report of a field survey carried out in selected areas of Mysore State, India. A co-operative project of the United Nations and the Government of India. New York: United Nations, Department of Economic and Social Affaires (Population Study, No. 34), 1961. Pp. 443.

«The Population Explosion», *National Review, A Journal of Fact and Opinion* (Des Moines, Iowa), July 27, 1965.

TUCKER, George, *Progress of the United States in Population and Wealth in Fifty Years.* New York: Press of Hunt's, 1843. Reprint in New York: Augustus M. Kelley, 1964. Pp. 211.

POST, Albert H., *Studien zur Entwicklungsgeschichte des Familienrechts.* Oldenburg: A. Schwartz, 1889. Pp. VIII, 368.

PRIVATE PROPERTY

See Economics, below, Ch. II, 5, p. 108.

SEX

See Population, above, p. 62; Psychoanalysis, above, p. 41; Social Ethics, below, p. 266.

CHESSER, Eustace, *The Cost of Loving*. London: Methuen, 1964. Pp. 223.
——, *Unmarried Love*. New York: David McKay, 1965. Pp. 177.
FILAS, Francis, S. J., *Sex Education in the Family*. Englewood Cliffs, New Jersey: Prentice-Hall, 1966. Pp. 112.
FRIBOURG, Arlette, *She Looks at Sex*. Translated by Dorothy BOLTON. London: Ebury Press, 1965. Pp. 160.
HAIRE, Norman (ed.), *Encyclopedia of Sexual Knowledge*. 2nd ed. London: Encyclopedaedic Press, 1965. Pp. 566.
KRICH, Aron M. (ed.), *The Sexual Revolution*. Philadelphia: Saunders, S. J. R., 1965. Pp. XXVIII, 225.
MARMOR, Judd (ed.), *Sexual Inversion: The Multiple Roots of Homosexuality*. New York: Basic Books, 1965. Pp. 358.
MONEY, John (ed.), *Sex Research*. New York: Holt, Rinehart and Winston, 1965. Pp. 260.
Sexual Hygiene and Pathology. 2nd revised edition. Philadelphia: Lippincott, 1965.
SCOTT, George Ryley, *Sex in Married Life: A Practical Book for Men and Women*. Revised edition. London: Luxor Press, 1965. Pp. 128.
SOROKIN, Pitirim A., *The American Sex Revolution*. Boston, Massachusetts: Porter Sargent Publisher, 1956. Pp. 186.
TAYLOR, Gordon Rattray, *Sex in History*. Revised edition. London: Panther Books, 1965. Pp. 335.
WILSON, John, *Logic and Sexual Morality*. Harmondsworth, England: Penguin Press, 1965.
WOOD, Frederic C., *Sex and the New Morality*. Glen Rock, New Jersey: Newman Press, 1968. Pp. 157.

VALUE

See Economics, below, p. 111; Sociology, below, p. 277. Idealistic Theories, above, p. 48.

In English

BOSANQUET, Bernard, *The Principle of Individuality and Value*. London: Macmillan Co., 1912. Pp. XXXVII, 409.
——, *The Value and Destiny of the Individual*. London: Macmillan Co., 1913. Pp. XXXII, 331.

Bouglé, C., *Leçons de sociologie sur l'évolution des valeurs.* Paris, 1922. English translation by H. S. Sellars, *The Evolution of Values: Studies in Sociology with Special Application to Teaching.* New York: Holt, 1926. Pp. XXXVII, 277.

Bronowski, J., *Sciences and Human Values.* New York: Harper and Row. 1954. Pp. 94.

Dewey, John, *Theory of Valuation.* Chicago: The University of Chicago Press, 1939. Pp. 67.

——, «Values, Liking and Thought», *Journal of Philosophy* (New York), XX, pp. 617- .

Ferguson, John, *Moral Values in the Ancient World.* London: Methuen, 1958.

Findlay, J. N., *Values and Intentions.* London: Humanities Press, 1961.

——, *Language, Mind and Value.* London: Humanities Press, 1963.

Gilson, Étienne, *Moral Values and Moral Life.* Translated by Leo Ward. St. Louis: Herder, 1931.

Gotshalk, D. W., *Patterns of Good and Evil: A Value Analysis.* Urban, Illinois: University of Illinois, 1964. Pp. 138.

——, *Human Aimes in Modern Perspective: Outlines of a General Theory of Value with Special Reference to Contemporary Social Life and Politics.* Yellow Springs, Ohio: The Antioch Press, 1966.

Hall, Everett Wesley, *What is Value? An Essay in Philosophical Analysis.* New York: Humanities Press, 1952. Pp. XIII, 255.

——, *Our Knowledge of Fact and Value.* Chapel Hill, North Carolina: University of North Carolina Press, 1961. Pp. 220.

——, *Categorical Analysis.* Ed. by E. M. Adams. Chapel Hill, North Carolina: University of North Carolina Press, 1964. Pp. 347.

Köhler, Wolfgang, *The Place of Value in the World of Facts.* New York: Liveright Publishing Co., 1398. Pp. IX, 418.

Lepley, Ray (ed.), *Value: A Cooperative Inquiry.* New York: Columbia University Press, 1949. Pp. IX, 487.

Lewis, C. I., *An Analysis of Knowledge and Valuation.* La Salle, Illinois: The Open Court Publishing Company, 1947. Pp. XXI, 567.

——, *The Ground and Nature of the Right.* New York: Columbia, 1955.

Mill, J. S., *Two Letters on the Measure of Value.* Baltimore: John Hopkins Press, 1936. Pp. 24.

Nietzsche, F. W., — see above, p. 29.

Oates, Whitney J., *Aristotle and the Problem of Value.* Princeton, New Jersey: Princeton University Press, 1963. Pp. X, 387. See also Aristotle, above, p. 8.

Osborne, H., *Foundations of the Philosophy of Value.* Cambridge: At the University Press, 1933. Pp. XXII, 132.

Perry, Ralph Barton, *General Theory of Value.* New York: Longmans, Green and Co., 1926. Reprint at Cambridge, Massachusetts: Harvard University Press, 1950. Pp. XVII, 702.

——, *Realms of Value: A Critique of Human Civilization.* Cambridge, Massachusetts: Harvard University Press, 1954. Pp. 497. See Naturalistic Ethics, above, p. 52.

Prall, David W., *A Study in the Theory of Value.* Berkeley: University of California Press, 1921. Pp. 290.

——, *The Present Status of Theory of Value*. Berkeley: University of California Press, 1923.

——, *Metaphysics and Value*. Berkeley: University of California Press, 1924.

——, *Naturalism and Morms*. Berkeley: University of California Press, 1925.

PRATT, J. B., *Reason in the Art of Living*. New York: The Macmillan Company, 1949. Pp. XIV, 303.

REID, John R., *A Theory of Value*. New York: Charles Scribner's Sons, 1938. Pp. 304.

ROBINSON, Richard, *An Atheist's Value*. Oxford: At the Clarendon Press, 1964. Pp. 256.

ROTENSTREICH, Nathan, *Spirit and Man: An Essay on Being and Value*. The Hague: Martinus Nijhoff, 1963. Pp. 257.

SAN JOSE STATE COLLEGE ASSOCIATES IN PHILOSOPHY (eds.), *In Quest of Value: Readings in Philosophy and Personal Values*. Chicago: Science Research Associates, 1963. Pp. IX, 514.

SCHLICK, Mauritz (1882-1936), *Fragen der Ethik*, 1930. English translation by S. RYNIN, *Problems of Ethics*. New York: Prentice Hall, 1939. Pp. XV, 217.

SESONSKE, Alexander, *Value and Obligation*. New York: Oxford University Press, 1966.

SHELDON, W. H., «An Empirical Definition of Value», *The Journal of Philosophy, Psychology and Scientific Method*, Vol. XI (1914).

SHIRK, Evelyn, *The Ethical Dimension: An Approach to the Philosophy of Values and Valuing*. New York: Appleton-Century-Crofts, 1965. Pp. 350.

URBAN, W. M., *Valuation: Its Nature and Laws*. New York: The Macmillan, 1909. Pp. XVIII, 433.

WARD, Leo, *Values and Reality*. New York: Sheed & Ward, 1935.

In Other Languages

BAUMBERGER, F., *Untersuchungen zur Enstehung des Wertproblems in der Philosophie des 19. Jahrhunderts*. Halle: T. Lotze, 1924.

BRENTANO, Franz Clemens, *Gesammelte Schriften*. 7 vols. Frankfurt a. M.: J. D.: Sauer Leander, 1852. See below, Index.

DÜHRING, Eugene, *Werth des Lebens*. Breslau: Trewendt, 1865. Pp. VIII, 235.

——, *Natürliche Dialektik. Neue Logische Grundlegungen der Wissenschaft und Philosophie*. Berlin: Mittler und Sohn, 1865. Pp. XII, 227.

EHRENFELS, Christian, *System der Werttheorie*. 2 vols. Leipzig: O. R. Reisland, 1897-1898.

LAVELLE, Louis, *Traité des valeurs*. 2 vols. Paris: Presses Universitaires de France, 1951-1955.

MEINONG, Alexius, *Psychologische-etische Untersuchung zur Werththeorie*. Graz: Leuschner und Lubensky, 1894. Pp. VIII, 107.

MISES VON, Ludwig, and Spiethoff, Arthur (eds.), *Problem der Wertlehre*. 2 vols. Munich and Leipzig: Duncker und Humblot, 1931-1933.

MÜNSTERBERG, Hugo, *Philosophie der Werte*. Leipzig: J. A. Barth, 1908. Pp. VIII, 486.

Poulantzas, Nicos, *Nature des choses et droit: essai sur la dialectique du fait et de la valeur*. Paris: Pichon, 1965.

Scheler, Max F., *Beiträge zur Feststellung der Beziehungen zwischen den logischen und ethischen Prinzipien*. Jena: B. Volpelius, 1899. Pp. 142.

———, *Der Formalismus in der Ethik und die materiale Wertethik*. 2 parts Halle: M. Niemeyer, 1916. Pp. VIII, 620. Ethical Personalism.

———, *Die Stellung des Menschen im Kosmos*. Darmstadt: O. Reichl, 1928. Pp. 114.

———, *Neuer Versuch der Grundlegung eines ethischen Personalismus*. 3. unveränderte Auflage. Halle: M. Niemeyer, 1927. Pp. XXVI, 648. 2 Tle. 4th ed. Bern: Francke, 1954. Pp. 678. First published in 1913-1916. See Phenomenology, in *PQS*. No. 5.

———, *Vom Umsturz der Werte*. 2 vols. 4th ed. Bern: A. Francke, 1955. Pp. 450. First published in 1918.

Lauer, J. Quentin, S. J., *The Triumph of Subjectivity: An Introduction to Transcendental Phenomenology*. New York: Fordham University Press, 1958. Pp. IX, 185.

Altmann, Alexander, *Die Grundlagen der Wertethik. Max Schelers Erkenntnis und Seinslehre in kritischer Analyse*. Berlin: Reuther und Reichard, 1931. Pp. 113.

Schorer E., *Die Zweckethik des hl. Thomas von Aquin als Ausgleich der formalistischen Ethik Kants und der materialen Wertethik Schelers*. Vechta in Oldenburg: Albertus-Magnus-Verlag der Dominikaner, 1937. Pp. 84.

WAR

See Military Force, below, p. 222.

Early Modern

Adams, Robert P., *The Better Part of Valor: More, Erasmus, Colet and Vives on Humanism, War and Peace*. Seattle, Washington: University of Washington Press, 1962. Pp. 363.

Vitoria de, Francisco, (1480-1546), *De Indiis et De iure belli relectiones*. Ed. by Ernest Nys. Washington: The Carnegie Institution of Washington, 1917. English translation by J. B. Scott, *The Spanish Origin of International Law: Francisco de Vitoria and His Law of Nations*. Oxford: The Clarendon Press, 1934. Pp. 475. First published in 1557.

———, *Relectiones morales duobus tomis comprehensae*. Cologne: Sumptibus A. Boetii, 1696. See below, p. 129.

Grotius, Hugo (1583-1645). *De jure Belli et pacis libri tres*. English translation, *The Rights of War and Peace*. New York: Universal Classics Library, M. Walter Dunne Publisher, 1901. A Translation by Francis W. Kelsey et al., *The Law of War and Peace*. New York: Bobbs-Merrill, 1963. Pp. 992.

———, *Prolegomena to the Law of War and Peace*. Translation of Grotius' introduction to *The Law of War and Peace* by F. W. KELSEY, taken from Carnegie edition. New York: Bobbs-Merrill, 1957. Pp. 64.

MACHIAVELLI, Niccolo, *I dialoghi dell' arte della guerra*. Florence: Heredi di Philippo di Giunta, 1521. English revised translation by Ellis FARNEWORTH, *The Art of War*. New York: Bobbs-Merrill, 1965. Pp. 352. See Politics, below, Ch. IV, p. 186.

SUAREZ, Francis, — see Scholastic Philosophy (commentators), in *PQS*, No. 5.

Late Modern

COLOMBOS, C. John. *Jeremy Bentham's Plan for an Universal and Perpetual Peace*. London: Sweet and Maxwell, 1927. Pp. III, 44.

Cox, Richard, Howard, *Locke on War and Peace*. Oxford: Clarendon Press, 1960. Pp. XX, 770.

KANT, I., *Zum ewigen Frieden*. Königsberg: F. Nicolovius 1795. English translation by Lewis W. BECK, *Perpetual Peace*. Indianapolis, Indiana: Bobbs-Merrill, 1957. Pp. XVIII, 59. See Politics, below, p. 184.

ROUSSEAU, J. J., «Du projet de paix perpetuel», in his *Œuvres politiques*. Paris: V. Lepetit, 1821. English translation by Edith M. NUTTALL, *A Project of Perpetual Peace*. London, 1927. See Politics, below, p. 181.

Contemporary

ADLER, Mortimer, *How to Think about War and Peace*. New York: Simon & Schuster, 1944. Pp. XXIII, 307.

BAKELESS, J., *The Economic Causes of Modern War*. New York: Moffat, Yard and Co., 1921. Pp. 265.

BEALES, A.C.F., *The History of Peace*. London: Dial Press, 1931. Pp. 355.

CLAUSEWITZ VON, Karl, *On War*. Translated by J. J. GRAHAM. 3 vols. London: Routledge & Kegan Paul. 1940-1949.

DEWEY, John. «The Future of Pacifism», *New Republic* (Washington, D. C.), July 28, 1917, pp. 358-360.

——, «What Outlawry of War is Not», *New Republic* (Washington, D. C.), October 3, 1923, pp. 149-152.

——, «War and a Code of Law», *New Republic* (Washington, D. C.), October 24, 1923, pp. 224-226.

——, «Outlawing Peace by Discussing War», *New Republic* (Washington, D. C.), May 16, 1928, pp. 370-371.

——, *Characters and Events*. 2 vol. London: Holt, 1929.

——, «Peace by Pact or Convenant?» *New Republic* (Washington, D. C.), March 23, 1932, pp. 145-147.

——, «Higher Learning and War», *Bulletin of the American Association of University Professors* (Washington, D. C.), 1939, pp. 613.

FEDOSEEV, P. N., *Istoricheskij materialism: sozialnaia filosofia sovremennoi burshuasii*. Moscow, 1960. English translation of an extract, «Contemporary Sociological Theories Concerning War and Peace», *Soviet Studies in Philosophy* (New York), 1962-1963, No. 3, pp. 3-24.

GIGON, H., *The Ethics of Peace and War*. London: Burns Oates & Washbourne, 1935. Pp. XII, 68.

GRISEZ, G. G., «Moral objectivity and the Cold War», *Ethics* (Chicago), 1960, No. 4 ,pp. 291-305.

HEMLEBEN, Sylvester Johns, *Plans for World Peace through Six Centuries.* Chicago: University of Chicago Press, 1943. Pp. 277.

HINSLEY, F. H., *Power and the Pursuit of Peace: Theory and Practice of Relations between States.* Cambridge: University Press, 1963. Pp. 416.

HOVCLAQUE, Emile L., *Deeper Cause of the War.* Translated by the author. London: Allen and Unwin, 1916. Pp. 158.

McDONALD, Lee Cameron, *Western Political Theory in the Modern World.* New York: Harcourt, 1962. Pp. 557.

MITCHELL, Timothy A., «War and Conscious Objection», *Social Justice Review* (St. Louis, Missouri: The Central Bureau, CCUA), 1968, pp. 147-154.

NORTHEDGE, F. S., «Peace, War, and Philosophy», in *The Encyclopedia of Philosophy* (8 vols. New York: The Macmillan Co., 1967), Vol. VI, pp. 63-67.

Principles for Peace. Washington, D.C.: National Catholic Welfare Conference, 1943.

RAMSEY, Paul, *War and Christian Conscience.* Durham, North Carolina: Duke University Press, 1961. See above, p. 46.

STAWELL, Florence M., *The Growth of International Thought.* London: Holt, 1929. Pp. 248.

STRATMANN, F., *The Church and War.* New York: Kennedy, 1928. Pp. XIII, 216.

VANN, Gerald, *Morality and War.* London: Bruns Oates & Washbourne, 1939. Pp. VII, 75.

WOODS, F. A., *Is War Diminishing?* Boston: Houghton Mifflin Co., 1915. Pp. XI, 105.

ARON, Raymond, *Paix et guerre entre les nations.* Paris: Calmann-Lévy, 1962. Pp. 800.

CONSTANTIN, Nicolas A., *Le rôle sociologique de la guerre et le sentiment national.* Paris: F. Alcan, 1907. Pp. 291.

CROCE, B., «Filosofia e guerra», *Critica* (Bari), No. 5, 1915.

DEL VECCHIO, Giorgio, *Studi su la guerra e la pace.* Milan: A. Giuffrè, 1959. Pp. 240.

GENTILE, Giovanni, *La filosofia della guerra.* Palermo: Ergon, 1914. Pp. 31.

——, *Guerra e fede.* Naples: Riccardi, 1919. Pp. XI, 381.

JOHNS, Max, *Krieg, Frieden und Kultur.* Berlin: Allgemeines Verein für deutsche Litteratur, 1893. Pp. XX, 432.

KUNZ, Josef L., *La problemática actual de las leyes de la guerra.* Valladolid: Universidad de Valladolid, 1955. Pp. 164.

MAGGIORE, Giuseppe, *Il valore etico della guerra.* Rome: Unione editrice, 1915. Pp. 19.

REGOUT, R., *La doctrine de la guerre juste de Saint Augustin à nos jours.* Paris: Pedone, 1934. Pp. 350.

RAVÀ, Adolfo, *Il problema della guerra e della pace: lezioni di storia delle dottrini politiche e scienza politica generale.* Padua: Università di Padova, 1932. Pp. 100.

——, *Le teorie filosofiche sullo stato.* Padua: Università di Padova, 1933. Pp. 88.

STEINMETZ, S. R., *Die Philosophie des Krieges.* Leipzig: J .A. Barth, 1907. Pp. XVI, 352.

Atom Bomb

STEIN, Walter, *Nuclear Weapons: A Catholic Response.* London: Burns and Oates, 1963. Pp. 151.

JASPERS, K., *Die Atombombe und die Zukunft des Menschen.* 2nd ed. München: Piper, 1958. Pp. 506.

WAGNER, Gerhart, *Die Forschung zwischen Wissen und Gewissen. Von der Verantwortung der Naturwissenschaft im Atomzeitalter.* Zürich: EVZ-Verlag, 1961. Pp. 64.

4. PERIODICALS

See General Philosophical Magazines, and also periodicals of related sciences of Ethics, below, Ch. II - VI; in *PQS*, No. 4.

(a) General

Endeavour: A Quarterly Designed to Record the Progress of the Sciences in the Service of Mankind. London: Millbank, 1942—.

Ethical Outlook. New York: American Ethical Union, 1914—.

Ethics: An International Journal of Social, Political and Legal Philosophy. Chicago: University of Chicago Press, 1890—.

Insight: Interdisciplinary Studies of Man. Quincy, Illinois: Quincy College (Dept. A), 1967—. Quarterly.

Journal of the History of Ideas. New York: City College, 1940—.

Ratio. London: Basil Blackwell, 1957—.

Esprit. Paris: 19, rue Jacob, 1932—.

Etyka. Warsaw: Panstwowe Wydawnictwo Naukowe, 1966—. Organ of the Instytut, Filosofia i Socjologia Polskiej Akademii Nauk.

Filosofia e Vita. Rome: Via Simon Saint Bon, 25, 1960—.

Freiburger Zeitschrift für Philosophie und Theologie. Freiburg, Switzerland: Paulus Verlag, 1954—.

Idea: mensile di cultura e politica sociale. Rome: G. Calogero, 1945—.

Morale et enseignement. Brussels: Institut de Philosophie, Université de Bruxelles, 1951—. Quarterly with variations.

Psyché: revue internationale des sciences de l'homme et de psychanalyse. Paris: 19 rue Monsieur, 1946—.

Revue de la Révolution. Revue mensuelle, historique, philosophique, économique, littéraire et artistique. Paris: C. d'Héricault et G. Bord, 1883-1889.

Revue de métaphysique et de morale. Paris: Librairie Armand Colin, 1893—.

Revue des sciences humaines. Lille, France: Faculté des Lettres de Lille, 1933—.

Revue des sciences philosophiques et théologiques. Paris: J. Vrin, 1907—.

(b) Special

Humanist. Yellow Spring, Ohio: American Humanist Association, 1941—.

Moral World: The Advocate of the Rational System of Society. Founded by Robert Owen. London 1845—.

Religious Humanism: A Quarterly Journal of Religious and Scientific Humanism. Yellow Springs, Ohio: The Fellowship of Religious Humanists affiliated with The American Ethical Union (105 W. North College Street), 1967—. Quarterly.

Progressive World. Los Angels, California: United Secularists of America, 1947—.

Self-Realization Magazine. Los Angeles, California: Self-realization Fellowship, 1925—.

Soviet Studies in Philosophy. New York: International Arts and Sciences Press (156 Fifth Ave.), 1962—.

The New Scholasticism. Washington, D.C.: The American Catholic Philosophical Association, 1927—.

Theosophy, Devoted to the Theosophical Movement and the Brotherhood of Humanity. Los Angles, California: Theosophy Co., 1912—.

The Thomist: A Theological and Philosophical Quarterly. Washington, D. C.— Baltimore, Maryland The Thomist Press, 1939—.

Angelicum. Rome: Pontificium Institutum Internationale Angelicum, 1924—.

Gregorianum: Commentarii de re theologica et philosophica. Rome: Pontificia Universitas Gregoriana, 1920—.

Il pensiero critico: problemi del nostro tempo. Milan: Istituto Editoriale Italiano, 1950—.

Rassegna di morale e di diritto. Rome: Scuola Tipografica Missionaria Domenicana, 1935-1941.

Rivista di filosofia e scienze affini. Bologne: Zamorani e Albertazzi, 1899-1908.

Rassegna di scienze filosofiche. Bari: Ermes, 1946—.

Responsabilità del sapere. Rome: Tipografia S. Giuseppe, 1947—.

Revue d'histoire et de philosophie religieuses. Paris: Presses Universitaires de France, 1921—.

Revue thomiste. Bruges, Belgium: Desclée De Brouwer, 1893—.

Sapientia: rivista tomista di filosofia. La Plata F. C. R., Argentina: Seminario Mayor San Jose, 1946—.

Voprosy Filosofii. Moscow: Akademiya Nauk SSSR, 1947—. Summaries in English.

Chapter II

ECONOMICS

Economics (from the Greek οἶκός, house, dwelling; and νόμος, law, ordinance; hence, οἰκονομία, affairs of managing a household) deals with questions pertaining to the ordering and promotion of private and public wealth.

Modern economics may be traced back to Jean Bodin (1553-1596), who advanced a quantitative theory of money. The combination of economics with politics seems to have been called political economics for the first time in Antony de Montchrétien's *L'économie politique,* 1615. However, the true inaugurator of modern economics is considered to be Adam Smith (1723-1790). The theories on solving economic problems multiply in the modern era. Some of them are listed in the Bibliography, below, Sections 3-4.

The philosophy of economics is interested in the notion, laws, and principles of economics. It also deals with the ethical implications of economics, and particularly the question of what economics should be in terms of human rights and duties. This aspect has become more pronounced in modern treatment of economics.

However, the ethical implications of economics come under heavy dispute in contemporary thought. There is a strong trend toward considering economics as ethically neutral and value-free, similar to sciences (see K. KLAPPHOLZ, Bibliography, p. 77).

The special problems of economics fall mainly in the categories of methodology, econometrics, money, private property, pure economics, underdeveloped countries, and slaves. These problems very often include ethical aspects, particularly with regard to justice, personal choice, policy-making, employment, and labor.

A specific ground for philosophical investigation is general principles of economy, which can be applied to all kinds of human actions, and not only to economics as a science in the proper sense. Such a principle is expressed, among other places, in Ockham's razor metaphor (beings are not multiplied without necessity — *entia non sunt multiplicanda sine necessitate*), in Leibniz's tenet that the greater success is obtainable by less effort, and in Goldschied's thesis concerning the saving of volitive energy (see Special Questions, below, p. 105).

Bibliography

1. INTRODUCTORY BIBLIOGRAPHIES

See Encyclopedias, below, 2 b; in *PQS*, No. 5; above, Ch. I, 1; Politics, below, Ch. IV, 1; Sociology, below, Ch. V, 1.

BURCHARDT, F. A., HICKS, J. R. *et al.*, *Bibliography in Economics for the Honour School of Philosophy, Politics and Economics.* Oxford: Basil Blackwell, 1948. Pp. 40.
International Bibliography of Economics. 8 vols. Ed. by l'ORGANISATION DES NATIONS UNIES (education). Paris: L'Imprimerie Union, 1955-1961. Works published in 1952-1959, and some previous works. Since 1960 Vol. IX-XII edited by INTERNATIONAL COMMITTEE FOR SOCIAL SCIENCES DOCUMENTATION. London: Stevens and Sons, 1962-1964—.

2. GENERAL STUDIES

(a) Histories

In English

BURNS, Arthur Robert, *Comparative Economic Organization.* New York: Prentice-Hall, Inc., 1955. Pp. XV, 766.
COLE, G. D. H., *A History of Socialist Thought.* 4 vols. From 1789-1931. London: Macmillan and Co. Ltd., 1955-1958.
GIDE, Charles and RIST, Charles, *Histoires des doctrines économiques depuis les physiocrates jusqu'à nos jours.* Paris, 1909. Authorized English translation by R. RICHARDS, *A History of Economic Doctrines from*

the Time of the Physiocrats to the Present Day. 2nd ed. Boston: D. C. Heath and Company, 1948. Pp. 800.

HEILBRONER, Robert L. (ed.), *The Great Economists: Their Lives and Their Conceptions of the World.* Revised edition. London: Eyre and Spottiswoode, 1955. Pp. 1955.

HOSELITZ, Bert F., SPENGLER, Joseph J., LETICHE, J. M. et al., *Theories of Economic Growth.* Glencoe, Illinois: Free Press, 1961. Pp. 340.

ROSTOW, W. W., *The Stages of Economic Growth: A Non-Communist Manifesto.* Cambridge: University Press, 1962. Pp. XI, 179.

SCHUMPETER, Joseph Alois, *Economic Doctrine and Method: An Historical Sketch.* Translatend from the German by R. ARIS. New York: Oxford University Press, 1954. Pp. 207. See Systematic Studies, below, b, in Other Languages.

——, *History of Economic Analysis.* New York: George Allen and Unwin, 1954. Pp. XXV, 1260.

SPENGLER, Joseph J. and ALLEN, William R., *Essays in Economic Thought: Aristotle to Marshall.* Chicago: Rand McNally and Company, 1960. Pp. 800.

The Cambridge Economic History of Europe. Ed. by John Clapham and and Eileen Power. 2 vols. Cambridge: Cambridge University Press, 1952. P. XV, 604.

UNWIN, George, *Studies in Economic History.* Ed. by R. H. TAWNEY. London: Royal Economic Society, 1927. Pp. LXXIV, 490. Reprint in New York: Augustus M. Kelly, 1958.

VINER, Jacob, *The Long View and the Short: Studies in Economic Theory and Policy.* Glencoe, Illinois: Free Press, 1958. Pp. 462.

WHITTAKER, Edmund, *Schools and Streams of Economic Thought.* Chicago: Rand McNally ad Company, 1960. Pp. 416.

Yale Economic Essays. New Haven, Connecticut: Yale University, Department of Economics, 1961—.

In Other Languages

COSSA, Luigi, *Histoire des doctrines économiques.* Paris: V. Giard et E. Brière, 1899. Pp. 574.

GIDE, Charles and RIST, Charles, — see above, In English.

KOVALEVSKY, Maksim M., *Die ökonomische Entwicklung Europas bis zum Beginn der kapitalistischen Wirtschaftsform.* 3 vols. Translated from the Russian by Leo MOTZKIN et al. Berlin: R. L. Prager, 1901-1905.

KRETSCHMANN, Griziotti, *Storia delle dottrine economiche.* Turin: Unione Tipografica — editrice torinese, 1949. Pp. XVI, 473.

——, *Storia delle dottrine economiche moderne.* Milan: J. Gorzanti, 1959. Pp. 195.

LUZZATTO, Gino (ed.), *Storia economica.* Turin: Unione tipografico-editrice torinese, 1936. Pp. XLVIII, 898.

SCHNEIDER, Erich, *Einführung in die Wirtschaftslehre.* 2 vols. Tübingen: Mohr, 1947-1949.

WEBER, Max, *Economia e società.* 2 vols. Milan: Ed. Comunità, 1961.

(b) Systematic Studies

See below, 3 and 5.

ALPERT, Paul, *Economic Development: Objectives and Methods.* New York: The Macmillan Company, 1963. Pp. 308.

CAREY, Henry Charles, *Principles of Political Economy.* 3 vols. Philadelphia: Carey, Lea and Blanchard, 1837-1840. Reprint in New York: Augustus M. Kelley, 1965.

CLAY, Henry, *Economics: Introduction for General Reader.* New York: The Macmillan Co., 1918. Pp. XVIII, 456.

COSSA, Luigi, *Guida allo studio dell' economia politica.* 2nd ed. Milan: Hoepli, 1877. Pp. VIII, 261. English translation by W. S. JEVONS, *Guide to the Study of Political Economy.* London: Macmillan and Co., 1880. First published in 1876. See Histories, above, a.

——, *Introduzione allo studio dell' economia politica.* 3rd. ed. Milan: Hoepli, 1892. Pp. XII, 594. English translation by Louis DYER, *Introduction to the Study of Political Economics.* London: Macmillan and Co., 1893.

DAHL, Robert Alan and LINDBLOM, C. E., *Politics, Economics, And Welfare.* New York: Harper, 1953. Pp. XXVI, 557.

DOBB, Maurice Herbert, *An Introduction to Economics.* London: Victor Gollancz, 1932. Pp. 143. See also Russia, p. 105.

——, *Political Economy and Capitalism: Some Essays in Economic Tradition.* London: G. Routledge and Sons, 1937. Pp. VIII, 359.

——, *Studies in the Development of Capitalism.* London. G. Routledge and Sons, 1946. Pp. IX, 1936.

GRAAFF DE, Johannes de Villiers, *Theoretical Welfare Economics.* London: Cambridge University Press, 1957. Pp. 178.

HADLEY, A. T., «Economic Science or Economics, or Political Economy», *Dictionary of Philosophy and Psychology,* ed. by James M. BALDWIN (3 vols. New York: Peter Smith, 1940), Vol. I, pp. 307-309.

KORNHAUSER, A., DUBIN, H. and Ross, A. M. (eds.), *Industrial Conflict.* New York: McGraw-Hill, 1954. Pp. 551.

NEWCOMB, Simon, *Principles of Political Economy.* New York: Harper and Brothers, 1886. Pp. XVI, 548. Reprint in New York: Augustus M. Kelley, 1966.

NICHOLSON, Joseph Shield, *Principles of Political Economy.* 3 vols. London: Macmillan Co., 1893-1901.

Palgrave's Dictionary of Political Economy. 3 vols. Ed. by Henry HIGGS. London: Macmillan and Co., 1928. Reprint in New York: A. M. Kelley, 1963.

PARETO, Vilfredo, *Cours d'économie politique.* 2 vols. Lüzern, Switzerland, 1896-1897.

——, *Manuale di economia politica, con una introduzione alla scienza sociale.* Milan: Società editrice Libreria, 1906. Pp. XII, 579.

RAYMOND, Daniel, *The Elements of Political Economy.* 2 vols. 2nd ed. Baltimore: F. Lucas, Jr. and E. J. Coale, 1823. Reprint in New York: Augustus M. Kelley, 1964.

SAMUELSON, Paul A., *Economics: An Introductory Analysis*. New York: Mc-Graw-Hill Company, Inc., 1961. Pp. 853.

SCHUMPETER, Joseph, *Capitalism, Socialism, and Democracy*. New York: Harper, 1950. Pp. XIV, 431. See Histories, above 2 a.

The New Encyclopedia of Social Reform. Ed. by W. D. P. BLISS. New York: Funk and Wagnalls Co., 1910. Pp. VI, 1321.

(c) Philosophy

See also above, 1; Particular Periods and Special Questions, below, 3-4.

In English

ARCHIBALD, G. C., «Welfare Economics, Ethics and Essentialism», *Economica*, New Series, 1959, pp. 316-327. Economics is not necessarly ethical.

ARROW, Kenneth Joseph, *Social Choice and Individual Values*. New York: Wiley, 1963. Pp. 124.

BONAR, James, *Philosophy and Political Economy in Some of Their Historical Relations*. 3rd ed. London: Macmillan, 1922. Pp. XVI, 410. First published in 1893.

BRAYBROOKE, David, «Economics and Rational Choice», *The Encyclopedia of Philosophy* (8 vols. New York: The Macmillan Co., 1967), Vol. II, pp. 454-458.

COATS, A. W., «Value Judgments in Economics», *Yorkshire Bulletin of Economic and Social Research*, 1964, pp. 53-67.

DAVENPORT, H. J., *Economics of Enterprise*. New York: The Macmillan Co., 1929.

HALÉVY, Élie, *La formation du radicalisme philosophique*. 3 vols. Paris: F. Alcan, 1901-1904. English translation in one volume by Mary MORRIS, *The Growth of Philosophic Radicalism*. New York: The Macmillan Co., 1928. Pp. XVII, 554.

HAYEK VON, Friedrich August, *Individualism and Economic Order*. Chicago: University of Chicago Press, 1949. Pp. VI, 272.

HUTCHISON, Terence Wilmot, *'Positive' Economics and Policy Objectives*. Cambridge, Massachusetts: Harvard University Press, 1964. Pp. 200. On value judgments in economics.

JOHNSTON, Herbart, *Business Ethics*. 2nd ed. New York: Pitman Publishing Corporation, 1961. Pp. XIII, 305.

KLAPPHOLZ, Kurt, «Value Judgments and Economics», *The British Journal for the Philosophy of Science*, 1964, pp. 97-114.

——, «Economics and Ethical Neutrality», *The Encyclopedia of Philosophy* (8 vols. New York: The Macmillan Co., 1967), vol II, pp. 451-454.

KNIGHT, Frank H., *The Ethics of Competition*. New York: Harper, 1935.

LITTLE, Ian Malcolm David, *A Critique of Welfare Economics*. 2nd ed. New York: Oxford University Press, 1957. Pp. 320.

MARSHALL, Alfred, *Principles of Economics*. 8th ed. London: Macmillan, 1936. Pp. XXXIV, 871. First published in 1890.

McCord Wright, David, «Economics», *A Dictionary of Social Sciences* (New York: The Free Press (Macmillan), 1965), pp. 226-227. Definitions of economics. See also «Economics» in *Encyclopedia Britanica*.

Mehta, Jamshed Kaikhusroo et al., *Studies in Economic Theory and Economic Philosophy*. Allhabad, India: Agarwal Press, 1956. Pp. 265.

——, *A Philosophical Interpretation of Economics*. London: G. Allen, 1962. Pp. 288.

Menyer, Carl, *Principles of Economics*. New York: The Macmillan Company, 1950.

Mises von, Ludwig, *Human Action: A Treatise on Economics*. London: William Hodge and Co., 1949. Pp. XV, 889.

Popper, Karl R., *The Open Society and Its Enemies*. 2 vols. London: Routledge and Kegan Paul, 1945.

——, *The Poverty of Historicism*. 2nd ed. London: Routledge and Kegan Paul, 1961. Pp. 166.

Robbins, Lionel Charles, *Essay on the Nature and Significance of Economic Science*. 2nd ed. London: Macmillan, 1935. Pp. XII, 144.

Robinson, Joan, *Economic Philosophy*. Chicago: Aldine Publishing Co., 1962. Pp. 150.

Samuelson, Paul Anthony, *Foundations of Economic Analysis*. Cambridge Massachusetts: Harvard University Press, 1947. Pp. XII, 447.

Schumpeter, Joseph Alois, *Capitalism, Socialism and Democracy*. 4th ed. London: G. Allen and Unwin, 1952. Pp. XIV, 431.

Sharp, Frank Chapman and Fox, Philip G., *Business Ethics: Studies in Fair Competition*. New York: Appleton-Century-Crofts, 1937. Pp. 316.

Sidgwick, Henry, *The Principles of Political Economy*. 3rd ed. London: Macmillan and Co., 1901. Pp. XXIV, 592. First published in 1883.

Veblen, Thorstein, «The Pre-conceptions of Economic Science», in his *The Place of Science in Modern Civilation* (New York: Viking Press, 1919), pp. 82-179.

Weber, Max, *The Theory of Social and Economic Organizations*. Translated by A. M. Henderson and Talcott Parsons, New York: Oxford University Press, 1947. Pp. X, 436.

——, *Grundriss der Sozialökonomik —, III abt.: Wirtschaft und Gesellschaft*. Tübingen: J. C. B. Mohr, 1925. Part I edited and translated, — see above.

Bendix, Reinhard, *Max Weber: An Intellectual Portrait*. New York: Doubleday, and Co., 1960. Pp. 480.

Rheinstein, Max (ed.), *Max Weber on Law in Economy and Society*. Cambridge, Massachussetts: Harvard University Press, 1954. Pp. LXXII, 363.

Schelting von, Alexander, *Max Webers Wissenschaftslehre*. Tübingen: J. C. B. Mohr, 1934. Pp. VIII, 420.

Wicksteed, Philip Henry, *The Common Sense of Political Economy*. 2 vols. London: Routledge and Kegan Paul, 1933.

In Other Languages

CROCE, B., *Aspetti morali della vita politica.* Bari: G. Laterza, 1928. Pp. 90. See Idealism, in *PQS*, No. 5.

——, *Filosofia della practica: economica ed etica.* 7th ed. Bari: G. Laterza, 1957. Pp. XX, 410.

CRONER, F., «Wissenschaftslogik und Wertproblematik», *Kölner Zeitschrift für Soziologie und Sozialpsychologie,* 1964, pp. 327-341.

DEMARIA, Giovanni, *Principi generali di logica economica.* Milan: C.E.A., 1944. Pp. XI, 484.

FANNO, Marco, *Principia di scienza economica.* 4th ed. Padua: Cedam, 1952.

FOSSATI, Eraldo, *Elementi di economia razionale.* Milan: A. Giuffrè, 1955. Pp. XI, 292.

KRAUS, Otto Josef, *Grundfragen der Wirtschaftsphilosophie. Eine analytische Einführung.* Berlin: Duncker und Humblot, 1962. Pp. 271.

RICHARD, A. F. Gaston, *La question sociale et le mouvement philosophique au XIX siècle.* Paris: A. Colin, 1914. Pp. XII, 363.

SCHACK, Herbert, *Wirtschaftsleben und Wirtschaftsgestaltung. Die Grundlagen der Wirtschafts- und Sozialphilosophie.* Berlin: Duncker und Humblot, 1963. Pp. 216.

STACKELBERG VON, Heinrich, *Grundlagen der theoretischen Volkswirtschaftslehre.* 2nd ed. Bern: A. Francke, 1948. Pp. XVI, 368.

(d) Excerpts from Original Writings

ABBOT, L. D. (ed.), *Masterworks of Economics.* Garden City, New York: Doubleday, 1953.

KORNHAUSER, A., DUBIN, R. and ROSS, A. M. (eds.), *Industrial Conflict.* New York: McGraw-Hill, 1954. Pp. 551.

3. PARTICULAR PERIODS

ANTIQUITY

(a) Ancient Orient

POLANYI, Karl, ARENSBERG, Conrad M. and PEARSON, Harry W. (eds.), *Trade and Market in the Early Empires.* Glencoe, Illinois: Free Press, 1957. Pp. XVIII, 382.

Book of the Dead. 3 vols. London: Kegan Paul and Co., 1897-1898. See Egypt, in *PQS*, No. 5.

Rig-Veda-Sanhita. 6 vols. Ed. by Max Müller. London: W. H. Allen and Co., 1849-1874.

PETERSON, P., *Handbook to the Study of the Rigveda.* Bombay: Department of Public Instruction, 1890.

The Bible: Old Testament, — see Jewish Philosophy, in *PQS*, No. 5.

(b) Ancient West

POHLMANN VON, Robert, *Geschichte der sozialen Frage und des Sozialismus in der antiken Welt.* 2 vols. 3rd ed. Munich: Ch. H. Beck, 1925.

GREECE

BOLKESTEIN, H., *Economic Life in Greece's Golden Age.* Translated from the Dutch and revised by E. J. JONKERS. Leiden, Holland: E. J. Brill, 1958. Pp. X, 168.

XENOPHON (c. 427-c. 355), «Economist», in Hermann Diels, *Die Vorsokratiker.* 3 vols. 4th ed. Berlin: Weidmannsche Buchhandlung, 1922.

XENOPHON, *Oeconomicus.* Ed. by J. THOMPSON and B. J. HAYES. 2nd ed. London: The Tutorial Series, 1888. Pp. 136.

KERN, F., *Über Xenophon.* Stettin: Dannenberg, 1874.

VOGEL, G., *Die Ökonomik des Xenophon.* Erlangen: M. Meneke, 1895. Pp. 85.

PLATO (429-348), *The Republic.* Translated and edited by F. M. CORNFORD. New York: Oxford University Press, 1945. Pp. 365. Communism; dependence of the state on economics.

——, *Laws.* 2 vols. Ed. by R. G. BURY. Cambridge, Massachusetts: Harvard University Press, 1952. Private property in Bk. I; population's problem in Bk. V.

ARISTOTLE (384-322), — see above, pp. 8-9.

——, *Aristotelis quae feruntur Oeconomica.* Ed. by F. SUSEMIHL. Leipzig: Teubner, 1887.

——, *The Politics and Economics of Aristotle.* Edited and translated by Edward WALFORD. London: H. G. Bohn, 1894. Pp. LXXX, 338.

ROME

ROSTOVTSEV, Mikhail Ivanovich, *Social and Economic History of the Roman Empire.* New York: Oxford University Press, 1926. Pp. XXVI, 696.

CICERO, Marcus Tullius (106-43 B. C.), *Fragmenta Ciceronis oeconomicorum e Xenophonte.* 1703.

——, *In Catilinam Orationes IV.* Ed. by J. W. VAN ROOYEN. 2 parts. Leiden, Holland: E. J. Brill, 1962. Pp. III, 63; II, 45.

——, *Pro T. Annio Milone oratio ad iudices.* Ed. by J. W. VAN ROOYEN. Leiden, Holland: E. J. Brill, 1963. Pp. XVI, 59.

——, *Oratio pro Murena.* Ed. by J. W. VAN ROOYEN and A. WITLOX. 2 parts, 3rd ed. Leiden, Holland: E. J. Brill, 1963. Pp. IV, 50; II, 34.

——, *De legibus libri tres.* A revised text with English notes. Cambridge: J. Hall and Son, 1881. Pp. VIII, 152.

JONKERS, E. J. (ed.), *Social and Economic Commentary on Cicero's Gnaei Pompei.* Leiden, Holland: E. J. Brill, 1959. Pp. X, 53.

——, (ed.), *Social and Economic Commentary on Cicero's De Lege Agraria Orationes Tres.* Leiden, Holland: E. J. Brill, 1963. Pp. VI, 148.

——, *Social and Economic Commentary on Cicero's 'Catilinaria'.* Leiden, Holland: E. J. Brill, 1967.

MIDDLE AGES

See *PQS,* No. 5; above, 2 a.

BEER, Max, *Social Struggles in the Middle Ages.* Translated by J. STEN-NING. New York: International Publishers, 1929. Pp. IX, 215.

MARITAIN, Jacques, *The Person and the Common Good.* New York: Charles Scribner's Sons, 1947. Pp. 98.

SPELTZ, G. H., *The Importance of Rural Life According to the Philosophy of St. Thomas Aquinas: A Study in Economic Philosophy.* Washington, D. C.: Catholic University of America, 1945. Pp. XVI, 184.

FEUDALISM: a system of land tenure by nobility from sovereign down to serf with specific rights and duties. This system is also a form of civilization, notably a specific political and social organization based on lord and vassal relationship.

BLOCH, Marc Léopold Benjamin (1888-1944), *La société féodale.* 2 vols. 3rd ed. 1957. English translation by L. A. Manyon, *Feudal Society.* Chicago: University of Chicago Press, 1961. Pp. XXI, 498.

COULBORN, Rushton, *Feudalism in History.* Princeton, New Jersey: Princeton University Press, 1956. Pp. 438.

LYON, Bryce Dale, *A Constitutional and Legal History of Medieval England.* New York: Harper, 1960. Pp. 671.

NORMAN, E. H., *Ando Shoeki and the Anatomy of Japanese Feudalism.* 2 vols. Tokyo, Japan: Tuttle Publishing Co., 1949.

PAINTER, Sidney, *Rise of the Feudal Monarchies.* Ithaca, New York: Cornell University Press, 1951. Pp. IX, 147.

——, *Studies in the History of the English Feudal Barony.* Baltimore: Johns Hopkins Press, 1943. Pp. XIV, 211.

STEPHENSON, Carl, *Mediaeval Feudalism.* Ithaca, New York: Cornell University Press, 1942. Pp. IX, 116.

LOT, Ferdinand and FAWTIER, Robert, *Histoire des institutions françaises au moyen âge.* 2 vols. Paris: Presses Universitaires de France, 1957-1958.

MITTEIS, Heinrich, *Lehnrecht und Staatsgewalt.* Weimar: H. Böhlaus, 1933. Pp. XVI, 714.

PETIT-DUTAILLIS, C., *La monarchie féodale en France et en Angleterre, Xe-XIIIe siècle.* Paris: Renaissance du livre, 1933. Pp. 496.

MODERN

See Contemporary, below.

(a) Comprehensive Studies

FELLNER, William, *Emergence and Content of Modern Economic Analysis.*
New York: McGraw-Hill, 1960. Pp. 459.

SMALL, Albion Woodbury, *The Cameralists, the Pioneers of German Social
Polity.* Chicago: The University of Chicago Press, 1909. Pp. XXV,
606.

SMART, William, *The Economic Annals of the Nineteenth Century, 1801-
1830.* 2 vols. Reprint in New York: Augustus M. Kelley, 1964.

SOMBART, Werner, *Der Bourgeois: Zur Geistesgeschichte des modernen Wirt-
schaftsmenschen.* Munich, Leipzig: Duncker und Humblot, 1913. Pp.
VII, 540. English translation by M. EPSTEIN, *The Quintessence of
Capitalism.* London: T. Fischer Unwin, 1915. Pp. 400.

BOHNEN, Alfred, *Die utilitaristische Ethik als Grundlage der modernen
Wohlfahrtsökonomik.* Göttingen: Schwartz, 1964. Pp. XVIII, 123.

FERRARA, Francesco, *Esame storico-critico di ecomomisti e dottrine economiche del secolo XVIII e prima metà del XIX.*

(b) Specific Systems

(aa) MERCANTILISTS (XVII-XVIII centuries) uphold the principle
that the state makes profit when like a merchant, it sells (exports) more than it buys (imports).

SCHMOLLER VON, Gustav Friedrich, *The Mercantile System and Its Histori-
cal Significance Illustrated Chiefly from Prussian History.* New
York: The Macmillan Co., 1896. Pp. IX, 95. Reprint in New York:
Augustus M. Kelley, 1966.

THOMAS, Parakunnel Joseph, *Mercantilism and the East India Trade.* London: P. S. King and Son, 1926. Pp. XVII, 176. Reprint in New York:
Augustus M. Kelley, 1965.

HECKSCHER, Eli F., *Der Merkantilismus.* 2 vols. Translated from the Swe-
dish by G. MACKENROTH. Jena: Fischer, 1932. First published in 1931.

Representatives

BODIN, Jean (1530-1596), *Paradoxon.* Paris: D. Duvallius, 1596. Pp. 100.
——, *Response aux Paradoxes de monsieur de Malestroit sur le faict des
monnoyes.* Paris: J. Du Puys, 1578.
——, *Les six livres de la Republique,* Paris: J. Du Puys, 1576. Pp. 759.
——, *Discours sur le rehaussement et diminution des monnoyes.* Four
parts in one volume. Paris: J. Du Pusy, 1578.

Bodin de Saint-Laurent, Jean, *Les idées monétaires* et commerciales de Jean Bodin. Bordeaux, 1907.

Castonnet des Fosses, Henril, *Jean Bodin, sa vie et ses œuvres*. Angers: Germain et G. Grassin, 1890. Pp. 40.

Colbert, Jean Baptiste (1619-1683), *Ordinance de la marine*. Proclaimed in 1685.

——, *Code Noire*. Proclaimed in 1685.

——, *Lettres, instructions et mémoires*. Ed. by Pierre Clément. 8 vols. Paris: Imprimerie Imperiale, 1861-1882.

——, *Lettres, instructions et mémoires de Colbert*. Ed. by P. Clément. 10 vols. Paris: Imprimerie Impériale, 1861-1882.

Mims, Stewart L., «Colbert's West India Policy», in *Yale Historical Studies*, No. 1. New Haven; Connecticut: Yale University Press, 1912. Pp. XIV, 385.

Clément, P., *Histoire de Colbert*. 2 vols. 3rd ed. Paris: Didier, 1892.

Neymarck, Alfred, *Colbert et son temps*. 2 vols. Paris: E. Dentu, 1877.

Montchrétien de, Antoine (1575-1621), *L'économie politique patronale: traité de l'économie politique dedié en 1615 au Roy*. Paris: E. Plon, 1889. Pp. CXVII, 398.

Mun, Thomas (1571-1641), *A Discourse of Trade, from England into the East-Indies*. London, 1621. Reprinted in New York: Columbia University Press, 1930. Pp. 58.

——, *England's Treasure by Foreign Trade is the Rule of our Treasure*. Written in 1630, published in 1664; reprinted in Oxford, 1928. Pp. XIII, 88.

Petty Sir, William (1623-1687), *A Treatise of Taxes and Contributions*. London: N. Brooke, 1662. Pp. 75.

——, *Five Essays in Political Arithmetic*. London: H. Mortlock, 1687.

——, «Verbum sapienti», in *The Political Anatomy of Irland*. London: D. Brown and W. Rogers, 1691. 2 pts.

——, *Sir W. Petty's Quantulumcunque concerning money*. London, 1695.

The Economic Writings of Sir William Petty. Ed. by C. H. Hull. Cambridge: University Press, 1899. Pp. XCI, 700.

The Petty Papers: Some Unpublished Writings. Ed. by the Marquis of Lansdowne. 2 vols. London: Constable and Co., 1927.

The Petty — Southwell Correspondence, 1676-1687. Ed. by the Marquis of Lansdowne. London: Constable and Co., 1928. Pp. XXXII, 343.

Strauss, Emil, *Sir William Petty: Portrait of a Genius*. New York: The Macmillan Co., 1954.

(bb) Physiocrats: natural resources (agriculture) are the foundation and measure of wealth and prosperity.

Higgs, Henry, *Bibliography of Economics, 1751-1775*. Cambridge: University Press, 1935. Pp. XXII, 742.

——, *The Physiocrats: Six Lectures on the French Economists of the Eigh-*

teenth Century. London: Macmillan and Co., 1897. Pp. X, 158.

MacCulloch, John Ramsay, *Treatises and Essays on Subjects Connected with Economical Policy.* With accounts of the lives and writings of Quesnay, A. Smith and Ricardo. 2nd ed. Edinburgh, 1859.

Daire, Louis François Eugène (ed.), *Économistes-financiers du XVIIᵉ siècle.* Paris: Collection des principaux économistes, 1843. Pp. VII, 1008.

——, *Physiocrates. Paris:* Collection des principaux économistes, 1846. Pp. LXXXVIII, 1027.

Güntzberg, Benedikt, *Die Gesellschafts und Staatslehre der Physiokraten.* Leipzig: Duncker und Humblot, 1907. Pp. XV, 144.

Hasbach, Wilhelm, *Die allgemeinen philosophischen Grundlagen der von François Quesnay and Adam Smith begründeten politischen ökonomie.* Leipzig: Duncker und Humblot, 1890. Pp. X, 177.

Weulersse, Georges, *Le mouvement physiocratique en France de 1756 à 1770.* 2 vols. Paris: F. Alcan, 1910.

——, *La physiocratie sous les ministères de Turgot et de Necker, 1774-1781.* Paris: 1950. Pp. XVI, 374.

Representatives

Quesnay, François (1694-1774), *Le droit naturel; analyse du tableau économique; maximes générales du gouvernement économique d'un royaume agricole; dialogues sur le commerce et les travaux des artisants.* Ed. by Louis F. E. Daire. Paris: Collections des principaux économistes, 1846.

—— *et al., Philosophie rurale, ou économie générale et politique de l'agriculture.* Amsterdam: Libraires associés, 1763. Pp. XXVI, 412.

——, *Physiocratie, ou constitution naturelle du gouvernement le plus anantageux au genre humain.* 2 vols. Ed. by Du Pont de Nemours. Paris: Merlin, 1768-1769.

——, *Œuvres économiques et philosophiques de François Quesnay.* Frankfurt a. M.: J. Baer, 1888. Pp. XXII, 815.

Bourthoumieux, Charles, *Essai sur le fondement philosophique des doctrines économiques: Rousseau contre Quesnay.* Paris: 1936. Pp. VIII, 140.

Maverick, Lewis A., *Chinese Influence Upon Quesnay and Turgot.* Claremont, California: Claremont Oriental Studies, 1942. Pp. 12. See China, below, 3.

Rasio, Stephane, *Discours de la méthode économique et correspondance avec M. P. Quesnay.* Grioux-les-Bains: 1939. Pp. 74.

Schelle, Gustave, *Du Pont de Nemours et l'école physiocratique.* Paris: Guillaumin, 1888. Pp. 456.

——, *Quesnay et le «Tableau économique».* Paris: L. Larose et L. Tenin, 1905. Pp. 32.

Turgot, Anne Robert Jacques (1727-1781), *Réflexions sur la formation et la distribution des richesses.* n.p., 1770. Pp. 136. English translation, *Reflections on the Formation and the Distribution of Riches.* New York: The Macmillan Co., 1898. Pp. XXII, 112.

——, *Œuvres de Turgot et documents le concernant.* Ed. by Gustave SCHELLE. 5 vols. Paris: F. Alcan, 1913-1923.

LODGE, Eleanor C., *Sully, Colbert and Turgot.* London: Methuen and Co., 1931. Pp. XVI, 263.

MAVERICK, Lewis A., — see Quesnay, above.

MAXWELL, Constantia E., *The Life and Work of Turgot.* London: G. Allen and Unwin, 1933.

LAFONT, Jean, *Les idées économiques de Turgot.* Bordeaux, 1912. Pp. 214.

NEYMARCK, A., *Turgot et ses doctrines.* 2 vols. Paris: Guillaumin et Cie, 1885.

SCHELLE, Gustave (ed.), *Turgot.* 5 vols. Paris, 1913-1933.

English School or Classic School of Economics, — see below.

(cc) ENGLISH SCHOOL or Classic School of Economics: labor and sacrifice are the fundamental contributors to production, but the cost of production lies also in the inheritent accumulation of capital.

SMITH, Adam (1723-1790), *Theory of Moral Sentiments.* 2nd ed. London: A. Millar, 1761. Pp. VIII, 436. First published in 1759.

——, *An Inquiry into the Nature and Causes of the Wealth of Nations.* 2 vols. London, 1776. Also 3 vols. in Dublin: Whitestone, 1776. Starting point of modern political economy.

——, *Essays on Philosophical Subjects.* Ed. by J. BLACK and J. HUTTON. London: T. Cadell and W. Davies, 1795. Pp. XCV, 244.

Adam Smith's Moral and Political Philosophy. Ed. by Herbert W. SCHNEIder. New York: Hafner, 1948. Pp. XXVII, 484.

The Works of Adam Smith. 5 vols. Ed. by Dugald STEWART. Edinburgh, 1811-1812.

The Whole Works of Adam Smith. A new edition. 5 vols. London: J. Richardson, 1922.

BONAR, James (ed.), *A Catalogue of the Library of Adam Smith.* London: Macmillan and Co., 1932. Pp. XXXIV, 218. First published in 1894.

——, «The Theory of Moral Sentiments by Adam Smith», *The Journal of Philosophical Studies* (London), Vol. I (1926), pp. 333-353.

HASEK, Carl William, *The Introduction of Adam Smith's Doctrine into Germany.* New York: Columbia University Press, 1925. Pp. 155.

JOHNSON, Edgar Jerome, *Predecessors of Adam Smith: The Growth of British Economic Thought.* Englewood Cliffs. New Jersey: Prentice-Hall, 1937. Pp. 426. Reprint in New York: Augustus M. Kelley, 1965.

LEAKE, Percy D., *Capital: Adam Smith — Karl Marx.* London: Gee and Co., 1933.

MORROW, Glenn R., *The Ethical and Economic Theories of Adam Smith: A Study in the Social Philosophy of the Eighteenth Century.* Ithaca, New York: Cornwell Pniversity Press, 1923.

——, «The Ethics of the Wealth of Nations». *The Philosophical Review* (Ithaca, New York), Vol. XXXIV (1923), pp. 609-612.

SCOTT, W. R., *Adam Smith as Student and Professor.* Glasgow: University Publications, 1937. Pp. XXIV, 445. With unpublished documents.

STEWART, Dugald, *Account of the Life and Writings of* Adam Smith, LL.D. London: T. Cadell and W. Davies, 1812. First published in Edinburgh: The Royal Society, 1793. Reprint, *Biographical Memoir of Adam Smith LL. D.* in New York: Augustus M. Kelley, 1966.

HASBACH, Wilhelm, *Untersuchungen über Adam Smith und die Entwicklung der politischen Ökonomie.* Leipzig: Duncker und Humblot, 1891. Pp. IX, 440.

WALCKER, Karl, *Adam Smith der Begründer der modernen Nationalökonomie. Sein Leben und seine Schriften.* Berlin: Liebmann, 1890. Pp. VI, 50.

French contributions to the Classic English School.

BASTIAT, Frédéric (1801-1850), *Œuvres complètes.* 7 vols. 2nd ed. Paris: Guillaumin, 1862-1864.
CANTILLON, Richard, *Essai sur le commerce.* London: Macmillan and Co., 1892. Pp. V, 430.
——, *Essais sur la nature du commerce en général.* Edited with an English translation by Henry HIGGS. London: Royal Economic Society, 1931. Pp. VIII, 394. First translation published in 1755.

LEGRAND, Robert, *Richard Cantillon: un mercantiliste précurseur des physiocrates.* Paris: V. Giard et E. Brière, 1900. Pp. Viii, 168.

(dd) SOCIALISM: speaking on distribution of goods by the state, since socialism holds that labor is the content of the cost of goods. The term first was used in its modern meaning by *Cooperative Magazine,* 1827 to designate doctrines opposed to liberal individualism, and in 1830 it was applied to the social theories of Robert Owen (1771-1858), Claude Henri de Saint-Simon (1760-1825) and François M. Ch. Fourier (1772-1837). Variants of socialism are communism and collectivism. However, the proper definition of socialism is very much disputable.

See also Socialism, below, Ch. V, 5, p. 267.

General Studies

Bibliographies

DOLLÉANS, Edouard and CROZIER, Michel, *Mouvement ouvrier et socialiste: chronologie et bibliographie, 1750-1918.* Paris: Les Éditions Ouvrières, 1949-1950. Pp. 380.

HEARNSHAW, F. J. C., «Book List» in his *A Survey of Socialism, Analytical, Historical and Critical.* (London: Macmillan and Co., 1928), pp. 449-466.

RALEA, Michel, *Révolution et socialisme: essai de bibliographie.* Paris: Presses Universitaires de France, 1923. Pp. 80.

STAMMHAMMER, Josef, *Bibliographie des Socialismus und Communismus.* 3 vols. Jena: G. Fischer, 1893-1909. New printing in Aalen: Zeller, 1963.

Encyclopedias, — see Sociology, below, Ch. V, 1, p. 230.

COMPÈRE-MOREL, Adéodat C. A. (ed), *Encyclopédie socialiste, syndicale et coopérative de l'Internationale ouvrière.* 8 vols. Paris: Publications Sociales, 1912-1913.

——, *Grand dictionnaire socialiste du mouvement politique et économique, national et international.* Paris: Publications Sociales, 1924. Pp. 1057.

Studies

In English

BEER, Max, *Allgemeine Geschichte des Sozialismus und der sozialen Kämpfe.* 6th ed. Berlin: Neuer deutscher Verlag, 1929. Pp. 789, English translation by Henry James STENNING, *Social Struggles.* 5 vols. London: Leonard Press, 1922-1925. Struggles in Antiquity, in the Middle Ages, Socialist Forerunners, in 1750-1860, Modern Socialism.

——, *History of British Socialism.* Philadelphia: William H. Allen, Bookseller, 1940.

BLISS, William D. P., *A Handbook of Socialism.* London: Swan Sonnenschein and Co., 1895. Pp. X, 291.

CATHREIN, Victor, *Socialism: Its Theoretical Basis and Practical Application.* Revised edition by Victor F. GETTELMAN. New York: Benzinger, 1904. Pp. 424. Critical.

COLE, George Douglas Howard, *History of Socialist Thought.* 7 vols. London: Macmillan Co., 1953-1960.

——, *The Meaning of Marxism.* Ann Arbor: University of Michigan Press, 1964. Pp. 301.

COLE, Margaret, «Socialism», in *The Encyclopedia of Philosophy* (8 vols. New York: The Macmillan Co., 1967), Vol. VII, pp. 467-470.

GRAY Sir, Alexander, *The Socialist Tradition — Moses to Lenin.* London: Longmans, Green and Co., 1946. Pp. XV, 568.

GRIFFITHS, Dan (ed.), *What Is Socialism? A Symposium.* London: Grant Richards, 1924. Pp. 102.

KIRKUP, Thomas, *A History of Socialism.* 5th ed. by Edward R. PEASE. London: A. and C. Black, 1913. Pp. XI, 490.

LAIDLER, Harry Wellington, *A History of Socialist Thought*. New York: Constable and Co., 1927. Pp. XXII, 713.

——, *Social-Economic Movements*. New York: The Thomas Y. Crowell Co., 1944. Pp. XX, 828.

LIPSET, Seymour Martin, *Agrarian Socialism*. Berkeley, California: University of California Press, 1950. Pp. XVII, 315.

LORWIN, L. L., *Labor and Internationalism*. London: G. G. Allen and Unwin, 1929. Pp. XVIII, 682.

MING, John, *The Morality of Modern Socialism*. New York: Benziger, 1909. Pp. 400. Critical.

MISES, Ludwig, *Die Gemeinwirtschaft. Untersuchungen über den Sozialismus*. Jena: G. Fischer, 1922. Pp. VIII, 503. English translation by J.

KAHANE, *Socialism: An Economic and Sociological Analysis*. 2nd ed. London: Jonathan Cape, 1951. Pp. 559.

RAVEN, Charles E., *Christian Socialism, 1848-1854*. London: Macmillan and Co., 1920. Pp. XII, 396.

SHAW, George B. et al., *Essays in Fabian Socialism*. London: Constable, 1932. Pp. VII, 326. Socialistic.

SKELTON, O. D., *Socialism: A Critical Analysis*. Boston: Houghton Mifflin, 1911. Pp. IX, 329.

STRACHEY, John, *The Theory and Practice of Socialism*. New York: Random House, 1936. Pp. 512.

SWEEZY, Paul, *Socialism*. New York: McGraw-Hill, 1949. Pp. XIII, 276.

LANGE, Oskar and TAYLOR, Fred M., *On the Economic Theory of Socialism*. Ed. by B. E. LIPPINCOTT. New York: Oxford University Press, 1938. Pp. VII, 143.

——, *Principles of Economics*. 9th ed. New York: Ronald Press, 1925. Pp. IX, 589.

In Other Languages

ADLER, Georg, *Geschichte des Sozialismus und Kommunismus von Plato bis zur Gegenwart*. Leipzig: C. L. Hirschfeld, 1899. Pp. X, 281.

ADLER, Max, Wegweiser, *Studien zur Geistesgeschichte des Sozialismus*. 5th ed. Vienna: Hess und Co., 1931. Pp. 389.

CATHREIN, Viktor, *Der Sozialismus. Eine Untersuchung seiner Grundlagen und seiner Durchführbarkeit*. 10th ed. Freiburg i.B.: Herder, 1910. Pp. XVIII, 520.

DENIS, Hector, *Histoire des systèmes économiques et socialistes*. 2 vols. Paris: V. Giard et E. Brière, 1904-1907.

DIEHL, Karl, *Über Sozialismus, Kommunismus und Anarchismus*. 3rd ed. Jena: G. Fischer, 1911. Pp. VI, 492.

DOLLÉANS, Édouard, *Histoire du mouvement ouvrier*. 2 vols. Paris: A. Colin, 1936-1939.

——, *Histoire du travail*. Paris: Domat-Montchrestien, 1943. Pp. 418.

HALÉVY, Élie, *Histoire du socialisme européen*. Paris: Gallimard, 1948. Pp. 368.

HERKNER, Heinrich, *Die Arbeitsfrage*. 2 vols. 8th ed. Berlin: W. de Gruyter und Co., 1922.

JAURÈS, Jean Léon (ed.), *Histoire socialiste (1789-1900)*. 13 vols. Paris: J. Rouff, 1901-1908.

KAUTSKY, Karl, *Vorläufer des neueren Sozialismus*. 2 vols. 2nd ed. Stuttgart: J. H. W. Dietz Nachfolger, 1909.

KELSEN, Hans, *Sozialismus und Staat*. 2nd ed. Leipzig: L. Hirschfeld, 1923. Pp. VIII, 208. First published in 1920. See also State, below, Ch. IV, p. 224.

LOUIS, Paul, — see France, below, p. 94.

LUKÁCS, Georg, *Geschichte und Klassenbewusstsein. Studien über Marxistische Dialektik*. Berlin: Der Malik-Verlag, 1923. Pp. 341. Classic Marxist study.

PARETO, Vilfredo, *I sistemi socialisti*. 2 vols. Milan: Istituto Editrice Italiano, 1917-1920.

STEGMANN, Carl and HUGO, C., *Handbuch des Socialismus*. 2 vols. Zürich: Verlags-Magazin, 1895-1896.

Collected Sources

Archiv für die Geschichte des Sozialismus und der Arbeiterbewegung. Ed. by Carl GRÜNBERG. 15 vols. Leipzig: L. Hirschfeld, 1910-1930.

Dokumente des Sozialismus. Ed. by E. BERNSTEIN. 5 vols. Berlin: Verlag der socialistischen Monatshefte, 1901-1905.

Die Neue Zeit. 41 vols. Stuttgart: J. H. W. Dietz, 1883-1923.

Forms of Socialism

The Critical School

SISMONDE, Jean C. L. (1773-1842), *La richesse commerciale*. 2 vols. Genève: J. J. Paschoud, 1803.

——, *Nouveaux principes d'économie politique*. 2 vols. Paris: Delaunay, 1819.

The Owenites and Cooperative Movement

OWEN, Robert (1771-1858), *An Address Delivered to the Inhabitants of New Lanark on the First of January, 1716*. 3rd ed. London: Printed for Longman, Hurst, Rees, Orme and Brown, 1817.

——, *Address to the Human Race*. London: Effingham Wilson, 1854. Pp. 24.

——, *The Book of the New Moral World, Containing the Rational System of Society, Founded on Demonstrable Facts*. London: E. Wilson, 1836. Pp. XXXII, 104.

——, *A New View of Society and Other Writings*. Ed. by G. D. H. Cole. New York: E. P. Dutton and Co., 1927. Pp. XX, 298.

——, *The Life of Robert Owen*. 2 vols. 2nd ed. London: Macmillan and Co., 1930. First published in 1857-1858.

Owen, Robert Dale (1801-1877), *The Debatable Land between this World and the Next*. London: Trübner, 1871. Pp. XVI, 440.

——, *An Outline of the System of Education at Lanark*. Glasgow: University Press, 1824. Pp. 103.

——, *Labor, in Its History and Prospects*. 2nd ed. New York: Fowlers and Wells, 1851. Pp. VI, 76. First published in Cincinnati: Herald of Truth Print, 1848.

——, *The Wrong of Slavery, the Right of Emancipation, and the Future of the African Race in the United States*. Philadelphia: J. B. Lippincott and Co., 1864. Pp. 246.

Bibliography of Robert Owen. 2nd ed. Aberystwith: National Library of Wales, 1925.

Rohl, Adolph, *Die Beziehungen zwischen Wirtschaft und Erziehung im Sozialismus Robert Owens*. Hamburg: H. Christians, 1930. Pp. 159.

The Saint-Simonians and the Beginning of Collectivism

Saint-Simon de, Claude Henri (1760-1825), *De la réorganisation de la société européenne*. Paris: A. Egron, 1814. With collaboration of A. Thierry, his pupil. Pp. XVIII, 112.

——, *L'Industrie*. 4 vols. Paris: Au bureau de l'administration, 1817-1818. Some essays are of A. Comte.

——, *La politique*. Paris: Corréard, 1819. Pp. XXVII, 521.

——, *Du système industriel*. Paris: A. A. Renouard, 1821. Pp. XX, 311.

——, *Catéchisme des industriels*. 3 cahiers. Paris: Sétier, 1823-1824.

——, *Nouveau christianisme*. Paris: Bossange père, 1825. Pp. VIII, 91.

——, *Travaux philosophiques, scientifiques et poétiques ayant pour objet de faciliter la réorganisation de la société européenne*. Paris: Corréard, 1822. Pp. 20.

——, *Selected Writings*. Edited and translated by F. M. H. Markham. New York: The Macmillan Co., 1953. Pp. LI, 116.

Œuvres de Saint-Simon et d'Enfantin. 47 vols. Paris: Dentu et Leroux, 1865-1878.

The Doctrine of Saint-Simon: An Exposition, First Years, 1828-1829. Translated by Georg G. Iggers. Boston: Beacon Press, 1958. Pp. XLVII, 286.

Shine, Hill, *Carlyle and The Saint-Simonians*. Baltimore, Maryland: Johns Hopkins Press, 1941. Pp. XIII, 191.

Charléty, Sébastien, *Histoire du Saint-Simonisme, 1825-1864*. Paris: Hachette, 1896. Pp. 498.

Leroy, M., *La vie véritable du comte H. de Saint-Simon (1760-1825)*. Paris: B. Grasset, 1925. Pp. 339.

Weill, Georges, *Un précurseur du socialisme: Saint-Simon et son œuvre*. Paris: Perrin et Cie, 1894. Pp. X, 247.

——, *L'école saint-simonienne: son histoire, son influence*. Paris: F. Alcan, 1896. Pp. 319.

ENFANTIN D', B. P. (1796-1864), — see SAINT-SIMON, above.
——, *Doctrine de Saint-Simon. Exposition.* 2nd ed. Paris: Au bureau de l'Organisateur, 1830. Pp. 431.
——, Correspondance philosophique et religieuse. Paris: Lacrampe, 1847. Pp. 217.

The Voluntary Socialists

FOURIER, François Marie Charles (1772-1837), *De l'anarchie industrielle et scientifique.* Paris: Librairie phailanstérienne, 1847. Pp. 79.
——, *L'harmonie universelle et le phalanstère.* 2 vols. Paris: Librairie phalanstérienne, 1849.
——, *Œuvres completes de Charles Fourier.* 2nd ed. 6 vols. Paris: La Phalange, 1841-1845.
Selections from the Works of Fourier. Translated by Julia FRANKLIN. London: Swan Sonnenschein and Co., 1901. Pp. 208.

BRISBANE, Albert, *Introduction to Fourier's Theory of Social Organization.* Philadelphia: C. F. Stollmeyer, 1876.

TRANSON, Abel L. E., *Charles Fourier's Theory of Attractive Industry, and the Moral Harmony of the Passions.* Translated from the French by H. DOHERTY. London, 1841.

BOURGIN, Hubert, *Fourier.* Paris: G. Bellais, 1905. Pp. 617.

FRIEDBERG, M., *L'influence de Charles Fourier sur le mouvement social contemporain en France.* Paris: M. Giard, 1926. Pp. 178.

LOUVANCOUR, Henri, *De Henri de Saint Simon à Charles Fourier.* Chartres: Durand, 1913. Pp. 452.

SILBERLING, Edouard, *Dictionnaire de sociologie phalansterienne. Guide des œuvres complètes de Charles Fourier.* Paris: M. Rivière, 1911. Pp. XI, 459.

BLANC, Louis Jean Joseph (1811-1886), *De l'organisation du travail.* Paris: Imprimerie nationale Discourses, 1848. Pp. 284.
——, *Catéchisme des socialistes.* Paris: Nouveau-Monde, 1949. Pp. 54.
——, *L'état et la commune.* Paris: Librairie Internationale, 1866. Pp. 62.

State Socialism

See Particular countries, below, 4, p. 102.

LASSALLE, Ferdinand Johann Gottlieb (1825-1864), *Das System der erworbenen Rechte, seine Versöhnung des positiven Rechts und der Rechtphilosophie.* 2 vols. Leipzig: F. A. Brockhaus, 1861.
——, *What is Capital?* Freely translated from Chapter 4 of *Herr Bastiat Schulze von Delitisch* by F. KEDDELL. Reprint. London: Justice Printery, 1889. Pp. 13.

——, *Gesamtwerke*. Ed. by E. BLUM. 10 vols. Leipzig: K. F. Pfau, 1899-1909.
——, *Reden und Schriften*. New edition by E. BERNSTEIN. 3 vols. Berlin: «Vorwärts», 1892-1893.
——, *Nachgelassene Briefe und Schriften*. Ed. by Gustav MAYER. 5 vols. Stuttgart, Berlin: Deutsche Verlags-Anstalt, 1921-1925.
Bismarck und Lasalle, ihre Briefwecksel und ihre Gespräche. Ed. by Gustav MAYER. Berlin: J. H. W. Dietz Nachfolger, 1928.

BRANDES, G., *Ferdinand Lassalle*. London: W. Heinemann, 1911. Pp. 242.

DAWSON, W. H., *German Socialism and Ferdinand Lassalle*. 3rd ed. London: Swan Sonnenschein, 1899. Pp. 312.

ONCKEN, Hermann, *Lassalle. Eine politische Biographie*. 4th ed. Stuttgart: Deutsche Verlags-Anstalt, 1923. Pp. VII, 562.

THIER, Erich, *Rodbertus, Lassalle, Adolph Wagner*. Jena: G. Fischer, 1930. Pp. IV, 128.

RODBERTUS-JAGETZOW, Johann Karl (1805-1875), — see also F. LASSALLE above.
——, *Sociale Briefe an von Kirchmann*. 2 vols. Berlin: Gerhard, Deutsche Verlags-Anstalt, 1850-1851. English translation by Julia FRANKLIN, *Overproduction and Crises*. 2nd ed. London: Swan Sonnenschein and Co., 1908. First translation published in 1898.
——, *Zur Erkärung und Abhülfe der heutigen Creditnoth des Grundbesitzes*. 2 vols. 2nd ed. Berlin: H. Bahr, 1893. First published in Jena, 1869.
Schriften von De Carl Rodbertus. 4 vols. New edition. Berlin, 1899.
——, *Neue Briefe über Grundrente, Rentprinzip und soziale Frage*. Ed. by Robert MICHELS. Karlsruhe: Bibliothek der Soziologie und Politik, 1926. Pp. VIII, 398.

GONNER, E. C. K., *The Social Philosophy of Rodbertus*. London: Macmillan and Co., 1899. Pp. XXI, 209.

CORNÉLISSEN, C., *Théorie de la valeur, avec une refutation des théories de Rodbertus, Karl Marx, Stanley Jevons et Böhm-Bewerk*. 2nd ed. Paris: Schleicher frères, 1913. First published in 1903. Pp. 413.

DIETZEL, H., *Karl Rodbertus*. 2 vols. Jena: G. Fischer, 1886-1888.

JENTSCH, Carl, *Rodbertus*. Stuttgart: F. Frommann, 1899. Pp. 259.

THIER, Erich, *Rodbertus, Lasalle, Adolph Wagner*. Leipzig: Frankstein und Wagner, 1930. Pp. 129.

(ee) NATIONAL POLITICAL ECONOMY
See also Particular Countries, below, 4.

England

CLAPHAM, John Harold, *The Economic History of Modern Britain*. 2nd ed. 3 vols. Cambridge: The University Press, 1926-1938.

BENTHAN, Jeremy (1748-1832), — see Utilitarianism, above, Ch. I, p. 26; below, Index.

——, *Analysis of Naturel Religion on the Temporal Happiness of Mankind*. Ed. by Phillip BEAUCHAMP (pseudonym of George GROTE) from the manuscripts of J. BENTHAM. London: R. Carlile, 1822. Pp. VIII, 140.

——, *Defence of Usury*. London: T. Payne and Son, 1787. Pp. 206.

——, *Economic Writings*. Ed. by W. Stark. 3 vols. London: Allen and Unwin, 1952.

HUME, David (1711-1776), — see Ethics, above, Ch. I, p. 22.

——, *Writings on Economics*. Ed. by Eugene ROTWEIN. Edinburgh: Nelson, 1955. Pp. CXI, 224.

LOCKE, John (1632-1704), — see Ethics, above, Ch. I, p. 22.

——, *Some Consideration of the Consequences of the Lowering of Interest and Raising the Value of Money*. London: A. and J. Churchill, 1692. Pp. 192.

——, *Several Papers relating to Money, Interest and Trade*. 2 parts. London: A. and J. Churchill, 1696.

——, *An Essay on the Governing Causes of the Natural Rate of Interest*. London: Printed for W. Owen, 1750. Pp. 62.

LARKIN, W. Paschal, *Property in the Eighteenth Century, with Special Reference to England and Locke*. Dublin: Cork University Press, 1930. Pp. XI, 252.

JAEGER, Georg, «Locke. Eine kritische Untersuchung der Ideen des Liberalismus und des Ursprungs nationalökonomischer Anschauungsformen». *Archiv für Geschichte der Philosophie* (Berlin), 1904. Pp. 176-195, 349-370, 534-560.

MILL, James (1773-1863), *Elements of Political Economy*. London: Printed for Baldwin, Cradock and Joy, 1821. Pp. XIII, 240.

——, *Analysis of the Phenomena of the Human Mind*. 2 vols. Ed. by A. BAIN *et al*. London: Longmans, Green, Reader and Dyer, 1869. Reprint in New York: Augustus M. Kelley, 1966.

MILL, John Stuart (1806-1873), — see Utilitarianism, above, p. 26.

——, *Principles of Political Economy*. 2 vols. 7th ed. London: Longmans and Co., 1871. First published in 1848.

BONAR, James, «The Economics of John Stuart Mill», *Journal of Political Economy* (Chicago), Vol. XIX (1911), Pp. 717-725.

GRUDE-OETTLI, Natalie, J. S., *Mill zwischen Liberalismus und Sozialismus*. Zürick: Bleicherode, 1936. Pp. 181.

RAY, Jean, *La méthode de l'économie politique d'après John Stuart Mill*. Paris: L. Tenin, 1914. Pp. 159.

ZUCCANTE, G., *Giovanni Stuart Mill e l'utilitarianismo*. Florence: Vallechi, 1922. Pp. 455.

RICARDO, David (1772-1823), *The High Price of Bullion, a Proof of the Depreciation of Banknotes*. London: J. Murray, 1810. Pp. 48.

——, *On the Principles of Political Economy and Taxation*. London: J. Murray, 1817. Pp. VIII, 590.

——, *On Protection to Agriculture*. 4th ed. London: J. Murray, 1822. Pp. 95.

——, *Economic Essays*. Ed. by E. C. K. GONNER. London: G. Bell and Sons, 1923. Pp. XXXVI, 315.

The Works of David Ricardo. Ed. by J. R. McCULLOCH. London: J. Murray, 1846. Pp. XXXIII, 584.

FRANKLIN, Burt and LEGMAN, George, *David Ricardo and Ricardian Theory: A Bibliographical Checklist*. New York: Burt Franklin, 1949. Pp. VI, 88.

HOLLANDER, J. H., *David Ricardo: A Centenary Estimate*. Baltimore: John Hopkins Press, 1910. Pp. IX, 137.

AMONN, Alfred, *Ricardo als Begründer der theoretischen Nationalökonomie*. Jena: G. Fischer, 1924. Pp. V, 122.

THEIS, Erich, *David Ricardos Verkennung und Adam Müllers Erkenntnis der wahren Krisengründe ihrer Zeit*. Düren: Dissertations-Buchdruckerei, 1938. Pp. IV, 49.

France

LOUIS, Paul, *Histoire du socialisme en France, 1789-1945*. Revised edition. Paris: M. Rivière, 1950.

PROUDHON, Pierre Joseph (1809-1865), *Qu'est-ce que la propriété ? Ou recherches sur le principe du droit et du gouvernement*. Paris: J. F. Brocard, 1840. Pp. XII, 244. See below, p. 110.

——, *De la création de l'ordre dans l'humanité*. Paris: Prevot, 1843. Pp. 582.

——, *Système des contradictions économiques ou philosophie de la misère*. 2 vols. Paris: M. Rivière, 1923. First published in 1846.

——, *Le droit au travail et le droit de propriété*. Paris: Garnier frères, 1848. Pp. 60.

——, *Philosophie du progrès, programme*. Bruxelles: A. Lebègue, 1853. Pp. 156.

——, *De la justice dans la Révolution et dans l'Église, nouveaux principes de philosophie pratique*. 3 vols. Paris: Garnier frères, 1858.

——, *Essai de philosophie pratique: la guerre et la paix*. 2 vols. Paris: Michel-Lévy frères, 1861.

——, *Œuvres complètes*. 26 vols. Paris: A. Lacroix, Verboeckhoven et Cie, 1867-1870.

BROGAN, D. W., *Proudhon*. London: H. Hamilton, 1934. Pp. 96.

LUBAC DE, Henri, *Proudhon et le Christianisme*. Paris: Edition du Seuil, 1945. Pp. 320. English translation by R. E. SCANTLEBURY, *The Un-Marxian Socialist: A Study of Proudhon*. London: Sheed and Ward, 1948. Pp. XVI, 304.

Bouglé, C., *La Sociologie de Proudhon.* Paris: Armand Colin, 1911. Pp. XVIII, 333.

Dolléans, Édouard, *Proud'hon.* Paris: Gallimard, 1948. Pp. 528.

Zévaès, Alexandre, *Histoire du socialisme et du communisme en France de 1871 à 1947.* Paris: Éditions France-Empire, 1948. Pp. 440.

Germany

See Politics, below, Ch. IV, p. 205; Dialectical Materialism, above, Ch. I, p. 38; also in *PQS*, No. 5.

Marx, Karl (1818-1883), *The Critique of Political Economy.* Chicago: Charles H. Kerr and Co., 1904. First published in 1859.

——, *Das Kapital. Kritik der politischen Oekonomie.* 3 vols. 4th ed. Hamburg: O. Meissner, 1890-1894. English translation by Samuel Moore, Edward Aveling and Ernest Utermann, *Capital.* 3 vols. Chicago: Charles H. Kerr and Co., 1915.

—— and Engels, Friedrich, *Manifest der kommunistischen Partei.* London, 1848. 6th ed., *Das kommunistische Manifest.* Berlin: Buchhandlung Vorwärts, 1901. Pp. 32. English translation by Eden and Cedar Paul, *The Communist Manifesto.* Ed. by D. Ryazanoff. New York: International Publishers, 1930. Pp. XI, 365.

Engels, Friedrich, *Der Ursprung der Familie, des Privateigentums und des Staat.* 8th ed. Stuttgart: J.H.W. Dietz, 1900. Pp. XXIV, 188. First published in 1884. English translation by Ernest Utermann, *The Origin of the Family, Private Property, and the State.* Chicago: Charles H. Kerr and Co., 1902. Pp. 217. The other translation by Lewis H. Morgan. New York: International Publishers, 1942. Pp. 176.

Karl Marx, Friedrich Engels, *Historisch-kritische Gesamtausgabe. Werke, Schriften, Briefe.* Ed. by D. Rjazanov. 3 sections. Moscow: Marx-Engels-Instituts, 1927-1936.

The Marxist Library: Works of Marxism-Leninism. Selected works of K. Marx and F. Engels. 5 vols. London: Martin Lawrence, 1932.

Karl Marx and Frederick Engels, *Selected Works.* 2 vols. Moscow: Foreign Language Publishing House, 1949-1950.

Bax, B., *The Ethics of Socialism.* 6th ed. London: Swan Sonnenschein und Co., 1907. Pp. XIII, 220. First published in 1889.

Cole, George D. H., *The Meaning of Marxism.* Revised edition of *What Marxism Really Meant.* London: Victor Gollancz, 1948. Pp. 302.

Dobb, Maurice Herbert, *Marx as an Economist.* New York: International Publishers, 1945. Pp. 32.

——, *Studies in the Development of Capitalism.* New York: International Publishers, 1947. Pp. IX, 396.

Croce, Benedetto, *Historical Materialism and the Economics of Marx.*New York: Macmillan, 1914. Pp. XXIII, 188.

——, «Comunismo e libertà», *Critica* (Bari), No. 3, 1937.

——, «Come nacque e come morì il Marxismo teorico in Italia (1895-1900)», *Critica* (Bari), Nos. 1-2, 1938.

——, *Come il Marx face passare il comunismo dell' utopia alla scienza.* Bari: Laterza, 1948.

GREGOR, A. James, *A Survey of Marxism.* New York: Random House, 1965. Pp. XIII, 370.

HICKS, John Richard, *Value and Capital.* 2nd ed. Oxford: Clarendon Press, 1946. Pp. IX, 340.

JOSEPH, H., *The Labor Theory of Value in Karl Marx.* London: Oxford University Press, 1923. Expository and critical.

KAUTSKY, Carl Johann, *The Economic Doctrines of Karl Marx.* Translated from the German by H. J. STENNING. 2nd ed. London: N.C.L.C. Publishing Society, 1936. Pp. VI, 252. First published in 1925.

LEFF, Gordon, *The Tyranny of Concepts: A Critique of Marxism.* Philadelphia: Dufour Editions, 1963. Pp. 203.

LENIN, V. I., *Marx, Engels, Marxism.* New York: International Publishers, 1935. Pp. XVI, 225.

LINDSAY, A., *Karl Marx's «Capital»,* London: Oxford University Press, 1925. Pp. 128. Expository and critical.

ROBINSON, Joan V., *An Essay on Marxian Economics.* London: Macmillan and Co., 1942. Pp. X, 121.

——, On Rereading Marx. Cambridge: Students' Bookshops, 1953. Pp. 23.

SHEED, Frank, *Communism and Man.* New York: Sheed & Ward, 1938. Pp. XIII, 247. Critical.

SHEEN, Fulton, *Communism and the Conscience of the West.* Indianapolis: Bobbs-Merrill, 1948. Pp. 247. Critical.

——, *Liberty, Equality, Fraternity.* New York: Macmillan, 1938. Pp. XIII, 187. Critical.

BASS, E., *Introduction critique au marxisme: perspectives marxistes, perspectives chrétiennes.* Paris: Colmar, 1954. Pp. 160.

CALOGERO, Guido, *Il metodo dell'economia e il marxismo.* Florence: La Nuova Italia, 1944.

FISCHER, Hugo, *Karl Marx und sein Verhältnis zu Staat und Wirtschaft.* Jena: Fischer, 1932. Pp. 102.

GRÉGOIRE, F., *Aux sources de la pensée de Marx.* Louvain: Institut Superieur de Philosophie, 1947. Pp. 204.

HAMMACHER, Emil, *Das philosophish-ökonomische System des Marxismus.* Leipzig: Duncker und Humblot, 1909. Pp. XI, 730.

KRANOLD, Albert, *Vom ethischen Gehalt der sozialistischen Idee und das Verhältnis des Marxismus zur Ethik.* Breslau: Schlesierdruck, 1930. Pp. 167.

LUKÁCS, Georg, *Geschichte und Klassenbewusstsein.* Berlin: Malik, 1923. Pp. 343.

MENDE, Georg: *Karl Marx' Entwicklung vom Revolutionaren Demo-kraten zum Kommunisten.* 2nd ed. Berlin: J. H. W. Dietz, 1955. Pp. 119.

VORLÄNDER, Karl, *Kant und Marx. Ein Beitrag zur philosophie des Sozialismus.* 2nd ed. Tübingen: J. C. B. Mohr, 1926. Pp. XII, 328.

——, *Karl Marx. Sein Leben und sein Werk.* Leipzig: F. Meiner, 1929. Pp. VIII, 332.

——, *Marx, Engels und Lassalle als Philosophen.* 3th ed. Berlin: J. H. W. Dietz, 1926. Pp. 119.

——, *Von Machiavelli bis Lenin.* Leipzig: F. Meiner, 1926. Pp. 286.

Poland

STEGMANN, Carl and HUGO, C., «Geschichte des socialistischen Bewegung in Polen», in their *Handbuch des Socialismus.* Zürich: Verlags-Magazin, *1895-1896.*

Russia

Communism, — see above, pp. 38, 95; below, p. 98.

FEDOROWICZ, Z., *Finanse w gospodarce socjalistycznej.* 6th ed. Warsaw: Panstwowe Wydawnictwo Naukowe, 1968. Pp. 574.

MARKERT, Werner *et al.* (eds.), *Sowjetunion: Das Wirtschaftssystem.* Graz: Böhlau Verlag. 1965. Pp. XVII, 587.

STRASZEWICZ, Ludwik (ed.), *Geografia gospodarcza europejskich krajow de-mokracji ludowej.* 2 vols. Warsaw: Panstwowe Wydawnictwo Eko-nomiczne, 1966-1968.

CONTEMPORARY

See Modern, above, 2; Philosophy, above, 1 b.

(a) Comprehensive Studies

In English

HOMAN, Paul T., *Contemporary Economic Thought.* New York: Harper and Brog, 1928. Pp. 475.

OAKESHOTT, Michael (ed.), *Social and Political Doctrines of Contemporary Europe.* 2nd ed. New York: The Macmillan Co., 1942. Pp. XXIII, 243.

ROEPKE, W., *La crisi sociale del nostro tempo.* Turin, 1946. English trans-lation by Annette and Peter SCHIFFER JACOBSOHN, *Social Crisis of Our Time.* London: W. Hodge, 1950. Pp. 260.

SELIGMAN, Ben B., *Main Currents in Modern Economics.* New York: The Macmillan Co., 1962.

In Other Languages

CROCE, B., *Filosofia della pratica, economica ed etica.* 7th ed. Bari: G. Laterza, 1957. Pp. XX, 410. See above, 1 b; Index.

FOSSATI, Eraldo (ed.), *Economia politica contemporanea.* Saggi in onore del Prof. Canillo Supino. 2 vols. Padua: A. Milani, 1930.

LUZZATTO, Gino, *Storia economica, dell'età moderna e contemporanea.* 3rd ed. Padua: Cedam, 1955. See Italy, below, 4.

——, (ed.), *Storia economica.* Turin: Unione tipografico-editrice torinese, 1936. Pp. XLVIII, 898.

Studi in onore di Gino Luzzatto. 4 vols. Milan: A. Giuffrè, 1949-1950.

MAYER, Hans, *Die Wirtschaftstheorie der Gegenwart.* 4 vols. Vienna, 1927-1928.

RÖPKE, Wilhelm, *La crisis social de nuestro tiempo.* Madrid: Revista de Occidente, 1947. Pp. 340. See above, In English.

——, *Die Ordnung der Wirtschaft.* New edition. Frankfurt a. M.: Shulte-Bulmke, 1948. Pp. 28.

(b) Specific Studies

(aa) COMMUNISM: insists on common property or on an equal distribution of income and wealth.

See Marxism, above, p. 95; also pp. 38, 144; Russia, China, below, pp. 103, 105, 151, 205, 215.

BERDIAEV, Nikolai A., *The Origin of Russian Communism.* New York: Charles Scribner's Sons, 1937. Pp. 239.

BETTIOL, Giuseppe, *The Philosophy of Communism.* New York: Fordham University Press, 1952. Pp. 308. Introduction by Charles Boyer.

BUKHARIN, Nikolai I. and PREOBRAZHENSKY, E., *The ABC of Communism.* Translated by Eden and Cedar Paul. London: The Communist Party of Great Britain, 1922. Pp. 422.

HAYEK VON, Friedrich August, *The Pure Theory of Capital.* London: Macmillan Co., 1941. Pp. XXXI, 454.

——, *The Road to Serfdom.* Chicago: Chicago University Press, 1944. Pp. XI, 250.

—— (ed), *Collectivist Economic Planning.* London. G. Routledge and Sons, 1935. Pp. 293.

—— et al., *Capitalism and the Historians.* Chicago: Chicago University Press, 1963. Pp. VII, 183.

KEYNES, John Maynard, *The General Theory of Employment, Interest and Money.* New York: Harcourt, Brace and World, 1965. Pp. XII, 408.

BOLZA, Hans, *Dialektische oder rationale Methoden in der Nationalökonomie.* Munich: Duncker und Humblot, 1936. Pp. 83.

POHORILLE, Maksymilian, *Ekonomia polityczna socjalizmu.* Warsaw: Panstwone Wydawnictwo Ekonomiczne, 1968. Pp. 834.

WAKAR, Aleksy, *Handel zagraniczny w gospodarce socjalistycznej.* Warsaw: Panstwowe Wydawmictwo Nauhowe, 1968. Pp. 329.

(bb) Theory of free competition: *laissez-faire* (let do) system.

Keynes, John Maynard, *The End of laissez-faire*. London: L. and V. Woolf, 1926. Pp. 53.

(cc) The Mathematical School: use of mathematical method and form in economic theory; economic reasoning by means of symbols.
See Econometrics, below, p. 106.

Bowley, Arthur L., *The Mathematical Groundwork of Economics: An Introductory Treatise*. Oxford: Milford Humphrey, 1924. Pp. 106.
Fisher, Irving, *Mathematical Investigations in the Theory of Value and Price*. New Haven, Connecticut: Yale University Press, 1925. Pp. 126. Reprint in New York: Augustus M.Kelly, 1965. First published in 1892.
Kühne, Otto, *Die matematische Schule in der Nationalökonomie*. Berlin: W. de Gruyter and Co., 1928.
Marshall, Alfred, — see Pure Theory, below, p. 110.
——, *The Pure Theory of Foreign Trade; The Pure Theory of Domestic Values*. London: Reprints of Scarce Tracts in Economics, 1930. Pp. 37. First published in 1879.
——, *Principles of Economics: An Introductory Volume*. 8th ed. London: Macmillan and Co., 1949. First published in 1890. Pp. XXXII, 731.
Pareto, Vilfredo, «Anwendungen der Mathematik auf Nationalökonomie», *Encyklopädie der mathematischen Wissenschaften* (6 vols. Leipzig: B. G. Teubner, 1898-1935), Vol. I, H. 7, (1902), pp. 1094-1120. Italian translation by Guido Sensini, *Applicazione della matematica all' economica politica*. Rome: Giornale degli economisti, 1906. Pp. 32.
——, «Economie mathématique», in *Encyclopédie des sciences mathématiques* (Paris, 1904-1916), Vol. I, 4, 4 (1911), pp. 591-640. See above p. 76.
Petty Sir, William, *Five Essays in Political Arithmetic*. London: H. Mortlock, 1687. Pp. 51.
——, *Political Arithmetic, or A Discourse Concerning the Value of Lands, People, etc.* London: R. Clavel and H. Mortlock, 1690. Pp. 117. See also Mercantilists, above, 2.

(dd) The Schools of Christian Inspiration: search after new solutions reconciled with basic Christian principles.
Corporativism, — see below, ee.

Ketteler von, Wilhelm Emmanuel (1811-1877), *Die Arbeitsfrage und das Christenthum*. 3rd ed. Mainz: F. Kirchheim, 1864. Pp. 212.
——, *Liberalismus, Socialismus und Christenthums Rede*. Mainz: F. Kirchheim, 1871. Pp. 20.
——, *Predigten*. Ed. by J. M. Raich. 2 vols. Mainz: F. Kirchheim, 1878.
——, *Ausgewälte Schriften*. Ed. by Johannes Mumbauer. 2nd ed. 3 vols. Munich: J. Kösel und F. Pustet, 1924.

BRAUER, Theodor, *Ketteler der deutsche Bischof und Sozialreformer.* Hamburg: Hanseat-Verlagsanstalt, 1927. Pp. 140.

PFÜLF, Otto, *Bischof Ketteler 1811-1877.* 3 vols. Mainz: F. Kirchheim, 1899.

LE PLAY, Pierre G. F. (1806-1882), *Les ouvriers européens.* 2nd ed. 6 vols. Tours: A. Mame, 1877-1879. First published in Paris: Imprimerie Impériale, 1855. Pp. 301.

——, *L'Organisation du travail.* Tours: A. Mame, 1870. Pp. XII, 561.

——, *Les réformes en Europe et le salut en France.* Tours: A. Mame, 1876. Pp. 300.

——, *La constitution essentielle de l'humanité.* Tours: A. Mame, 1881. Pp. XVI, 328.

BAUNARD, Louis, *Frédéric Le Play, la foi et ses victoires.* 2 vols. Paris: Poussielgue frères, 1882-1894. In Vol. II, P. Le Play.

RIBBE DE, Charles, *Le Play d'après sa correspondance.* Paris: Firmin-Didot, 1984. Pp. 454.

VIGNES, J. B. Maurice, *La science sociale d'après les principes de Le Play et de ses continuateurs.* 2 vols. Paris: Bibliothèque sociologique, Internationale, 1897.

(ee) THEORIES OF A CORPORATIVISM: uphold that the state should be organized into corporations and not left to discrete individuals. Corporation consists of a group of individuals authorized to work for certain purposes as a legal unity.
See The Owenites, above, p. 89.

BENNETT, Walter Hartwell, *American Theories of Federalism.* Alabama: University of Alabama Press, 1964. Pp. 227. Sovereignty stressed.

BERLE, Adolf A. and MEANS, G. C., *The Modern Corporation and Private Property.* New York: The Macmillan Co., 1933. Pp. 396. See below, p. 101.

BOWEN, Ralph, *German Theories of the Corporative State.* New York: Mc-Graw-Hill Book, Co., 1947.

FIELD, George Lowell, *The Syndical and Corporative Institutions of Italian Fascism.* New York: Columbia University Press, 1938. Pp. 209. See also Fascism, below, Ch. IV, p. 217.

HENN, Harry G., *Handbook of the Law of Corporations and Other Business Enterprises.* St. Paul, Minnesota: West Publishing House, 1961. Pp. Pp. 735.

MASON, Edward Sagendorph (ed.), *The Corporation in Modern Society.* Cambridge, Massachusetts: Harvard University Press, 1960. Pp. 335.

METLAKE, George (Laux, John Joseph), *Christian Social Reform.* Philadelphia: The Delphin Press, 1912. Pp. IV, 246.

OLECK, Howard L. and HIGGINS, W. R., *Modern Corporation Law.* 5 vols. Indianapolis, Indiana: The Bobbs-Merrill Co., 1958.

RAVEN, Charles, E., *Christian Socialism, 1848-1854.* London: Macmillan and Co., 1920. See Socialism, above, p. 86.

SCHMIDT, Carl Theodore, *The Corporate State in Action: Italy under Fascism.* New York: Oxford University Press, 1939. Pp. 173.

BAGALÁ, G., *Fascismo e corporativismo, essenza e definizione: Lineamenti di filosofia politica.* Bologne: Cantelli, 1942. See also Politics (Fascism), below, Ch. IV, 203.

BATTAGLIA, Felice, «Ancora sulla corporatività come essenza assoluta dello Stato», *Archivio di Studi corporativi*, No. 3, 1936.

FOSSATI, Eraldo, *Linee di economia Corporativa.* Florence: Carlo Cya, 1937. Pp. 92.

SÁNCHEZ-APPELLANIZ VALDERRAMA, Francisco, «Los presupuestos antropológicos y sociológicos del federalismo», *Anales de la Universidad Hispalense*, 1962, pp. 49-89.

Fascism, — see p. 217.

Hitlerism, — see p. 211.

Spain, — see p. 221.

(ff) CAPITALISM: is the economic system characterized by the operation of the owner of capital (capitalist) for private profit. Capital is an aggregate of non-personal means of production: land, industrial plants, mines, etc.

BERLE, Adolf Augustus, *The Twentieth Century Capitalist Revolution.* New York: Harcourt, Brace and Co., 1954. Pp. 192.

——, *Power without Property: A New Development in American Political Economy.* New York: Harcourt, Brace and Co., 1959. Pp. 184.

COX, Oliver Cromwell, *Foundations of Capitalism.* New York: Philosophical Library, 1959. Pp. 500.

HARBRECHT, Paul P., *Pension Funds and Economic Power.* New York: Twentieth Century Fund, 1959. Pp. 328.

KEYNES, J. M., *The General Theory of Employment, Interest and Money.* New York: Harcourt, Brace and Co., 1936. Pp. XII, 403.

MASON, Edward Sagendorph (ed.), *The Corporation in Modern Society.* Cambridge, Massachusetts: Harvard University Press, 1960. Pp. 335.

SCHUMPETER, Joseph Alois, *Capitalism, Socialism and Democracy.* New York: Harper, 1942. Pp. X, 381.

SWEEZY, Paul Marior, *The Theory of Capitalist Development: Principles of Marxian Political Economy.* New York: Oxford University Press, 1942. Pp. XIV, 398.

TAWNEY, Richard Henry, *Religion and the Rise of Capitalism: A Historical Study.* New York: Harcourt, Brace and Co., 1926. Pp. X, 337.

SOMBART, W., *Der moderne Kapitalismus.* 3 vols. Munich: Duncker & Humblot, 1928.

——, *Sozialismus und soziale Bewegung.* 9th ed. Jena: G. Fischer, 1920. Pp. XII, 308.

4. PARTICULAR COUNTRIES

See National Political Economy, above, p. 92; Particular
Periods, p. 79.

AMERICA

U.S.A.

BERLE, Adolf A., *The American Economic Republic.* New York: Harcourt,
   Brace and World Inc., 1963. Pp. XV, 247.

BERNSTEIN, Samuel, *The First International in America.* New York: Augustus M. Kelley, 1965. See also France, below.

BLODGET, Samuel, *Economica: A Statistical Manual for the United States
   of America.* Washington, D. C.: Printed for the Author, 1806. Pp.
   VIII, 202, XIV. Reprint in New York: Augustus M. Kelley, 1960.

BOGUE, Donald J. and BEALE, Calvin L., *Economic Areas of the United States.* New York: The Macmillan Co., 1961. Pp. XC, 1162.

CALLENDER, Guy S., *Selections from the Economic History of the United
   States, 1765-1860.* Reprint in New York: Augustus M. Kelley, 1965.
   Pp. XVIII, 819.

COMMONS, John Rogers *et al., History of Labor in the United States.* 4 vols.
   New York: The Macmillan Co., 1918-1935. Reprint in New York:
   Augustus M. Kelley, 1966.

HICKS, John Richard *et al., The Social Framework of the American Economy: An Introduction to Economics.* 2nd ed. New York: Oxford University Press, 1955. Pp. XVI, 309.

LIST, Georg Friedrich, *Outlines of American Political Economy.* Philadelphia: S. Parker, 1927. Pp. 40. Reprint in New York: Augustus M.
   Kelley, 1964.

ONEAL, James, *American Communism: A Critical Analysis of Its Origin,
   Development and Program.* New York: Hanford Press, 1927. Pp. 256.

SOBEL, Robert, *The Big Board: A History of the New York Stock Market.*
   New York: The Macmillan Co., 1965. Pp. XIII, 395.

TUCKER, George, *Progress of the United States in Population and Wealth.*
   New York: Press of Hunt's. Boston: Little and Brown 1943. Pp. 211.
   Reprint in New York: Augustus M. Kelley, 1964. See Population,
   above, Ch. I, p. 62.

Latin America

ALEXANDER, Robert J., *Organized Labor in Latin America.* New York: Free
   Press of Glencoe, 1965. Pp. X, 274.

JONES, Tom B. and WARBURTON, Elizabeth Anne, *A Bibliography on South
   American Economic Affairs.* Minneapolis: University of Minnesota
   Press, 1955. Pp. XV, 146.

Poppino, Rollie, *International Communism in Latin America: A History of the Movement*. New York: Free Press of Glencoe, 1964. Pp. VIII, 247.

Withers, William, *The Economic Crisis in Latin America*. New York: Free Press of Glencoe, 1964. Pp. X, 307.

CHINA

Jacobs, Dan N. and Baerwald, Hans H., *Chinese Communism: Selected Documents*. New York: Harper and Row, 1963. Pp. VIII, 242.

Eckstein, Alexander, *The National Income of Communist China*. New York: Free Press of Glencoe, 1961. Pp. 215.

—— (ed.), *Economic Trends in Communist China*. Chicago: Aldine Publishing Co., 1967. Pp. 800.

Lee, M. P. H., *The Economic History of China*. New York: Columbia University, 1921. Pp. 461.

Maverick, Lewis Adams, *China: A Model for Europe*. 2 vols. San Antonio, Texas: Paul Anderson Co., 1946. Vol. I, China's economy and government admired by seventeenth and eighteenth century Europeans. Vol. II, Despotism in China, a translation of F. Quesnay's *Le Despotisme de la Chine*.

The Ethics of Confucius: The Sayings of the Master and His Disciples upon the Conduct of the «Superior Man». Ed. by Miles Meander Dawson. New York: G. P. Putnam's Sons, 1915. Pp. XXI, 323.

The Living Thought of Confucius. Ed. by Alfred Doeblin. London: Longmans, Green and Co., 1940. Pp. 182.

ENGLAND

Ashley Sir, William James, *An Introduction to English Economic History and Theory*. 2 vols. 2nd ed. London: Longmans, Green and Co., 1892-1893. Reprint in New York: Augustus M. Kelley, 1966.

Beer, Max, *A History of British Socialism*. 2 vols. New edition. London: G. G. Bell and Sons, 1929. First published in 1919-1920.

Clapham, John Harold, *The Economic History of Modern Britain*. 2nd ed. 3 vols. Cambridge, England: The University Press, 1926-1938.

Cole, G. D. H., *A Short History of the British Working Class Movement, 1789-1927*. 3 vols. New edition. London: George Allen and Unwin, 1932.

Eden Sir, Frederic Morton, *The State of the Poor or An History of the Labouring Classes in England from the Conquest to the Present Period*. 3 vols. London: J. Davis, 1797. Reprint in New York: Augustus M. Kelley, 1966.

Hoffman, Walther, *British Industry, 1700-1950*. Translated by W. O. Henderson and W. H. Chaloner, Oxford: B. Blackwell, 1955. Pp. XXIII, 338. Reprint in New York: Augustus M. Kelley, 1965.

Lyon, B. D., — see above, p. 81.

Nicholls Sir, George, *A History of the English Poor Law*. 3 vols. New edition. London: P. S. King and Son, 1898-1909. Reprint in New York: Augustus M. Kelley, 1966.

FRANCE

BERNSTEIN, Samuel, *The Beginning of Marxist Socialism in France*. New York: Russel and Russell, 1965. Pp. XXVIII, 229.

CLAPHAM, John Harold, *The Economic Development of France and Germany*. 4th ed. Cambridge, England: The University Press, 1936.

LOT, Ferdinand and Fawtier, Robert, *Histoire des institutions françaises au Moyen âge*. 2 vols. Paris: Presses Universitaires, 1957. See Feudalism, above, p. 77.

MOON, Parker, Thomas, *The Labor Problem and the Social Catholic Movement in France*. New York: The Macmillan Co., 1921. Pp. XIV, 473.

LOUIS, Paul, *Histoire du socialisme en France, 1789-1945*. Revised edition. Paris: M. Rivière, 1950.

GERMANY

CLAPHAM, J. H., — see France, above.

MEHRING, Franz, *Geschichte der deutschen Sozialdemokratie*. 4 vols. 12th ed. Stuttgart: J. H. W. Dietz, 1922.

ROSCHER, Wilhelm, *Geschichte der Nationalökonomie in Deutschland*. Munich: Oldenbourg, 1874. Pp. VIII, 1085.

——, *System der Volkswirtschaft*. 2 vols. Stuttgart: J. G. Gotta, 1912-1913.

INDIA

ROSEN, George, *Industrial Change in India: Industrial Growth, Capital Requirements, and Technological Change, 1937-1955*. Glencoe, Illinois: Free Press, 1958. Pp. 243.

ITALY

LUZZATTO, Gino, *Storia economica d'Italia*. Rome: Edizioni Leonardo, 1949. English translation by Philip JONES, *An Economic History of Italy, from the Fall of Roman Empire to the Beginning of the Sixteenth Century*. New York: Barnes and Noble, 1961. Pp. 180.

——, *Storia economica d'Italia: il medioevo*. Florence: G. S. Sansoni, 1963. Pp. VIII, 307.

——, *Studi di storia economica veneziana*. Padua: Cedam, 1954. Pp. VI, 310.

MICHELS, Roberto, *Storia critica del movimento socialista italiano dagli inizi fino al 1911*. Florence: La Voce, 1926. Pp. X, 463.

JAPAN

NORMAN, E. H., *Ando Shoeki and the Anatomy of Japanise Feudalism*. 2 vols. Tokyo, Japan: Tuttle Publishing Co., 1949.

ROSOVSKY, Henry, *Capital Formation in Japan*. New York: Free Press of Glencoe, 1961. Pp. XIII, 358.

POLAND

Powszechna historia gospodarcza. Warsaw: Wydawnictwa Universytetu Warszauskiego, 1968.
Przedsiebiorstwo w polskim systemie spoteczno-ekonomicznym. Warsaw: Panstwowe Wydawnictwo Ekonomiczne, 1967. Pp. 646. Collective edition.
SZELIGA, Zygmunt, *Podstawy wiedzy ekonomicznej w Polsce wspolczesnej.* Warsaw: Panstwowe Zaklady Wydawnictw Szkolnych, 1968. Pp. 242.

RUSSIA

See China, above.

DOBB, Maurice Herbert, *Russian Economic Development since the Revolution.* 2nd ed. London: Labour Research Department, 1928. Pp. XII, 437.
——, *Soviet Economic Development since 1917.* 2nd ed. London: Routledge and Kegan Paul, 1951. Pp. VII, 476.
MASARYK, T. G., *Russland und Europa.* 2 vols. Jena: G. Fischer, 1913. English translation by Eden and Cedar PAUL, *The Spirit of Russia.* New York: The Macmillan and Co., 1919.
——, *Die philosophischen und soziologischen Grundlagen des Marxismus.* Vienna: C. Konegan, 1899. Pp. XV, 600.
Readings on the Soviet Economy. Ed. by Franklyn D. HOLZMAN. 2nd printing. Chicago: Rand McNally and Company, 1963. Pp. XI, 763. Good guide to Bibliography.
ROSTOW, W. W., *The Stages of Economic Growth: A Non-Communist Manifesto.* Cambridge, Massachusetts: Harvard University Press, 1960.

5. SPECIAL QUESTIONS

BUSINESS ETHICS

See Philosophy, above, p. 77.

CHRISTIANITY AND ECONOMICS

See also Private Property, below, p. 108.

STAMP, Josiah, *Christianity and Economics. New York: The Macmillan* Company, 1938. Pp. X, 194.
TAWNEY, R. H., *Religion and the Rise of Capitalism.* New York: Penguin Books, 1947. Pp. 280.
TROELTSCH, E. D., «Die Soziallehren der christlichen Kirchen und Gruppen», in *Gesammelte Schriften,* Vol. I. 3rd ed. Tübingen, 1923. English trans-

lation by Olive Wyon, *The Social Teaching of the Christian Churches.* 2 vols. London: Allen and Unwin, 1931.

Weber, Max, *The Protestant Ethic and the Spirit of Capitalism.* Translated from the German by Talcott Parsons. London: G. Allen and Unwin, 1930. Pp. 292.

Fanfani, Amintore, *Catholicism, Protestantism and Capitalism.* London: Sheed and Ward, 1935. Pp. V, 224.

ECONOMETRICS

Econometrics adds empirical testing to mathematical economy by the way of statistical methodology.

See the Mathematical School, above, p. 99.

Fogel, Robert William, *Railroads and American Economic Growth: Essays in Econometric History.* Baltimore, Maryland: The Johns Hopkins Press, 1964. Pp. XV, 296.

Tinbergen, Jan, *Econometrics.* Translated from the Dutch by H. Rijken van Olst and H. A. M. Somers. London: G. G. Allen and Unwin, 1951. Pp. XII, 258.

——, *Dynamics of Business Cycles: A Study in Economic Fluctuation.* Chicago: University of Chicago Press, 1950. Pp. X, 366.

Tintner, Gerhard, *Econometrics.* New York: John Wiley and Sons, 1952. Pp. XIII, 370.

MONEY

Burns, Arthur R., *Money and Monetary Policy in Early Times.* New York: A. A. Knopf, 1927. Pp. XIII, 517. Reprint in New York: Augustus M. Kelley, 1966.

Davis, Andrew, *Colonial Currency Reprints, 1682-1751.* 4 vols. Boston: Prince Society, 1910-1911. Reprint in New York: Augustus M. Kelley, 1964.

Fisher, Irving, *The Nature of Capital and Income.* New York: The Macmillan Co., 1906. Pp. XXI, 427. Reprint in New York: Augustus M. Kelley, 1965.

——, *The Theory of Interest.* New York: The Macmillan Co., 1930. Pp. XXVII, 566. Reprint in New York: Augustus M. Kelley, 1963.

Keynes, J. M., *The General Theory of Employment, Interest and Money.* New York: Harcourt, Brace, 1965. Pp. XII, 403.

Monroe, Arthur E., *Monetary Theory before Adam Smith.* Cambridge, Massachusetts: Harvard University Press, 1923. Pp. XI, 312. Reprint in New York: Augustus M. Kelly, 1966.

Powell, Ellis T., *The Evolution of the Money Market, 1385-1915.* London: The Financial News, 1915. Pp. XV, 732. Reprint in New York: Augustus M. Kelley, 1966.

Wilson, Thomas, *A Discourse Upon Usury.* London: G. Bell and Sons, 1925. Pp. VIII, 392. Reprint in New York: Augustus M. Kelley, 1963.

POLITICAL ECONOMY

This is a study and a practice of the management of the entire state or nation treated as the estate, «household» of the ruling body; such a management combines the question of prices and market with political theory.

See Introduction, above, p. 73; Systematic Studies, above, p. 76.

PRINCIPLE OF ECONOMY

Principle of Economy or law of simplicity: greater success with smallest expenditure.

Studies

HÖFFDING, Harold, *Der Totalitätsbegriff. Eine erkenntnistheoretische Untersuchung.* Leipzig: O. R. Reisland, 1917. Pp. III, 126.
HÜRTH, F., «Totalitätsforderung und Totalitätsgesetz», *Scholastik*, 1935, pp. 321 ff.
JANKÉLÉVITCH, V., «Signification spirituelle du principe d'économie», *Revue philosophique*, 1928, pp. 88-126.
NINK, Kasper, *Ontologie.* Freiburg im B.: Herder, 1952. Pp. 494.

Representatives

Ancient and Medieval

ARISTOTLE, *Metaphysics*, V, 25-26.
    ST. THOMAS, *In Metaph*, 1, 21 nos. 1093-1108.
OCKHAM, William, — see above, p. 17.
——, *Commentary on the Sentences*, Prologue, q. 1: «Pluralitas non est ponenda sine necessitate».

Modern

AVENARIUS, R., *Philosophie als Denken der Welt gemäss dem Prinzip des kleinsten Kraftmasses.* 2nd ed. Berlin: Guttentag, 1903. Pp. 85.
GOLDSCHIED, Rudolf, *Entwicklungswerttheorie, Entwicklungsökonomie, Menschenökonomie.* Leipzig: W. Klinkhardt, 1908. Pp. XXXVI, 218.
LEIBNIZ, Gottfried Wilhelm, *Discourse on Metaphysics.* Translated by George R. MONTGOMERY. Chicago: The Open Court Publishing Co., 1902. Pp. XXI, 272.
MACH, E., «Die ökonomische Natur der physikalischen Forschung», in *Populärwissenschaftliche Vorlesungen.* 2nd ed. Leipzig: J. A. Barth, 1897. Pp. IX, 344.

——, *Die Mechanik in ihrer Entwicklung historisch-kritisch dargestellt*. 3rd ed. Leipzig: F. A. Brockhaus, 1897. Pp. XII, 505. First published in 1883. See also AVENARIUS, above.

VAIZEY, John, *The Economics of Education*. New York: Free Press of Glencoe, 1962. Pp. 165.

PRIVATE PROPERTY

Comprehensive Studies

ALLUNTIS, Felix, «Private Property and Natural Law», *Studies in Philosophy and the History of Philosophy* (   ), 1963, pp. 189-210.

BARTLETT, J. V. *et al. (eds.)*, *Property: Its Duties and Rights, Historically, Philosophically and Religiously Regarded*. New edition. London: Macmillan Co., 1922.

BENN, Stanley I., «Property», in *The Encyclopedia of Philosophy* (8 vols. New York: The Macmillan Co., 1967). Vol. VI, pp. 491-494.

DURKHEIM, Émile, *Leçons de sociologie physique des mœurs et du droit*. Paris: Presses Universitaires de France, 1953. Pp. XLVIII, 264. English translation by Cornelia Brookfield, *Professional Ethics and Civic Morals*. London: Routledge and Kegan Paul, 1957. Pp. XLIV, 228.

HONORÉ, A. M. «Ownership», in Anthony Gordon GUEST (ed.), *Oxford Essays in Jurisprudence*. New York: Oxford University Press, 1961. Pp. 292.

NOYES, Charles Reinold, *The Institution of Property: A Study of the Development, Substance and Arrangement of the System of Property in Modern Anglo-American Law*. New York: Longmans, Green and Co., 1936. Pp. XIV, 645.

RENNER, Karl, *Die Rechtsinstitute des Privatrechts und ihre soziale Funktion*. Tübingen: 1929. English translation by Agnes SCHWARZSCHILD, *The Institutions of Private Law*. Ed. by Otto Kahn-Freund. London: Routledge and Kegan Paul, 1949. Pp. VIII, 307.

ROSS, Alf, *On Law and Justice*. Translated by Margaret Dutton. London: Stevens and Sons, 1958. Pp. 383.

SCHLATTER, Richard Bulger, *Private Property: The History of an Idea*. New Brunswick, New Jersey: Rutgers University Press, 1951. Pp. 283.

SIMPSON, A. W. B., «The Analysis of Legal Concepts», *Law Quarterly Review*, 1964, pp. 535-558.

SKRZYDLEWSKI, Bernard, «Le problème du droit à la propriété privée», *Divus Thomas* (Piacenza), 1963, pp. 241-252.

Specific Studies

Antiquity

CUSSACK, Sr. Mary T., O. P., *The Significance of a Changing Concept of Ownership in Social and Economic Planning*. Washington, D. C.: The Catholic University of America Press, 1940. Pp. 146.

DENMAN, D. R., *Origins of Ownership: A Brief History of Land Owner-ship and Tenure in England from Earliest Times to Modern Era.* London: George Allen and Wunwin, Ltd., 1958. Pp. 190.

LAURÉ, Martin John, *Property Concepts of the Early Hebrews.* Iowa City, Iowa: University of Iowa, 1915.

Middle Ages

McDONALD, William J., *The Social Value of Property according to St. Thomas Aquinas.* Washington, D. C.: The Catholic University of America Press, 1959.

BABIN, Eugene, «Saint Thomas d'Aquin et le droit de propriété: incompré-hension générale du problème», *Revue de l'Université Laval (Que-bec)*, 1952-1953, pp. 706-718.

Modern

BERLE, A. A. and MEANS, G. C., *The Modern Corporation and Private Property.* New York: The Macmillan Co., 1933. Pp. XIII, 396.

BRAYBROOKE, David, «Economics and Rational Choice», in *The Encyclope-dia of Philosophy* (8 vols. New York: The Macmillan Co., 1967), Vol. II, pp. 454-458.

CHESHIRE, Geoffrey Chevalier, *The Modern Law of Real Property.* 4th ed. London: Butterworth and Co., 1937. Pp. XLVIII, 850. First published in 1925.

ELY, Richard Theodore, *Property and Contract in Their Relations to the Distribution of Wealth.* 2 vols. London: Macmillan Co., 1914.

GRACE, Frank, *The Concept of Property in Modern Christian Thought.* Ur-bana, Illinois: The University of Illinois Press, 1953. Pp. 173.

HEGEL, G. W. F., *Philosophy of Right.* Translated by T. M. KNOX. Oxford: At the Clarendon Press, 1942. See below, p. 138.

HUME, David, *Treatise of Human Nature.* Ed. by L. A. SELBY-BIGGE. 2nd ed. Oxford: Oxford University Press, 1896.

LEO XIII, *Rerum Novarum.* Rome: The Vatican, 1891. English translation in Washington, D. C.: National Catholic Welfare Conference, n.d. New York: The Paulist Press, n.d.

La «Rerum Novarum», *Enciclica sulla questione operatia.* Ed. with commentary by V. ARCOZZI. Rome: Studium, 1929.

CASTELEIN, Auguste, *Leon XIII et la question sociale.* Brussels: A. De-wit, 1914. Pp. XI, 149.

LOCKE, John, *Two Treatises of Government.* Ed. by Peter LASLETT. London: Cambridge University Press, 1960. Pp. 520. See below, p. 180.

CZAJKOWSKI, Casimir J., *The Theory of Private Property in John Locke's Political Philosophy.* Notre Dame, Indiana: University of No-tre Dame, 1941. Pp. VIII, 108.

MARX, Karl, «Economic and Philosophical Manuscripts», in *Karl Marx: Early Writings*. Edited and translated by T. B. BOTTOMORE. New York: McGraw-Hill, 1964. Pp. 227.

——, *Economic and Philosophic Manuscripts of 1844*. Ed. by Dirk J. STRUIK, translated by Martin MILLIGAN. New York: International Publishers, 1964. Pp. 255.

MILL, John Stuart, *Principles of Political Economy*. 7th ed. London: Longmans, 1867. Pp. XX, 591. See Socialism, below.

PIUS XI, *Quadrogesimo anno*. Rome: The Vatican 1931. English translation in Washington, D. C.: National Catholic Welfare Conference, 1931.

PIUS XII, *Summi Pontificatus*. Rome: The Vatican, 1939. English translation, *Summi Pontificatus: Functions of the State in the Modern World*. Washington: National Catholic Welfare Conference, 1939.

BRUFAN, Prat Jaime, «Senso attuale del diritto di proprietà nel pensiero pontificio», *Rivista internazionale di filosofia del diritto* (Milan), 1962, pp. 701-718.

Social Creed. U.S.A.: Federal Council of the Churches of Christ in America, 1932.

Social Ideals of the Churches. U.S.A.: Federal Council of the Churches of Christ in America, 1932.

JARLOT, G., S. J., «Propriété, droit naturel et bien commun: Les pauvres ont-ils des droits?», *Nouvelle revue théologique* (Tournai), 1963, pp. 618-630.

PROUDHON, Pierre J., *Qu'est-ce que la propriété?* Paris J. F. Brocard, 1840. Pp. XII, 244. See above, p. 94.

ROUBIER, Paul, *Le droit de la propriété industrielle*. 2 vols. Paris: Recueil Sirey, 1952-1954.

PURE ECONOMICS

Theory of rules and economic worth free from ideological and sociological elements.

KOOPMANS, Tjalling C., *Three Essays on the State of Economic Science*. New York: McGraw-Hill, 1957. Pp. 231.

MARSHALL, Alfred, *The Pure Theory of Foreign Trade; The Pure Theory of Domestic Values*, 1879. London: Reprints of Scarce Tracts in Economics, 1930. See The Mathematical School above, p. 99.

ROBINSON, Joan, *Economic Philosophy*. Chicago: Aldine Publishing Co., 1962. Pp. 150.

DEL VECCHIO, Giorgio, *Lezioni di economia pura*. Padua: Cedam, 1938.

PANTALEONI, Muffeo, *Principi di economia pura*. 2nd ed. Florence: Barbera, 1894. Pp. 376. First published in 1889.

WALRAS, Léon, *Eléments d'économie politique pure, ou théorie de la richesse sociale*. 4th ed. Paris: R. Pichon et R. Durand-Auzias, 1926. Pp. XX, 491. First published in Lausanne, 1874.

SLAVES

See Colonies, below, Ch. IV, pp. 214, 222.

SOCIALISM

See above, pp. 86, 91; Private Property, above, p. 108.

MILL, John Stuart, *Socialism, Being a Collection of His Writings on Socialism, Democracy, the Rights of Property in Land and the Enfranchisement of Women.* Ed. by W. D. P. BLISS. New York: The Humbold Publishing Co., 1891. Pp. IX, 214.

CASTELEIN, Auguste, *Léon XIII et la question sociale.* Brussels: A. Dewit, 1914. Pp. XI, 149. See LEO XIII, above, p. 102.

UNDERDEVELOPED COUNTRIES

BRAND, Wilhelm, *The Struggle for a Higher Standard of Living: The Problem of the Underdeveloped Countries.* New York: The Macmillan Co., 1958.

FRANKEL, H., «The Economic Impact on Underdeveloped Societies», in *Essays on International Investments and Social Change.* New York: Oxford University Press, 1953.

BERQUE, Jacques, «Valeurs de la décolonisation», *Revue de métaphysique et de morale* (Paris), 1963, pp. 302-318.

MARCUSE, Herbert, «Idéologie et société industrielle avancée», *Méditations* (Paris), 1962, pp. 57-71.

VALUE

See Philosophy, above, p. 77; Social Ethics, below, pp. 266; Value, pp, 64, 277.

ARCHIBALD, G. C., «Welfare Economics, Ethics and Essentialism», *Economica*, New Series, 1959, pp. 316-327. Economics is not necessarily ethical.

COATS, A. W., «Value Judgments in Economics», *Yorkshire Bulletin of Economic and Social Research*, 1964, pp. 53-67.

HICKS, John Richard, *Value and Capital.* 2nd ed. New York: Oxford University Press, 1946. Pp. IX, 340.

HUTCHISON, T. W., *'Positive' Economics and Policy Objectives.* Cambridge, Massachusetts: Harvard University Press, 1964. Pp. 200.

KLAPPHOLZ, Kurt, «Value Judgments and Economics», *The British Journal for the Philosophy of Science*, 1964, pp. 97-114.

——, «Economics and Ethical Neutrality», in *The Encyclopedia of Philosophy* (8 vols. New York: The Macmillan Co., 1967), Vol. II, pp. 451-454.

LITTLE, Ian Malcolm David, *A Critique of Welfare Economics*. 2nd ed. New
     York: Oxford University Press, 1957. Pp. 363.
LUCE, Robert Duncan and RAIFFA, Howard, *Games and Decisions*. New York:
     Columbia University Press, 1957. Pp. 509.
ROBBINS, L. C., *An Essay on the Nature and Significance of Economic
     Science*. 2nd ed. London: Macmillan Co., 1935. Pp. XII, 144.

6. PERIODICALS

See above, Ch. I, 4; below, Ch. IV, 6.

(a) International

Economica. London: London School of Economics and Political Sciences,
     1921—.
International Economic Review. Osaka, Japan: Economic Federation. Phi-
     ladelphia: University of Pennsylvania, 1960—.
Journal of Political Economy. Chicago: University of Chicago Press, 1892—.
Metroeconomica, International Review of Economics. Trieste, Italy: L.
     Cappelli, 1950—.
Quarterly Journal of Economics. Cambridge, Massachusetts: Harvard Uni-
     versity Press, 1886—.
Études économiques. Mons, Belgium: L'Institut Supérieur Commercial, 1923—.
Nouvelle revue d'économie contemporaine. Formerly, *Économie contem-
     poraine*. Paris: 2, rue Montesquieu, 1950—.
Problèmes économiques, sélections de presses française et etrangère. Paris:
     Direction de la conjoncture et des études économiques, 1948—.
Recherches économiques de Louvain. Formerly, *Bulletin de l'Institut de
     Recherches économiques et sociales*. Louvain: Centre de Recherches
     économiques (Place Mgr Ladeuze), 1929—.
Revue d'économie politique. Paris: Librairie Sirey, 1887—.

(b) National

America, — see above, a.

England

National Institute Economic Review. London: National Institute of Eco-
     nomic and Social Research, 1959—.

France, — see above, a.

Italy

Studi e richerche. Rome: Via Paganini, 1961 —.

Poland

Ekonomista: czasopismo poswiecone nauce i potrzebom zycia. **Warsaw:** Panstwowe Wydawnictwo Naukowe, 1900— 1965—.
Kwartalnik historii Kultury materialnej. Warsaw: Pånstwowe Wydawnictwo Naukowe, 1952-1968.

Russian

Moskovski Universiteit. Vestnik. Jerija ekonomika, filosofia. Moscow: Leninskije Gory, 1946—.
Problems of Economics: Selected Articles from Soviet Economics Journals. English translations. New York: International Arts and Sciences Press (156 Fifth Ave.), 1958—.
Soviet Studies: A Quarterly Review of the Social and Economic Institutions of the U.S.S.R. Oxford: Basil Blackwell, 1949—.

Chapter III

LAW

Law has traditionally been closely connected with philosophical studies. Beginning in the nineteenth century, however, it became increasingly separated from philosophy and more technical. Notwithstanding this development, law remains a constant subject of philosophical interest.

The chief questions in regard to law concern its notion, origin, definition, foundation, classification, methods, objective judicial value, processes, obligation, sanction, relationship to ethics, customs, and function in various phases and aspects of human life.

In the Bibliography below, we list books and periodicals related to the history and philosophy of law and its special aspects, according to the particular periods, schools, and specific questions.

Bibliography

1. INTRODUCTORY BIBLIOGRAPHIES

An Index to Legal Periodical Literature. Ed. by Leonard A. JONES (before 1887 to 1932). Boston: Charles C. Soule, 1888—. Contination by other editors, among them in New York: H. W. Wilson Co., 1964—.

BEARDSLEY, Arthur S. and ORMAN, Oscar C., *Legal Bibliography and the Use of Law Books.* 2nd ed. Brooklyn: The Foundation Press, 1947. Pp. 653.

DIAS, R. W. M., *Bibliography of Jurisprudence.* 2nd ed. London: Butterworth and Co., 1964. Pp. 234.

HICKS, Frederick C., *Materials and Methods of Legal Research with Bibliographical Manual.* 2nd ed. Rochester, New York: The Lawyers Co-operative Publishing Company, 1933. Pp. XVI, 651.

POUND, Roscoe, *A Bibliography of Procedural Reform, Including Organization of Courts.* Chicago: Northwestern University Press, 1917. Reprint from *Illinois Law Review,* Vol. XI, No. 7, pp. 451-463.

Annuario bibliografico di filosofia del diritto. Milan: A. Giuffrè, 1967—. Vol. I: Bibliography 1965, Rassegne internazionali. Pp. XX, 459.

CONTE, Amedeo G., «Bibliografia di logica giuridica, 1936-1960», *Rivista internazionale di filosofia del diritto,* 1961, pp. 120-144; 1962, pp. 45-46.

STOLLREITHER, Konrad, *Internationale Bibliographie der juristischen Nachschlagewerke.* Frankfurt a. M.: Vittorio Klostermann, 1955. Pp. 595.

2. GENERAL STUDIES

(a) Histories

See also particular Countries, below, 4.

In English

GOLDING, M. P., «History of Philosophy of Law», *The Encyclopedia of Philosophy* (8 vols. New York: The Macmillan Co., 1964), Vol. VI, pp. 254-264.

MACDONNELL Sir, John and MANSON, Edward William Donoghue (eds.), *Great Jurists of the World.* 2 vols. London: Little, Brown and Co., 1914. Biographies.

NUSSBAUM, Arthur, *A Concise History of the Law of Nations.* New York: The Macmillan Co., 1947. Pp. XI, 361.

PLUCKNETT, Theodore F. Th., *A Concise History of the Common Law.* 2nd ed. London: Butterworth and Co., 1936. Pp. XXV, 679.

POUND, Roscoe, *Interpretations of Legal History.* Cambridge: The University Press, 1923. Pp. XVII, 171. See also Philosophy, below, c.

SEAGLE, William, *History of Law.* New York: Tudor Publishing Co., 1946. Pp. XV, 439.

——, *Men of Law from Hammurabi to Holmes.* New York: The Macmillan Co., 1947. Pp. 391. See also Philosophy, below, c.

VINOGRADOV, Pave G., *Outlines of Historical Jurisprudence.* 2 vols. London: Humphrey Milford, 1920-1923.

——, (ed.), *Oxford Studies in Social and Legal History.* Oxford: Clarendon Press, 1909—.

WIGMORE, John Henry, *A Panorama of the World's Legal Systems.* Washington, D. C.: Washington Law Book Co., 1936. Pp. XXIII, 1206. First published in Saint Paul, 1928.

In Other Languages

DEL VECCHIO, Giorgio, *Contributi alla storia del pensiero giuridico e filosofico.* Milan: A. Giuffrè, 1963. Pp. 383.

DECUGIS, Henri, *Les étages du droit des origines à nos jours.* 2nd ed. 2 vols. Paris: Recueil Strey, 1946.

GAGNER, Sten, *Studien zur Ideengeschichte der Gesetzgebung*. Stockholm: Almqvist & Wiksell, 1960. Pp. 404.

GRANERIS, Giuseppe, *La filosofia del diritto nella sua storia e nei suoi problemi*. Rome: Desclée et Cie, 1961. Pp. 258.

RAVÀ, A., — see below, p. 153.

ROUBIER, Paul, *Théorie générale du droit: histoire des doctrines juridiques et philosophie des valeurs sociales*. Paris: Recueil Sirey, 1946. Pp. 283.

TRUYOL Y SERRA, Antonio, *Historia de la filosofía del derecho y del estado*. Vol. I, De les origenes a la baja edad media. 3rd ed. Madrid: Revista de Occidente, 1961. Pp. XXVIII, 416.

VILLEY, Michel, *Leçons d'histoire de la philosophie du droit*. 2nd ed. Paris: Dalloz, 1962. Pp. 318. First published in 1957.

(b) Systematic Studies

See History, above, a; Philosophy, below, c; Special, below, 3-4.

In English

AMOS, Sheldon, *A Systematic View of the Science of Jurisprudence*. London: Longmans and Co., 1872. Pp. XXII, 545.

——, *The Science of Law*. London: H. S. King and Co., 1874. Pp. XX, 417.

——, *Science of Politics*. 3rd ed. London: Kegan Paul, Trench, Trübner and Co., 1906. Pp. VIII, 490.

BEDAN, Hugo A., «Law, Legal Systems, and Legal Rules», in *Memorias del XIII Congresso Internacional de Filosofia* (Mexico: Universidad Nacional Autonoma de Mexico, 1964), Vol. VIII, pp. 17-27.

HOHFELD, Wesley Newcomb, *Fundamental Legal Conceptions*. Ed. by Walter W. COOK. New Haven, Connecticut: Yale University Press, 1920. Pp. 114.

HOLLAND, Thomas Erskine, *Elements of Jurisprudence*. 12th ed. Oxford: Clarendon Press, 1916. Pp. XXVI, 458.

HOLMES, Oliver W., «The Path of the Law», in *Collected Legal Papers*. New York. Harcourt, 1920.

JOLOWICZ, Herbert Felix, *Lectures on Jurisprudence*. London: University Institute of Advanced Legal Studies, 1963. Pp. XXI, 391.

KOCOUREK, Albert, *An Introduction to the Science of Law*. Boston: Little, Brown and Co., 1930. Pp. XII, 343.

LLOYD, Dennis, *Introduction to Jurisprudence*. London: Praeger, 1960. Pp. XXIII, 482.

PATON Sir, George Whitecross, *A Text-Book of Jurisprudence*. 2nd ed. New York: Oxford University Press, 1951. Pp. 527.

PATTERSON, Edwin Wilhite, *Jurisprudence: Men and Ideas of the Law*. New York: Foundation Press, 1953. Pp. 649.

POLLOCK Sir, Frederick, *Jurisprudence and Legal Essays*. London: St. Martin's Press, 1962. Pp. XLVIII, 244.

POUND, Roscoe, *Law and Morals*. 2nd ed. Chapel Hill, North Carolina: The University of North Carolina Press, 1926. Pp. 144. First published in 1923.

——, *Outlines of Lectures on Jurisprudence*. 4th ed. Cambridge, Massachusetts: Harvard University Press, 1928. Pp. VI, 136.

——, *Ideal Element in Law*. Calcutta: University of Calcutta Press, 1958. Pp. 370.

——, *Introduction to the Philosophy of Law*. New Haven, Connecticut: Yale University Press, 1959. Pp. 209.

——, *Law Finding through Experience and Reason*. 3 lectures. Athens, Georgia; University of Georgia Press, 1960. Pp. 65.

——, *A Bibliography of the Writings of Roscoe Pound, 1940-1960*. Cambridge, Massachusetts: Harvard University Press, 1960.

SALMOND Sir, John William, *Jurisprudence*. 8th ed. London: Sweet and Maxwell, 1930. Pp. XVIII, 580.

SCOTT, James Brown, *Law, the State, and the International Community*. 2 vols. New York: Columbia University Press, 1939.

STREET, Thomas Atkins, *The Foundations of Legal Liability: A Presentation of the Theory and Development of Common Law*. 3 vols. Northport, New York: Wedward Thompson Co., 1906.

Studies in History, Economics and Public Law. New York: Columbia University Press, 1891—.

Studies in Economics and Political Science. London: School of Economics and Political Science, 1896—.

STUMPF, Samuel Enoch, *Morality and the Law*. Nashville, Tennessee: Vanderbilt University Press, 1966. Pp. 247.

WIGMORE, John Henry, *Wigmore's Code of the Rules of Evidence in Trials at Law*. 3rd ed. Boston: Little, Brown and Co., 1942. Pp. LXXIV, 620.

In Other Languages

BINDER, Julius, *Zur Lehre vom Rechtsbegriff*. Darmstadt: Wissenschaftliche Buchgeselschaft, 1963. Pp. 35. Reprint from *Logos*, Vol. XVIII (1929).

COING, Helmut, *Die obersten Grundsätze des Rechtes*. Heidelberg: Lambert Schneider Verlag, 1947. Pp. 155. See also philosophy, below, c.

ENGISCH, Karl, *Einführung in das juristische Denken*. 3rd ed. Stuttgart: Kohlhammer, 1964. Pp. 256.

HUSSERL, Gerhart, *Recht und Welt*. Frankfurt a.M.: Klostermann, 1964. Pp. 375.

MARIN, Pérez, «Pascual, Las nuevas estructuras en el orden juridico», *Crisis* (Madrid), 1962. Pp. 277-302.

(c) Philosophy

See also Histories, above, a: Special Question, below, 5; definition of law, *ibid*.

In English

ALLEN Sir, Carleton Kemp, *Law in the Making*. 5th ed. Oxford: Clarendon Press, 1951. Pp. XXXII, 626. First published in 1927.

BEROLZHEIMER, Fritz, *Rechtsphilosophische Studien*. Munich: C. H. Beck, 1903. Pp. VI, 167.

——, *System der Rechts- und Wirtschaftsphilosophie*. 5 vols. Munich: C. H. Beck, 1904-1907. English translation of vol. II by R. S. JASTROW, *The World's Legal Philosophies*. Boston: The Boston Book Co., 1912. Pp. 490.

BODENHEIMER, Edgar, *Jurisprudence: The Philosophy and the Method of the Law*. Cambridge, Massachusetts: Harvard University Press, 1962. Pp. 402.

CAIRNS, Huntington, *The Theory of Legal Science*. Chapel Hill: The University of North Carolina Press, 1941. Pp. VIII, 155.

——, *Law and Social Science*. London: Kegan Paul, Trench, Trubner and Co, 1935. Pp. XIV, 279.

——, *Legal Philosophy from Plato to Hegel*. Baltimore: John Hopkins Press, 1949. Pp. XV, 582.

——, «Philosophy as Jurisprudence», in Paul SAYRE (ed.), *Interpretations of Modern Legal Philosophies* (New York: Oxford University Press 1947), pp. 52-69.

CARDOZO, Benjamin Nathan, *The Nature of the Judicial Process*. New Haven, Connecticut: Yale University Press, 1932. Pp. 180. First published in 1921. See Natural Law, below, p. 164.

——, *The Growth of the Law*. New Haven, Connecticut: Yale University Press, 1934. Pp. 145. First published in 1921.

——, *The Paradoxes of Legal Science*. New York: Columbia University Press. 1930. Pp. 142. First published in 1928.

COHEN, Felix, *Ethical Systems and Legal Ideals: An Essay on the Foundation of Legal Criticism*. New York: Falcon Press, 1933. Pp. XI, 303.

COHEN, Hermann Joseph, *The Origins of Order and Law*. London: E. Wilson, 1923. Pp. VII, 86.

——, *The Spirit of Our Law*. Revised ed. London: Methuen and Co., 1932. Pp. XV, 293. First published in 1922.

COHEN, Morris Raphael, *Reason and Law*. New York: The Macmillan Co., 1961. Pp. 224. See also Natural Law, below, p. 164.

DAVITT, Thomas E., *The Nature of Law*. St. Louis, Missouri: Herder, 1951. Pp. 274.

DEL VECCHIO, Giorgio, «Truth and Untruth in Morals and Law», in Paul SAYRE (ed.), *Interpretations of Modern Legal Philosophies* (New York: Oxford University Press, 1947), pp. 143-166.

FRIEDRICH, Carl Joachim, *The Philosophy of Law in Historical Perspective*. 2nd ed. Chicago: University of Chicago Press, 1963. Pp. 296.

GEWIRTH, Alan, *Political Philosophy*. New York: The Macmillan Co., 1965. Pp. 123.

GOLDING, Martin P., *The Nature of Law*. New York: Random House, 1966. Pp. X, 276. See also Histories, above, 2 a.

HÄGERSTRÖM, Axel Anders Theodor, *Inquiries into the Nature of Law and Morals*. Translated by C. D. BROAD. Copenhagen, Denmark: Munksgaard, 1953. Pp. 377.

HART, H. L. A., «Problems of Philosophy of Law», *The Encyclopedia of Philosophy* (8 vols. New York: The Macmillan and Co., 1967), Vol. VI, pp. 264-276.

——, *The Concept of Law.* New York: Oxford University Press, 1961. Pp. 274.

——, *Punishment and Responsability: Essays in the Philosophy of Law.* New York: Oxford University Press, 1968.

Hook, Sidney (ed.), *Law and Philosophy: A Symposium.* New York: New York University Press, 1964. Pp. 344.

Jhering von, Rudolf, *Die Normen und ihre Übertretung.* Leipzig: Breitkopf und Härtel, 1872.

——, *Der Kampf um's Recht.* Wien: Manz, 1872. Pp. VI, 100. English translation from the fifth German edition by John J. Lalor, *The Struggle for Law.* 2nd ed. Chicago: Callaghan and Co., 1915. Pp. III, 138.

——, *Der Zweck im Recht.* 2 vols. 4th ed. Leipzig: Breitkopf und Härtel, 1904-1905. English translation by Isaac Husik, *Law as a Means to an End.* Boston: The Boston Book Co., 1913. Pp. 483. Translation of the first volume of the fourth German edition. German edition first published in 1877-1883.

Kelsen, Hans, — see below, pp. 150, 158.

Kohler, Josef, *Lehrbuch der Rechtsphilosophie.* 3rd ed. Berlin: W. Rothschild, 1923. Pp. XXIV, 300. English translation by Adalbert Albrecht, *Philosophy of Law.* Boston: The Boston Book Company, 1914. Pp. 390. See also Ancient Studies, 2 a.

Montesquieu (Secondat de), Charles Louis, *De l'esprit des lois.* 2 vols. Geneva: Barillot et fils; 1748. English translation by Thomas Nugent, *The Spirit of Laws.* 2 vols. 10th ed. London: J. Collingwood, 1823.

Pound, Roscoe, *Interpretations of Legal History.* Cambridge: The University Press, 1923. Pp. XVIII, 171. See also Histories, above, 2 a.

——, *Law and Morals.* 2nd ed. Chapel Hill, North Carolina: The University of North Carolina Press, 1926. Pp. 144. First published in 1924.

——, *An Introduction to the Philosophy of Law.* Revised edition. New Haven, Connecticut: Yale University Press, 1954. Pp. VIII, 201. First published in 1922.

Sayre, Paul L. (ed.), *Interpretations of Modern Legal Philosophies.* New York: Oxford University Press, 1947. Pp. IX, 807. See Modern below, p. 129.

Seagle, William, *The Quest for Law.* New York: Alfred Knopf, 1941. Pp. XV, 439. See also Histories, above, 2 a.

Stone, Julius, *The Province and Function of Law: Law as Logic, Justice and Social Control.* A Study in Jurisprudence. Sydney: Associated General Publications, 1946. Pp. LXIV, 918. See other edition, Realistic School, below, 3 Contemporary, 149.

Vinogradov, Pavel G., *Common Sense in Law.* 2nd ed. London: Oxford University Press, 1946. Pp. 192. First published in 1914.

In Other Languages

Battaglia, F., *Corso di filosofia del diritto.* 3 vols. Rome: Il Foro Italiano, 1940-1947.

——, *Il concetto del diritto.* Rome: Società editrice del Foro Italiano, 1962. Pp. VI, 405.

Bobbio, N., *Introduzione alla filosofia del diritto.* Torino: G. Giappischelli, 1948. See also Phenomenological School, below, 3 Contemporary, bb.

——, *Lezioni di filosofia del diritto ad uso degli studenti.* Torino: G. Giappischelli, 1946. Pp. 224.

COING, Helmut, *Grundzüge der Rechtsphilosophie.* Berlin: W. de Gruyter, 1950. Pp. XI, 302. See also Systematic, above, b.

DEL VECCHIO, G., *Lezioni di filosofia del diritto.* 11th ed. Milan: Giuffrè, 1962. Pp. XII, 403.

DI CARLO, F., *Filosofia del diritto.* 3rd ed. Palermo: Palumbo, 1953. Pp. 168. First published in 1940.

ENGISCH, Karl, *Wahrheit und Rechtigkeit im juristischen Denken.* Munich: Hueber, 1963. Pp. 23.

GALÁN Y GUTIERREZ, E., *Introductión al estudio de la filosofia juridica.* Madrid: Graficas Gonzalez, 1947. Pp. 671.

JHERING VON, Rudolf, — see In English, above.

KAUFMANN, Arthur, — see General Theory of Law, below, p. 158.

LEGAZ Y LACAMBRA, Luis, *Horizontes del pensamiento juridico.* Estudios de Filosofia del Derecho. Barcelona: Editorial Bosch, 1947. Pp. 584.

——, *Introducción a la ciencia del Derecho.* Barcelona: Editorial Bosch, 1943. Pp. 639.

——, *Rechtsphilosophie.* Translated by Wolfram and Gertrud KROMER. Neuwied, Rhein: Luchterhand, 1965.

LEONI, Bruno, *Lezioni di Filosofia del diritto.* Multiple volumes. Pavia: Viscontea, 1948.

LEVI, Alessandro, «Teoria del diritto e filosofia del diritto», *Rivista internazionale di filosofia del diritto* (Milan), 1923, No. 5.

L'idée de philosophie politique. Ed. by Pierre ARNAUD, Paul BASTID, Henri BATIFFOL, et al. Paris: Presses Universitaires de France, 1965. Pp. 193.

PASINI, Dino, *Vita e forma nella realità del diritto.* Milan: A. Giuffrè, 1964. Pp. VIII, 228.

PASSERIN D'ENTRÈVES, Alessandro, «Morale, diritto ed economia», in *Studi in oncre di F. Coletti.* Pavia: Università, 1937.

PERELMAN, Ch. (ed.), *Les antinomies en droit.* Bruxelles: Brylant, 1965. Pp. 404.

POULANTZAS, Nicos, *Nature des choses et droit: essai sur la dialectique du fait et de la valeur.* Paris: Pichon, 1965.

RADBRUCH, Gustav, *Vorschule der Rechtsphilosophie.* Ed. by Arthur KAUFMANN. 3rd ed. Göttingen: Vandenhock and Ruprecht, 1965. Pp. 123.

RAVÀ, Adolfo, *Lezioni di filosofia del diritto.* 3 vols. 6th and 4th eds. Padua: Università di Padova, 1934-1938.

REALE, Miguel, *Filosofia do direito.* Vol. I, Propedeutica filosofica ad usum jurisprudentiae. São Paulo: Edicão Saraiva, 1953. Pp. 256.

RICHARD, Antoine F. G., *Essai sur l'origine de l'idée de droit.* Paris: E. Thorin, 1892. Pp. XXIII, 263.

RIPERT, G., *Le déclin du droit: études sur la législation contemporaine.* Paris: Librairie générale de droit et de jurisprudence, 1949. Pp. VIII, 226.

SERTILLANGES, Antonin Dalmace, *La philosophie des lois.* Paris: Editions Alsatia, 1946. Pp. 124. See also Scholastic Philosophy in *PQS*, No. 5.

SFORZA, Cesarini W., *Guida allo studio della filosofia del diritto.* Rome, 1949.

SÖHNGEN, Gottlieb, *Grundfragen einer Rechtstheologie.* Munich: Pustet, 1962. Pp. 168.

UTZ, Arthur F., *Sozialethik.* Vol. II, Rechtsphilosophie. Heidelberg, Kerle, 1963. Pp. XIV, 409. International Bibliography included. See also Social Ethics, in Sociology, below, p. 267.

VERDROSS, Alfred E., *Abendländische Rechtsphilosophie.* Vienna: J. Springer, 1958. Pp. X, 270.

ZIPPELIUS, Reinhold, *Das Wesen des Rechtes.* Munich: C. H. Beck, 1965. Pp. 157.

(d) Excerpts from Selected Writings

HALL, Jerome, *Readings in Jurisprudence.* New York: Bobbs-Merrill Co., 1938. Pp. XIX, 1183.

HOOK, Sidney (ed.), *Law and Philosophy: A Symposium.* New York: New York University Press, 1964. Pp. 344. See Philosophy, above, 1 c.

POUND, Roscoe (ed.), *Readings in Roman Law and the Civil Law and Modern Codes as Developments thereof: An Introduction to Comparative Law.* 2nd ed. Cambridge, Massachusetts: Harvard University Press, 1914. Pp. VII, 159.

Readings on the History and System of the Common Law. 3rd ed. Rochester, New York: The Lawyers Cooperative Publishing Co., 1927. Pp. XX, 731.

SAYRE, Paul (ed.), *Interpretations of Modern Legal Philosophies. Essays in Honor of Roscoe Pound.* Oxford: University Press, 1947. Pp. IX, 807. See also Modern, below, p. 129.

KAUFMANN, Rich (ed.), *Rechtsidee und Recht. Rechtsphilosophische und ideen-geschichtliche Bemühungen aus fünft Jahrzehnten.* Göttingen: Schwarz und Co., 1961. Pp. XLVIII, 400.

3. PARTICULAR PERIODS

ANTIQUITY

(a) Comprehensive Studies

MAINE Sir, Henry J. S., *Ancient Law: Its Connection with the Early History of Society and Its Relation to Modern Ideas.* New edition. New York: Oxford University Press, 1931. Pp. XXVIII, 344.

KOHLER, Josef, *Rechtsvergleichende Studien über das islamitische Recht, das Recht der Berbern, das chinesische Recht und das Recht auf Ceylon.* Berlin: C. Heymann, 1889. Pp. 252.

(b) Specific Studies

Primitive Law, — see Special Questions, below, p. 166.

(aa) EAST

Assyria-Babylonia

JOHNS, Claude H. W., *Babylonian and Assyrian Laws: Contracts and Letters.* New York: Charles Scribner's Sons, 1904. Pp. XVIII, 424.

Oldest Code of Laws in the World. Translated by C. H. W. JOHNS. New York: Charles Scribner's Sons, n.d. Also Edinburgh: T. and T. Clark, 1903. Pp. XII, 88.

The Code of Hammurabi. Edited and translated by Robert Francis HARPER. Chicago: University of Chicago Press, 1904. Pp. XV, 192.

CRUVEILHIER, Pierre (ed.), *Recueil de lois assyriennes.* 3 vols. Paris: P. Geuthner, 1926-1929.

——, *Introduction au Code d'Hammourabi.* Paris: E. Leroux, 1937. Pp. 177.

CUQ, E., *Études sur le droit babylonien, les lois assyriennes et les lois hittites.* Paris: Recueil Sirey, 1929.

FURLANI, Giuseppe, *La civiltà babilonese e assira.* Rome: L'Istituto per l'Oriente, 1929. Pp. VIII, 518.

—— (ed.), *Leggi dell' Asia Anteriore. antica.* Rome: L'Istituto per l'Oriente, 1929. Pp. XII, 113.

KOHLER, Joseph and PEISER, Felix Erst, *Aus dem babylonischen Rechtsleben.* 4 vols. Leipzig: E. Pfeiffer, 1898.

MEISSNER, Bruno, *Babylonien und Assyrien.* 2 vols. Heidelberg: C. Winter, 1920-1925.

Hebrews

BEVAN, Edwyn Robert, SINGER, Charles *et al. (eds.), The Legacy of Israel.* New York: Oxford University Press, 1927. Pp. XXIX, 551.

COOK, S. A., *Laws of Moses and the Code of Hammurabi.* London: A. and C. Clark, 1903. Pp. XVIII, 307.

POWIS, J. M., *The Origin and History of Hebrew Law.* Chicago: University of Chicago Press, 1931.

WARBURTON, William, *The Divine Legation of Moses.* Ed. by R. HURD. 10th ed. 3 vols. London: T. Tegg, 1846. First published in 2 vols., London, 1738-1741.

EBERHARTER, Andreas, *Das Ehe- und Familien-Recht der Hebräer.* 2 vols. Munster: Aschendorffsche Buchhandlung, 1914. Pp. X, 205.

FASSEL, Hirsch B., *Das Mosaisch-Rabbinische Civilrecht.* 2 vols. Vienna: L. Sommer, 1852-1854.

HILDESHEIMER, Esriel Erich, *Das judische Geselschaftsrecht.* Leipzig: O. Harrassowitz, 1930. Pp. XIII, 172.

MÜLLER, David Heinrich, *Die Gesetze Hammurabis und ihr Verhältnis zur mosaischen Gesetzgebung sowie zu den XII Tapfeln.* Vienna: A. Hölder, 1903. Pp. 286.

RAPAPORT, Mordche W., *Der Talmud und sein Recht.* 2nd ed. Berlin: L. Lamm, 1912. Pp. VIII, 149.

RUBIN, Simon, *Das talmudische Recht auf den verschiedenen Stufen seiner Entwiclung.* 2 vols. Vienna: Nibur-Verlag, 1920-1938.

(bb) West

GRONINGEN VAN, B. A. and MEIJERS, E. M. *et al.* (eds.), *Symbolae ad jus et historiam antiquitatis pertinentes.* Leiden, Holland: E. J. Brill, 1946. Pp. VIII, 410.

HILDENBRAND, Karl, *Geschichte und System der Rechts- und Staatsphilosophie. Das klassische Altertum.* Aalen: Scientia Verlag, 1962. Pp. XX, 642.

LEONI, Bruno, *Lezioni di filosofia del diritto: il pensiero antico.* Multiple volumes. Pavia: Viscontea, 1949.

McILVAIN, Charles H., *The Growth of Political Thought in the West.* New York. The Macmillan Co., 1932. Pp. 417.

SCHELTEMA, H. J. (ed.), *Florilegium iurisprudentiae Graeco-Romanae.* Leiden, Holland: E. J. Brill, 1950. Pp. 61.

Greece

CALHOUN, George Miller and DELAMERE, Catherine, *A Working Bibliography of Greek Law.* Cambridge, Massachusetts: Harvard University Press, 1927. Pp. XIX, 144.

BONNER, Robert J. and SMITH, G. E., *The Administration of Justice from Homer to Aristotle.* Chicago: University of Chicago Press, 1930—. Pp. 399.

CALHOUN, G. M., *The Growth of Criminal Law in Ancient Greece.* Bereley, California: University of California Press, 1927. Pp. X, 149.

——, *Introduction to Greek Legal Science.* Ed. by Francis de Zulueta. New York: Oxford University Press, 1944. Pp. V, 86.

BEAUCHET, Ludovic, *Histoire du droit privé de la république athénienne.* 4 vols. Paris: Chevalier-Marescq, 1897.

LIPSIUS, Justus Hermanus, *Das attische Recht und Rechtsverfahren.* 3 vols. Leipzig: O. R. Reisland, 1905-1915.

WOLF, Erik, *Griechisches Rechtsdenken.* 3 vols. Frankfurt a.M.: Klostermann, 1950-1956.

Representatives

PRE-SOCRATICS, — see Plato, below.

BARKER, Ernest, *Greek Political Theory: Plato and His Predecessors.* London: Methuen and Co., 1918. Pp. XIII, 403.

HAMBURGER, Max, *The Awakening of Western Legal Thought.* Translated by Bernard MIALL. New York: W. W. Norton and Company, 1942. Pp. XXIII, 167.

CREMONA, Antonio, «La norma juridica nella filosofia morale e nella dottrina politica dei sofisti», *Rivista internazionale di filosofia del diritto* (Milan), 1960, pp. 139-142.

XENOPHON (c. 434-355 B. C.) Ἀπομνημονεύματα. *Xenophon's Memorabilia of*

Socrates. With notes and introduction by R. D. C. Robins. New York: D. Appleton and Co., 1868.

——, *Memorabilia.* Ed. by Josiah R. Smith on the basis of the Breitenbach-Mücke edition. Boston and London: Ginn and Co., 1903. Pp. XIX, 270. See above, p. 80.

Plato (429-348): considers law as a rule about good and evil which is the public decree assuring order in the State. See above, Ch. I, 2, p. 7; Politics, below, Ch. IV, 2, p. 181.

——, *Laws.* 2 vols. Ed. by Edwin Bourdieu England. Manchester: University Press, 1921. For definition of law, see *Laws,* 644 D, 875 D.

Cairns, Huntington, «Plato», in his *Legal Philosophy from Plato to Hegel* (Baltimore: The Johns Hopkins Press, 1949), pp. 29-76.

Davis, Morris, «The Place of Law in Projected Platonic Cities», *Symbolae Osloenses* (Oslo), 1960, pp. 72-85.

Wild, John Daniel, *Plato's Modern Enemies and the Theory of Natural Law.* Chicago: University of Chicago Press, 1953. Pp. 259.

Aristotle (384-322): treats law as a rule of orderly conduct, and an ideal of reason tending toward common good. — See Ethics, above, Ch. I, 2, pp. 8-9; Politics, below Ch. IV, 2, p. 181.

——, *Politics.* Translated by Benjamin Jowett. Ed. by Max Lerner. New York: Modern Library, 1943. Pp. 337. For description of law, see *Politics,* 1280-1292.

Lachance, Louis, *La conception de droit selon Aristotle et St. Thomas.* Ottawa, Montreal: Editions du Lévrier, 1948. Pp. 336.

Ravà, Adolfo, *La filosofia del diritto di Aristotele.* Padua: G. U. F., 1935.

——, *Lezioni di filosofia del diritto.* 4 vols. Padua: A. Milani, 1931-1937.

Siegfried, Walter, *Der Rechtsgedanke bei Aristoteles.* Zürich: Schulthess, 1947. Pp. III, 99.

Rome

See also Modern, below.

Buckland, William Warwick, *A Textbook of Roman Law from Augustus to Justinian.* 2nd ed. Cambridge: University Press, 1932. Pp. XIV, 756. First published in 1921.

Buckland, William Warwick and McNair, Arnold Duncan, *Roman Law and Common Law: A Comparison in Outline*. 2nd ed. Cambridge: University Press, 1952. Pp. XX, 439. First published in 1936.

Jolowicz, Herbert Felix, *Historical Introduction to the Study of Roman Law*. New York: The Macmillan Co., 1932. Pp. XXI, 545.

Kantorowicz, Hermann U. and Buckland, William W. (eds.), *Studies in the Glossators of the Roman Law*. New York: The Macmillan Co., 1938. Pp. XVI, 323. See Medieval, below.

Pound, Roscoe (ed.), *Readings in Roman Law and the Civil Law and Modern Codes as Developments thereorf*. 2nd ed. Cambridge, Massachusetts: Harvard Univessity Press, 1914. Pp. VII, 159.

Schulz, Fritz, *Principles of Roman Law*. Translated by Marguerite Wolff. New York: Oxford University Press, 1936. Pp. XVI, 268.

——, *History of Roman Legal Science*. New York: Oxford University Press, 1946. Pp. XVI, 358.

Wenger, Leopold, *Institutes of the Roman Law of Civil Procedure*. Revised edition. Translated by Otis Harrison Fisk. New York: Veritas Press, 1940. Pp. XXIX, 440. See also below, In Other Languages.

Brasiin, Otto, «Aspects philosophiques du droit romain,» in *Mélanges en honeur de Jean Dabin* (2 vols. Paris: Editions Sirey, 1963), Vol. I, pp. 27-31.

Bonfante, Pietro, *Manuale di storia del diritto romano*. 2nd ed. Milan: Società editrice, 1909. Pp. XVI, 862.

Cuq, E., *Manuel des institutions juridiques des romains*. Paris: Plon, 1928. Pp. 956.

Guibal, Maurice Philibert, *De l'influence de la philosophie sur le droit romain et la jurisprudence de l'époque classique*. Paris: Recueil Sirey, 1937. Pp. 238.

Jhering von, Rudolph, *Der Geist des römischen Rechts auf den verschiedenen Stufen seiner Entwicklung*. 5th ed. 3 vols. Leipzig: Breitkopf und Härtel, 1888-1898.

Mitteis, Ludwig, *Antike Rechtsgeschichte und romantisches Rechtsstudium*. Vienna: C. Fromme, 1917. Pp. 23.

Wenger, Leopold, *Der heutige Stand der römischen Rechtswissenschaft*. Enlarged edition. Munich. Münchener Beiträge zur Papyrusforschung und antiken Rechtsgeschichte, 1927. Pp. X, 113.

——, *Die Quellen des römischen Rechts*. Vienna: Österreichische Akademie der Wissenschaften, 1953. Pp. XVIII, 973.

Representatives

Stoics, — see Ethics, above, Ch. I, 2, p. 11.

Cicero, Marcus Tullius (106-43 B. C.): considers law as a command or prohibition which agrees with right reason and nature, and thus may have universal application.

——, *De Republica,* — see below, Ch. IV, 3, p. 182.

——, *De Legibus libri tres.* A revised text with English notes. Cambridge: J. Hall and Son, 1881. Pp. VIII, 152. For description of law, see *De legibus,* I, 15; III, 22, 33.

Hunt, Harold Arthur Kinross, *Humanism of Cicero.* London: Cambridge University Press, 1954. Pp. 221.

Ulpian, Domitius (c. 170-228): law is the art of the good and the equitable. He distinguishes *ius civile* (right of a community) from *ius gentium* (right common to all societies) and *ius naturale (right common to all).* See below, *The Digest of Justinian,* I, 1,1.

——, *D. Ulpiani Fragmenta.* Ed. by E. Huschke. Leipzig: Teubner, 1861.

The Commentarius of Gaius and Rules of Ulpian. Translated with notes by J. T. Abdy and Bryan Walker. Cambridge: University Press, 1885. Pp. XXVI, 501.

Justinian I (Emperor of the East 527-565): what pleases the king has the force of law.

——, *Corpus Juris Civilis Justinianei.* 6 vols. Lyon: J. et P. Cavellat, 1627.

——, *Digestorum seu Pandectarum libri quinquaginta.* Atrebat: E. Vignon, 1735. English translation by C. H. Munro, *The Digest of Justinian.* 2 vols. Cambridge: University Press, 1904. For the definition of law, see *Digest,* I, 4, 1.

Holmes, William Gordon, *The Age of Justinian and Theodor.* 2nd ed. 2 vols. London: G. Bell and Sons, 1912. First published in 1905.

Ure, Percy Neville, *Justinian and His Age.* Harmondsworth: Penguin Books, 1951. Pp. 262.

MIDDLE AGES

See Scholastic Philosophy, in *PQS,* No. 5; Sovereignty, below, Ch. III, 5, p. 168.

(a) Comprehensive Studies

Carlyle, Sir, Robert Warrand, and Carlyle, A. J., *History of Medieval Political Theory in the West.* 6 vols. London: W. Blackwood and Sons, 1903-1936. See also Politics, below, Ch. IV, 2 Middle Ages.

Gierke von, Otto Friedrich, *Political Theories of the Middle Ages.* Translated by Frederic William Maitland. Cambridge: University Press, 1900. Pp. LXXX, 197.

Savigny von, Friedrich Carl, *Geschichte des römischen Rechts im Mittelalter.* 2 vols. Heidelberg: Mohr und Zimmer, 1815-1816. English translation by C. Cathcart, *The History of the Roman Law During the Middle Ages.* Vol. I. Edinburgh: A. Black, 1829.

ULLMANN, Walter, *The Mediaeval Idea of Law*. London: Methuen, 1946. Pp. XXXIX, 220.
VINOGRADOFF, Pavel G., *Roman Law in Medieval Europe*. 2nd ed. Oxford: Clarendon Press, 1929. First published in 1909. Pp. VII, 135.

(b) Specific Studies

KANTOROWICZ, Hermann U. and BUCKLAND, William W. (eds.), *Studies in the Glossators of the Roman Law*. Newly discovered writings of the twelfth century. New York: The Macmillan Co., 1938. Pp. XVI, 323.
MITTEIS, Heinrich, *Politische Prozesse des früheren Mittelalters in Deutschland und Frankreich*. Heidelberg: C. Winter, 1927. Pp. 124.

Representatives

AUGUSTINE ST. (354-430): insists on *ius divinum* and *ius naturale*, God's authority and natural law.
See Ethics, above, Ch. I, 2, p. 14.

GRATIAN, *Decretum*. Venice: N. Bevilaqua, 1567. Pp. 1320.

THOMAS ST., AQUINAS (1224/5-1274): law is a promulgated ordinance of reason for the common good made by him who has care of the community.
See Ethics, above, Ch. I, 2, p. 15.

——, AQUINAS, *Summa theologiae*, II/I, qq. 90-97. See below, p. 184.

DI CARLO, Eugenio, *Attualità della dottrina giuridica e politica di S. Tommaso*. Agrigento: Libreria Tipografica di G. Onorato, 1952. Pp. 15.
O'CONNOR, D. I., *Aquinas and Natural Law*. New York: St. Martin's Press, 1968. Pp. 96.

LOTTIN, O., *Le droit naturel chez saint Thomas d'Aquin et ses prédécesseurs*. Bruges, 1931.

TREVES, Renato, «Intorno alla dottrina morale e giuridica di S. Tommaso d'Aquino», *Studi Urbinati* (Rome), No. 1, 1938.

SUAREZ, Francis, — see Modern, below,

MODERN

(a) Comprehensive Studies

FRANK, Jerome, *Law and the Modern Mind*. 6th printing. London: Stevens and Sons, 1949. Pp. XXXI, 368.
JENNINGS, William Ivor, *Modern Theories of Law*. New York: Oxford University Press, 1933. Pp. VI, 229.

Morris, C., «Four Eighteenth Century Theories of Jurisprudence», *Vanderbilt Law Review*, 1960, pp. 101-116

Sayre, Paul L. (ed.), *Interpretations of Modern Legal Philosophies*. New York: Oxford University Press, 1947. Pp. IX, 807.

Savigny von, Friedrich Carl, *System des heutigen römischen Rechts*. 8 vols. Berlin: Veit, 1840-1849.

——, *Vom Beruf unserer Zeit für Gesetzgebung und Rechtswissenschaft*. 3rd ed. Heidelberg: J. C. B. Mohr, 1840. Pp. X, 198.

(b) Specific Studies

(aa) Renaissance

Foriers, Paul, «Les utopies et le droit», in *Les utopies à la Renaissance* (Paris: Presses Universitaires de France, 1963), pp. 231-261.

Vitoria de Francis (1845-1546), see above, p. 67.

Mendizábal, Alfredo, «On Everlasting Values of the Spanish School of Natural Law (F. de Vitoria)», in Paul Sayre (ed.), *Interpretations of Modern Legal Philosophies* (New York: Oxford University Press, 1947), pp. 498-520.

Bodin, Jean (1530-1596), — see below, p. 131.

Suarez, Francis (1548-1617): distinguishes laws in the prescriptive and descriptive sense. Prescriptive law is a common precept, which is just, stable and promulgated by God in the last result; descriptive laws are laws metaphorically only.

See Ethics, above, Ch. I, 2, p. 17.

——, *Tractatus de legibus ac de Deo legislatore*. Coimbra: D. Gomez de Loureyro, 1612. Pp. 1266. For the definition of the Law, see *De Legibus*, I, 12-20.

——, *Selections*, 2 vols. Ed. by G. L. Williams *et al.* Oxford: Clarendon Press, 1944.

Francisco Suarez: Addresses in Commemoration of His Contribution to International Law and Politics. Washington, D. C.: Catholic University of America, 1933. Delivered, April 30, 1933. Pp. 54.

Hearnshaw, Fossey John Cobb (ed.), *Social and Political Ideas of Some Great Thinkers of the Renaissance and the Reformation*. New York: Brentano, 1926. Pp. 215.

Scott, James B., *The Spanish Conception of International Law and of Sanctions*. 2 parts. Washington, D. C.: Carnegie Endowment for International Peace, 1934. Part I, Francisco de Vitoria; Part II, Francisco Suarez.

ABBOT, Robert (ed.), *De suprema potestate regia: Exercitationes habitae in Academia Oxoniensi, contra Robertum Bellarminum et Franciscum Suarez.* London: Ioannes Billiius, 1619. Pp. 197.

AMBROSETTI, Giovanni, *La filosofia delle Leggi di Suarez.* Rome. Editrice Studium, 1948. Vol. I.

BOURRET, E., *De l'origine du pouvoir d'après saint Thomas et Suarez.* Paris: C. Douniol, 1875. Pp. 55.

MEDINA OLMOS, Manuel, *La obra juridica del Padre Suarez.* Granada: Imp. Escuela del Ave Maria, 1917. Pp. XIX, 225.

RECASÉNS SICHES, L., *La filosofia del derecho de Francisco Suarez, con un estudio previo sobre antecedentes en la Patristica y en la Escolastica.* Madrid: Victoriano Suarez, 1927. Pp. 168.

ROMMEN, H., *Die Staatslehre des Franz Suarez, S. J.* Munich: M. Gladbach, 1927. Pp. XV, 383.

Vitoria et Suarez: Contribution des théologiens au droit international moderne. Paris: A. Pédone, 1939. Pp. XII, 279.

GROTIUS, Hugo (1583-1645), — see below, p. 188.

——, *De iure belli ac pacis libri tres, in quibus ius naturae et gentium, item iuris publici praecipua explicantur.* Paris: N. Buon, 1625. Pp. 786. Ed. by J. MORRICE, *Hugo Grotius of the Rights of War and Peace.* 3 vols. London: D. Brown, 1715.

——, *De iure praedae.* Ed. by H. G. HAMAKER. Hague: M. Nijhoff, 1868. Pp. XVI, 359. English translation from the original manuscript of 1604 by Gladys L. WILLIAMS and Walter H. ZEYDEL, *Commentary on the Law of Prize and Booty.* 2 vols. Oxford: Clarendon Press, 1950.

POUND, Roscoe, «Grotius in the Science of Law», *American Journal of International Law* (Concord, New Hampshire), 1925, pp. 685-688.

THOMASIUS, Christian (1655-1728), — see Politics, below, Ch. IV, 2, p. 189.

——, *Institutiones iurisprudentiae divinae.* 3 vols. Frankfurt: M. G. Weidmann, 1688.

——, *Dissertatio inauguralis iuris gentium de Templariorum ordine sublato.* Halle: Salfedius, 1705. Pp. 64.

——, *Fundamenta iuris naturalis.* 7th ed. Halle: Salfedius, 1730. Pp. 460.

——, *Vernünftige und christliche, aber nicht scheinheilige Thomasische Erwägungen über allerhand gemischte philosophische und iuristische Händel.* 3 vols. Halle: Salfedius, 1723-1725.

——, *Delineatio historiae iuris romani et germanici.* Erfurt: J. A. Lorber, 1750. Pp. 72.

BATTAGLIA, Felice, *Cristiano Thomasius filosofo e giurista.* Rome: Il Foro Italiano, 1936. Pp. 444.

Del Bo, D., «Le dottrine giuridiche di Cristiano Thomasius», *Rivista di filosofia neoscolastica* (Milan), No. 1, 1939.

(bb) RATIONALISM: reason provides self-evidently true juridical principles or generalizations.

BODIN, Jean (1530-1596): law is the command of the sovereign as sovereign who must respect the law of nature, dictated by God.

——, *Les six livres de la République.* Paris: Jacques du Puys, 1577. Pp. 759. English translation by Richard KNOLLES, *The Six Books of a Commonweale* (sic). London: Adam Islip, 1606. Pp. 794.

CUDWORTH, Ralph (1617-1688), *A Treatise Concerning Eternal and Immutable Morality.* London: J. and J. Knapton, 1731. Pp. XX, 303. See Ethics, above, Chapter I, 2, p. 20.

CUMBERLAND, Richard (1732-1811), *De legibus naturae disquisitio philosophica.* London: E. Flesher, 1672. Pp. 421. English translation by John MAXWELL, *A Treatise of the Laws of Nature.* London: R. Philipps, 1727. Pp. CIXVIII, 377.

HOBBES, Thomas (1588-1679); laws are the commands of the sovereign.
See Ethics, above, Ch. I, 2, p. 21.

——, *Leviathan.* Ed. by Michael OAKESHOTT. New York: The Macmillan Co., 1962. Pp. 511. First published in 1651.
——, *The Elements of Law Natural and Politic.* Ed. by Ferdinand TONNIES. Cambridge: University Press, 1928. Pp. XVII, 195. First published in 1650.
——, *A Brief of the Art of Rhetoric.* With a Discourse of the Laws of England. Oxford: D. A. Talboys, 1823. Pp. 394.

BALOGH, E., «Note on Thomas Hobbes», in SAYRE, Paul (ed.), *Interpretations of Modern Legal Philosophies* (New York: Oxford University Press, 1947), pp. 29-42.

CAIRNS, Huntington, «Hobbes», in his *Legal Philosophy from Plato to Hegel* (Baltimore: The Johns Hopkins Press, 1947).

LEIBNIZ, Gottfried W. (1646-1716): law is a norm established for the commonwealth characterizing the structure of society.

——, *Codex juris gentium diplomaticus, in quo tabulae authenticae actorum publicorum, tractatuum, aliarumque rerum majoris momenti per Europam gestarum... continentur, a fine seculi undecimi ad nostra usque tempora.* 2 vols. Hanover: S. Ammon, 1693-1700.
——, *Caesarini Fuerstenerii de iure suprematus ac legationis principum Germaniae.* S. 1., 1679. Pp. 245. Leibniz' pseudonym.

——, *Caesarinus Fürstenerius von des Kaisers Jurisdiction.* S. 1., 1747. Pp. IV, 84. Leibniz' pseudonym.

——, «Nova methodus discendae docendaeque jurisprudentiae: ratio corporis juris reconcinnandi», in *Variorum opuscula ad cultiorem jurisprudentiam adsequendam pertinentia* (9 vols. Pisis, 1769-1771), Vol. II.

——, «Gedanken von Verbesserung der römischen Rechts Gelehrtheit», in Christian B. Buder (ed.), *Nützliche Sammlung verschiedener meistens ungedruckter Schriften.* Frankfurt: C. H. Cuno, 1735. Pp. 136.

Grua, Gaston, *Jurisprudence universelle et théodicée selon Leibniz.* Paris: Presses Universitaires de France, 1953. Pp. 548.

Hartmann, Gustav, *Leibniz als Jurist und Rechtsphilosoph.* Tübingen: H. Laupp, 1892. Pp. 121.

Mollat, G. (ed.), *Rechtsphilosophisches aus Leibnizens ungedruckten Schriften.* Leipzig: Cassel, 1885. Pp. VII, 96.

Zimmermann, Robert, *Das Rechtsprinzip bei Leibnitz.* Vienna: W. Braumüller, 1852. Pp. 70.

Pufendorf, Samuel (1632-1694): law is the fruit of the will of the sovereign, but its ultimate principle is the will and omnipotence of God.

See above, Ch. I, 2, p. 20.

——, *Elementorum jurisprudentiae universalis libri duo.* 2 vols. Oxford: Clarendon Press, 1931. Vol. I, Reproduction of the edition of 1672; Vol. II, English translation by William A. Oldfather. First editions published in Hague: A. Vlacq; 1660. 2nd revised edition in 1672.

——, *De officio hominis et civis juxta legem naturalem libri duo.* 2 vols. New York: Oxford University Press, 1927. First published in London: A. Junghans, 1673. Pp. 240. English translation by A. Tooke, *The Whole Duty of Man according to the Law of Nature.* 5th ed. London: R. Gosling, 1735.

——, *De iure naturae et gentium libri octo.* London: A. Junghans, 1672. Pp. 1227. English translation by Basil Vennet et al., *Of the Law of Nature and Nations.* 2nd ed. Oxford: A. and J. Churchill, 1710. Pp. 724.

——, *Specimen controversiarum circa ius naturale ipsi nuper notarum.* Upsala: D. van der Mylen, 1678. Pp. 270.

Phillipson, Coleman, *The Great Jurists of the World. XIV, Samuel Pufendorf.* London: Society of Comparative Legislation, 1919. Pp. 33.

Spinoza, Baruch (1632-1677): law is an order of life. However, his philosophy of law was not finished.

See Ethics, above, Ch. I, 2, p. 19; Politics, below, Ch. IV, 2, p. 191.

——, *Lucii Antistii Constantis de jure ecclesiasticorum liber singularis.* Alethopoli: Caius Valerius Pennatus, 1665. Pp. 162.

CAIRNS, Huntington, «Spinoza», in his *Legal Philosophy from Plato to Hegel*. (Baltimore: The Johns Hopkins Press, 1949), pp. 272-294.

GALLICET CALVETTI, Carla, «I diritti della persona umana nel *Tractatus theologico-politicus* di Spinoza», in *Studi di filosofia e di storia della filosofia in onore di Francesco Olgiati* (Milan: Vita e Pensiero, 1962), pp. 321-344.

WOLFF, Christian (1679-1754), *Ius gentium methodo scientifica pertractatum*. Magdeburg: Renger, 1749. Pp. 849. Leibniz' affiliation, — see above, p. 19.

——, *Ius gentium*. New edition. 8 vols. Frankfurt: Renger; Societas Veneta, 1764-1766.

——, *Institutiones iuris naturae et gentium*. Magdeburg: Renger, 1754. Pp. 782.

(CC) EMPIRICAL SCHOOL: generalizations of law have to be obtained from its particularization, given in experience.

Early Empiricism

BACON, Francis (1561-1626): insists on certainty as the condition of the existence of law. This certainty is provided by the directives of a competent authority.
See above, p. 21; Index.

——, «De justitia universali, sive de fontibus iuris», in the Book VIII of his *De dignitate et augmentis scientiarum libri IX*. London: Ioannes Haviland, 1623. English translation by D. Caulfield HERON, *Lord Bacon's Tractat on Universal Justice*. Dublin: Hodges and Smith, 1852. Pp. 38.

——, *The Elements of the Common Laws of England*. 2 parts. London: The Assignes of I. More, Esq., 1630.

——, *Exemplum tractatus de fontibus iuris, and Other Latin Pieces of Lord Bacon*. Translated by James GLASSFORD. Edinburgh: Waygh and Innes, 1823. Pp. IX, 192.

——, *Essays, or Counsels Civil and Moral*. Ed. by Samuel H. REYNOLDS. Oxford: At the Clarendon Press, 1890. Pp. XXIX, 405.

CAIRNS, Huntington, «Francis Bacon», in his *Legal Philosophy from Plato to Hegel* (Baltimore: The Johns Hopkins Press, 1949), pp. 205-245.

BODIN, Jean (1530-1596), — see Rationalism, above.

HOBBES, Thomas (1588-1679), — see Rationalism, *ibid.*; Empiricism, above, p. 20.

Classic Empiricism

GRAY, John Chipman, *The Nature and Sources of the Law*. 2nd ed. New York: The Macmillan Co., 1921. Pp. XVIII, 348. First published in 1904.

HOLLAND Sir, Thomas Erskine, *The Elements of Jurisprudence*. 13th ed. Oxford: The Clarendon Press, 1928. Pp. XXVI, 458.

MAINE Sir, Henry J. S., *Lectures on the Early History of Institutions*. London: John Murray, 1875. Critical.

SALMOND, John William, *Jurisprudence, or the Theory of Law*. 10th ed. London: Sweet and Maxwell, 1937. Pp. XX, 753.

AUSTIN, John (1790-1859): law is a command of a sovereign.

——, *Lectures on Jurisprudence, or the Philosophy of Positive Law*. 5th ed. 2 vols. London: J. Murray, 1885. First published from the original manuscripts in 3 vols., 1861-1863.

——, *The Province of Jurisprudence Determined*. London: J. Murray, 1832. Pp. 391.

BROWN, J., *The Austinian Theory of Law*. London, 1920.

BENTHAM, Jeremy (1748-1832): describes law as an expression of the will of the sovereign.
See Ethics, above, Ch. I, 2, p. 26.

——, *An Introduction to the Principles of Morals and Legislation*. London: T. Payne and Son, 1789. Pp. 9-335.

——, Codification proposed. London: J. M. Greery, 1882. Pp. 78.

——, *Leading Principles of a Constitutional Code for Any State*. London: A. J. Valpy, 1823. Pp. 13.

——, *Justice and Codification Petitions*. London: Robert Heward, 1829.

——, «On the Influence of Time and Place in Matters of Legislation», *The Works of Jeremy Bentham*. Ed. by John BOWRING. 11 vols. Edinburgh: W. Tait, 1838-1843.

——, *The Limits of Jurisprudence Defined*. Ed. by Charles W. EVERETT. New York: Columbia University Press, 1945.

——, *A Comment on the Commentaries: A Criticism of William Blackstone's Commentaries on the Laws of England*. Ed. by Charles W. EVERETT. Oxford: Clarendon Press, 1928. Pp. VII, 253.

Bentham's Theory of Legislation. Edited and translated by Charles Milner ATKINSON. 2 vols. London: Oxford University Press, 1914.

HOLDSWORTH Sir, William S., *Bentiam's Place in English Legal History*. Reprinted from the *California Law Review* (Berkeley, California), 1940.

BLACKSTONE Sir, William (1723-1780), *Commentaries on the Laws of England*. 4 vols. Ed. by Francis HARGRAVE. Oxford: Clarendon Press, 1765-1769. See also England, below, p. 143.

——, *An Abridgment of Blackstone's Commentaries on the Laws of England*. Ed. by J. E. EARDLEY. London: J. Hatchard and Son, 1822. Pp. VIII, 304.

——, *An Analysis of the Laws of England*. 4th ed. Oxford: Clarendon Press, 1759. Pp. LXX, 189. First published in 1756.

LOCKE, John (1632-1704): considers law as a rule, a measure of conduct established by authority, which takes into consideration individual's rights.

——, *Essays on the Law of Nature*. Ed. by W. VON LEYDEN. Oxford: Clarendon Press, 1954. Pp. XI, 292. The Latin with a translation and notes. First written in 1676.

——, *Two Treatises of Government*. A critical edition by Peter LASLETT. Cambridge: University Press, 1960. Pp. XII, 520. First published in 1690.

——, *The Two Charters Granted by King Charles II to the Proprietors of Carolina*. Drawn by John LOCKE. London: R. Parker, 1705. Pp. 60.

——, *An Essay Concerning Human Understanding*. 2nd ed. London: Printed for A. and J. CHURCHIL, 1664. Pp. 407. First published in 1690.

——, *Elements of Natural Philosophy*. London: J. Thomson, S. Dampier and B. Bland, 1750. Pp. VII, 64.

BYRNE, James W., — see above, p. 22.

CAIRNS, Huntington, *Legal Philosophy from Plato to Hegel* (Baltimore: The Johns Hopkins Press, 1949), pp. 335-361.

ALLOGIO, Sabino, «La filosofia giuridica di Giovanni Locke», *Opusculi filosofi di «Sabina»*. Canosa di Puglia, No 5, 1949.

BOBBIO, Norberto, *Locke e il diritto naturale*. Turin: G. Giappichelli, 1963. Pp. 287.

GRONDIN, Max, *Les doctrines politiques de Locke et les origines de la déclaration des droits de l'homme de 1789*. Ribérac: F: Réjou, 1920. Pp. 101.

SMYRNIADIS, Bion, *Les doctrines de Hobbes, Locke et Kant sur le droit d'insurrection, esquisse d'une théorie du droit d'insurrection*. Paris: La vie universitaire, 1921. Pp. XXXV, 217.

HUME, David (1711-1776): law is a body of precepts.
See Ethics in General, above, Ch. I, 2, p. 22.

——, *Enquiry concerning the Principles of Morals*. London: A. Millar, 1751. Pp. 253.

——, *Essays, Moral, Political and Literary*. Ed. by T. H. GROSE. 2 vols. London: Longmans, Green and Co., 1875.

REID, Thomas, *Essays on the Powers of the Human Mind*. 3 vols. Edinburgh: Bell and Bradfute, 1803.

Stewart, John B., *The Moral and Political Philosophy of David Hume.* New York: Columbia University Press, 1963. Pp. VIII, 422.

Castiglione, Silvane, «Diritto naturale e diritto positivo in David Hume», *Rivista internazionale di filosofia del diritto* (Milan), 1962, pp. 79-82.

Molinari, Ernesto, «Diritto e linguaggio in Hume», *Rivista internazionale di filosofia del diritto* (Milan), 1962, pp. 400-402.

Montesquieu de Secondat, Charles (1689-1755): laws are regulations which necessarily arise from the nature of things.

——, *Lettres persanes.* 2 parts in one volume. Amsterdam: P. Brunel, 1721.
——, *Considérations sur les causes de la grandeur et de la décadence des Romains.* Amsterdam: J. Desbordes, 1734. Pp. 277.
——, *De l'esprit des loix.* 2 vols. Geneva: Barrillot et fils, 1748. For the definition of Law, see *The Spirit of the Laws,* I, 1. See below, p. 193.

Burke, Edmund, *Reflections on the Revolution in France.* London: J. Dodsley, 1790. Pp. IV, 356.

Fletcher, Frank Thomas Herbert, *Montesquieu and English Politics* (1750-1800). New York: Longmans Green and Co., 1940. Pp. 286.

Levin, Lawrence Meyer, *Political Doctrine of Montesquieu's Esprit des Lois: Its Classical Background.* New York: Institute of French Studies, 1936. Pp. XIII, 359.

Morgan, Charles, *Liberty of Thought and the Separation of Powers: A Modern Problem Considered in the Context of Montesquieu.* Oxford: Oxford University Press, 1948. Pp. 20.

Stark, Werner, *Montesquieu: Pioneer of the sociology of knowledge.* London: Routledge and Kegan Paul, 1960. Pp. 214.

(dd) Idealism: there are mental principles underlying all positive laws.

Critical School: law is an autonomous function of the mind; its material content varies with experience.

Kant, Immanuel (1724-1804): treats law as a harmony of wills effected by general rules oriented toward safeguard of freedom.
See Politics, below, Ch. IV, 2, p. 197. PQS. No. 5.

——, *Zum ewigen Frieden, ein philosophischer Entwurf.* Königsberg: F. Nicolovius, 1795. English translation by Lewis W. Beck, *Perpetual Peace.* Indianapolis, Indiana: Bobbs-Merrill Co., 1957. Pp. 59.
——, *Metaphysische Anfangsgründe der Rechtslehre.* Königsberg: F. Nicolovius, 1797. Pp. XII, 236.

Kant's Principles of Politics. Translated by W. Hastie. Edinburgh: T. Clark, 1891.

Cairns, Huntington, «Kant», in his *Legal Philosophy from Plato to Hegel* (Baltimore: The Johns Hopkins Press, 1949), pp. 390-463.

Cohen, M. R., «A Critique of Kant's Philosophy of Law», in *The Heritage of Kant.* Ed. by G. T. Whitney and D. F. Bowers. Princeton, New Jersey: Princeton University Press, 1939. Pp. X, 426.

Schwarz, Wolfgang, «Kant's Philosophy of Law and International Peace», *Philosophy and Phenomenological Research* (Philadelphia), 1962-1963, pp. 71-80.

Bobbio, Norberto, *Diritto e stato nel pensiero di Emanuele Kant.* Torino: G. Giappichelli, 1957. Pp. 285.

Horn, Adam, *Immanuel Kants ethish-rechtliche Eheauffassung. Eine Rechtfertigung seines Eherechts.* Düsseldorf: Nolte-Verlag, 1936. Pp. 66.

Negri, Antonio, *Alle origini del formalismo giuridico: Studio sul problema della forma in Kant e nei giuristi Kantiani tra il 1789 e il 1802.* Padua: Cedam, 1962. Pp. VIII, 399.

Neuburger, Adalbert, *Legalität und Moralität. Mit besonderer Berücksichtung von Kant und Shaftesbury.* Metzingen: Inaugural Dissertation, 1931. Pp. 131.

Radbruch, Gustav, *Grundzüge der Rechtsphilosophie.* Leipzig: Quelle and Mayer, 1914. Pp. XI, 215.

Stammler, Rudolf (1856-1938): law is a volition binding without exception.

——, *Lehrbuch der Rechtsphilosophie.* Berlin: W. de Gruyter and Co., 1922. Pp. XIV, 392.
——, *Rechts- und Staatstheorien der Neuzeit. Leitsätze zu Vorlesungen.* Leipzig: Vereinigung der Wissenschaftlichen Verleger, 1917. Pp. 88.

Idealistic evolutionist School: law can be explained only in terms of its social processes or evolution.

Battaglia, Felice, «Romanticismo giuridico», *Rivista internationale di filosofia del diritto* (Milan), No. 2, 1929.
——, «Linee di sviluppo del pensiero filosoficogiuridico in Kant e in Hegel», *Rivista internazionale di filosofia del diritto* (Milan), No. 6, 1931.
——, «Oggettività e valori nell' idealismo assoluto», in *Filosofi italiani contemporanei.* Como: Marzorati, 1944.
Gierke von, Otto Friedrich, *Das deutsche Genossenschaftsrecht.* 4 vols. Berlin: Weidmann, 1868-1913.

FICHTE, J. G. (1762-1814): considers law as a relationship between men.
See Politics, below. IV, 2, p. 198.

——, *Grundlage des Naturrechts nach den Principien der Wissenschaftslehre*. 2 parts. Leipzig: C. E. Gabler, 1796-1797.
——, «Wissenschaftslehre und das System der Rechtslehre, vorgetragen an der Universität zu Berlin in den Jahren 1804, 1812 und 1813». Ed. by I. H. FICHTE as 2nd vol. of his *Johann Gottlieb Fichte's nachgelassene Werke*. 3 vols. Bonn: A. Marcus, 1834-1835. English translation by A. E. Kroeger. London: Trübner, 1889. Pp. X, 505.
——, *Rechtslehre. Nach der Handschrift*. Ed. by Hans Schulz. Leipzig: F. Meiner, 1920. Pp. VIII, 176.

COULMAS, Peter, *Fichtes Idee der Arbeit*. Hamburg: Hansischer Gildenverlag, 1939. Pp. 74.

LÉON, Xavier, *Fichte et son temps*. 3 vols. Paris: A. Colin, 1922-1927.

OESTEREICH, Heinrich, *Freiheitsidee und Rechtsbegriff in der Philosophie von Johann Gottlieb Fichte*. Jena: Frommann, 1935. Pp. VIII, 100.

SCHNEIDER, Fritz, *J. G. Fichte als Sozialpolitiker*. Halle: C. A. Kaemmerer und Co., 1894. Pp. III, 80.

HEGEL, George W. F. (1770-1831): treats law as an unfolding of the idea of right, or else as an expression of general will.
See also Politics, below, Ch. IV, 2, p. 32; in *PQS*, No. 5.

HEGEL, G. W. F., *Encyclopädie der philosophischen Wissenschaften in Grundriss*. 2nd ed. Heidelberg: A. Oswald, 1827. Pp. XLII, 544. First published in 1817.
——, *Grundlinien der Philosophie des Rechts*. Berlin: Duncker, 1821. English translation by T. M. KNOX, *Philosophy of Right*. Oxford: At the Clarendon Press, 1942.
——, *Recht, Staat, Geschichte*. Eine Auswahlung aus seinen Werken. Ed. by Friedrich BÜLOW. Stuttgart: Kröner, 1964. Pp. VIII, 515.

CAIRNS, Huntington, «Hegel», in his *Legal Philosophy from Plato to Hegel* (Baltimore: The Johns Hopkins Press, 1949), pp. 503-550.

REYBURN, Hugh A., *The Ethical Theory of Hegel: A Study of the Philosophy of Right*. Oxford: Clarendon Press, 1921. Pp. XX, 271.

SANDARS, T. C., *Hegel's Philosophy of Right*. 4 vols. London: J. W. Parker and Son, 1855-1858.

STIRLING, James Hutchison, *Lectures on the Philosophy of Law*. London: Longmans, Green and Co., 1873. Pp. V, 139.

Maggiore, Giuseppe (ed.), *G. F. W. Hegel: Filosofia del diritto*. Excerpts and commentary. Florence: Vallecchi, 1926.

SAVIGNY VON, Friedrich Karl (1779-1861): considers law as spontanious development of subconscious forces.

——, *Of the Vocation of Our Age for Legislation and Jurisprudence.* Translated from the German by Abraham HAYWARD. London: Littlewood and Co., 1831. Pp. 192.

> GRAY, John Ch., *The Nature and the Sources of the Law.* 2nd ed. New York: The Macmillan Co., 1921. Pp. XVIII, 348. See Empiricism, above, p. 133.

CROCE, B., — see Contemporary Idealistic School, below, p. 141.

NIETZSCHE, F. W. (1844-1900), — see Superman-Ethics, above, Ch. I, 2, p. 29.

(ee) POSITIVISM: legal generalizations are tentative, but legal particular facts can be known with some certainty due to experience of their utility; thus the rules posited by the state are legal rules alone.

See also Neo-Postivism, below, p. 149.

England, France, Italy.

AUSTIN, John, — see Empiricism, above, p. 135.

BECCARIA, Cesare (1738-1794).
——, *Opere diverse.* 2 vols, Naples: G. Gravier, 1770.
——, *An Essay on Crimes and Punishments.* Translated from the Italian, with commentary attributed to Msgr. DE VOLTAIRE. Philadelphia: Bell, 1778. Pp. 352.

COMTE, August (1798-1857), — see Politics, below, Ch. IV, 3, p. 189.
——, *Cours de philosophie positive.* 6 vols. Paris: Rouen frères, 1830-1842.
——, *Système de politique positive.* 4 vols. Paris: L. Mathias, 1851-1854.

> CAIRNS, Huntington, «Comte», in his *Legal Philosophy from Plato to Hegel* (Baltimore: The Johns Hopkins Press, 1949).

> MILL, John Stuart, *Auguste Comte and Positivism.* 3rd ed. London: Trübner and Co., 1882. Pp. 200.

HUME, David, — see Empiricism, p. 135.
MILL, John Stuart (1806-1873), — see Politics, below, Ch. IV, 3, p. 196.
Freedom, below, Ch. I, 3, p. 60.
——, *Thoughts on Parliamentary Reform.* 2nd. ed. London: J. W. Parker and Son, 1859. Pp. 58.
——, *On Liberty.* New York: The Bobbs-Merrill Co., 1956. Pp. XXVIII, 141. First published in 1859.
——, *Speech on the Admission of Women to the Electoral Franchise,* May 20, 1867. London: Trübner and Co., 1867. Pp. 18.

——, *The Subjection of Women*. London: Longmans, Green, Reader, and Dyer, 1869. Pp. 188.

——, *Speech in Favour of Women's Suffrage*, January 12, 1871. Edinburgh, 1873.

——, *Dissertations and Discussions: Political, Philosophical, Historical*. 4 vols. Boston: W. V. Spencer, 1865-1868.

——, *Chapters and Speeches on the Irish Land Question*. London: Longmans, Green, Reader and Dyer, 1870. Pp. 125.

HOLYOAKE, George Jacob, *A New Defence of the Ballot in Consequence of Mr. Mill's Objections to it*. London: Book Store, 1868. Pp. 8.

WHITE, Carlos, *Ecce Femina: An Attempt to Solve the Women Question, Being an Examination of Arguments in Favor of Female Suffrage by John Stuart Mill and Others*. Boston, Massachusetts: Ice and Shepard, 1870. Pp. 258.

RESCHER, Nicholas, — see Justice, below, p. 161.

JACOBS, Herbert, *Rechtsphilosophie und politische Philosophie bei John Stuart Mill*. Bonn: Bouvier, 1965.

Germany

BINDING, Karl (1841-1920): considers law as the classification of legal volition which is a source of law.

——, *Die Normen und ihre Übertretung*. 4 vols. Leipzig: F. Meiner, 1914-1919.

JHERING VON, Rudolf (1818-1892): considers law as a sum of the constraining precepts in the state.

——, *Law as a Means*. 2 vols. translated from the German by I. HUSIK. Boston: The Boston Book Co., 1913. See Philosophy, above, p. 120.

Marxism, — see below, Contemporary, p. 144.

CONTEMPORARY

See Modern, above.

(a) Comprehensive Studies

CAIRNS, Huntington, «Jurisprudence as Philosophy», in his *Legal Philosophy from Plato to Hegel* (Baltimore: The Johns Hopkins Press, 1947), pp. 551-567.

POUND, Roscoe, «Twentieth Century Ideas as to the End of Law», *Harvard Legal Essays* (Cambridge, Massachusetts), 1934.

SAYRE, Paul (ed.), *Interpretations of Modern Legal Philosophies*. New York: Oxford University Press, 1947. Pp. IX, 807. See Modern, above.

ALLOGIO, S., *Le nuove teorie del diritto*. Milan: Albrighi e Segati, 1925. Pp. 280.

DIEZ ALEGRIA, José Maria, *Etica, derecho e historia: el tema ius naturalista en la problematica contemporanea*. 2nd ed. Madrid: Razón y Fe, 1963. Pp. 225.

LARENZ, Karel, *La filosofia contemporánea del derecho y del Estado*. Translation by E. GALÁN Y GUTIÉRREZ and A. TRUYOL SERRA. Madrid: Imp. de Galo Saez, 1942. Pp. 232.

POPOFF, Peter, «Uber das Wesen und die Besonderheiten des modernen Rechtsnormativismus», *Deutsche Zeitschrift für Philosophie* (Berlin), 1962, pp. 140-1414.

RECASÉNS SICHES, Luis, *Direcciones contemporaneas del pensamiento juridico*. Barcellona: Editorial Labor, 1929. Pp. 238.

——, *Los temas de la filosofia del derecho*. Barchellona, 1934.

——, *La filosofia del derecho en el siglo XX*. Mexico, 1944.

TOBEÑAS, J. C., Prospettivi filosofiche giuridiche del pensiero contemporaneo», *Jus*, 1959, pp. 445-450.

(b) Specific Studies

(aa) IDEALISTIC SCHOOL: law is only explicable through its evolution, or social processes.

See Modern, above, p. 136.

CAPPOZZI, Gino, *La mediazione come divenire e come relazione: Etica e diritto nella problematica dell' immanentismo*. Naples: E. Jovene, 1961. Pp. XV, 348.

LAZZARO, Giorgio, «Sul diritto come forma», *Rivista internazionale di filosofia del diritto* (Geneva), 1962, pp. 636-655.

MAGGIORE, Giuseppe, *Il diritto e il suo processo ideale*. Palermo: Diorenza, 1916. Pp. VIII, 140.

——, *L'interpretazione delle leggi come atto creativo*. Palermo: Ergon, 1914. Pp. 28.

——, *L'unità del mondo nel sistema del pensiero*. Palermo: Fiorenza, 1914. Pp. 282.

——, *Saggi di filosofia giuridica*. Palermo: Fiorenza, 1914. Pp. 100.

Representatives

CROCE, Benedetto (1866-1952), «Riduzione della filosofia del diritto alla filosofia dell' economia», *Atti di Accademia Pontaniana*, 1907. Also in CROCE's *Filosofia della pratica*. Bari: Laterza, 1909.

——, «La filosofia del diritto nella facoltà di giurisprudenza», *Critica* (Bari), No. 2, 1907.

——, «Obiezioni alla mia tesi sulla natura del diritto», *Critica* (Bari), No. 2, 1908.

——, *Filosofia della pratica, economia ed etica*. 4th ed. Bari: Laterza, 1932. First published in 1909. Pp. XIX, 415.

——, «Intorno alla mia teoria del diritto», *Critica* (Bari), No. 6, 1914.

——, «A proposito del diritto internazionale», *Critica* (Bari), No. 4, 1916.
——, «Filosofia e storia del diritto», *Critica* (Bari), No. 1, 1918.

Ascoli, M., *Intorno alla concezione del diritto nel sistema di Benedetto Croce*. Rome: Treves, 1925.

Chiaramonte, N., «Il problema della filosofia del diritto in Benedetto Croce», *Rivista di filosofia mazziniana*, 1928.
Poggi, A., «Sulla teoria giuridica di B. Croce», *Archivio di storia della filosofia*, No. 1, 1932.

Treves, R., *Benedetto Croce y el problema filosofico del derecho*. Buenos Aires, 1942.

Del Vecchio, Giorgio (1878-   ), *I presupposti filosofici della nozione del diritto*. Bologne: Zanichelli, 1905.
——, *Il concetto del diritto*. Bologne: Zanichelli, 1906. Pp. 150.
——, *Il concetto della natura e il principio del diritto*. Turin: Bocca, 1908. English translation by J. Lisle, *The Formal Basis of Law*. New York: The Macmillan Co., 1921.
——, *Sui caratteri fondamentali della filosofia politica del Rousseau*. 3rd ed. Geneve: Carlivi, 1912. Pp. 15.
——, «Sui principi generali del diritto», *Archivio giuridico* (Bologne), 1921.
——, *Lezioni di filosofia del diritto*. 4th ed. Milan: Giuffrè, 1948. 3rd ed. published in 1936. Pp. VIII, 399.
——, «Diritto ed etica», *Atti IX Congresso nazionale di filosofia, Padova, 1934*. Padua: Cedam, 1935.
——, *Justice, droit, état, études de philosophie juridique*. Paris: Librairie du Recueil Sirey, 1938.

Studi filosofico-giuridici dedicati a Giorgio Del Vecchio. 2 vols. Modena: Società tipografica Modenese, 1930-1931.

Gentile, G. (1875-1944), — see Fascism, below, Ch. IV, 5, p. 219.
——, *La riforma della dialettica hegeliana, ed altri scritti*. 2nd ed. Messina: Principato, 1923. Pp. VI, 279.
——, «Riforme costituzionali e fascismo», in his *Che cosa é il fascismo?* Florence: Vallecchi, 1925. Pp. 262.
——, «Fascismo e idealismo», *Educazione fascista*, No. 10, 1926.
——, *Fascismo e cultura*. Milan: Treves, 1928. Pp. 205.
——, *Origin e dottrina del fascismo*. 3rd ed. Rome: Fascista di Cultura, 1934. Pp. 107. First published in 1929.
——, «La filosofia e il codice penale», *Critica* (Bari), No. 2, 1907.

Di Carlo, Eugenio, «I principi fondamentali della filosofia del diritto secondo il profesore Gentile», *Circolo Giuridico*, 1920.

——, «Il principio della derivazione dei diritti nel pensiero del Rosmini, del Petrone e del Gentile», *Il circolo Giuridico L. Sampolo*. (Palermo: Università de Palermo, 1956), pp. 9-54.

Maggiore, Giuseppe, «Il problema del diritto nel pensiero di Giovanni Gentile», *Giornale critico della filosofia italiana* (Florence), Nos. 1-2, 1947.

KÖHLER, Joseph (1849-1919), *Philosophy of Law*. Translated from the German by Adalbert ALBRECHT. New York: The Macmillan Co., 1914. Pp. 340.

LASSON, Georg (ed.), *Hegel. Eigenhändige Randbemerkungen zu seiner Philosophie*. Leipzig: F. Meiner, 1930. Pp. VII, 124.

«Zum 70. Geburtstag Georg Lassons», *Kantstudien*, 1932.

PARESCE, Enrico, *La genesi ideale del diritto: saggio sulla attuazione spontanea del diritto e la sua creatività*. Milan: Giuffré, 1938. Pp. 161.

——, *La problematica storica della filosofia del diritto*. Messina: Ferrara, 1949.

RAVÀ, Adolfo (1879-1957), *Introduzione alla filosofia del diritto*. Rome: Athenaeum, 1919. Pp. 44.

——, «Diritto, Stato ed etica», *Atti di IX Congresso nazionale di Filosofia* (Padua: Cedam), 1934.

——, *Breve storia della filosofia del diritto*. Padua: Cedam, 1949.

(bb) PHENOMENOLOGICAL SCHOOL OR INTUITIONISM: law is grasped immediately in our conscience with its real and sociological aspects.

COSSIO, Carlos, «Phenomenology of the Judgment: An Introduction to the Egological Theory of Law». Translated by Richard W. TYLER, in Paul SAYRE (ed.), *Interpretations of Modern Legal Philosophies* (New York: Oxford University Press, 1947), pp. 85-129. See also General Theory of Law, below, p. 148.

AMSELEK, Paul, *Méthode phénoménologique et théorie du droit*. Paris: Librairie générale de droit et de jurisprudence. 1964. Pp. 55.

BOBBIO, N., «Aspetti odierni della filosofia giuridica in Germania», *Rivista internazionale di filosofia del diritto* (Milan), Nos. 4-5, 1934.

Representatives

BOBBIO, Norberto, *L'indirizzo fenomenologico della filosofia sociale e giuridica*. Turin: Istituto giuridico, 1934. Pp. 157.

——, *Scienza e tecnica del diritto*. Turin: Istituto giuridico della R. Università, 1934. Pp. 51.

——, *L'analogia nella logica del diritto*. Turin: Istituto giuridico, 1938. Pp. 216.

——, «L'interpretazione delle leggi e la ragion di Stato», in *Scritti giuridici in onore di Santi Romano*. Padua: Cedam, 1939.

——, *Lezioni di filosofia del diritto*. Turin: Giappichelli, 1945.

——, *Introduzione alla filosofia del diritto*. Turin: Giappichelli, 1948.

HUSSERL, Edmund G. A. (1859-1938), *Ideen zu einer reinen Phänomenologie und phänomenologischen Philosophie*. 2 parts .Halle: M. Niemeyer, 1922. English translation by W. R. Boyce GIBSON, *Ideas: General Introduction to Pure Phenomenology*. New York: The Macmillan Co., 1931. Pp. 465.

——, *Logische Untersuchungen.* 2nd ed. 2 vols. Halle: M. Niemeyer, 1913-1921.

Bobbio, N., «La filosofia di Husserl e la tendenza fenomenologica», *Rivista di filosofia* (Turin), No. 1, 1935.

Pedroli, Guido, *La fenomenologia di Husserl.* Turin: Taylor, 1958. Pp. 210.

Kaufmann, Arthur, — see General Theory of Law, below, 158.

Reinach, Adolf (1883-1918). *Die apriorischen Grundlagen des bürgerlichen Rechts.* 2nd ed. Halle: M. Niemeyer, 1922. Pp. 847.

Scheler, Max F., (1874-1928), *Abhandlungen und Aufsätze.* 2 vols. Leipzig: Der Neue Geist Verlag, 1915.

——, *Schriften zur Soziologie und Weltanschauungslehre.* Leipzig: Der Neue Geist Verlag, 1923. Pp. XI, 176.

——, *Der Formalismus in der Ethik und die Materiale Wertethik. Neuer Versuch der Grundlegung eines ethischen Personalismus.* 2nd ed. Halle: M. Niemeyer, 1927. Pp. XXVI, 648. See also Value, above, Chapter I, 3.

Koehle, Eckhard J., *Personality: A Study according to the Philosophies of Value and Spirit of M. Scheler and N. Hartmann.* Newton, New Jersey: Benedictine Monastery, 1941. Pp. XII, 231.

Bobbio, N., «La fenomenologia secondo Max Scheler», *Rivista di filosofia* (Turin), No. 3, 1936.

——, «La personalità di Max Scheler», *Rivista di filosofia* (Turin), No. 2, 1948.

Pedroli, Guido, *Max Scheler della fenomenologia alla sociologia.* Turin: Edizioni di Filosofia, 1952. Pp. VI, 132.

(cc) Marxism: law evolves on the basis of economical struggle; thus the will of the class, if elevated to a statute, becomes a law.

Vychinsky, A. Y., *The Law of the Soviet State.* Translated by Hugh Babb. New York: The Macmillan Co., 1948. Pp. 749.

Cerroni, Umberto, «La critica di Marx alla filosofia hegeliana del diritto pubblico», *Rivista internazionale di filosofia del diritto* (Milan), 1961, pp. 281-308.

Ferandez Cuesta, R., «Marxismo y derecho», *Revista de estudios politicos,* 1960, pp. 5-30.

Renner, Karl, *Marxismus, Krieg und Internationale.* 2nd ed. Stuttgart: J. H. W. Dietz, 1918. Pp. VIII, 387.

——, *Die Rechtsinstitute des Privatrechts und ihre soziale Funktion.* Tübingen: Mohr, 1929. Pp. XII, 181.

Stoyanovitch, K., *Marxisme et droit.* Paris: Librairie generale de droit et jurisprudence, 1964. Pp. 50.

Vincent, Jean Marie, «Vers une théorie marxiste du droit moderne», *Les Temps Modernes* (Paris), 1964, Pp. 219-220, 552-576.

Representatives

See above, pp. 38, 95, below, 205.

Marx, Karl and Engels, Friedrich, *The Communist Manifesto*. Translated by Eden and Cedar Paul. New York: International Publishers, 1930. Pp. XI, 365.

(dd) Pragmatism: law is a part of society; it rests on psychological concepts of interests and social notions of «drives»; hence, no legal autonomy.

See Philosophical Systems in *PQS*, No. 5.

Allen, Carleton Kemp, «Justice and Expediency», in Paul Sayre (ed.), *Interpretations of Modern Legal Philosophies* (New York: Oxford University Press, 1947), pp. 15-28.

Cowan, Thomas A., «Legal Pragmatism and Beyond», in Paul Sayre (ed.), *Interpretations of Modern Legal Philosophies* (New York: Oxford University Press, 1947), pp. 130-142.

Representatives

Dewey, John (1859-1952), «Nature and Reason in Law», *International Journal of Ethics*, October 1914, pp. 25-32.

——, «Force, Violence, and Law», *New Republic* (Washington, D. C.), January 22, 1916, pp. 295-297. Reprinted in his *Characters and Events*, ed. by Joseph Ratner (New York: Henry Holt and Co., 1929), pp. 636-641.

——, «War and a Code of Law», *New Republic* (Washington, D. C.), October 24, 1923, pp. 224-226. See also War, above, p. 68.

——, «Logical Method and Law», *Philosophical Review* (Cornell University, New York), November, 1924, pp. 560-572.

——, «The Historic Background of Corporate Legal Personality», *Yale Law Journal* (New Haven, Connecticut), April, 1926, pp. 655-673.

——, *Character and Events: Popular Essays in Social and Political Philosophy.* Ed. by Joseph Ratner. 2 vols. New York: Henry Holt and Co., 1929. Contains also essays on law.

——, «Justice Holmes and the Liberal Mind», in *Mr. Justice Holmes*, ed. by Felix Frankfurter (New York: Coward McCann, 1931).

——, «Letter on Suggestion that People Should Vote for Man rather than for Party», *New York Times* (New York), February 15, 1931, p. 2.

——, *Are Sanctions Necessary to International Organizations?* Yes, *Raymond Leslie Buell*; No, *John Dewey*. New York: Foreign Policy Association, 1932. Pp. 39.

——, «To Replace Judge Cardozo», *New Republic* (Washington, D. C.), March 9, 1932, pp. 3-4, 15.

——, «Prospects for a Third Party», *New Republic* (Washington, D. C.), July 27, 1932, pp. 278-280.

——, *New York and the Seabury Investigation.* New York: The City Affairs Committee of New York, 1933. Pp. 48.

——, «Letter to Roosevelt on Unemployment Problem», *New York Times* (New York), June 11, 1934, pp. 2.

——, «Toward Administrative Statesmanship», *Social Frontier*, February 1935, No. 6.

——, *Not Guilty: Report of the Commission of Inquiry into the Charges Made Against Leon Trotsky in the Moscow Trials.* New York: Harpers, 1937. Pp. 422.

——, *German Philosophy and Politics.* Revised edition. New York: G. P. Putnam's Sons, 1942. First published in 1915. Pp. 134.

——, The Public and Its Problems. 2nd ed. Chicago: Gateway Books, 1946. Pp. XII, 224. First published in 1927.

TEBALDESCHI, Ivanhoe, *Socialità e diritto nel pensiero di John Dewey.* Rome: Arte e storia, 1957. Pp. 77.

TOZZI, Antonio, «Intorno ad alcune considerazioni di J. Dewey sul diritto naturale», *Rivista internazionale di filosofia del diritto* (Milan), 1962, pp. 205-209.

HOLMES, Oliver Wendell, Jr. (1841-1935), *The Common Law.* 32nd ed. Boston: Little, Brown and Co., 1938. Pp. XVI, 422. First published in 1881.

——, «The Path of the Law», in *The American Pragmatists: Selected Writings,* ed. by Milton R. KONVITZ and Gail KENNEDY (New York: Meridian Books, Inc., 1960), pp. 144-166. Originally an address first published in *Harvard Law Review,* 1896, pp. 451-418.

——, *Law in Science and Science in Law.* Boston, 1899. A paper read before the New York State Bar Association, January 17, 1899.

——, *Speeches.* Boston: Little, Brown and Co., 1918. Pp. VI, 103.

——, *Collected Legal Papers.* New York: Harcourt, Brace and Co., 1920. Pp. 316.

——, *The Dissenting Opinions.* New York: The Vanguard Press, 1929. Pp. XVIII, 314.

——, *Representative Opinions of Mr. Justice Holmes.* Ed. by Alfred LIEF. New York: The Vanguard Press, 1931. Pp. XXII, 319.

——, *The Judical Opinions of Oliver Wendell Holmes.* Selected excerpts, 1883-1902. Ed. by Harry C. SCHRIVER. Buffalo, New York: Dennis and Co., 1940. Pp. XVI, 360.

——, *Holmes-Pollock Letters.* The correspondence, 1874-1932. Ed. by Mark DE WOLFE HOWE. 2 vols. Cambridge, Massachusetts: Harvard University Press, 1941.

FRANKFURTER, Felix, *Mr. Justice Holmes and the Supreme Court.* 4th printing. Cambridge, Massachusetts: Harvard University Press, 1938. Pp. 139. 2nd ed., 1961, pp. 112.

RICHARDSON, Dorsey, *Constitutional Doctrines of Justice Oliver Wendell Holmes.* Baltimore: John Hopkins University Press, 1924. Pp. 105.

WIENER, Philip P., «Evolutionary Pragmatism in Holme's Theory of Law», in his *Evolution and the Founders of Pragmatism* (New York: Harper, 1965), pp. XII, 288.

JAMES, William (1842-1910), *The Will to Believe, and Other Essays in Popular Philosophy*. New edition. New York: Longmans, Green and Co., 1937. First published in 1897. Pp. XVII, 332. See Ethics, above, Chapter I, 2, p. 40.

PEIRCE, Charles S. (1839-1914), *The Philosophy of Peirce: Selected Writings*. Ed. by Justus BUCHLER. London: Kegan Paul and Co., 1940. Pp. XVI, 386.

——, *Chance, Love and Logic: Philosophical Essays*. Ed. by Morris R. Cohen. London: Kegan Paul and Co., 1923. Pp. XXXIII, 318.

HASS, William Paul, O. P., *The Conception of Law and the Unity of Peirce's Philosophy*. Fribourg, Switzerland: The University Press, 1964. Pp. XII, 144.

POUND, Roscoe (1870-1964), «Mechanical Jurisprudence», *Columbia Law Review*, 1908, pp. 605-610.

——, «A Theory of Social Interests», *Papers and Proceedings of the American Sociological Society*, 1921, pp. 16-45.

——, *An Introduction to the Philosophy of Law*. New Haven: Yale University Press, 1922. Pp. 307.

——, *Law and Morals*. 2nd ed. London: H. Milford, 1926. Pp. 144. First published in 1924.

——, *The Spirit of the Common Law*. Boston: Marshall Jones Co., 1931. Pp. XV, 224. First published in 1921.

——, *Interpretations of Legal History*. Cambridge, Massachusetts: The University Press, 1923. Pp. XVII, 171. See also Histories, above, p. 116.

——, *Contemporary Juristic Theory*. Claremont, California: Pomona College, 1940. Pp. VIII, 83.

——, *Social Control through Law*. New Haven, Connecticut: Yale University Press, 1942. Pp. 138.

——, *Administrative Law: Its Growth, Procedure and Significance*. Pittsburgh: University of Pittsburgh Press, 1942. Pp. 138.

SETARO, Franklyn Christopher, *A Bibliography of the Writings of Roscoe Pound*. Cambridge, Massachusetts: Harvard University Press, 1942. Pp. VI, 193.

PATTERSON, Edwin W., «Pound's Theory of Social Interests», in Paul SAYRE, *Interpretations of Modern Legal Philosophies* (New York: Oxford University Press, 1947), pp. 558-573.

REHBINDER, Manfred, «Roscoe Pound (1870-1964)», *Juristenzeitung*, 1965, pp. 482-484.

(ee) SOCIOLOGICAL SCHOOL: law originates from positive, social facts.

CAIRNS, Huntington, *Law and the Social Sciences*. New York: Harcourt, Brace and Co., 1935. Pp. XIV, 279.

COHEN, Morris Raphael, *Law and the Social Order: Essays in Legal Philo-sophy*. New York: Harcourt, Brace and Co., 1933. Pp. XII, 403.

EHRLICH, Eugen (1862-1922), *Fundamental Principles of the Sociology of Law*. Translated by Walter L. MOLL. Cambridge, Massachusetts: Harvard University Press, 1936. Pp. XXXVI, 541.

HECK VON, Philipp, *Begriffs-bildung und Interessenjurisprudenz*. Tübingen: Mohr, 1932. Pp. VIII, 228.

LLEWELLYN, Karl N. (1893-1962) *The Cheyenne Way: Conflict and Case Law in Primitive Jurisprudence*. Norman: University of Oklahoma Press, 1941. Pp. 360.

——, *A Realistic Jurisprudence*. New York: Columbia Law Review 1930 Reprint for Columbia Law Review, April 1930.

POUND, Roscoe, *Social Control Through Law*. New Haven, Connecticut: Yale University Press, 1942. Pp. 138. See Pragmatism, above.

TIMASHEFF, Nicolas S., *An Introduction to the Sociology of Law*. Cambridge, Massachusetts: Harvard University Press, 1939. Pp. XIV, 418.

DURKHEIM, Emile, *Leçons de sociologie: physique des mœurs et du droit*. Paris: Presses Universitaires de France, 1953. Pp. XLVIII, 264.

(ff) NATURAL LAW THEORIES: laws are founded on natural law. See below, p. 164.

The Natural Law Forum. Notre Dame: Indiana: Notre Dame Law School, 1956—.

(gg) REALISTIC SCHOOLS: legal phenomena must be understood in empirical terms, and based on social facts rather than on legal concepts, since laws are an instrument of government.

ROGAT, Yosal, «Legal Realism», *The Encyclopedia of Philosophy* (8 vols. New York: The Macmillan Co., 1967), Vol. IV, pp. 420-421.

TARELLO, Giovanni, *Il realismo giuridico americano*. Milan: Giuffrè, 1962. Pp. X, 254.

Representatives

BINGHAM, Joseph Walter (1878-   ), «What Is the Law ?», *Michigan Law Review*, 1912, pp. 1-25, 109-121.

FRANK, Jerome (1889-1957), *Law and the Modern Mind*. 2nd ed. New York: Coward-McCann, 1942. Pp. XXXI, 368. First published in 1930.

——, *Courts on Trial: Myth and Reality in American Justice*. Princeton, New Jersey: Princeton University Press, 1949. Pp. XII, 441.

FULLER, Lon Luvois, *Law in Quest of Itself*. Chicago: Foundation Press, 1940. Pp. VII, 147.

——, *The Morality of Law*. New Haven, Connecticut Yale University, School of Law, 1964. Pp. 202.

——, «American Legal Realism», *University of Pennsylvania Law Review*, 1934, pp. 429-462.

GRANT, Gilmore, «Legal Realism: Its Cause and Cure», *Yale Law Journal,* 1961, pp. 1037-1048.

GRAY, John Chipman, *The Nature and Sources of Law.* 2nd ed. New York: The Macmillan Co., 1927. Pp. XVIII, 348. First published in 1909.

HART, Herbert Lionel Adolphus, *Concept of Law.* New York: Oxford University Press, 1961. Pp. 263.

HÄGERSTRÖM, Axel A. T. (1868-1939), *Inquiries into the Nature of Law and Morals.* Translated by C. D. BROAD. Copenhagen, Denmark: Munksgaard, 1953. Pp. 377.

JHERING VON, Rudolf, — see Philosophy, above 2, c, p. 120.

LLEWELLYN, Karl Nickerson, *Jurisprudence: Realism in Theory and Practice.* Chicago: University of Chicago Press, 1962. Pp. 531.

LUNDSTEDT, Anders V. Chelm, *Legal Thinking Revised.* Stockholm: Almqvist, 1956. Pp. 420.

OLIVECRONA, Karl, *Law as Fact.* Copenhagen, Denmark: Munksgaard, 1939. Pp. 220.

ROSS, Alf., *On Law and Justice.* Translated by Margaret DUTTON. Barcley California: University of California Press, 1959. Pp. 383.

STONE, Julius, *The Province and Function of Law: Law as Logic, Justice, and Social Control: A Study in Jurisprudence.* Cambridge, Massachusetts: Harvard University Press, 1950. Pp. LXIV, 918.

Marxism, — see above, p. 144.

Pragmatism, — see above, p. 145.

Sociological School, — see above, p. 147.

Neopositivism, — see below.

School of Vienna, — see below.

Neo-positivistic School: no way to verify the truth or falsity of a proposition that law is right by nature and not by conviction.

See Realistic School, above; School of Vienna, below; Positivism, above, p. 139.

AUSTIN, John, — see Empiricism, above, p. 134.

AYER, Alfred Jules, *Language, Truth and Logic.* 2nd ed. London: Victor Gallancz, 1946. Pp. 160. First published in 1936.

FEINBERG, Joel, «Analytic Jurisprudence», in *The Encyclopedia of Philosophy* (8 vols. New York: The Macmillan Co., 1967), Vol. I, pp. 109-111.

HART, H. L. A., «Legal Positivism», *The Encyclopedia of Philosophy* (8 vols. New York: The Macmillan Co., 1967), Vol. IV, pp. 418-420.

SUMMERS, Robert S., «'Is' and 'Ought' in Legal Philosophy», *Philosophical Quarterly* (Dundee, Scotland), 1963, pp. 157-161.

SHUMAN, Samuel I., *Legal Positivism: Its Scope and Limitations.* Detroit: Wayne State University Press, 1963. Pp. 265.

Bobbio, Norberto, «Ancora sul positivismo giuridico», *Rivista di Filosofia* (Turin), 1962, pp. 335-345.
——, *Il positivismo giuridico*. Turin: Cooperativa Libraria universitaria torinese, 1965. Pp. 377.
Husson, Léon, «L'expérience dans les sciences humaines, Droit», in *L'Expérience* (Paris: Albin Michel, 1964), pp. 221-244.
Kalinowski, Georges, *Introduction à la logique juridique: éléments de sémantique juridique, logique des normes et logique juridique*. Paris: Pichon, 1965. Pp. 188.
Kelsen, Hans, «Was ist juristischer Positivismus ?», *Juristenzeitung*, 1965, pp. 465-469.
Tarello, Giovanni, *Il realismo giuridico americano*. Milan: Giuffrè, 1962. Pp. X, 254.

School of Vienna: maintains, among others, dualism between Being (*Sein*) and ought to be (*Sollen*) and endeavors to apply the method free from political and axiological influences. The School is influenced by Kant and Phenomenology.

See also Neo-positivistic School, above.

Engisch, Karl, *Logische Studien zur Gesetzeanwendung*. Heidelberg: C. Winter, 1963. Pp. 126.
Kelsen, Hans, — see General Theory of Law, below, p. 159.

Bustamante y Montoro, A. S., «Kelsenism», in Paul Sayre (ed.), *Interpretations of Modern Legal Philosophies* (New York: Oxford University Press, 1947), pp. 43-51.

Simitis, Spiros, «*Zum Problem einer juristischen Logik*», *Ratio* (Oxford, England), 1960, pp. 52-82.

(hh) Relativism: law has relation to the values which man tries to realize, but there appear antinomies among the values, which lead toward relativism.

Radbruch, Gustav (1878-1949), *Vorschule der Rechtsphilosophie*. Ed. by A. Kaufmann. 3nd. ed. Göttingen: Vandenhoeck und Ruprecht, 1965. See above, p. 121.

Marxism, — see above, p. 144.

Pragmatism, — see above, p. 145.

4. PARTICULAR COUNTRIES

EAST

See Ancient Period, above, p. 122; Islam, below; in *PQS.* No. 5.

Assyria-Babylon

DELAPORT, Louis Joseph, *La Mesopotamie: les civilisations babylonienne et assyrienne.* Paris: Renaissance du livre, 1923. English translation by V. Gordon CHILDE, *Mesopotamia: The Babylonian and Assyrian Civilization.* New York: A. A. Knopf, 1925. Pp. XVI, 371.

WIGMORE, John Henry, *A Panorama of the World's Legal System.* Washington, D. C.: Washington Law Book Company, 1936. Pp. XXIII, 1206. See above, p. 118.

China

See Dialectical Materialism, above, Ch. I, p. 38.

CHANG, Ch'ung-en, *Anglo-Chinese Law Dictionary.* 2 vols. Tientsin, 1936.

DEWEY, John, — see Politics, below, Ch. IV, 3, p. 209.

——, «China and Disarmament», *Chinese Students' Monthly,* November, 1921, pp. 16-17.

——, «Shrewd Tactics are Shown in Chinese Plea», *Baltimore Sun,* November 23, 1921.

——, «Four Principles for China Regarded as but Framework», *Baltimore Sun,* November 23, 1921.

RIASANOVSKY, Valentin A., *Fundamental Institutions of Chinese Civil Law.* Translated from the Russian by M. N. LOOTSKY. Tientsin, 1938. Pp. 310.

——, *The Modern Civil Law of China.* 2 vols. Harbin: Zaria, 1927-1928.

India

MAYNE, John Dawson, *The Criminal Law of India.* 4th revised edition by S. SWAMINADHAM. Madras: Higginbothams, 1914. Pp. CXXX, 296, 1089.

——, *A Treatise on Hindu Law and Usage.* 10th ed. Madras: Higginbotham, 1922. Pp. LXXX, 1057.

MULLA, Dinshah Fardunji, *Principles of Hindu Law.* 9th ed. Calcutta: The Eastern Law House, 1940. Pp. LIX, 731.

Islam

MANSOOR, M., *Legal and Documentary Arabic Reader with Explanatory Notes, Exercises, Vocabularies and Model Answers.* 2 vols. Leiden, Holland: E. J. Brill, 1965.

MULLA, Dinshah F., *Principles of Mahomedan Law.* 11th ed. Calcutta: The Eastern Law House, 1938. Pp. XXVII, 280.

Japan

BECKER DE, Joseph Ernest, *The Principles and Practice of the Civil Code of Japan: A Complete Theoretical and Practical Exposition of the Motifs of the Japanese Civil Code.* London: Butterworth and Co., 1921. Pp. XXIX, 853.

SANSOM, George Bailly, *Japan: A Short Cultural History.* 4th impression. New York: D. Appleton-Century Company, 1938. Pp. XVI, 537.

WIGMORE, John Henry (ed.), *Materials for the Study of Private Law in Old Japan.* Tokyo: The Asiatic Society of Japan, 1892. See also Assyria, above.

MAGNINO, Leo, «Sulle moderne correnti filosofiche e giuridiche in Giappone», *Rivista internazionale di filosofia del diritto* (Milan), 1955, pp. 791-801.

Mongolia

RIAZANOVSKY, Valentin A., *Customary Law of the Mongol Tribes.* Harbin: Artistic Printing House, 1929. Pp. 306. Mongols, Buriats, Kalmucks.

——, *Fundamental Principles of Mongol Law.* London: K. Paul, Trench, Trubner and Co., 1937. Pp. 338.

WEST

America

POUND, Roscoe, *National Law Library.* 6 vols. New York: Collier, 1939. See below.

TREVES, Ranato, «Rassegna bibliografica della filosofia del diritto nell' America Latina, 1939-1948», *Rivista internazionale di filosofia del diritto* (Milan), Nos. 2-3, 1949.

COHEN, Morris Raphael, *A Critical Sketch of Legal Philosophy in America.* New York: New York University Press, 1937. Pp. 319.

DEWEY, John, «The Issues at Washington», *Baltimore Sun*, November 14-17, 1921. See also Pragmatism, above, p. 39.

——, «Shall we Join the League ?», *New Republic* (Washington, D. C.), March 7, 1923, pp. 36-37.

——, «Shall the United States Join the World Court ?», *Christian Century* (Chicago, Illinois), October 18, 1923, pp. 1329-1334.

Pound Roscoe, *Criminal Justice in America*. New York: H. Holt and Co., 1930. Pp. XIV, 226.

——, *The Formative Era of American Law*. Boston: Little, Brown and Company, 1938. Pp. See also Criminal Law, below, p. 14.

Kunz, Josef Laurenz, *La filosofia del derecho latino-americano en el siglo XX*. Translated by Luis Recaséns Siches. Buenos Aires: Losada, 1951. Pp. 228.

Stumpf, S. E., «L'élément nouveau dans la philosophie américaine du droit», in *La théologie chrétienne et le droit*. Paris: Sirey, 1960. Pp. VI, 250.

England

Laws, — see *British Museum Catalog:* «England, Laws», cf. above, p. VIII.

Barker, Ernest, *The Ideas and Ideals of the British Empire*. Cambridge: The University Press, 1941. Pp. VIII, 167.

Blackstone Sir, William, *Commentaries on the Laws of England*. Ed. by William Carey Jones. 2 vols. San Francisco, California: Bancroft-Whitney Co., 1916.

Cohen, Hermann J., *Spirit of Our Laws: British Justice at Work*. Ed. by A. F. G. Ransome. 3rd ed. London: Methuen, 1933. Pp. XV, 293.

Hale, Sir, Matthew, *An Analysis of the Law... of England*. 3rd ed. London: T. Waller, 1739. Pp. 148.

Holdsworth, William (ed.), *A History of English Law*. 12 vols. London: Methuen and Co., 1903-1938.

——, *Some Makers of English Law*. New York: The Macmillan Co., 1939. Pp. XI, 308.

Mullalla, James, *A Delineation of the British Constitution from the Origin to the Present Period*. 3 vols. Dublin: Printed for the Author, 1798-1801.

Pocock, John G. A., *The Ancient Constitution and the Feudal Law: A Study of English Historical Thought in the Seventeenth Century*. Cambridge: Cambridge University Press, 1957. Pp. 261.

Pollock Sir, Frederick, *The Law of Torts*. 15th ed. London: Stevens and Sons, 1951. Pp. XLV, 480. First published in 1887.

——, *The History of English Law before the Time of Edward I*. 2 vols. Cambridge, Massachusetts: The University Press, 1923. First published in 1895.

Ravà, Adolfo, *Storia delle dottrine politiche*. 2 vols. Padua: Università di Padova, 1932-1933. Vol. I: Le dottrine del secolo XVII in Inghilterra e in Ollanda. Vol. II: I monarchi.

France

Amos Sir, Maurice Sheldon, and Walton, Frederick Parker, *Introduction to French Law:* Oxford: The Clarendon Press, 1935. Pp. IX, 398.

Beauchet, Ludovic, *Histoire de l'organisation judiciaire en France, époque franque*. Paris: A. Rousseau, 1886. Pp. IV, 499.

FouILLÉE, Alfred J. E., SPENCER, A. W. *et al.* (ed.), *Modern French Legal Philosophy*. Translated by Franklin W. SCOTT and Joseph P. CHAMBERLAIN. New York: The Macmillan Co., 1921.

GLASSON, Ernest Désiré, *Histoire du droit et des institutions de la France*. 8 vols. Paris: F. Pichon, 1887-1903.

——, *Histoire du droit et des institutions politiques, civiles et judiciaires de l'Angleterre, comparés au droit et aux institutions de la France depuis leur origine jusqu'à nos jours*. 6 vols. Paris: G. Pédone-Lauriel, 1882-1883.

LAFERRIÈRE, Firmin J., *Essai sur l'histoire du droit français depuis les temps anciens jusqu'à nos jours*. 2 vols. New edition. Paris: Guillaumin, 1885.

Germany

BRUNNER, Heinrich, *Deutsche Rechtsgeschichte*. 2 vols. 2nd ed. Munich: Duncker und Humblot, 1906-1928.

——, *Grundzüge der deutschen Rechtsgeschichte*. 8th ed. Munich: Duncker und Humblot, 1928. Pp. XI, 348.

Deutsches Rechtswörterbuch. Ed. by the Preussische Akademie der Wissenschaften. 7 vols. Weimar: Böhlau, 1914-1931.

GIERKE von, Otto, *Das deutsche Genossenschaftsrecht*. 4 vols Berlin: Weidmann, 1868-1913. English partial translation by F. M. MAITLAND, *Political Theories of the Middle Ages*. Cambridge: Cambridge University Press, 1900. Also translation of other parts by Ernest BARKER, *Natural Law and the Theory of Society*. 2 vols. Cambridge: Cambridge University Press, 1934.

KELSENISM, — see above, p. 150.

KLECATSKY, Hans; MARCIC, René and SCHAMBECK, Herbert (eds.), *Die Wiener Rechtstheoretische Schule*. Vienna: Europa Verlag, 1968. Pp. XII, 1201. Works of Hans Kelsen, Adolf Merkl, Herbert Schambeck.

LEHR, Ernest, *Elements de droit civil germanique, considerés en eux-mêmes et dans leurs rapports avec la legislation française*. Paris: E. Plon, 1875. Pp. XX, 464.

LENZ, George (ed.), *Deutsches Staatsdenken im 18. Jahrhundert*. Neuwied, Rhein: Luchterhand, 1965.

SCHRÖDER, Richard, *Lehrbuch der deutschen Rechtsgeschichte*. Ed. by Eberhard von KÜNSSBERG. 7th ed. Berlin: De Gruyter, 1932. Pp. X, 1172.

Italy

BATTAGLIA, F., — see above, pp. 120, 137.

BOBBIO, Norberto, «La filosofia del diritto in Italia nella seconda metà del secolo XIX», *Bolletino dell'Istituto di filosofia del Diritto*. No. 3, 1942.

ORECCHIA, Rinaldo, *La filosofia del diritto nelle università italiane, 1900-1965*. Milan: A. Giuffrè, 1967. Pp. XLIII, 467.

Croce, B., — see above, p. 141.

Del Vecchio, — see above, p. 142.

Gentile, G., — see above, p. 142.

Poland

Encyklopedia prawa obowiazujacego w Polsce. Ed. by D. Peretiakowicz. Poznan: Fiszer & Majewski, 1923—.

Kock, Zdzislaw, *Skorowidz przepisow prawnych, ogtoszonych w Dzienniku Ustaw i Monitorze Polskim w latach 1918-1939 i 1944-1967*. Warsaw: Panstwowe Wydawsnictwo Prawnicze, 1968.

Kutrzeba, Stanislaus, *Historya ustroju Polski w zarysie*. 4 vols. Lwow: B. Poloniecki, 1908-1917. 6th ed. Warsaw, 1925.

——, *Polskie prawo polityczne wedlug traktatow*. 2 vols. Cracow: Gebethner & Wolff, 1923.

——, *Historya źródel dawnego prawa polskiego* [History of the Sources of Ancient Polish Law]. 2 vols. Lwow: B. Poloniecki, 1925-1926.

Maciejowski, Waclar Aleksander, *Historya prawodastw slowianskich*. 6 vols. 2nd ed. Warsaw: The Author, 1856-1865. Supplement in 1872. First published in 1833-1835. German translation by F. J. Buss and M. Nawrocki, *Slavische Rechtsgeschichte*. 4 vols. Stuttgart: Rieger, 1835-1839.

Waskiewicz, Hanna, «Die Rechtsphilosophie der polnischen Aufklärung», in *Atti del XII Congresso internazionale di Filosofia* (Venice, 12-18 September, 1958. Florence: Sansoni), Vol. XII, pp. 477-484.

Russia

See Dialectical Materialism, above, pp. 38, 95, 145.

Kovalevsky, Mausim M., *Modern Customs and Ancient Laws of Russia*. London: D. Nutt, 1891. Pp. X, 260.

Schlesinger, Rudolf, *Soviet Legal Theory: Its Social Background and Development*. New York: Humanities Press, 1951. Pp. 312.

Soviet Legal Philosophy. Translated by Hugh W. Bobb. Cambridge, Massachusetts: Harvard University Press, 1951. Pp. 465.

Stuchka, Petr Ivanovich, «The Revolutionary Part Played by Law and the State: A General Doctrine of Law», in *Soviet Legal Philosophy* (Cambridge, Massachusetts: Harvard, 1951), pp. 17-69. See above, and below.

Götz, Leopold Karl, *Das Russische Recht*. 4 vols. Stuttgart: F. Enke, 1910-1913.

Legaz y Lacambra, Luis, *El comunismo y el Derecho naturale*. La Coruna: Ediciones de la Delegacion Provincial de Education Popular, 1944. Pp. 14.

Lehr, Ernest, *Elements de droit civil russe*. 2 vols. Paris: E. Plon, 1877-1890. Russia, Poland, Baltic Provinces.

Sergeyevich, V. I., *Russkiya yuridicheskiya drevnosti* (Russian juridical antiquity), 3 vols. 2nd ed. St. Petersburg, 1900-1903.

Stoyanovich, K., *Marxisme et droit*. Paris: Pichon, 1964. Pp. 406.

——, *La philosophie du droit en U.R.S.S. (1917-1953)*. Paris: Pichon, 1965. Pp. 284.

Stucka, Pasukanis, Vysinsky-Strogovic, *Theorie sovietiche del diritto*. Ed. by Umberto Cerroni. Milan: Giuffrè, 1964. Pp. 320.

5. SPECIAL QUESTIONS

COMPARATIVE LAW

GUTTERIDGE, H. C., «The Province of Comparative Law», in Paul Sayre (ed.), *Interpretations of Modern Legal Philosophies* (New York: Oxford University Press, 1947), pp. 303-312.

BARBEY, Jean P., *Le conflit des lois en matière de contrats dans le droit des États-Unis d'Amérique et le droit anglais comparés au droit français*. Paris: Rousseau et Cie, 1938. Pp. 360.

——, *Le rôle du droit comparé dans le droit international privé*. Paris: Rousseau et Cie, 1937.

BODIN, Jean, — see Modern-Empiricism above, 3 Modern, p. 133.

LAMBERT, Edouard, *Études de droit commun législatif ou droit civil comparé*. Paris: V. Giard et E. Brière, 1903. Pp. XXIV, 427.

——, *L'enseignement du droit comparé: sa coopération au rapprochement entre la jurisprudence française et la jurisprudence anglo-américaine*. Lyon: A. Rey, 1919. Pp. 118.

——, *Le Congrès international de droit comparé de 1932: le travaux de la section générale, souvenirs d'un congressiste*. Lyon: A. Rey, 1934. Pp. 122.

MONTESQUIEU, Ch., — see above, 3 Modern, p. 136.

SARFATTI, Mario, *Introduzione allo studio del diritto comparato*. Turin: Giappichelli, 1933. Pp. 133.

SAUSER — HALL, Georges, *Fonction et méthode de droit comparé*. Geneva: A. Kündig, 1913. Pp. 113. Originally Inaugural Lecture at the University of Neuchâtel, October 23, 1912.

CONTRACTS

BARKER, Ernest (ed.), *Social Contract: Essays by Locke, Hume and Rousseau*. New York: Oxford University Press, 1947. Pp. LXIII, 440. See also Otto F. GIERKE, below, p. 164.

BUCKLAND, William Warwick and FINCH, Gerard Brown (eds.), *A Selection of Cases on the English Law of Contracts*. 2nd ed. by R. T. WRIGHT and W. W. BUCKLAND. Cambridge: University Press, 1896. Pp. XII, 867.

GOUGH, J. W., *The Social Contract: A Critical Study of Its Development*. Revised edition. New York: Oxford University Press, 1957. Pp. 259. First published in 1936.

LASLETT, Peter, «Social Contract», in *The Encyclopedia of Philosophy* (8 vols. New York: The Macmillan Co., 1967), Vol. VII, pp. 465-467.

POLLOCK Sir, Frederick, *The Principles of Contract*. 13th ed. Ed. by Percy H. WINFIELD. London: Stevens and Sons, 1950. Pp. XLIII, 610.

ROUSSEAU, Jean Jacques, — see below, pp. 194, 241.

WILLISTON, Samuel, *Treatise on the Law of Contracts*. Revised edition. 8 vols. New York: Baker, Voorhis and Co., 1936.

CRIMINAL LAW

See Responsibility. — see below.

BENTHAM, Jeremy, *The Rationale of Punishment.* London: Robert Heward, 1830. Pp. XV, 441.

——, *Rationale of Reward.* London: J. and H. L. Hunt, 1825. Pp. VIII, 352.

CALHOUN, George Miller, *The Growth of Criminal Law in Ancient Greece.* Berkeley, California: University of California Press, 1927. Pp. X, 149. See also Ancient Law, above, p. 124.

EDWARDS, James L.J., *Mens Rea in Statutory Offenses.* London: Macmillan Co., 1955. Pp. 298.

FEINBERG, Joel, «Problematic Responsability in Law and Morals», *Philosophical Review,* 1962, pp. 340-351.

HALL, Jerome, *Studies in Jurisprudence and Criminal Theory.* New York: Oceana Publications, 1958. Pp. 300.

——, *General Principles of Criminal Law.* New York: The Bobbs-Merrill Co., 1960. Pp. 642.

POUND, Roscoe, *Criminal Justice in America.* New York: H. Holt and Company, 1930. Pp. XIV, 194.

WARBURTON, Henry P. I., *A Selection of Leading Cases in the Criminal Law.* 6th ed. London: Stevens and Sons, 1932. Pp. XXVIII, 476. First published in 1892.

WILLIAMS, Gllanville L., *Criminal Law.* London: Stevens and Sons, 1953. Pp. XLIV, 736.

BARATTA, Alessandro, *Antinomie giuridiche e conflitti di coscienza, contributo alla filosofia e alla critica del diritto penale.* Milan: A. Giuffrè, 1961. Pp. 143.

FEUERBACH, Paul J. A., *Lehrbuch des gemeinen in Deutschland gültigen peinlichen Rechts.* 14th ed. Giessen: Heyer, 1847. Pp. XXXII, 878. First published in 1801.

——, *Über Philosophie und Empirie in ihrem Verhältnisse zur positiven Rechtswissenschaft.* Landshut: J. Attenkofer, 1804. Pp. 100.

KAUFMANN, Arthur, *Das Schuldprinzip. Eine strafechtlichrechtsphilosophische Untersuchung.* Heidelberg: Winter, 1961. Pp. 288.

KLEIN, Ritter E. F., *Grundsätze des gemeinen deutschen und preussischen peinlichen Rechts.* Halle. Schwetschke und Sohn, 1796.

MAGGIORE, Giuseppe, *L'unità delle scuole di diritto penale.* Palermo: Fiorenza, 1918. Pp. 62.

SEWING, Johannes, *Studien zur Todesstrafe im Naturrecht.* Bonn. Rohrscheid, 1966. Pp. 172.

DEFINITION OF LAW

See Philosophy, above, p. 118; Particular Periods, above, p. 122.

AUSTIN, John, *The Province of Jurisprudence Determined.* London: John Murray, 1832. Page. XX, 391, LXXVI.

BENTHAM, Jeremy, *The Limits of Jurisprudence Defined.* New York: Columbia University Press, 1945. Pg. XXII, 358.

——, *A Comment on the Commentaries*. Oxford: Clarendon Press, 1928. Pp. VII, 253.

GRAY, John Chipman, *The Nature and Sources of the Law*. 2nd ed. New York: The Macmillan Co., 1921. Pp. XVIII, 348. First published in 1904.

HART, Herbert Lionel Adolphus, *The Concept of Law*. Oxford: Clarendon Press, 1961. Pp. 263.

KANTOROWICZ, Hermann, *The Definition of Law*. Cambridge: University Press, 1958. Pp. 112.

KELSEN, Hans, *General Theory of Law and State*. Translated by Anders WEDBERG. Cambridge, Massachusetts: Harvard University Press, 1945. Pp. XXXIII, 516.

THOMAS, Aquinas, *Summa theologiae*, II/I, qq. 90-97. See above, p. 128.

WOLLHEIM, Richard, «The Nature of Law», *Political Studies*, 1954, pp. 128-142.

GENERAL THEORY OF LAW

Studies

FRIEDMAN, Wolfgang Gaston, *Legal Theory*. 4th ed. London: St. Martin's Press, 1960. Pp. XX, 564.

JONES, John Walter, *Historical Introduction to the Theory of Law*. New York: Oxford University Press, 1940. Pp. XI, 304.

——, *Nazi Conception of Law*. New York: Oxford University Press, 1939. Pp. 31.

KORKUNOV, Nikolai M., *General Theory of Law*. Translated by W. G. HASTINGS. 2nd ed. New York: The Macmillan Co., 1922. Pp. XXVIII, 524. First published in 1909.

BAGOLINI, Luigi, «Dommatica, teoria generale e filosofia del diritto», *Rivista internazionale di filosofia del diritto* (Geneva), 1963, pp. 3-24. See also following pages.

BUSTAMANTE Y MONTORO, Antonio S., *Teoria general del derecho*. 2nd ed. Havana: Editorial «Alfa», 1940. See School of Vienna, above, p. 150.

CARNELUTTI, Francesco, *Teoria generale del diritto*. 2nd ed. Rome: Società editrice del «Foro italiano», 1946. Pp. 480.

HAESAERT, J., *Théorie générale du droit*. Paris: Recueil Sirey, 1950. Pp. 501.

KAUFMANN, Arthur, *Die ontologische Begründung des Rechtes*. Darmstadt: Wissenschaftliche Buchgesellschaft, 1965. Pp. 742.

LEVI, Alessandro, «Per l'insegnamento della filosofia e della teoria generale del diritto», *Rivista internazionale di filosofia del diritto* (Milan), 1924, No. 1.

RUIZ MORENO, Martin T., *Filosofia del Derecho*. Buenos Aires: Editorial G. Kraft Ilda, 1944. Pp. 524.

Representatives

Forerunners, — see Modern Empirical Schools, above, p. 133.

COSSIO, Carlos, *La teoria egologica del derecho y el concepto juridico de libertad*. Buenos Aires: Losada, 1944. Pp. 448.

——, «Sobre as relacôes da filosofia do direito com a ciência juridica», *Boletin do Ministerio da justiça* (Lisbon), 1947, No. 3. pp. 5-26.

KAUFMANN, Felix, *Logik und Rechtswissenschaft. Grundriss eines Systems der reinen Rechtslehre.* Tübingen: J. C. B. Mohr, 1922. Pp. XI, 134.

——, *Die Kriterien des Rechtes.* Tübingen: J. C. B. Mohr, 1924. Pp. VIII, 164.

KELSEN, Hans, — see also Politics, Chapter IV, 5, p. 224.

——, *General Theory of Law and State.* Translated by Anders WEDBERG. Cambridge, Massachusetts: Harvard University Press, 1945. Pp. XXXIII, 516.

——, *Hauptprobleme der Staatsrechtslehre, entwickelt aus der Lehre von Rechtssatze.* Tübingen: J. C. B. Mohr, 1911. Pp. XXVII, 709.

——, *Rechtswissenschaft und Recht. Erledigung eines Versuch zu Überwindung der 'Rechtsdogmatik'.* Vienna: F. Deuticke, 1922. Pp. 135.

——. «Théorie générale du droit international public», in *Recueil des Cours de l'Académie de droit international* (Paris), 1923.

——, *Allgemeine Staatslehre.* Berlin: Julius Springer, 1925. Pp. XVI, 433.

——, *Die philosophischen Grundlagen der Naturrechtslehre und des Rechtspositivismus.* Leipzig: Pan-Verlag, 1928. Pp. 78.

——, *Reine Rechtslehre.* Vienna: Deuticke, 1934. Pp. XIV, 236.

——, «The Pure Theory of Law», *Law Quarterly Review* (London), 1935, pp. 517.

EBENSTEIN, William, *Die Rechtsphilosophische Schule der reinen Rechtslehre.* Prague: Taussi, 1938. Pp. 180.

——, *The Pure Theory of Law.* Madison, Wisconsin: University of Wisconsin Press, 1945. Pp. XII, 211.

HALI, J., «Integrative Jurisprudence», in *Interpretations of Modern Legal Philosophies* (Ed. by P. L. SAYRE in, New York: Oxford University Press, 1947), pp 319-320.

JORGENSEN, Jorgen, *The Development of Logical Empiricism.* Chicago: University of Chicago Press, 1951. Pp. 100. Also in *International Encyclopedia of Unified Science: Foundation of the Unity of Science* (Chicago: University of Chicago Press), Vol. II, No. 9.

GÓMEZ, Otalora, G., «Introduction a la 'Teoria pura del derecho' de Hans Kelsen», in *Universitas* (Bogota), 1954, pp. 105-228.

JÖCKEL, Wilhelm, *Hans Kelsen rechtstheoretische Methode.* Tübingen: J. C. B. Mohr, 1930. Pp. VIII, 214.

LEGAZ Y LACAMBRA, Luis, *Kelsen: Estudio critico de la teoria pura del Derecho y del Estado de la Escuela de Viena.* Barcelona: Libreria Bosch, 1933. Pp. 371.

SCARPELLI, U., «Società e natura nel pensiero di Hans Kelsen», in *Rivista internazionale della filosofia del diritto* (Milan), 1954, pp. 767-780.

SCHALLER, Leodegar M., *Der Rechtsformalismus Kelsens und die thomistische Rechtsphilosophie.* Freiburg, Switzerland: University of Freiburg, 1949. Pp. 92.

TREVES, Renato, *Il fondamento filosofia della dottrina pura del diritto di Hans Kelsen.* Turin: Istituto giuridico d'Università, 1934.

VONLANTHEN, Albert, *Zu Hans Kelsens Anschauung über die Rechts-norm*. Berlin: Duncker and Humblot, 1965. Pp. 92.

ZAMPETTI, P. L., *Metafisica e scienza del diritto nel Kelsen*. Milan: Giuffrè, 1956. Pp. 180.

MERKEL, Adolf, *Teoria general del derecho administrativo*. Translation by E. IMAZ. Madrid: Edit. «Revista de Derecho Privado», 1935. Pp. XXIII, 496.

SCHREIER, Fritz, *Concepto y formas fundamentales del derecho*. Buenos Aires: Losada, 1942. Pp. 285.

VERDROSS, Alfred, *Die Einheit des rechtlichen Weltbildes auf Grundlage der Völkerrechtsverfassung*. Tübingen: J. C. B. Mohr, 1923. Pp. XII, 171.

——, *Die Verfassung der Völkerrechtsgemeinschaft*. Vienna: Julius Springer, 1926. Pp. X, 228.

INTERNATIONAL LAW

AGO, Roberto, «Positive and International Law», *American Journall of International Law*, 1957, pp. 691-733.

CAIRNS, Huntington, «Foreword, A Symposium in Juristic Bases for International Law», *Iowa Law Revue* (Iowa City), No. 3, 1946.

DEWEY, John, «Ethics and International Relations», *Foreign Affaires* (New York), March 15, 1923, pp. 85-95.

EPPSTEIN, John, *The Catholic Tradition and the Law of Nations*. Washington, D. C.: Catholic Association for International Peace, 1935. See also International Relations, above, Chapter IV, p. 221.

GROTIUS, Hugo, — see above, p. 130.

KUNZ, Joseph L., *Völkerrechtswissenschaft und reine Rechtslehre*. Leipzig: F. Deuticke, 1923. Pp. 86.

——, «On the Theoretical Basis of the Law of Nations», in *Grotius Society: Problem of Peace and War* (London, 1925), pp. 115-142.

——, *Die Anerkennung von Staaten und Regierungen im Völkerrecht*. Stuttgart: W. Kohlhammer, 1928. Pp. 218.

——, *Die Staatenverbindungen*. Stuttgart: W. Kohlhammer, 1929. Pp. VIII, 818.

——, «The Law of Nations, Static and Dynamic», *American Journal of International Law* (Concord, New Hamshire), 1933, pp. 630-650.

——, «The Problem of Revision in International Law», *American Journal of International Law* (Concord, New Hamshire), 1939, pp. 33-55.

McDOUGAL, Myres S., LASSWELL, Harold D., VLASIC, Ivan A., *Law and Public Order in Space*. 2nd printing. New Haven, Connecticut: Yale University Press, 1964. Pp. XXVI, 1147.

NORGAARD, Carl Aage, *The Position of the Individual in International Law*. Copenhagen: Ejnar Munksgaard, 1962. Pp. 325.

NUSSBAUM, Arthur, *Principles of Private International Law*. New York: Oxford University Press, 1943. Pp. XVI, 288.

——, *A Concise History of the Law of Nations*. New York: The Macmillan Co., 1947. Pp. XI, 361.

POUND, Roscoe, *Philosophical Theory and International Law*. Lyon: Bibliotheca Visseriana, 1923. Lecture. Pp. 20.

SCOTT, James Brown (ed.), *Cases on International Law Selected from Decisions of English and American Courts*. Boston: Boston Book Co., 1902. Pp. LXVII, 961.

——, *The Catholic Conception of International Law: Francesco de Vitoria,
   Founder of the Modern Law of Nations; Francesco Suarez, Founder
   of the Modern Philosophy of Law in General and in Particular of
   Law of Nations.* Washington, D. C.: Georgetown University Press,
   1934. Pp. 494. See Scholastic Philosophy, in *PQS*, No. 5.
—— (ed.), *The Classics of International Law.* 44 vols. Washington: George-
   town University, 1911-1950.
SUAREZ, Francis, — see above, p. 129.
TAMMELO, Ilmar, «The Rule of Law and the Rule of Reason in International
   Legal Relations», *La théorie de l'argumentation* (Louvain: Nauwe-
   laerts, 1963. Pp. 614), pp. 335-368.
VITORIA DE, Francis, — see above, p. 67, cf. 129.
WALKER, Tomas Alfred, *The Science of International Law.* London: C. J.
   Clay, 1893. Pp. XVI, 544.
——, *A History of the Law of Nations.* Cambridge: University Press,
   1899.

KUNZ, Jozef L., — see above.
Les fondateurs du droit international, leurs œuvres, leurs doctrines. Paris:
   1904. Pp. XXXI, 691. F. de Vitoria, A. Gentilis, F. Suarez, M. Grotius, Zouch, S. Pufendorf, Bynkershoek, Ch. Wolf.

JUSTICE

See Responsibility, below.

BLACKSHIELD, Anthony, «Empiricist and Rationalist Theories of Justice»,
   Archiv für Rechts-Sozialphilosophie (Bern), 1962, pp. 25-93.
CARDOZO, Benjamin N., *Law is Justice: Notable Opinions.* Ed. by A. L.
   SAINER. New York: 100 Grand St., 1938. Pp. XV, 441.
DEL VECCHIO, Giorgio, *Justice: An Historical and Philosophical Essay.*
   Translated by Lady GUTHRIE. Edinburgh: University Press, 1952. Pp.
   258.
DEWEY, John, «Fiat Justitia, Ruat Coelum», *New Republic* (Washington, D.
   C.), September 29, 1917. pp. 237-238.
——, «Psychology and Justice», *New Republic* (Washington, D. C.), No-
   vember 23, 1927. pp. 9-12. See also Pragmatism, above, Ch. I, 2, p. 38.
GARLAN, Edwin Norman, *Legal Realism and Justice.* New York: Columbia
   University Press, 1941. Pp. XII, 161.
GRINDEL, Carl W., «Social Justice in the Modern World», *Memorias del
   XIII Congresso Internacional de Filosofia.* Mexico, D. F., 7-14 Sep-
   tember, 1963 (7 vols. Mexico: Universidad Nacional Autonoma de
   Mexico, 1963-1964), Vol. VII, pp. 79-87.
KELSEN, Hans, «Metamorphoses of the Idea of Justice», in Paul SAYRE (ed.),
   Interpretations of Modern Legal Philosophies (New York: Oxford
   University Press, 1947), pp. 390-418.
——, *Justiz und Verwaltung.* Vienna: J. Springer, 1929. Pp. II, 25.
——, *What is Justice? Justice, Law and Politics in the Mirror of Science.*
   Berkeley, California: California University Press, 1957. Pp. 397.

Pound, Roscoe, *Justice according to Law*. New York: The Evening Post Job
    Printing Office, 1914. Pp. 61.
Rescher, Nicholas, *Distributive Justice: A constructive Critique of the Uti-
    litarian Theory of Distribution*. Indianopolis, Indiana: Bobbs-Merrill
    Co., 1966. Pp. 184.
Ross, Alf., *On Law and Justice*. London: Macmillan Co., 1958.
Schumacher, L. S., *The Philosophy of the Equitable Distribution of Wealth*.
    Washington, D. C.: The Catholic University of America Press, 1949.
Stammler, Rudolf, *Theory of Justice*. Translated by Isaac Rusik. New York:
    The Macmillan Co., 1925. Pp. XII, 591.

Battaglia, Felice, «Alcune osservazioni sul fondamento del contratto»,
    Rendiconti di Accademia delle scienze dell'Istituto di Bologna. Bo-
    logne: Cl. Scienze morali, 1943.
Croce, B., «Giustizia internazionale», *Critica* (Bari), No. 5, 1928.
Kriele, Martin, *Kriterien der Gerechtigkeit. Zum Problem der Rechtsphi-
    losophie und politischen Relativismus*. Berlin: Duncker und Hum-
    blot, 1963. Pp. 109.
Perelman, Chaim, *Justice et raison*. Brussels: Presses Universitaires de Bru-
    xelles, 1963. Pp. 256.
Soto, Dominicus, *Libri decem de iustitia et iure*. Lyon: J. Juncta, 1559.
    Also Venice (Venetiis): Gratiosus Perehainus, 1568. Pp. 275.

LAW AND RELIGION

Christianity, — see Politics, below, Ch. 5, p. 214.

Judaism, — see Jewish Philosophy, in *PQS*, No. 5.

Cohen, Abraham (ed.), *Everyman's Talmud*. London: J. M. Dent and Sons,
    Ltd., 1932. Pp. XII, 420.

Alvarez, Romero C. J., *Humanismo juridico cristiano*. Madrid: Instituto
    «Luis Vives» de Filosofia, 1964. Pp. 138.
Bautain, Louis E. M., *Philosophie des lois au point de vue chrétien*. 3rd
    ed. Paris: Didier, 1863. First published in 1860. Pp. VIII, 431.
Cohen, Élie, *La question juive devant le droit international public*. Paris:
    Éditions de la Vie Universitaire, 1922. Pp. 308.
Cohen, Hermann, *Deutschtum und Judentum, mit grundlegenden Betrach-
    tungen über Staat und Internazionalismus*. Giessen: A. Topelmann,
    1916. Pp. 59.

LAW AND SOCIOLOGY

See Sociology, below, Ch. V, 5, p. 273.

Cohen, Morris Raphael, *Law and The Social Order: Essay in Legal Philo-
    sophy*. New York: Harcourt, Brace and Co., 1933. Pp. XII, 403.
Ehrlich, Eugen, *Grundlegung der Soziologie des Rechts*. Munich: Dunker
    und Humblot, 1913. Pp. 409. English translation by Walter L. Moll,

Fundamental Principles of the Sociology of Law. Cambridge, Massachusetts: Harvard University Press, 1936. Pp. XXXVI, 541.

——, *Die juristische Logik.* Tübingen: J. C. B. Mohr, 1925. Pp. VIII 337.

GIERKE VON, Friedrich, *Natural Law and the Theory of Society,* 1500 to 1800. 2 vols. Translated by Ernest BARKER. Cambridge: University Press, 1934.

GURVITCH, Georges D., *Sociology of Law.* New York: Philosophical Library, 1942. Pp. XX, 309.

POUND, Roscoe, — see Pragmatism, above, p. 147.

RENNER, Karl, *Die Rechtsinstitute des Privatrechts und ihre soziale Funktion.* Tübingen: J. C. D. Mohr, 1929. Pp. XII, 181. English translation by Agnes SCHWARZSCHILD, *The Institutions of Private Law and Their Social Function.* London: Routledge and Kegan Paul, 1949. Pp. VIII, 307.

METHOD

BACON, Francis, — see Modern, Empirical School, above, 3, p. 133.

CAIRNS, Huntington, «Philosophy as Jurisprudence: Methodology», in his *Legal Philosophy from Plato to Hegel* (Baltimore: The Johns Hopkins Press, 1949), pp. 1-16, see also 555-566.

COHEN, Morris R., «The Place of Logic in the Law», *Harvard Law Review* (Cambridge, Massachusetts), 1916, pp. 622-629.

LEIBNIZ, G. W., — see Modern Rationalism, above, 3, p. 131.

RADIN, Max, *Law as Logic and Experience.* New Haven, Connecticut: Yale University Press, 1940. Pp. IX, 171.

SIDGWICK, Henry, *The Methods of Ethics.* 7th ed. London: Macmillan Co., 1901. 7. Pp. XXXVI, 536. See Ethics, above, Chapter I, p. 4.

BATTAGLIA, Felice, «Metodo realistico e metodo giuridico nella scienza del diritto pubblico», *Rivista internazionale di filosofia del diritto* (Milan), No. 3, 1938.

CAAMANO MARTINEZ, José, «Il metodo della filosofia del diritto», *Rivista internazionale di filosofia del diritto* (Milan) 1962, pp. 805-807,

CALOGERO, Guido, «La metodologia del naturalismo giuridico», *Archivio di studi corporativi,* No. 2, 1940.

CARNELUTTI, Francesco, *Metodologia del diritto.* Padua: Cedam, 1939. Pp. 116.

GÉNY, François, *Méthode d'interprétation et sources en droit privé positif.* Paris: A. Chevalier-Marescq, 1889. Pp. XIII, 606. See International, Positive and Private Law, below.

GERMANN, Oskar Adolf, *Probleme und Methoden der Rechtsfindung.* Bern: Stämpfli, 1965. Pp. 418.

KELSEN, Hans, *Über Grenzen zwischen juristischer und soziologischer Methode.* Tübingen: J. C. B. Mohr, 1911. Pp. III, 64.

RASOVSKY, Adolf, *Ethos und Naturrecht. Eine Untersuchung zur Methodik.* Vienna: Europa Verlag, 1964. Pp. 190.

REINACH, Adolf, *Die apriorischen Grundlagen des bürgerlichen Rechts.* Halle: M. Niemeyer, 1922. Pp. 847.

SAUSER-HALL, Georges, *Fonction et méthode de droit comparé.* Geneva: A. Kündig, 1913. Pp. 113. See also Comparative Law, above.

SCHNEIDER, Egon, *Logik für Juristen. Die Grundlagen der Denklehre und der Rechtsanvendung.* Berlin: Vahlen, 1965.

TREVES, Renato, «Il metodo teologico nella filosofia e nella scienza del diritto», *Rivista internazionale di filosofia del diritto* (Milan), No. 4, 1933.

NATURAL, POSITIVE AND PRIVATE LAWS

In English

BOURKE, Vernon J., «Natural Law and the Contemporary Mind», in *Teaching Thomism Today* (Washington, D. C.: The Catholic University of America Press, 1963), pp. 307-329.

CARDOZO, Benjamin, N., *The Nature of the Judicial Processes.* New Haven, Connecticut: Yale University Press, 1932. Pp. 180. See also Philosophy, above, p. 119.

——, *The Paradoxes of Legal Science.* New York: Columbia University Press, 1928. Pp. V, 142.

CHROUST, Anton-Hermann, «On the Nature of Natural Law», in Paul SAYRE (ed.), *Interpretations of Modern Legal Philosophies* (New York: Oxford University Press, 1947), pp. 70-84.

COHEN, Morris Raphael, *Reason and Nature.* 2nd ed. New York: The Macmillan Co., 1964. Pp. 470.

——, *Reason and Law.* New York: The Macmillan Co., 1961. Pp. 224.

ENTRÈVES D', H. P., *Natural Law: An Introduction to Legal Philosophy.* London: Longmans, 1951. Pp. 126.

GRAY, John Chipman, *Nature and Sources of the Law.* 2nd ed. New York: The Macmillan Co., 1927. Pp. XVIII, 348.

GIERKE, Otto F., *Natural Law and the Theory of Society.* 2 vols. New York: The Macmillan Co., 1934. See above, p. 154.

HOBBES, Thomas, — see Modern, above, 3, p. 131.

HOLMES, Oliver W., Jr., *The Common Law.* 32nd printing. Boston: Little, Brown and Co., 1938. Pp. XVI, 422. First published in 1881.

LASERSON, Max M., «Positive and 'Natural' Law and Their Correlation», in *Interpretations of Modern Legal Philosophies,* ed. by Paul SAYRE (New York: Oxford University Press, 1947), pp. 434-449.

LOCKE, John, — see above, p. 135.

POLLOCK Sir, Frederick, *The Expansion of the Common Law.* London: Stevens and Sons, 1904. Pp. VII, 164.

——, *The Law of Torts: A Treatise on the Principles of Obligations Arising from Civil Wrongs in the Common Law.* 14th ed. London: Stevens and Sons, 1939. Pp. XLVI, 504.

POUND, Roscoe, *The Spirit of the Common Law.* Boston: Marshall Jones Co., 1931. Pp. XV, 224. First published in 1921.

ROMMEN, Heinrich Albert, *Die ewige Widerkehr des Naturrechts.* 2nd ed. Munich: J. Kösel, 1947. English translation by Thomas R. HANLEY, *The Natural Law: A Study in Legal and Social History and Philosophy.* London: B. Herder Book Co., 1949. Pp. XI, 290.

STRAUSS, L., *Natural Right and History.* Chicago: University of Chicago Press, 1953. Pp. 327.

The Natural Law Forum, — see Periodicals, below, p. 171.

WRIGHT, Benjamin Fletcher, *American Interpretations of Natural Law.* Cambridge, Massachusetts: Harvard University Press, 1931. Pp. X, 360.

In Other Languages

AUER Albert, «Naturrechts Probleme der Gegenwart», *Salzburger Jahrbuch für Philosophie* (Salzburg), 1959, pp. 21-55.

BATTAGLIA, F., *La crisi del diritto naturale.* Venice: La Nuova Italia, 1929. Pp. 181.

BOBBIO, Norberto, *Il diritto naturale nel sec. XVIII.* Turin: Giappichelli, 1947. Pp. 167.

CASTIGLIONE, Silvana, «Diritto naturale e diritto positivo in David Hume», *Rivista internazionale di filosofia del diritto* (Milan), 1962, pp. 79-82. See also Empirical School, above, 3 Modern, p. 136.

CATHREIN, Viktor, *Recht: Naturrecht und positives Recht.* 2nd ed. Freiburg i. B.: Herder, 1909. Pp. VII, 327.

COING, Helmut, *Naturrecht als wissenschaftliches Problem.* Wiesbaden: Steiner, 1965. Pp. 28.

DEL VECCHIO, Giorgio, *Il concetto della natura e il principio del diritto.* 2nd ed. Bologne: Zanichelli, 1922. Pp. X, 191.

FICHTE, J. G., *Grundlage des Naturrechts nach Principien der Wissenschaftslehre.* 2 parts in one volume. Leipzig: C. E. Gabler, 1796-1797. See Idealistic School, above, 3, p. 138.

FLEISCHER, Johann Lorenz, *Institutiones iuris naturae et gentium.* Leipzig: Apud J. S. Heinsium 1741. Pp. 640.

FLÜCKIGER, Feliks, *Geschichte des Naturrechtes.* Zürich: Evangelischer Verlag, 1954. Pp. 475.

FORIERS, Paul, «Le juste et le droit naturel: essai de definition d'un droit naturel positif», *Revue internationale de Philosophie* (Paris), 1963, pp. 335-352.

GALÁN Y GUTIÉRREZ, E., *Jus naturae.* Valladolid: Meseta, 1954. Pp. 652.

GASPARRI, P., *Gli interessi umani e il diritto.* Bologne: C. Zuffi, 1951. Pp. 181.

GÉNY, François, *Méthode d'interprétation et sources en droit privé positif, essai critique.* Paris: A. Chevalier-Marescq, 1889. Pp. XIII, 606.

HAMEL, Edouardo, S. J., *Loi naturelle et loi du Christ.* Bruges-Paris: Desclée De Brouwer, 1964. Pp. 171.

KELSEN, H., «Naturrecht und positives Recht», *Internazionale Zeitschrift für Theorie des Rechtes,* 1927-1928. Pp. 71-138. See also General Theory, above.

LARENZ, Karl, *Rechtsperson und subjectives Recht.* Berlin: Junker und Dunnhaupt, 1935. Pp. 40.

LECLERCQ, Jacques, *Leçons de droit naturel.* 4 vols. Louvain: Presse Universitaire, 1947.

——, «Les équivoques du droit naturel», *Revue internationale de Philosophie* (Paris), 1963, pp. 271-286.

LEINWEBER, Adolph, *Gibt es ein Naturrecht?* Hamburg: Cram, de Gruyter and Co., 1965. Pp. 216.

MESSNER, Johannes, *Das Naturrecht. Handbuch der Geselschaftsethik und Wirtschaftsethik.* 5th ed. Vienna: Tyrolia-Verlag, 1966. Pp. 1372.

PASSERIN D'ENTRÈVES, A., *La dottrina del diritto naturale*. Milan: Edizioni di Communità, 1962. Pp. 192. First published in 1954.

PUFENDORF, — see Rationalism, above, 3, p. 132.

RENNER, Karl, *Die Rechtsinstitute des Privatrechts und ihre soziale Funktion*. Tübingen: J. C. B. Mohr, 1929. Pp. XII, 181. See law and Sociology, above; Marxism, above, p. 144.

RYFFEL, Hans, *Das Naturrecht*. Bern: Lang und Cie, 1944. Pp. 160.

SANCHEZ DE LA TORRE, Angel, *Los Griegos y el derecho natural*. Madrid: Editoria Tecnos, 1962. Pp. 344.

SAUTER, Johannes, *Die philosophischen Grundlagen des Naturrechts*. Vienna: Springer, 1932. Pp. IV, 231.

SCHILLING, Otto, *Naturrecht und Staat nach der Lehre der alten Kirche*. Paderborn: Görres-Geselschaft, 1914. Pp. VIII, 247.

SCHMOLZ VON, Franz Martin (ed.), *Das Naturrecht in der politischen Theorie*. Vienna: Springer-Verlag, 1963. Pp. 168. — See also Politics (Philosophy), below, Chapter IV, 1 c.

SCHULTZ-EWERTH, Erich and ADAM, Leonhard (eds.), *Das Eingeborenrecht*. 2 vols. Stuttgart: Strecker und Schröder, 1929-1930.

SOKOLOWSKI, Paul, *Die Philosophie im Privatrecht*. Halle: M. Niemeyer, 1902. Pp. XV, 616.

THOMAS S., AQUINAS, — see above, 3 Middle Ages.

VILLEY, Michel, «Observations d'un historien sur le droit naturel classique», *Archiv für Rechts- und Sozialphilosophie*, 1965, pp. 19-35.

WOLF, Erik, *Das Problem der Naturrechtslehre. Versuch einer Orientierung*. 3rd ed. Karlsruhe: C. F. Müller, 1964. Pp. XV, 219.

WOLFF, Christian, *Ius naturae methodo scientifica pertractatum*. 8 vols. Frankfurt: Societas Veneta, 1764-1766. See Rationalism, above 3, p. 133.

PRIMITIVE LAW

See Natural Law, above.

HARTLAND, Edwin Sidney, *Primitive Law*. London: Methuen and Co., 1924. Pp. VI, 222.

KOCOUREK, Albert und WIGMORE, John H. (ed.), *Primitive and Ancient Legal Institutions*. Boston: Little, Brown and Company, 1915. Pp. XII, 704.

MALINOWSKI, Bronislaw, *Crime and Custom in Savage Society*. New York: Harcourt and Co., 1926. Pp. XII, 132. First published in 1926. Trubner and Co., 1927. Pp. XIV, 285.

——, *Sex and Repression in Savage Society*. London: K. Paul, Trench,

——, *The Sexual Life of Savage in North-Western Melanesia: An Ethnographic Account of Courtship. Marriage and Family Life*. 3rd ed. 2nd impression. London: G. Routledge and Sons, 1932. First published in New York by Halcyon House, 1929. Pp XXVIII, 603.

——, *The Foundations of Faith and Morals: An Anthropological Analysis of Primitive Beliefs and Conduct*. London: Oxford University Press, 1936. Pp. 62.

TORDAY, Emil, *African Races*. London: Williams and Norgate, 1930. Pp. IV, 385.

Post, Albert Hermann, *Grundriss der ethnologischen Jürisprudenz.* 2 vols. Oldenburg: A Schwartz, 1894-1895.

PURE LAW

Pure Law: free from any ideological and sociological elements; legal system is simply a system of norms.

See General Theory of Law, above, p. 158.

Ebenstein, William, *The Pure Theory of Law.* Madison, Wisconsin: University of Wisconsin Press, 1945. Pp. XII, 211.
Kelsen, Hans, — see General Theory, above, p. 159.
Radbruch, Gustav (1878-1949), — see Relativism, above, p. 150.
Silving, Helen, «Law and Fact in the Light of the Pure Theory of Law», in Paul Sayre (ed.), *Interpretations of Modern Legal Philosophies* (New York: Oxford University Press, 1947), pp. 642-667.

RESPONSABILITY

Anscombe, Gertrud Elisabeth Margaret, *Intention.* Ithaca, New York: Cornell University Press, 1958. Pp. 93.
Aristotle, *Nicomachean Ethics.* See above, Ch. I, 2, p. 8.
Austin, John, «Ifs and Cons», *Proceedings of the British Academy,* 1956, pp. 109-132.
Bayne, David Cowan, *Conscience, Obligation, and the Law.* Chicago: Loyola University Press, 1966. Pp. 287.
Carnes, J. R., «Why Should I Obey the Law ?», *Ethics.* Chicago, 1960. Pp. 14-26.
Davis, Philip E., *Moral Duty and Legal Responsibility.* New York: Appleton-Century-Crofts, 1966. Pp. 320.
Ginet, Carl, «Can the Will Be Caused ?», *Philosophical Review,* 1962, pp. 49-52.
Green, Thomas Hill, *Lectures on the Principles of Political Obligation.* New impression. New York: Longmans, Green and Co., 1901. Pp. XXIV, 252.
Hart, Henry, «The Aims of the Criminal Law», *Law and Contemporary Problems,* 1958, pp. 405-441. Moral guilt is condition of crime.
——, «Legal Responsibility and Excuses», in Sidney Hook (ed.), *Determinism and Freedom in the Age of Modern Science.* New York: New York University Press, 1958. Pp. 237. Amendment of his previous view.
——, «Decision, Intention, and Causality», *Mind* ,1958, pp. 1-12.
——, *Punishment and Responsibility.* New York: Oxford University Press, 1968. Pp. 224.
Kaufman, A. S., «Ability», *Journal of Philosophy,* September 12, 1963, pp. 537-551.
——, «Practical Decision», *Mind,* 1966, pp. 25-44.
——, «Responsibility, Moral and Legal», in *The Encyclopedia of Philosophy* (8 vols. New York: The Macmillan Co., 1967), Vol. VII, pp. 183-188.

LEONI, Bruno, *Freedom and the Law*. Princeton, New Jersey: Van Nostrand, 1961. Pp. 204.

MORRIS, Herbert (ed.), *Freedom and Responsibility: Readings in Philosophy and Law*. Stanford, California: Stanford University Press, 1961. Pp. 547. Extensive bibliography.

SKINNER, Burrhus Frederic, *Science and Human Behavior*. New York: The Macmillan Co., 1953. Pp. 461.

SZASZ, Thomas Stephen, *Law, Liberty and Psychiatry: An Inquiry into the Social Uses of Mental Health Practices*. New York: The Macmillan Co., 1963. Pp. 281.

TAYLOR, Richard, «I Can», *Philosophical Review*, 1960, pp. 78-89.

WHITE, W. A., *Insanity and the Criminal Law*. London: Macmillan and Co., 1923. Pp. 281.

WOOTTON OF ABINGER, Barbara Frances, *Social Science and Social Pathology*. New York: The Macmillan Co., 1959. Pp. 400.

FAUCONNET, Paul, *La responsabilité*. Paris: F. Alcan, 1920. Pp. XXVI, 400. See also Ethics, Freedom, above, Chapter I, 3, p. 62.

Humanität und politische Verantwortung. Zürich. Eugen Rentsch, 1964. Pp. 312.

REVOLUTION

DRACHKOVITCH, M. M. (ed.), *The Revolutionary Internationals, 1864-1943*. New York: Oxford University Press, 1967.

MARCUSE, Herbert, *Reason and Revolution: Hegel and the Rise of Social Theory*. London: Oxford University Press, 1941. Pp. XII, 431.

SHAULL, R., *Revolution: Heritage and Contemporary Option*. New York: The Macmillan Co., 1967.

SOVEREIGNTY

BENN, Stanley I., «Sovereignty», in *The Encyclopedia of Philosophy* (8 vol. New York: The Macmillan Co., 1967), VII, 501-505.

COHEN, Hymen Ezra, *Recent Theories of Sovereignty*. Chicago: University of Chicago Press, 1937. Pp. IX, 169. Bibliography.

FIGGIS, J. N., *Theory of the Divine Right of Kings*. 2nd ed. Cambridge: University of Cambridge, 1914. Pp. XI, 406. First published in 1896.

GOODENOUGH, Erwin Ramsdell, *The Political Philosophy of Helenistic Kingship*. New Haven, Connecticut: Yale University, Department of Classics, 1928.

REES, W. J., «The Theory of Sovereignty Restated», in P. LASLETT (ed.), *Philosophy, Politics and Society*. New York: The Macmillan Co., 1956. Pp. 184.

RIESENBERG, Peter N., *The Inalienability of Sovereignty in Medieval Political Thought*. New York: Columbia University Press, 1956. Pp. 204.

SIMON, Yves, *A General Theory of Authority*. Notre Dame, Indiana: University of Notre Dame Press, 1962. Pp. 167.

GALIZIA, Mario, *La teoria della sovranità dal medioevo alla Rivoluzione francese*. Milan, A. Giuffrè, 1951. Pp. VIII, 545.

KELSEN, Hans, *Das Problem der Souveränität und die Theorie des Volker-rechtes.* 2nd ed. Tübingen: J. C. B. Mohr, 1928. Pp. XII, 320. First published in 1920.
KRABBE, Hugo, *Lehre des Rechtssouveränität.* Groningen, Netherlands, 1906.

6. PERIODICALS

(a) Bibliographical

See above, p. 112.

Current Legal Bibliography. A selected list of books and articles received by the Harvard School Library. Cambridge, Massachusetts: Langdell Hall, 1960—.
Index to Foreign Legal Periodicals. London: Institute of Advanced Legal Studies, 1960—.
Index to Legal Periodicals. New York: H. W. Wilson Co., 1908—.
Index to Periodical Articles Related to Law. Selected from Journals and included in the Index to legal periodicals. Hackensack, New Jersey: Law Library Service (57 Leuning St.), 1958—.

(b) General

American Bar Association Journal. Chicago: 1155 E. Sixtieth Street, 1915—.
American Journal of Comparative Law. Ann Arbor, Michigan: University of Michigan, 1952—.
Cambridge Law Journal. London: Stevens and Sons, Ltd., 1921—.
Canadian Bar Review. Toronto, Canada: Osgoode Hall Law School, 1923—.
Columbia Law Review. New York: Columbia University, 1965—.
Cornell Law Quarterly. Ithaca, New York: Cornell University, College of Law, 1915—.
Ethics: An International Journal of Social, Political and Legal Philosophy. Chicago: University of Chicago Press, 1890—.
Federal Bar Journal. Washington, D. C.: Federal Bar Association, 1931—.
Fordham Law Review. New York: School of Law, Fordham University, 1914—.
Harvard Law Review. Cambridge, Massachusetts: Harvard Law Review Association, 1887—.
Georgetown Law Journal. Washington, D. C.: Georgetown Law Journal Association, 1932—.
Juridical Review. Edinburgh, Scotland: W. Green and Son, 1889—.
Law and Contemporary Problems. Durham, North Carolina: Duke University School of Law, 1933—.
Law Quarterley Review. London: Stevens and Sons, Ltd. (3 Chancery Lane), 1885—.
St. John's Law Review. Brooklyn, New York: St. Thomas More Institute for Legal Research, 1926—.

The Catholic University Law Review. Washington, D. C.: The Catholic University of America Press, 1950—.
University of Chicago Law Review. Chicago: University of Chicago Press, 1933.
Yale Law Journal. New Haven, Connecticut: Yale Law Journal Co., 1891—.
Archives de philosophie du droit et de sociologie juridique. Paris: Recueil Sirey, 1931—.
Archiv für Rechts- und Sozialphilosophie. Berlin: W. Rothschild, 1907—.

Bollettino dell'Istituto di Filosofia del Diritto dell'Università di Roma. Rome: University of Rome, 1940-1943.

Jus: rivista di science giuridiche. Milan: Università Cattolica del Sacro Cuore, 1940—.
Rassegna di morale e di diritto. Rome: Scuola Tipografica Missionaria Domenicana, 1935-1941.
Revista de derecho y ciencias sociales. Buenos Aires, Argentina: Las Heras 2176, 1954—.
Rivista internazionale di filosofia del diritto. Geneva — Milan: A. Giuffrè, 1921—.

(c) Special

International Law

American Journal of International Law. Washington, D. C.: American Society of International Law, 1907—.
Foreign Affairs: An American Quarterly Review. New York: Council of Foreign Relations (58 E. 68th Street), 1922—.
International and Comparative Law Quarterley. London: Society of Comparative Legislation (1 Temple Gardens), 1952—.

Journal du droit international. Paris: Éditions Techniques, 1874—.
Jus Gentium: diritto internazionale. Rome, Italy: Casella Postale 410, 1950—.
Revue critique de droit international. Paris: Recueil Sirey, 1905—.
Revue de droit international et de droit comparé. Brussels, Belgium: Institut Belge de Droit Comparé, 1869—.
Rivista internazionale di filosofia del diritto. Milan, Geneva: Tipografia Sociale, 1921—.
Zeitschrift für ausländisches öffentliches Recht und Völkerrecht. Stuttgart, Germany: W. Kohlhammer Verlag, 1929—.

Other Laws

Canadian Current Law. Toronto, Canada: Burroughs and Co., 1948—.
Catholic Lawyer. Brooklyn, New York: St. John's University School of Law, 1955—.
Journal of Criminal Law. Baltimore, Maryland: International Association of Arson Investigators, 1910—.

Journal of Family Law. Louisville, Kentucky: University of Louisville
   School of Law, 1961.
Journal of Legal Education. Organ of Association of American Law Schools.
   Durham, North Carolina: Faculty of Law, Duke University, 1948—.
Medico-Legal Journal. Organ of Medico-Legal Society. Cambridge: W.
   Heffer and Sons, 1901—.
M.U.L.L. Modern Uses of Logic in Law. New Haven, Connecticut: Yale Law
   School, 1959—.
Soviet Law and Governement. New York: International Arts and Sciences
   Press (156 Fifth Ave.), 1962—.
The Natural Law Forum. Notre Dame, Indiana: Notre Dame Law School,
   1956—.

Osteuropa-Recht. Stuttgart, Germany: Deutsche Geselschaft für Osteuro-
   pakunde, 1955—.
Revue critique de droit criminal. Liège: L. Grandmont — Donders, 1881—.
Revue de droit pénal et de criminologie. Brussels, Belgium: Palais de Justice, 1907—.

CHAPTER IV

POLITICS

Politics (from πολίς, city) as a science treats the state, its activity, and the participation of the citizens in the governing of the community. Philosophy is interested in these activities, and considers them in general as distinguished from the practices of an individual politican. Therefore, a philosopher of politics reflects on its internal logic and its differences from, and relationship to other activities and to moral responsibility.

As a result, the problem of the philosophy of politics concerns the formulation, justification, and classification of the rules governing empirical political practices, the nature of the state, its rights, its functions, and its relation to its members. Some of these problems include the question of morality. These philosophical aspects involved in politics can be properly treated only when based on politics itself.

However, particular philosophical trends, chiefly in contemporary times have their own views of the task and methods of political philosophy. Among them is the opinion expressed by analytical philosophy that philosophy ought to be concerned with the conceptual structure of our thinking and our language rather than with the evaluation, presuppositions and percepts of action and policies. These views, of course, are open to further discussions.

Among the main philosophical contributors to political questions are Plato (429-348 B. C.), Aristotle (384-322 B. C.), St. Thomas Aquinas (1225-1274), Niccolo Machiavelli (1469-1527), Giovanni Battista Vico (1668-1744), Immanuel Kant (1724-1804), Georg W. F. Hegel (1770-1831), Karl Marx (1818-1883), and Benedetto Croce (1866-1952). However, each period of human history forms its own schools with outstanding representatives.

The same can be said of particular countries. Basic evidence
to this effect is provided in the bibliography listed below.

Bibliography

See Economics, above, Ch. II, 1; Law, above Ch. III, 1; Sociology, below, Ch. V, 1.

1. INTRODUCTORY INFORMATIONS

Bibliographies

International Bibliography of Political Science. 13 vols. — Paris: UNESCO;
   also Chicago: Aldine Publishing Co., 1953-1964—.
International Political Science Abstracts. 14 vols. — Oxford: Basil Black-
   well, 1951-1964.
DUNNER, Joseph (ed.), *Dictionary of Political Science.* New York: Philoso-
   phical Library, 1964. Pp. XXII, 585.
SPERBER, Hans and TRITTSCHUH, Travis, *American Political Terms.* Detroit:
   Wayne State University Press, 1962. Pp. VIII, 516.

Encyclopedias

GOULD, Julius and KOLB, William L. (eds.), *A Dictionary of the Social Scien-
   ces.* New York: The Free Press, 1964. Pp. XVI, 761.
TALLMAN, Marjorie, *Dictionary of Civics and Government.* New York: The
   Philosophical Library, 1953. Pp. 291.

AMAYA, Florencio J., *Diccionario politico, sociologico y filosofico argentino.*
   Mendoza, Argentina: Cuyo, 1946. Pp. 520.
Encyclopédie politique de la France et du monde. 4 vols. 3rd. ed. Paris:
   L'encyclopédie coloniale et maritime, 1951.
Handwörterbuch der Staatwissenschaften. Ed. by Ludwig ELSTER, Adolf
   WEBER and Friedrich WIESER. 9 vols. Jena: Gustav Fischer, 1923-1929.
Staatslexikon. Recht, Wirtschaft, Geselschaft. Ed. by Görres-Geselschaft.
   7 vols. New edition. Freiburg im Br.: Herder, 1960-1963. First publis-
   hed in 1901-1904.

2. GENERAL STUDIES

(a) Histories

See also Philosophy, below c; Ancient, Medieval and Modern
Histories, below, 3.

In English

ABBO, John A., *Political Thought: Men and Ideas.* Westminster, Maryland: The Newman Press, 1960. Pp. 450.

BLAKEY, R., *The History of Political Literature from the Earliest Time.* 2 vols. London, England: Bentley, 1855. Reprint. Dubuque, Iowa: Wm. Brown Reprint Library, 1962.

BOWLE, John, *Western Political Thought.* New York: Oxford University Press, 1948. Vol. I: An Historical Introduction from the Origins to Rousseau. Pp. 460.

BRECHT, Arnold, *Political Theory: The Foundations of Twentieth-Century Political Thought.* Princeton, New Jersey: Princeton University Press, 1959. Pp. 603.

CATLIN, George, *The Story of the Political Philosophers.* New York and London: Whittlesey House, McGraw-Hill Book Publishing Company, Inc., 1939. Pp. 810.

COOK, Thomas Ira, *History of Political Philosophy from Plato to Burke.* New York: Prentice-Hall, Inc., 1937. Pp. 725.

DOYLE, Phyllis, *A History of Political Thought.* New York: Holt, 1933. Pp. 335. Bibliography. Reprint in London: Jonathan Cape, 1948.

EASTON, David, *A Systems Analysis of Political Life.* New York: John Wiley and Sons, Inc., 1965. Pp. 507.

EBENSTEIN, W., *Great Political Thinkers: Plato to the Present.* New York: Holt, Rinehart and Winston, 1951. Pp. XIX, 903.

EISENSTADT, S. N., *The Political Systems of Empires: The Rise and Fall of the Historical Bureaucratic Societies.* New York: The Macmillan Co., 1963. Pp. 524.

ENGELMANN, Geza, *Political Philosophy from Plato to Jeremy Bentham.* Translated from the German by Karl Frederick GEISER. New York and London: Harper & Brothers, 1927. Pp. 400. Bibliography.

FOSTER, Jones and LANCASTER, L. W., *Masters of Political Thought.* 3 vols: Boston: Houghton, Mifflin Co., 1959. Vol. I: FOSTER, Michael, *Plato to Machiavelli;* Vol. II: JONES, W. T., *Machiavelli to Bentham;* Vol. III: LANCASTER, Lane W., *Hegel to Dewey.* New edition, s. p. Vol. I, 1961. Pp. IX, 302.

GETTELL, Raymond Garfield, *History of Political Thought.* New York: Appleton-Century Crofts, 1953. Pp. 425.

GIERKE VON, Otto Frederick, *The Development of Political Theory.* Translated by Bernard FREYD. New York: W. W. Norton & Company, Inc., 1939. Pp. 364.

HACKER, Andrew *et al.* (eds.), *History and Sources of Western Political Thought.* 12 vols. New York: The Macmillan Co., 1964—.

HEARNSHAW, Fossey John Cobb, *The Development of Political Ideas.* Revised edition. London: Nelson Classics, 1937. Pp. 151.

——, *Some Great Political Idealists of the Christian Era.* London: G. G. Harrap and Co., 1937. Pp. 273.

JONES, W. T., *Masters of Political Thought.* 2 vols. 2nd ed. Boston: Houghton, 1947. Pp. 388.

LITTELL, Franklin H., *From State Church to Pluralism.* Garden City, New York: Doubleday Anchor, 1962. Pp. 174.

MARVICK, Dwaine (ed.), *Political Decision-Makers.* New York: The Macmillan Co., 1961. Pp. 347.

MAZEY, Chester Collins, *Political Philosophies.* New York: The Macmillan Company, 1954. Pp. 712.

PARKINSON, Cyril Northcote, *The Evolution of Political Thought.* Boston: Houghton Mifflin, 1958. Pp. 327.

PLAMENATZ, John Petrov, *Man and Society: Political and Social Theory.* 2 vols. New York: McGraw-Hill, 1963.

POLLOCK Sir, Frederick W., *An Introduction to the History of the Science of Politics.* New edition. London: Macmillan and Co., 1911. Pp. XII, 138. First published in 1883.

SABINE, George Holland, *A History of Political Theory.* New York: Holt, Rinehart and Winston, 1961. Pp. 948. Bibliography. First published in 1938.

SCHMANDT, Henry J., *A History of Political Philosophy.* Milwaukee: Bruce Publishing Co., 1960. Pp. 499. Bibliography.

SIDGWICK, Henry, *The Development of European Polity.* Ed. by Eleanor M. Sidgwick. London: Macmillan and Co., 1903. Pp. XXVI, 454.

VEREKER, Charles, *The Development of Political Theory.* London: Hutchinson, 1957. Pp. 230.

WALZER, Michael, *The Revolution of the Saints: A Study in the Origins of Radical Politics.* London: Weidenfeld & Nicolson, 1966. Pp. XII, 332.

In Other Languages

BATTAGLIA, Felice, *L'ineamenti di storia delle dottrine politiche.* Rome: Il Foro Italiano, 1936.

BENEYTO, Juna, *Historia de las doctrinas politicas.* Madrid: Aguilar, 1948. Pp. 475.

BRUNELLO, B., *Dottrine politiche.* Brescia: Morcelliana, 1955. Pp. 456.

CHEVALLIER, Jean Jacques, *Les grandes œuvres politiques: de Machiavel à nos jours.* Paris: A. Colin, 1949. Pp. XIII, 406. Bibliography.

GUMPLOWICZ, Ludwig, *Geschichte der Staatstheorien.* Innsbruck: Wagner, 1926. Pp. XI, 592. First published in 1905.

——, *Philosophisches Staatsrecht.* Vienna: Manzische Hofbuchhandlung, 1877. Pp. VI, 195.

——, *Allgemeines Staatsrecht.* Innsbruck: Wagner, 1907. Pp. XV, 540.

HIPPEL VON, Ernst, *Geschichte der Staatsphilosophie.* 2 vols. 2nd ed. Meisenheim am Glan: A. Hain, 1958.

HOLSTEIN, Gunther, *Historia de la filosofia politica.* Translated by Luis LEGAZ LACAMBRA. Madrid: Instituto de Estudios politicos, 1950. Pp. 300.

JANET, Paul A., *Histoire de la science politique dans ses rapports avec la morale.* 5th rev. ed. by G. PICOT. 2 vols. Paris: F. Alcan, 1925. First published in 1858.

MOSCA, G., *Storia delle dottrine politiche.* 6th ed. Bari: Laterza, 1951. Pp. 379.

SCHILLING, K., *Geschichte der Staats- und Rechtsphilosophie.* Berlin: Junker und Dunnkaupt Verlag, 1937. Pp. 216.

THEIMER, Walter, *Geschichte der politischen Ideen.* Bern: Francke, 1955. Pp. 500.

(b) Systematic Studies

In English
224

BANFIELD, Edward C., *Political Influence. Glencoe,* Illinois: Free Press, 1961. Pp. 354.

CATLIN, George Edward Gordon, *Political and Sociological Theory and Its Applications.* Ann Arbor, Michigan: University of Michigan Press, 1964. Pp. 118.

——, *Systematic Politics: Elementa Politica and Sociologica.* Toronto: University of Toronto Press, 1962. Pp. 434.

——, *The Science and Method of Politics.* Hamden, Connecticut: Shoe String Press, 1964. Pp. 360.

CHARLESWORTH, James C. (ed.), *Contemporary Political Analysis.* New York: The Free Press (Macmillan), 1967.

FLATHMAN, Richard E., *The Public Interest: An Essay Concerning the Normative Discourse of Politics.* New York: John Wiley and Sons, 1967. Pp. 197.

FRIEDRICH, Carl Joachim, *The Public Interest.* New York: Atherton Press, 1962. Pp. 256.

——, *Man and His Government: An Empirical Theory* New York: McGraw-Hill, 1963. Pp. 737. Good bibliography.

——, *The Philosophy of Law in Historical Prospective.* 2nd ed. Chicago: University of Chicago Press, 1963. Pp. 296.

KORNHAUSER, William, *The Politics of Mass Society.* Glencoe, Illinois: Free Press, 1959. Pp. 256.

LASKI, Harold Joseph, *A Grammar of Politics.* 4th ed. London: G. Allen and Unwin, 1938. Pp. XXVII, 672. First published in 1925.

SIDGWICK, Henry, *The Elements of Politics.* 4th ed. London: Macmillan and Co., 1897. Pp. XXXV, 665. First published in 1891.

In Other Languages

BRUNELLO, Bruno, *Introduzione alla politica.* Bologne: Cappelli, 1948. Pp.
——, *Problemi della politica come scienza.* Bologne: Riccardo Patron, 384.
1961. Pp. 216.

DUVERGER, Maurice, *Introduction à la politique.* Paris: Gallimard, 1964. Pp.

FRIEDRICH, C. J., *Die politische Wissenschaft.* Freiburg: Alber, 1961. Pp. 450.

LEONE, Enrico, *Teorie della politica.* 2 vols. Turin: Bocca, 1931.

MAGGIORE, Giuseppe, *La politica.* Bologne: Zanichelli, 1941. Pp. 390.

MOSCA, Gretano, *Elementi di scienza politica.* 6th ed. 2 vols. Bari: G. Laterza, 1953.

VIDAL, Enrico, «Considerazioni sul problema dei rapporti tra politica, morale, diritto ed economia», in *Scritti di sociologia e politica in onore di Luigi Sturzo.* Bologne: Zanichelli, 1953.

(c) Philosophy

See Special Questions, below, 5, p. 213.

In English

APTER, David E. (ed.), *Ideology and Discontent*. New York: The Macmillan Co., 1964. Pp.342.

BANFIELD, Edward C., *The Moral Basis of a Backward Society*. Glencoe, Illinois: Free Press, 1958. Pp. 204.

BARKER Sir, Ernest, *Principles of Social and Political Theory*. New York: Oxford University Press, 1951. Pp. VIII, 284.

BENN, Stanley I., «Nature of Political Philosophy», in *The Encyclopedia of Philosophy* (8 vols. New York: The Macmillan Co., 1967), Vol. VI, pp. 387-392.

—— and PETERS, R. S., *Principles of Political Thought*. New York: Collier Books, 1964. See State, below, 5, p. 223.

BOSANQUET, Bernard, *The Philosophical Theory of the State*. London: Macmillan and Co., 1920. Pp. LXII, 320. Also 4th ed. New York: St. Martin's Press, 1923. Pp. 345.

BRAYBROOKE, David and LINDBLOM, Charles E., *A Strategy of Decision*. New York: Free Press of Glencoe, 1963. Pp. IX, 268.

CATLIN, George E. G., *A Study of the Principles of Politics*. New York: The Macmillan Co., 1930. Pp. 469. See Rationalism, below, 3, p. 190.

DEININGER, Whitaker T., *Problems in Social and Political Thought: A Philosophical Introduction*. New York: The Macmillan Co., 1965. Pp. 480.

GREAVES, Harold Richard Goring, *Foundations of Political Theory*. London: Allen and Unwin, 1958. Pp. 208.

HAMPSHIRE, Stuart, *Thought and Action*. New York: Viking, 1960. Pp. 276.

HOOK, S., *Political Philosophy*. Englewood Cliffs, New Jersey: Prentice-Hall, 1965. Pp. 128.

LASLETT, Peter (ed.), *Philosophy, Politics and Society*. New York: The Macmillan Co., 1956. First Series. Pp. 184.

—— and Cummings, Philip W., «History of Political Philosophy», in *The Encyclopedia of Philosophy* (8 vols. New York: The Macmillan Co., 1967), Vol. III, pp. 370-387.

—— and RUNCIMAN, W. G. (eds.), *Philosophy, Politics and Society*. New York: Barnes and Co., 1963. Second Series. Pp. 229.

MACPHERSON, Crawford, *The Political Theory of Possessive Individualism: Hobbes to Locke*. New York: Oxford University Press, 1962. Pp. 310.

McCOY, Charles N. R., *The Structure of Political Thought*. New York: McGraw-Hill Co., 1963. Pp. 328.

McPHEE, William N., *Formal Theories of Mass Behavior*. New York: Free Press of Glencoe, 1963. Pp. 244.

MURRAY, Alexander R. M., *An Introduction to Political Philosophy*. 2nd ed. Philadelphia: Dufour Editions, 1962. Pp. 240.

NEWMAN, Jeremiah, *Political Morality*. Chicago: Scepter Press, 1963. Pp. 459.

OAKESHOTT, Michael Joseph, *Rationalism in Politics*. London: Methuen, 1962. Pp. 333.

POPPER, Karl Raimund, *The Open Society and Its Enemies*. 2 vols. 4th ed. London: Routledge and Kegan Paul, 1962. First published in 1945.

RUNCIMAN, Walter Garrison, *Social Science and Political Theory*. London: Cambridge University Press, 1963. Pp. 200.

SRZEDNICKI, J., «Basic political concepts», *Philosophical Quarterly*, 1963, pp. 229-237.

STRAUSS, Leo, *What is Political Philosophy?* New York: The Macmillan Co. (The Free Press), 1959. Pp. 315.

STURZO, Luigi, *Politique et Morale*. Paris: Les Cahiers de la Nouvelle Journée, 1938. English translation by Barbara BARCLAY CARTER, *Politics and Morality*. London: Burns, Oates and Co., 1938. Pp. VII, 235.

POLLOCK, Robert C. (ed.), «Luigi Sturzo: An Anthology of His Writings», *Thought* (New York), 1953, pp. 165-208.

VAUGHAN, Charles Edwyn, *Studies in the History of Political Philosophy, Before and After Rousseau*. 2 vols. New York: Longmans, Green and Co., 1925.

WALLAS, Graham, *Human Nature in Politics*. 4th ed. London: Constable and Co., 1948. Pp. XXII, 301. First published in 1908.

WELDON, Thomas Dewar, *The Vocabulary of Politics*. London: Penguin Books, 1953. Pp. 119.

WOLIN, Sheldon and SLUSSER, R. M. *Politics and Vision*. Boston: Little, Brown and Co., 1960. Pp. 529.

In Other Languages

ARNAUD, Pierre *et al.* (eds.), *L'idée de philosophie politique*. Paris: Presses Universitaires de France, 1965.

ARANGUREN, Jose L. L., *Etica y politica*. Madrid: Guadarrams, 1963. Pp. 319.

BATTAGLIA, F., *Morale e storia nella prospetiva spiritualistica*. Bologna: C. Zuffi, 1953. Pp. 259.

CURIEN, Gilles, *La morale en politique*. Paris: Plon, 1962.

DEL VECCHIO, Giorgio, *L'état et le droit: essais de philosophie politique*. Paris: Balloz, 1964.

FAZIO-ALLMAYER, Vito, *Etica e politica*. Palermo: G. U. F., 1942.

FISCHER, Hugo, *Wer soll der Herr der Erde Sein? Eine politische Philosophie*. Stuttgart: Seewald Verlag, 1962. Pp. 408.

HENNIS, Wilhelm, *Politik und praktische Philosophie. Eine Studie zur Rekonstruktion der politischen Wissenschaft*. Berlin: Luchterhand, 1963. Pp. 131.

SANTONASTASO, G., «Le ideologie politiche». *Rassegna di scienze filosofiche* (Bari, Rome), 1958, Pp. 31-43.

SCHMÖLZ VON, Franz Martin, *Zerstörung und Rekonstruktion der politischen Ethik*. Munich. Beck, 1963. Pp. VIII, 152.

(ed.), *Das Naturrecht in der politischen Theorie*. Vienna: Springer-Verlag, 1963. Pp. 168. See Natural Law, above, Ch. III, 5, p. 164.

WATKINS, J. W. N., «Epistemology and Politics», *Proceedings of Aristotelian Society* (London), 1957-1958, Pp. 79-102.

(d) Excerpt from Selected Writings

See also Particular Periods, below, 3.

ANDERSON, Thornton, *Jacobson's Development of American Political Thought: A Documentary History.* 2nd ed. A-C-C Political Science Series, 1961. Pp. 659.

CHANDLER, Albert R. (ed.), *The Clash of Political Ideals: A Sourcebook on Democracy and the Totalitarian State.* 3rd ed. New York: Appleton-Century-Crofts, 1957. Pp. 374.

ECKSTEIN, Harry and Apter, David E. (eds.), *Comparative Politics: A Reader.* New York: Free Press of Glencoe, 1963. Pp. 746.

EULAU, Heinz, ELDERSVELD, Samuel J. and JANOWITZ, Morris (eds.), *Political Behavior: A Reader in Theory and Research.* New York: The Macmillan Co., 1956.

GEWIRTH, Alan (ed.), *Political Philosophy.* New York: The Macmillan Co., 1965. Pp. 123.

Great Political Theories. London: Methuen, 1947—.

LASLETT, Peter (ed.), *Philosophy, Politics and Society: A Collection.* Oxford: Basil Blackwell and Mott, 1962. Pp. 229.

QUINTON, Anthony (ed.), *Political Philosophy.* New York: Oxford University Press, 1967. Pp. 198.

ROSENAU, James N. (ed.), *International Politics and Foreign Policy: A Reader in Research and Theory.* New York: Free Press of Glencoe, 1961. Pp. 511.

SOMMERVILLE, J. and SONTONI, Ronald (eds.), *Social and Political Philosophy: Readings from Plato to Ghandi.* Garden City, New York: Doubleday Anchor, 1963. Pp. 545.

SNYDER, Richard C. and BRUCK, H. W. (eds.), *Foreign Policy Decision Making: An Approach to the Study of International Politics.* New York: Free Press of Glencoe, 1962. Pp. VII, 274.

WAHLKE, John C. and EULAN, Heinz (eds.), *Legislative Behavior: A Reader in Theory and Practice.* New York: The Macmillan Co., 1959. Pp. 413.

WOLFF, Robert P. (eds.), *Political Man and Social Man: Readings in Political Philosophy.* New York: Random House, 1966. Pp. 512.

3. PARTICULAR PERIODS

ANTIQUITY

(a) Comprehensive Studies

BARKER Sir, Ernest (ed.), *From Alexander to Constantine.* New York: Oxford University Press, 1956. Pp. XXV, 505.

GRENE, David, *Man in His Pride: A Study in the Political Philosophy of Thucydides and Plato.* Chicago: University of Chicago Press, 1950. Pp. XII, 230.

——, *Greek Political Theory.* Chicago: University of Chicago Press, 1965.

KAGAN, Donald, *The Great Dialogue: A History of Greek Political Thought from Homer to Polybius.* New York: The Macmillan Co., 1965. Pp. XI, 274.

—— (ed.), *Sources in Greek Political Thought from Homer to Polybius.* New York: The Macmillan Co., 1965.

McILLWAIN, Charles Howard, *The Growth of Political Thought in the West, from the Greeks to the End of the Middle Ages.* New York: The Macmillan Company, 1932. Pp. 520.

GLOVER, T. R., *Democracy in the Ancient World.* London: Macmillan Co., 1927. Pp. 263.

(b) Specific Studies

(aa) GREECE: small city-state assures political good.

PLATO (429-348 B. C.), — see Ethics, above, Ch. I, 2, p. 7; Law, above, Ch. III, 3, p. 125.

——, *Republic.* Translated by Paul SHOREY. 2 vols. Cambridge, Massachusetss: Harvard University Press, 1930. Reprint in 1943, 1946.

——, *Statesman.* Translated by J. B. SKEMP. London: Routledge and Kegan Paul, 1952. Pp. 244.

BARKER, Ernest, *Greek Political Theory: Plato and His Predecessors.* 3rd ed. London: Methuen and Co., 1947. First published in 1918. Pp. XIII, 403. See also ARISTOTLE, below.

FOSTER, M. B., *The Political Philosophies of Plato and Hegel.* Oxford: Clarendon Press, 1935. Pp. XII, 207.

LEVINSON, Ronald Barlett, *In Defense of Plato.* Cambridge, Massachusetts: Harvard University Press, 1953. Pp. 674.

WILD, J. D., *Plato's Modern Enemies and the Theory of Natural Law.* Chicago: University of Chicago Press, 1953. Pp. XI, 259.

GENTILE, Marino, *La politica di Platone.* Padua: Cedam, 1940. Pp. 230.

HIPPEL VON, Ernst, *Der Sinn des Staates und die Lehre von den Staatsformen bei Plato.* Langensalza: H. Beyer, 1927. Pp. 22.

KROHN, A., *Der platonische Staat.* Halle: R. Mühlmann, 1876. Pp. XIII, 386.

LÜDKE, G., *Über das Verhältnis von Staat und Erziehung in Platos* πολιτεία. Berlin: Trenkel, 1908. Inaugural dissertation, pp. 39.

ARISTOTLE (384-322 B. C.), — see Ethics, above, Ch. I, 2, p. 8.

Aristotle's Politics. Translated by B. JOWETT. Oxford: At the Clarendon Press, 1931. Pp. 355. Also translated by Ernest BARKER, *The Politics of Aristotle.* Oxford: At the Clarendon Press, 1946.

——, *On the Constitution of Athens.* Ed. by F. G. KENYON. London: G. Bell and Sons, 1891. Pp. XLIII, 126.

The Constitution of the Athenians by the Old Oligarchy and by Aristotle: A New Interpretation. Ed. by Livio Catalio Stecchine. Glencoe, Illinois: The Free Press, 1950. Pp. 112.

Barker Sir, Ernest, *The Political Thought of Plato and Aristotle.* New York: G. P. Putnam's Sons, 1906.

Newman, William Lambert, *The Politics of Aristotle.* Two Prefatory Essays, and Notes Critical and Explanatory. 4 vols. Oxford: The Clarendon Press, 1887-1902.

Defourny, Maurice, *Aristotle: Étude sur la «Politique».* Paris: G. Beauchesne et ses fils, 1932. Pp. XX, 559.

Dreizehnter, A., *Untersuchungen zur Textgeschichte der aristotelischen Politik.* Leiden, Holland: E. J. Brill, 1962. Pp. XVI, 81.

Jaeger, Werner Wilhelm, *Paideia: Die Formung des griechischen Menschen.* New edition. 3 vols. Berlin: W. de Gruyter und Co., 1954.

(bb) Judaism: biblical partriarchalism (obedience), chosen people, and divine power of kings.

See Law, above, Ch. III, 3, p. 123.

(cc) Rome: cosmopolitan character of natural law.

Cicero, Marcus Tullius (106-43 B. C.), — see Law, above, Ch. III, 3, p. 126.

——, *De Re Publica,* c. 46 B. C. With an English translation by Clinton Walker Keyes. London: W. Heinemann, 1928. Pp. 533.

Stoics, — see Ethics, Ch. I, 2, p. 11; Natural Law, above, Ch. III, 5, p. 164.

(dd) Patristic: just men are the true membres of the City of God.

See Ethics, above, Ch. I, 2, p. 14.

Augustine Saint (354-430), *De Civitate Dei,* written between 410-423. English translation by John Healey, *The City of God.* London: J. M. Dent and Sons, 1931. Pp. 267. See also Middle Ages, below, p. 172.

Deane, Herbert, Andrew, *The Political and Social Ideas of St. Augustine.* New York: Columbia University Press, 1963. Pp. 356.

Figgis, John Neville, *The Political Aspects of St. Augustine's City of God.* London: Longmans and Co., 1921. Pp. 132.

Combes, G., *La doctrine politique de saint Augustin.* Paris: Plon, 1927. Pp. VIII, 482.

Schilling, Otto, *Die Staats- und Soziallehre des hl. Augustinus.* Freiburg i. B.: Herder, 1910. Pp. X, 280.

MIDDLE AGES

See Scholastic Philosophy and Medieval Histories in *PQS,* No. 5.

Predominant idea is that of two swords, or else pope-emperor, the former has supremacy in supernatural, the latter in natural matter.

(a) Comprehensive Studies

In English

CARLYLE, Robert W. and CARLYLE, A. J., *A History of Mediaeval Political Theory in the West.* 6 vols. Edinburgh and London: W. Blackwood and Sons, 1903-1936.

DUNNING, W., *A History of Political Theories, Ancient and Mediaeval.* New York: The Macmillan Co., 1930. Pp. XXV, 360. See also Modern, below.

GIERKE VON, Otto Friedrich, *Political Theories of the Middle Ages.* Translated by Frederic W. Maitland. New York: The Macmillan Co., 1938. Pp. LXXX, 197.

LERNER, Ralph, MAHDI, Muhsin and FORTIN, Ernest L. (eds.), *Medieval Political Philosophy: A Sourcebook.* New York: The Macmillan C., 1963. Pp. 544.

LEWIS, Ewart K. (ed.), *Miedieval Political Ideas.* 2 vols. London: Routledge and Paul, 1954.

——, *History and Sources of Medieval Political Thought.* New York: The Macmillan Co., 1967.

MORRALL, John B., *Political Thought in Medieval Times.* London: Hutchinson, 1958. Pp. 122.

TROELTSCHE, Ernst, *The Social Teaching of the Christian Churches.* Translated from the German by Olive WYON. 2 vols. London: The Macmillan Co., 1931.

In Other Languages

BATTAGLIA, Felice, «Il pensiero politico medievale», in *Questioni di storia medievale.* Milan: Marzorati, 1946.

CROSA, E., *Il principio della sovranità populare dal medioevo alla Revoluzione francese.* Turin: Bocca, 1915. Pp. VIII, 269.

FLORI, Ezio, *Il trattato «De regimine principum» e le teorie politiche di S. Tommaso.* Bologne: Zanichelli, 1928. Pp. 106.

PASSERIN D'ENTRÈVES, Alessandro, *Appunti di storia delle dottrine politiche: la filosofia politica medievale.* Turin: Giappichelli, 1934. Pp. 238.

RAVÀ, Adolfo, *Lezioni di storia delle dottrine politiche: le dottrine politiche da S. Tommaso alla prima metà del secolo XIV.* Padua: Cedam, 1925.

——, *Compendio di storia delle dottrine politiche.* Padua: Università di Padova, 1933. Pp. 234.

(b) Specific Studies

FEUDALISM, — see above, Ch. II, 3, p. 81.

AUGUSTINE SAINT, — see Ancient, above, pp. 81, 128.

DANTE, Alighieri (1265-1321), *De Monarchie*, c. 1313. Ed. by E. MOORE with an introduction on Dante's political theory by W. H. V. READE. Oxford: At the Clarendon Press, 1916. Pp. XXXI, 376.

JOHN OF SALISBURY (1315/20-1180), *Policraticus*. 2 vols. Oxford: At the Clarendon Press, 1909. First published in 1159.

——, *Metalogicon*. Ed. by C. C. J. WEBB. Oxford: At the Clarendon Press, 1929. See also *Patrologia Latina* (J. P. MIGNE), Vol. CXCIX, cf. above, p. 14.

WEBB, C. C. J., *John of Salisbury*. London, 1932.

MARSILIUS OF PADUA (d. between 1336/43), *Defensor pacis*. English translation by Alan GEWIRTH, *Defender of Peace*. New York: Columbia University Press, 1956. First published in 1346.

BATTAGLIA, Felice, «I politici curialisti del tempo di Giovanni XXII (Marsilio da Padova)», *Ricerche religiose*, No. 3, 1927.
——, *Marsilio da Padova e la filosofia politica del Medioevo*. Florence: Le Monnier, 1928. Pp. 278.

THOMAS SAINT, Aquinas (1224/5-1284): the power of the monarch should be controled by the magistrates, representatives of the people: the Church's power over state is indirect. See above, Ch. I, 2, p. 15.

——, *De regimine principium*, c. 1266.

——, *Commentaries*, — see Ethics, above, Chapter I, 2 Middle Ages, p. 14, cf. particularly on Aristotle's Politics and Ethics.

——, *Selected Political Writings*. Ed. by Alessandro PASSERIN D'ENTRÈVES. Translated by J. G. DAWSON. Oxford: Basil Blackwell, 1948. Pp. XXXVI, 199.

DEMONGEOT, Marcel, *Le meilleur régime politique selon saint Thomas*. Paris: A. Blot, 1928.

KURZ, Edelbert, *Individuum und Gemeinschaft beim heiligen Thomas von Aquin*. Freiburg i. M.: Kösel und Pustet, 1933. Pp. 163.

FLORI, Ezio, — see above, p. 183.

MICHEL, G.; *La notion thomiste du bien commun*. Paris. 1932.

ROCCA DELLA, Guglio, *La politica in s. Tommaso*. Naples: Rispoli, 1934. Pp. 206.

ROLAND-GOSSELIN, B., *La doctrine politique de saint Thomas d'Aquin*. Paris: M. Rivière, 1928.

SCHILLING, Otto, *Die Staats- und Soziallehre des hl. Thomas von Aquin*. Paderborn: F. Schöningh, 1923. Pp. X, 285.

Suarez, Francis (1548-1617): the monarch (ruler, political sovereignty) is necessary for human society, but political authority of the individuals, although derived ultimately from God, depends on the agreement of the people. See Law, above, Ch. III, 3, p. 129.

——, *De legibus*, — see above, p. 129.

Battaglia, Felice, «Società civile ed autorità nel pensiero di Francesco Suarez», *Rivista internazionale di filosofia del diritto* (Milan), 1950, pp. 213-234.

Zimmermann, Michel A., *La crise de l'organisation internationale à la fin du moyen âge*. Hague: Academy of International Law, 1933. Pp. 317

MODERN

Predominant idea: secular natural law.

(a) Comprehensive Studies

In English

Dunning, William A., *Political Theories from Luther to Montesquieu*. New York: The Macmillan Co., 1905. Pp. X, 459. Bibliography.

Gooch, George P., *English Democratic Ideas in the Seventeenth Century*. Ed. by H. J. Laski. Cambridge : Cambridge University Press, 1927. Pp. 315.

Hallowell, John H., *Main Currents in Modern Political Thought*. New York: Henry Holt and Co., 1950. Pp. XII, 759.

Harrison, W., *Conflict and Compromise: History of British Political Thought, 1593-1900*. New York: Free Press of Glencoe, 1965. Pp. XII, 269.

—— (ed.), *Sources in British Political Thought, 1593-1900*. New York: Free Press of Glencoe, 1965. Pp. VIII, 289.

Hearnshaw, Fossey John Cobb (ed.), *Social and Political Ideas of Some Great Thinkers of the Renaissance and the Reformation*. New York: Henry Holt and Co., 1923. Pp. 215.

—— (ed.), *Political Principles of Some Notable Prime Ministers of the Nineteenth Century*. Lectures. London: Macmillan and Co., 1926. Pp. IX, 300.

MacIver, Robert Morrison, *The Modern State*. Oxford: At the Clarendon Press, 1926. Pp. XII, 504.

Woodward, E. L., *The Social and Political Ideas of Some Great Thinkers of the Sixteenth and Seventeenth Centuries*. Lectures delivered in London, 1925-1926. Ed. by F. J. C. Hearnshaw. London, 1925.

In Other Languages

Barni, Jules Romain, *Histoire des idées morales et politique en France au XVIIIe siècle*. 2 vols. Paris: Germer-Baillière, 1865-1867.

CROCE, B., *Storia dell' età barocca in Italia*. Bari: G. Laterza, 1929. Pp. XII, 508.

Les doctrines politiques modernes. New York: Brentano's, 1947. Pp. 322.

LENZ, George (ed.), *Deutsches Staatsdenken im 18. Jahrhundert*. Neuwied Rhein: Luchterhand, 1965. Pp. 434.

SOLARI, Gioele, *La scuola del diritto naturale nelle dottrine etico-giuridiche dei seccoli XVII e XVIII*. Turin: Bocca, 1904.

(b) Specific Studies

(aa) RENAISSANCE,

See Modern, above, a; also above, p. 129.

ALLEN, John William, *A History of Political Thought in the Sixteenth Century*. London: Reprinted London: Lippincott, 1957. Pp. 527.

FIGGIS, John Neville, *Political Thought in the Sixteenth Century*. London: Longmans, Green and Co., 1904.

HEARNSHAW, Fossey John Cobb (ed.), *Social and Political Ideas of Some Great Thinkers of the Renaissance and the Reformation*. New York: Henry Holt and Co., 1923. Pp. 215.

BRUNELLO, Bruno, *Il pensiero politico italiano del settecento*. Messina: Principate, 1942.

BODIN, Jean (1530-1596), *Les six livres de la république*. Paris: I. du Puys, 1583. Pp. 1060. English translation and edition by K. D. MACRAE. Cambridge, Massachusetts: Harvard University Press, 1962. First published in 1576. See Law above, Chapter III, 3 Modern, p. 131.

MACHIAVELLI, Niccolò (1469-1527): is it better to be loved than to be feared ?

——, *Il principe*. Written in 1513, published in Rome: Antonio Blado, 1532. Edited in Italian also by L. H. BURD. Oxford: At the Clarendon Press, 1891. English translation by Edward DACRES, *Nicholas Machiavelli's Prince*. London: Daniel Pakeman, 1640. Pp. 305. Among other translations is that of Robert Caponigri, Chicago, Regnery, 1963; Leslie J. WALKER, *Discourses*, 2 vols London, Routledge and Kegan Paul, 1950.

——, *I dialoghi dell' arte della guerra*. Florence: Heredi di Philippo di Giunta, 1521. English translation by Peter WHITEHORNE, *The Arte of Warre*. London: Ihon Kingston, 1560. A recent translation by Ellis FARNEWORTH, *The Art of War*. New York: Bobbs-Merrill Co., 1965. Pp. 352. See Ethics, above, Chapter I, 3 War, p. 67.

——, *Discorsi di Niccolò Machiavelli sopra la prima deca di Tito Livio*. 3 vols. Milan: N. Bettoni, 1830.

——, *The Historical, Political, and Diplomatic Writings*. Translated by Christian E. DETMOLD. 4 vols. Boston: James R. Osgood and Co., 1882.

——, *Machiavelli*. The Tudor Translation. London: David Nutt, 1905.

——, *Œuvres politique*. Paris: Lavigne, 1842. Pp. XXIV, 380.

——, *Œuvres politique*. Paris: Gerdès, 1847. Pp. 480.

——, *Œuvres politiques*. Paris: Charpentier, 1851. Pp. XXXII, 590.

——, *Opere*. 11 vols. Milan: L. Mussi, 1810-1811.

The _Chief Works of Machiavelli and Others. Edited and translated by Allan H. GILBERT. 3 vols. Durham, North Carolina: Duke University Press, 1964.

BUTTERFIELD, H., Statecraft of Machiavelli. London: Bell, 1955. Pp. 167. First published in 1940.

GILBERT, Felix, «Machiavelli Nicolò», in The Encyclopedia of Philosophy (8 vols New York: The Macmillan Co., 1967), Vol. V, pp. 119-121.

MEINECKE, Friedrich, Machiavellism: The Doctrine of Reason d'Etat and Its Place in Modern History. Translated by Douglas SCOTT. London: Routledge, 1957. Pp. 438.

PREZZOLINI, Giuseppe, Vita di Nicolò Machiavelli fiorentino. Verona: Mondadori, 1934. Pp. 257. English translation by Ralph ROEDER, Nicolo Machiavelli, The Florentine. London: G. P. Putnam's Sons, 1928.

SFORZA, Carlo, The Living Thoughts of Machiavelli. New York: Longmans, Green and Co., 1940. Pp. 161.

STRAUSS, Leo, Thoughts on Machiavelli. New York: The Macmillan Co., 1958. Pp. 348.

BATTAGLIA, Felice, «Studi sulla politica di Machiavelli», Nuovi studi di diritto, economia e politica, Nos. 1-6, 1927-1928; Nos. 1-2, 1929.

——, «Post illa machiavellica: Risposta al prof. Carista», Rivista internazionale di filosofia del diritto, No. 3, 1932.

BRUNELLO, Bruno, Machiavelli e il pensiero politico del Rinascimento. Bologne: Patron, 1964. Pp. 219.

CHABOD, Federico, «Del «Principe» di Nicolao Machiavelli», Nova Rivista Storica. (Milan: Albrighi e Segati), 1926.

CROCE, B., Pagine sulla guerra. New edition. Bari: G. Laterza, 1928. Pp. 358.

NORSA, Achille, Il principio della forza nel pensiero politico di Niccolo Machiavelli seguito da un contributo bibliografico. Milan: Hoepli, 1936. Pp. XCV, 248.

QUADRI, Goffredo, Niccolo Machiavelli e la costruzione politica della coscienza morale. Florence: La Nuova Italia, 1948. Pp. 253.

SASSO, Gennaro, Niccolò Machiavelli. Geschichte seines politischen Denkens. Stuttgart. Kohlhammer, 1965. Pp. 416.

Reaction to Machiavelism

BOTERO, Giovanni (1544-1617), Della ragion di Stato. New edition by C. MORANDI. Bologne: Capelli, 1930. First published in 1589. Pp. 367.

——, De regia sapientia. Milan: P. Pontius, 1583. Pp. 115.

——, Politia Regia. Marburg: P. Egenolphus, 1620. Pp. XXIV, 252.

CHABOD, Federico, Giovanni de Botero. Rome: A. R. E., 1934.

DE LUCA, Luigi, Stato e Chiesa nel pensiero politico di Giovanni Botero. Rome: Danesi, 1946.

MATTEI DE, R., «Il problema della Ragion di Stato», in *Rivista internazionale della filosofia del diritto* (Geneva), 1951, pp. 333-356.

CAMPANELLA, Tommaso (1568-1639), *Aforismi politici*. Ed. by L. FIRPO. Turin: Giappichelli, 1941.

——, *De Monarchia hispanica discursus*. Amsterdam: L. Elzevirius, 1640. Pp. VIII, 560.

——, *Antireneti*. Ed. by L. FIRPO. Florence: Sansoni, 1945.

——, *Discorsi ai principi d'Italia*. Ed. by L. FIRPO. Turin: Chiantore, 1945.

FIRPO, L., *Ricerche campanelliane*. Florence: Sansoni, 1947.

JACOBELLI ISOLDI, A. M., *Tommaso Campanella: la crisi della coscienza. in sé*. Milan: N. Zanichelli, 1953.

MATTEI DE, Rodolfo, *la politica di Campanella*. Rome: Garroni, 1927. Pp. 240.

TREVES, P., *La filosofia politica di T. Campanella*. Bari: G. Laterza, 1930. Pp. 248.

GROTIUS, Hugo (Groot de, Huig, 1583-1645) — see Law above, p. 130.

——, *De iure belli ac pacis libri tres*. Paris: W. Buon, 1625. English edition by George G. WILSON, *Law of War and Peace*. Concord, New Hamsher, 1941.

——, *De iure praedae commentarius*. Chapter, Mare Liberum, published in 1609; the rest in 1868. The Hague: Hagae Comitum, 1868. New edition with commentary. 2 vols. Oxford: Clarendon Press, 1950.

FRIEDMANN, Wolfgang, «Grotius Hugo», in *The Encyclopedia of Philosophy* (8 vols. New York: The Macmillan Co., 1967), Vo. III, pp. 393-395.

MEULEN, Jacob, *Concise Bibliography of Hugo Grotius*. Leyden: A. W. Siithoff, 1925. Pp. 88.

Huig de Groot: Essays on His Life and Works Selected for the Occasion of the Tercentenary of His De jure belli ac pacis (1625-1925). Ed. by A. LYSEN. Leyden. E. J. Brill, 1925.

AMBROSETTI, Giovanni, *I presupposti teologici e speculativi delle concezioni giuridiche di Grozio*. Bologne: N. Zanichelli, 1955.

CORSANO, A., *Ugo Grozio: L'umanista, il teologo, il giurista*. Bari: G. Laterza, 1948.

JOUBERT, J., *Étude sur Grotius*. Paris: Domat-Montchrestien, 1938. Pp. 112.

LABROUSSE, R., «Il problema dell' originalità di G. Grozio», in *Rivista internazionale di filosofia del diritto* (Geneva), 1951, No. 2.

WOLF, Erik, *Grosse Rechtsdenker der deutschen Geistesgeschichte*. 3rd ed. Tübingen: Mohr, 1951. Pp. V, 739.

SUAREZ, Francis (1548-1617), — see above, p. 185; Law, above, Ch. III 3, p. 129; Ethics, Ch. I, 2, p. 17.

THOMASIUS, Christian (1655-1728), — see Law, above, Ch. III, 3, p. 130.

——, *Delineatio iuris romani et germanici.* Erfurt: J. A. Lorber, 1750. Pp. 72.

BATTAGLIA, Felice, *Christiano Thomasius filosofo e giurista.* Rome: Il Foro Italiano, 1936. Pp. 444.

——, «Marsilio da Padova nell' interpretazione di Cristiano Thomasius», *Rivista internazionale di filosofia del diritto* (Geneva), No. 4-5, 1933.

VICO, Giambattista (1668-1744), — see History in *PQS*, No. 5.
——, *New Science.* Translated by T. G. BERGIN and M. I. FISCH. New York: Doubleday, 1964.

CROCE, B., *The Philosophy of Giambattista Vico.* Translated by R. G. COLLINGWOOD. New York: The Macmillan Co., 1913.

Per il II Centenario della «Scienza Nuova». Special issue of the *Rivista internazionale di filosofia del diritio* (Geneval), 1925.

ZUCCOLO, Ludovico (1568-1630), «Della Ragion di Stato», *Politici e moralisti del Seicento.* Bari: G. Laterza, 1930.

Reformation, — see Christianity, below, 5, p. 214.

Utopianism: imaginary, impractical and ideal proposals completely different from ordinary thinking.

BUBER, Martin, *Paths in Utopia.* Translated by R.F.C. HULL. New York: The Macmillan Co., 1950. Pp. 152.
KATEB, George, «Utopias and Utopianism», in *The Encyclopedia of Philosophy* (New York: The Macmillan Co., 1967), Vol. VIII, pp. 212-215.
MANNHEIM, Karl, *Ideologie und Utopie.* Bonn: F. Cohen, 1929. Pp. X, 250. English translation by Louis WIRTH and E. SHILS, *Ideology and Utopia: An Introduction to Sociology of Knowledge.* New York: Harcourt, Brace and Co., 1936. Pp. XXXI, 318. See below, p.
POLAK, Fred L., *The Images of the Future.* 2 vols. Translated by Elsie BOULDING. New York and Leiden: Sijthoff, 1961.

Representatives

MORE Sir, Thomas, (1478-1535), *The Utopia.* Ed. by H. B. COTERILL: translated by Ralph ROBINSON. New York: St. Martin's Press, 1908. Pp. 284. First published in 1516; emended edition in 1556.

MOSCA, Gaetano, «L'utopia di Tommaso Moro et il pensiero comunista moderno", in *Scritii in onore di Antonio Scialoia.* Milan: Villardi, 1928.

(bb) RATIONALISM,
See Ethics, above, Ch. I, 2, p. 18.

GIERKE VON Otto Friedrich, *Natural Law and the Theory of Society, 1500 to 1800.* 2 vols. Translated by Ernest BARKER. Cambridge: The University Press, 1934.

FILMER Sir, Robert (c. 1653): all people are naturally subordinated.

——, *The Anarchy of a Limited or Mixed Monarchy, Or A Succinct Examination of the Fundamentals of Monarchy.* (London), 1648. Pp. 39.
——, *The Free-holders Grand Inquest. Touching Our Sovereign Lord the King and His Parliament.* London: Printed in the year 1680. Pp. 326.
——, *Observations concerning the Original and Various Forms of Government.* London: sold by T. Axe, 1696.
——, *Observations upon Aristoteles Politiques.* London: Printed for R. Chiswell, 1680. Pp. 141.
——, *Patriarcha; or, The Natural Power of King.* London: Printed for R. Chiswell, 1680. Pp. 141.

HOBBES, Thomas (1588-1679): monarchy is to be preferred.
See Ethics, above, Ch. I, 2, p. 21.

——, *Leviathan.* London: Printed for Andrew Ckooke, 1651. Pp. 394. Edited also by Michael OAKESHOTT in Oxford, 1947.
——, *De Corpore Politico or the Elements of Law, Moral and Politick.* (sic). London: Ram-Alley, 1650. Pp. 195. Edited by Richard S. PETERS, *Body, Man, and Citizen.* New York: Collier, 1962.
——, *Elementa philosophia de cive.* Amsterdam: L. Elzevirus, 1647. Pp. 407.
——, *The Moral and Political Works.* Ed. by Dr. BLACKBOURNE. London: Printed in year 1750. Pp. XVIII, 697.
——, *The Elements of Law, Natural and Politic.* Ed. by Ferdinand TONNIES. London: Simpkin, Marshall and Co., 1889. Pp. XVI, 226. Edited also in Cambridge: University Press, 1928. Pp. XVII, 195.

GRAHAM, William, *English Political Philosophy from Hobbes to Maine.* 5th ed. London: E. Arnold, 1919. Pp. 415. First published in 1899.

MACPHERSON, C. B., *Political Theory of Possessive Individualism: Hobbes to Locke.* New York: 1962.

STRAUSS, L., *The Political Philosophy of Hobbes: Its Basis and Its Genesis.* English translation from the German by Elsa M. SINCLAIR. New edition. Chicago: University of Chicago Press, 1952. Pp. XX, 172.

WARRENDER, Howard, *Political Philosophy of Hobbes.* New York: Oxford University Press, 1957. Pp. 346.

BIANCA, Giovanni, *Diritto e Stato nel pensiero di T. Hobbes.* Naples: Humus, 1946.

NARDO, Giuseppe, *Spinoza: il pensiero politico e religioso in rapporto con Hobbes.* Rome: Editrice Italia, 1947. See also Spinoza, below.

PACCHI, Arrigo, *Convenzione e ipotesi nella formazione della filosofia naturale di Thomas Hobbes.* Milan: Giuffrè, 1966. Pp. 252.

POLIN, Raymond, *Politique et philosophie chez Thomas Hobbes.* Paris: Presses Universitaires de France, 1952. Pp. XX, 267.

SPINOZA, Baruch (1632-1677): the wise sovereign must look for the well-being of the people.

See Ethics, above, Ch. I, 2, p. 19; Modern History of Philosophy, in *PQS*, No. 5.

——, *Tractatus theologico-politicus.* Hamburg: H. Künraht, 1670. Pp. 234.

——, *Tractatus politicus.* Posthumously published in Amsterdam, 1677. New edition. Hilversumi: S. H. de Roos, 1928. Pp. III, 113. English translation by W. MACCALL, *A Treatise on Politics.* London: 1854. Also in *The Chief Works of Benedict de Spinoza.* English translation by R. H. M. ELWES, 2 vols. London: G. Bell and Sons, 1883-1884. Vol. I: Tractatus; Vol. II: De intellectus emendatione.

——, *Political Works.* Ed. by A.G. WERNHAM. New York: Oxford University Press, 1958. Pp. 463.

FEUER, Lewis Samuel, *Spinoza and the Rise of Liberalism.* Boston: Beacon Press, 1958. Pp. 323.

McSHEA, Robert, J., *The Political Philosophy of Spinoza.* New York: Columbia University Press, 1968. Pp. 214.

POLLOCK Sir, Frederick, *Spinoza: His Life and Philosophy.* 2nd ed. reprint. New York: American Scholar Publications, 1966. Pp. XXIV, 427.

WOLFSON, H. A , *Philosophy of Spinoza.* 2 vols. New York: Meridian Books, 1958.

HORN, J. E., *Spinoza Staatslehre.* New edition. Aalen: Scientia Verlag, 1964. Pp. XII, 201.

NARDO, Giuseppe, *Spinoza: il pensiero politico e religioso in rapporto con Hobbes.* Rome: Editrice Italia, 1947.

LEIBNIZ, Gottfried Wilhelm (1646-1716). City of God, or the harmonious unity of spirits as a result of the moral world within the natural world, which is the best possible in the present circumstances.

See Ethics, above, Ch. I, 2, p. 20, cf. 131.

——, *Scriptores rerum brunsvicensium.* 3 vols. Hanover: N. Foerster, 1707-1711.

——, *Codex iurius gentium diplomaticus.* 2 vols. Hanover: G. Freytag, 1693 1700.

——, *De expeditione Aegyptiaca Ludovico XIV Franciae Regi proponenda.* Ed by O. Klopp. Hannover: Klindworth, 1864. Pp. CII, 432. English summary, *A Summary Account of Leibnitz's Memoir Addressed to Lewis the Fourteenth Recommending to the Monarch the Conquest of Egypt, as conducive to the establishment of a Supreme Authority over the Governments of Europe.* London, 1803.

——, *Wybór króla w Polsce.* Translation from the Latin. Paris: Cendrowicz, 1843. Pp. 95.

Naërt, Emilienne, *La pensée politique de Leibniz.* Paris: Presses Universitaires de France, 1964. Pp. 116.

(cc) Empiricism

See Empiricism in Ethics, below, Ch. I, 2, p. 21; War above, Ch. I, 3, p. 67; Rationalism, above, p. 190.

Cassirer, Ernst, *The Philosophy of the Enlightenment.* Translated by Fritz C. A. Koelln and James P. Pettegrove. Princeton, New Jersey: Princeton University Press, 1951. Pp. 380.

Halévy, Élie, *The Growth of Philosophic Radicalism.* Translated by Mary Morris. London: Faber and Gwyer, 1928. Pp. XVII, 554.

Talmon, J. L., *The Origins of Totalitarian Democracy.* 3 vols. London: Secker and Warburg, 1952.

Grotius, H., — see Renaissance, above, p. 188.

Locke, John (1632-1704): the government has its right and power from the consent of the people expressing themselves lawfully through the majority of their representatives. Natural law is the basis of man's rights.

——, *Two Treatises of Government.* New York: Hafner, 1947. First revised and published in 1689. Also edited by Peter Laslett in London: Cambridge University Press, 1960. Pp. 520.

——, *Treatise of Civil Government and A Letter Concerning Toleration.* Ed. by Charles L. Sherman. New York: Appleton-Century, 1959. Pp. 224.

Cox, Richard H., *Locke's Theory of International Relations.* Chicago: University of Chicago Press, 1955. Pp. IV. 184.

Czajkowski, C. J., *The Theory of Private Property in John Locke's Political Philosophy.* Notre Dame, Indiana: University of Notre Dame, 1941. Pp. VIII, 108. See also Private Property, above, Ch. II, 5.

Gough, John W., *John Locke's Political Philosophy.* Oxford: Clarendon Press, 1956. Pp. VII, 204.

Green, John Park, *The Philosophic Premises of Locke's Politics: The Doctrine of the Law of Nature.* Chicago: University of Chicago, 1953. Pp. III, 178.

LAMPRECHT, Sterling P., *The Moral and Political Philosophy of John Locke*. New York: Russell and Russell, 1962. Pp. VIII, 168. First published in 1918.

MACPHERSON, Crawford B., *The Political Theory of Possessive Individualism*. Hobbes to Locke. Oxford: Clarendon Press, 1962. Pp. 310.

HUME, David (1711-1776): the state and its institutions develop out of man's instincts and needs.
See Empiricism, below, Ch. I, 2, p. 22.

——, *Political Essays*. Ed. by Charles W. HENDEL. New York: Bobbs-Merrill, 1953. Pp. 230. Excerpts from Hume's *Political Discourses*.
——, *Political Discourses*. Edinburgh: R. Fleming, 1752.
——, *Essays, Moral and Political*. 3rd. ed. Edinburgh: A. Kincaid, 1748. First published by R. FLEMING, in 1741.

BAGOLINI, Luigi, «Esperienza guiridica e politica nel pensiero di David Hume», in *Studi Senesi* (Siena), 1947. Reprint in 1948.

VLACHOS, Georges, *Essai sur la politique de Hume*. Paris: Dumat-Monchrestien, 1955. Pp. 250.

MONTESQUIEU, Charles Louis de Secondat (1689-1755): natural law is the basis of legal system.

——, *Considérations sur les causes de la grandeur des Romains et de leur décadence*. Paris: Garnier frères, 1945. Pp. XIX, 221. First published in Amsterdam, 1734.
——, *De l'esprit des lois*. 2 vols. Paris: Garnier frères, 1945. First published in Geneva: Barrillot et fils, 1748. English translation by Franz NEUMANN, *Spirit of the Laws*. 2 vols. New York: Hafner, 1949.
——, *Défense de l'esprit des lois*. Geneva: Barillot et fils, 1750. Pp. 207.
——, *Œuvres complètes*. Ed. by A. MASSON. 3 vols. Paris: Gallimard, Nagel, 1950-1955.

CABEEN, David Clark, *Montesquieu: A Bibliography*. New York: Public Library, 1947. Pp. 87.

SHACKLETON, Robert, *Montesquieu: A Critical Biography*. New York: Oxford University Press, 1961. Pp. 432.

STARK, Werner, *Montesquieu: Pioneer of the Sociology of Knowledge*. London: Routledge, 1960. Pp. 214.

ALTHUSSER, Louis, *Montesquieu: La politique et l'histoire*. 2nd ed. Paris: Presses Universitaires de France, 1965. Pp. 120.

DURKHEIM, E., *Montesquieu et Rousseau précurseurs de la sociologie*. Paris: M. Rivière, 1953. First published in 1892.

Rousseau, Jean Jacques (1712-1778): attempts to reconcile the will of the individual with that of the society.
See also Sociology, below, p. 241, cf. 153.

——, *The First and Second Discourses.* Edited and translated by Roger D. Masters and Judith R. Masters. New York: St. Martin's Press, 1964. Pp. 354. First published in 1751-1755.

——, *Du contrat social.* Amsterdam: M. M. Rey, 1762. Pp. VIII, 324. English translation by Willmoore Kendall, *Social Contract.* Chicago: H. Regnery, 1954. Pp. 171.

——, *Œuvres politiques.* Paris: V. Lepetit, 1821. Discours sur l'origine et les fondaments de l'inégalite; Du contrat social; Discours sur l'économie politique; Extrait du projet de paix perpétuel; Jugement; Considérations sur le gouvernement de Pologne; Lettres à M. Butta Foco.

——, *The Political Writings.* Ed. by C. E. Vaughan. 2 vols. New edition. New York: John Wiley and Sons, 1962. First English edition published in Cambridge, University Press, 1915.

Barker Sir, Ernest (ed.), *Social Contract: Essays by Locke, Hume and Rousseau.* New York: Oxford University Press, 1951. Pp. LXIII, 440.

Chapman, John William, *Rousseau: Totalitarian or Liberal?* New York: Columbia University Press, 1956. Pp. 154.

Masters, Roger D., *The Political Philosophy of Rousseau.* Princeton, New Jersey: Princeton University Press, 1968. Pp. 488.

Brunello, Bruno, «Idee sociali ed economiche nel Rousseau», *Rivista internazionale di filosofia del diritto* (Geneva), No. 6, 1935.

Cotta, Sergio, «Philosophie et politique dans l'œuvre de Rousseau: un essai d'interpretation», *Archiv für Rechts- und Sozialphilosophie* (Bern), 1963, pp. 171-189.

Pecelli, Diego, «Società e natura nel Discorso sull' ineguaglianza di J. F. Rousseau», *Rivista internazionale di filosofia del diritto* (Geneva), 1963, pp. 201-217.

Rousseau et la philosophie politique. Ed. by P. Arnaud, H. Barth, P. Burcelin, S. Cotta, L. G. Crocker, R. Derathé et al. Paris: Presses Universitaires de France, 1965. Pp. 255.

Weissel, Bernhard, *Von wem die Gewalt in den Staaten herrührt.* Beiträge zu den Auswirkungen der Staats- und Geselschaftauffassungen Rousseaus auf Deutschland im letzten Viertel des 18. Jahrhunderts. Berlin: Rütten und Loening, 1963. Pp. 336.

(dd) Federalism: organization of the communities (States) into larger unities of two governements, one dealing with the communities diversified territorially, the other with these communities as united together. The powers of the governements

are assuming various forms: early City Leagues, Federal States (Bundsstraat), Commonwealth of Nations, United States of
America, and Soviet Union.

See Particular Countries, below, 4, p. 209.

BELOFF, Max, *Public Order and Popular Disturbances, 1660-1714*. London:
Oxford University Press, H. Milford, 1938. Pp. VIII, 168.

BOWIE, Robert R. and FRIEDRICH, Carl (eds.), *Studies in Federalism*. Boston:
Little, Brown and Co., 1954. Pp. XLII, 887.

BURKE, Edmund (1729-1797), *Reflexion on the Revolution in France*. 3rd ed.
London: J. Dodsley, 1790. Pp. IV, 356.

——, *The Works of the Right Honourable Edmund Burke*. 4 vols. Boston:
John West, 1806-1807.

CLARK, Jane Perry, *The Rise of New Federalism*. New York: Columbia
University Press, 1938. Pp. XVIII, 347.

COOKE, J. E. (ed.), *The Federalist*. Middletown, Connecticut: Wesleyan
University Press, 1961. Pp. XXX, 672.

HAMILTON, Alexander (1757-1804), *Hamiltonian Principles*. Extracts from
his writings. Boston: Little, Brown and Co., 1928. Pp. XIX, 188.

——, *A Letter from Phocion to the Considerate Citizens of New York, on
the Politics of the Day*. New York: Samuel London, 1784. Pp. 19.

——, *The Works Comprising his Most Important Official Reports*. An im-
proved edition of The Federalist, on the new Constitution written
in 1788. 3 vols. New York: Williams and Whiting, 1810.

  HACKER, Louis Morton, *Alexander Hamilton in the American Tradition*. New York: McGraw-Hill, 1957. Pp. 273.

JAY, John (1817-1894), *America Free or America Slave*. An address. New
York Tribune, 1856. Pp. 20.

—— *The Dawson's «Federalist»*. Letter. New York: Evening Post, 1864.
Pp. 8.

——, *Our Duty to Freedom*. New York: Cooper Institute, 1865. Pp. 7.

——, *Our Triumph and Our Duties*. New York: Pierrpont House, 1864. Pp.
6.

——, *The Correspondence and Public Papers*. 4 vols. New York: G. P.
Putman, 1890-1893.

JEFFERSON, Thomas, — see below, p. 209.

MACMAHON, Arthur Whittier (ed.), *Federalism Mature and Emergent*. New
York: Doubleday, 1955. Pp. 557.

MADISON, James (1749-1812), *An Examination of the British Doctrine Which
Subjects to Capture a Natural Trade Not Open in Time of Peace*.
London: J. Johnson and W. J. Richardson, 1806. Pp. 200.

——, *The Writings of James Madison, Comprising His Public Papers and
Private Correspondence*. 9 vols. New York: G. P. Putnam's Sons,
1900-1910.

MOGI, Sobel, *The Problem of Federalism: A Study in the History of Political Theory*. 2 vols. New York: The Macmillan Co., 1931.

PAINE, Thomas (1737-1809), *The Rights of Man*. 2 parts. London: J. S. Jordan, 1791-1792. Pp. 171, 178.

——, *Paine's Complete Works.* 3 vols. Boston: J. P. Mendum, 1878.
——, *The Writings of Thomas Paine.* Ed. by Moncure Daniel Conway. 4
  vols. New York: G. P. Putman, 1894-1896.
Wheare, Kenneth Clinton, *Federal Governement.* 3rd. ed. New York:
  Oxford University Press, 1953. P. 278.

(ee) Utilitarianism

See Ethics, above, Ch. I, 2, p. 25.

Bentham, Jeremy (1748-1832): motives of acts are irrelevant,
the consequences matter.

——, *A Fragment on Government, being an examination of what is deli-
  vered on the subject of government in general in the Introduction
  to Sir W. Blackstone's Commentaries.* 2nd ed. enlarged. London:
  W. Pickering and E. Wilson, 1823. Pp. LII, 143. First published in
  1776.
——, *An Introduction to the Principles of Morals and Legislation.* Oxford:
  Clarendon Press, 1892. Pp. XXXV, 378. First published in 1789.
——, *Essay on Political Tactics.* London: T. Payne, 1791. «Essay 6» of an
  unpublished larger work.
——, *A Pleas for Constitution.* London: Maurnan and Hatchard, 1803. Pp.
  IX, 68.
——, *Constitutional Code for the Use of All Nations, and all Govern-
  ments Professing Liberal Opinions.* London: printed for the Author,
  1928. Pp. VII, 253.
——, *The Utilitarians: Principles of Morals and Legislation.* New York:
  Doubleday and Co., 1961. Together with J. St. Mill's *On Liberty*
  and Utilitarianism. Pp. 600.

Mill, John Stuart (1806-1873): the only freedom is to pursue
our own good in our own way, so long as we do not attempt to deprive others of theirs.
See Postivism, above, Ch. III, 3 Modern, p. 139; Ethics-
Utilitarianism, above, Ch. I, 2, p. 26.

——, *Utilitarianism, On Liberty, and Essay on Bentham together with Se-
  lected Writings of Jeremy Bentham and John Austin.* Ed. by Mary
  Warnock. New York: Meridian Books, 1962. Pp. 352.
Essays on Politics and Culture. Ed. by Gertrude Himmelfarb. Garden City,
  New York: Doubleday, 1962. Pp. 494.

Cowing, Maurice, *Mill and Liberalism.* London: Cambridge University Press, 1963. Pp. 161.

Jones, W. T., *Masters of Political Thought.* Boston: Houghton Mifflin Co., 1960. Vol. II: Machiavelli to Bentham. Pp. 388.

McCloskey, H. J., «Mill's Liberalism», *Philosophical Quarterly* (A-
malner, India), 1963, pp. 143-156.

MILLER, Kenneth E., «John Stuart Mill's Theory of International Relations», *Journal of the History of Ideas* (New York), 1961, pp. 493-514.

HIFFLER, F., *Staat und Geselschaft bei Mill, Marx, Lagarde*. Berlin: Junker und Dünnhaupt, 1934. Pp. 239.

JACOBS, Herbert, *Rechtsphilosophie und politische Philosophie bei John Stuart Mill*. Bonn: Bouvier, 1965. Pp. 230.

NIETZSCHE, F. W., — see Superman Ethics, above. Ch. I, 2, p. 29.

SIDGWICK, Henry (1838-1900): freedom is the sole end of governmental interference.
See above, p. 51.

——, *The Elements of Politics*. 4th ed. London: Macmillan Co., 1919. Pp. XXXV, 665. First published in 1891.
——, *The Development of European Polity*. London: Macmillan Co., 1903. Pp. XXVI, 454.

(ff) IDEALISM
See above, Ch. I, 2, p. 32; *PQS*, No. 5.

GERBI, A., *La politica del romanticismo: le origini*. Bari: G. Laterza, 1932. Pp. VII, 257.

England
See below, p. 210.

German

See Idealism in Ethics, above, Ch. I, 2, p. 32; Law, above, Ch. III, 3, p. 136.

KANT, Immanuel (1724-1804): obligation is the condition of the existence of the state.

——, *Zum ewigen Frieden, ein philosophischer Entwurf*. New edition. Königsberg: F. Nicolovius, 1796. Pp. 112. First published in 1795. English more recent translation by Lewis W. BECK, *Perpetual Peace*. Indianapolis, Indiana: Bobbs-Merrill Co., Inc., 1957. Pp. XIV, 59.
——, *Metaphysische Anfangsgrunde der Rechtslehre*. Königsberg: F. Nicolovius, 1797. Pp. XII, 236. English translation by Translation by W. HASTIE, *The Philosophy of Law*. Edinburgh: T. and T. Clark, 1887. Pp. XXXVI, 265.
Kant's Principles of Politics. Translated by W. Hastie. Edinburgh: T. Clark, 1891.

CARRITT, Edgar Frederick, *Morals and Politics: Theories of Their Relation from Hobbes and Spinoza to Marx and Bosanquet.* Oxford: Clarendon Press, 1935. Pp. 216.

——, *The Theory of Morals.* London: Oxford University Press, 1928. Pp. XII, 144.

SCIACCA, G. M., *L'idea della libertà fondamento della coscienza etico-politica in Kant.* Palermo: Palumbo, 1963. Pp. 258.

WEIL, E. *et al.*, *La philosophie politique de Kant.* Paris: Presses Universitaires de France, 1962. Pp. 188.

WOLFF, E., «La philosophie politique de Kant», *Archives de Philosophie* (Paris), 1963, pp. 621-624.

FICHTE, Johann Gottlieb (1762-1814): the state is a groundwork of interests and a means for the rightful, legal relation among men: the Germans are destined to lead nations to the kindom of God on the earth.
See above, pp. 32, 138.

——, *Reden an die deutsche Nation.* New edition. Tübingen: H. Leupp, 1869. Pp. XX, 203. English translation, *Addresses to the German Nation.* La Salle, Illinois: Open Court Publishing Co., 1923.
——, *Das System der Sittenlehre nach den Principien der Wissenschaftslehre.* Leipzig: C. E. Gabler, 1798. PP. XVIII, 494. English translation By A. E. KROEGER, *The Science of Ethics as Based on the Science of Knowledge.* New edition. London: Kegan Paul, 1907.
——, *Der geschlossene Handelsstaat. Ein philosophischer Entwurf als Anhang zur Rechtslehre.* Tübingen: J. C. Cotta, 1800. Pp. 290. :
——, *Johann Gottlieb Fichtes Sämmtliche Werke.* Ed. by I. H. FICHTE. 8 vols. Berlin: Veit, 1845-1846. Vol. III-IV, Rechts- und Sittenlehre.

ENGELBRECHT, H. C., *Johann Gottlieb Fichte: A Study of His Political Writings with Special Reference to His Nationalism.* New York: Columbia University Press, 1933.

GLÜCKSOHN, Moses, *Fichtes Staats- und Wirtschaftslehre.* Bern: Universität Bern, 1910. Pp. 91.

LEIBHOLZ, Gerhard, *Fichte und der demokratische Gedanke.* Freiburg i. Br.: J. Boltze, 1921. Pg. IV, 100.

MEYER, J. B., *Fichte, Lasalle und der Socialismus.* Berlin: C. Habel, 1878. Pp. 64.

RICKERT, H., «Die philosophischen Grundlagen von Fichtes Sozialismus», *Logos*, 1922-1923, pp. 149-180.

SCHNEIDER, Fritz, *J. G. Fichte als Sozial-politiker.* Halle: C. A. Fremmerer, 1894. Pp. 82.

STRECKER, Heinrich Wilhelm Reinhard, *Die Anfänge von Fichtes Staatsphilosophie.* Leipzig: F. Meiner, 1916. Pp. V, 228.

VLACHOS, Georges, *Fédéralisme et raison d'état dans la pensée internationale de Fichte*. Paris: Éditions Pédone, 1948. Pp. 208.

WEBER, Marianne, *Fichtes Sozialismus und sein Verhältnis zur Marx'schen Doktrin*. Freiburg i. Br.: J. C. B. Mohr, 1900. Pp. VII, 122.

WINDELBAND, Wilhelm, *Fichtes Idee des deutschen Staates*. Freiburg i. Br.: J. E. B. Mohr, 1890. Pp. 31.

HEGEL, Georg W. F. (1770-1831): the state is the culmination of the progressive dialectical development where man becomes truly free.
See, above, pp. 32, 138.

——, «Über die wissenschaftliche Behandlungsarten des Naturrechts, seine Stelle in der praktischen Philosophie und seine Verhältnis zu der positiven Rechtswissenschaften», *Kritiker Journal der Philosophie* (Ed. by Schelling and Hegel), Vol. II, Heft 2-3, 1802.

——, *Grundlinien der Philosophie des Rechts*. Berlin: Nicolai, 1820. English translation by T. M. KNOX, *Philosophy of Right*. Oxford: Clarendon Press, 1942.

——, *Kritik der Verfassung Deutschlands*. Aus dem handschriftlichen Nachlasse des Verfassers. Ed. by Georg MOLLAT. Kassel: T. G. Fischer, 1893. Pp. VII, 143.

——, *Political Writings*. Translated by T. M. KNOX with an introductory essay by Z. A. PELCZYNSKI. New York: Oxford University Press, 1964. Pp. 337.

CAIRNS, H., *Legal Philosophy from Plato to Hegel*. Baltimore: John Hopkins University Press, 1949. Pp. XV, 583.

CROCE, B., see Italian, below, p. 201.

FOSTER, M. B., *The Political Philosophies of Plato and Hegel*. Oxford: Clarendon Press, 1935.

FLEISCHMANN, Eugène, *La philosophie politique de Hegel, sous forme d'un commentaire des Fondements de la philosophie du droit*. Paris: Plon, 1964. Pp. VIII, 404.

GERBI, A., *La politica del romanticismo: le origini*. Bari: G. Laterza, 1932. Pp. VII, 257.

GIESE, Gerhardt, *Hegel und der preußische Staat*. Leipzig: Teubner, 1930. Pp. 32.

HALLER, Hermann, *Hegel und der nationale Machtstaatsgedanke in Deutschland*. Ein Beitrag zur politischen Geistesgeschichte. New edition. Aalen: Zeller, 1963. Pp. VI, 210.

Hegel's Lehre vom Staat und seine Philosophie der Geschichte in ihren Hauptresultaten. Berlin: A. Förstner, 1837. Pp. 99.

ILTING, Karl Heinz, «Hegels Auseinandersetzung mit der aristotelischen Politik», *Philosophisches Jahrbuch* (Munich), 1963, pp. 38-58.

KAMPFER, Walter, «Die Kritik Hegels an der Staatsauffassung Karl Ludwig von Hallers», in *Festgabe Max Obrecht* (Solothurn, 1961), Pp. 23-43.

LÖWITH, Karl (ed.), *Die Hegelsche Linke*. Stuttgart and Bad Connstaltt: F. Fromann, 1962. Pp. 288. Texts from H. HEINE, A. RUGE, M. HESS, M. STIRNER, B. BAUER, L. FEUERBACH, K. MARX, S. KIERKEGAARD.

LÜBBE, Hermann (ed.), *Die Hegelsche Rechte*. Stuttgart and Bad Connstatt: F. Frommann, 1962. Pp. 330. Text from F. W. CARORÉ, *et al.*

PASSERIN D'ENTRÈVES, A., *Il fondamento della filosofia giuridica di G. G. F. Hegel*. Turin: Gobetti, 1924. Pp. 134.

ROSENZWEIG, F., *Hegel und der Staat*. 2 vols. Munich: Berlin: R. Oldenbourg, 1920.

SCHEUNER, Ulrich, «Hegel und die deutsche Staatslehre des 19. und 20. Jahrhunderts», *Studium Berolinense* (Berlin), 1960, pp. 129-151.

WEIL, Erich, *Hegel et l'état*. Paris: Université de Paris, 1950. Pp. 118.

English and American Idealism

BARKER, Ernest, *Reflections on Government*. New York: Oxford University Press, 1942. Pp. XVI, 424.

MILNE, A. J. M., *The Social Philosophy of English Idealism*. London: Allen and Unwin, 1962. Pp. 320.

BOSANQUET, Bernard (1848-1923): social coercion is true freedom.

——, *The Philosophical Theory of the State*. London: Macmillan and Co., 1899. Pp. XVIII, 342. See also State, below, p. 223.

HOUANG, F., *Le Néo-hégélianisme en Angleterre: la philosophie de Bernard Bosanquet*. Paris: J. Vrin, 1954. Pp. 232.

GREEN, Thomas Hill (1836-1882): the state is the embodiment of citizens' rights and should hasten the idea of treating others as the end.

——, *Lectures on the Principles of Political Obligation*. London: Longmans, Green and Co., 1901. Pp. XXIV, 252.

——, *The Works of Thomas Hill Green*. Ed. by R. L. NETTLESHIP. 3 vols. London: Longmans, Green and Co., 1889-1890.

RICHTER, Melvin, *The Politics of Conscience: T. H. Green and His age*. Cambridge, Massachusetts: Harvard University Press, 1964. Pp. 415.

HOBHOUSE, Leonard Trelawney (1864-1929), *Liberalism*. New York: H. Holt and Co., 1911. Pp. 254.

——, *The Elements of Social Justice*. New York: H. Holt and Co., 1922. Pp. VIII, 247. See also State, below, p. 223.

——, *Morals in Evolution: A Study in Comparative Ethics.* New edition. New York: H. Holt and Co., 1915. Pp. 648.

——, *Social Evolution and Political Theory.* New York: Columbia University Press, 1911. Pp. IX, 218.

Hobson, John Atkinson and Ginsberg, Morris, *L. T. Hobhouse, His Life and Work.* London: Allen and Unwin, 1931. Pp. 360.

Royce, Josiah (1855-1916), *The World and the Individual.* New York: The Macmillan Co., 1900. Pp. XVI, 588.

——, *The Philosophy of Loyalty.* New York: The Macmillan Co., 1936. Pp. XIII, 409. First published in 1908.

Smith, John Edwin, *Royce's Social Infinite.* New York: Liberal Arts, 1950. Pp. XIII, 176.

Italian Idealism

See Renaissance, above 3 Modern, p. 186; Idealism, above, Ch. I, 2 p. 48.

Croce, B., — see Law, above, Ch. III, 3, p. 141.

——, *Filosofia della pratica: Economica ed etica.* 4th ed. Bari: G. Laterza, 1932. Pp. XX, 394. English translation by D. Ainslie, *Philosophy of the Practical, Economic and Ethic.* London: Macmillan, 1913. Pp. XXXIX, 592.

——, «Intorno alla storia degli studi sociali e politici», *Critica* (Bari), No. 2, 1905.

——, «Contro l'astrattismo e il materialismo politico», *Critica* (Bari), No. 3, 1912.

——, *Cultura e vita morale: intermezzi polemici.* Bari: G. Laterza, 1914. Pp. 224.

——, «I limiti della dottrina dello stato come potenza», *Critica* (Bari), No. 3, 1916.

——, «Ancora filosofia e politica», *Critica* (Bari), No. 6, 1923.

——, *Elementi di politica.* Bari: G. Laterza, 1925. Pp. 117.

——, *Riduzione della filosofia del diritto alla filosofia dell' economia.* Naples: R. Ricciardi, 1926. Pp. XXXII, 94.

——, *Etica e politica.* Bari: G. Laterza, 1931. Pp. 415. English translation by Salvatore J. Castiglione, *Politics and Morals.* New York: Philosophical Library, 1945. Pp. 204.

——, *Pagine politiche.* Bari: Laterza, 1945. Pp. 154.

——, *Pensiero politico e politica attuale.* Bari: G. Laterza, 1946. Pp. 188.

——, *Storiografia e idealità morale.* Bari: G. Laterza, 1950.

Antoni, Carlo, *Commento a Croce.* Venice: Neri Pozza, 1955. Pp. 254.

Bobbio, Norberto, «Benedetto Croce e il liberalismo», *Rivista di filosofia* (Bologne), 1955, pp. 261-286.

Mautino, A., *La formazione della filosofia politica di Benedetto Croce.* Turin: Einaudi, 1941.

Parente, A., *Il pensiero politico di Benedetto Croce e il nuovo Liberalismo.* Naples, 1944.

Gentile, Giovanni, — see Ch. III, 3, p. 142; Facism, below, p. 219.

——, «Politica e filosofia», *Politica*, 1918.

——, *Guerra e fede: frammenti politici.* Naples: Ricciardi, 1919. Pp. XI, 381.

——, *Dopo la vittoria: novi frammenti politici.* Rome: La Voce, 1920. Pp. VIII, 216.

——, «Realismo e fatalismo politico», *Politica*, No. 2, 1920.

——, «Stato etico e statolatoria», *Giornale critico della filosofia* (Florence, Italy), No. 5, 1924.

——, «Idealismo e umanismo», *Giornale critico della filosofia* (Florence, Italy), No. 3, 1926.

——, «The Philosophy of the Modern State», *Spectator* (London), 3 Nov. 1928.

——, «La filosofia e lo Stato», in *Atti VII Congresso nazionale di filosofia, Rome, 1929.* Milan: Bestetti e Tuminelli, 1929.

——, «Il concetto di Stato in Hegel», *Nuovi Studi di diritto, economia e politica*, No. 6, 1931.

——, «Hegel, Orestano e il fascismo», *Educazione fascista*, No. 6, 1933.

——, «Politica ed economia», in his *Origini e dottrina del fascismo.* 3rd ed. Rome: Istituto nazionale di cultura, 1934.

——, *Dottrina politica del fascismo.* Padua: Cedam, 1937. Pp. 22. See also Fascism, below, p. 219.

——, «La filosofia del fascismo», *Il libro italiano nel mondo*, Nos. 5-6, 1941.

——, *Genesi e struttura della società.* Florence: Sansoni, 1946.

CIRELL-CZERNA, R., «Riflessioni sul concetto di società e di stato nell' ultima fase del pensiero gentiliano», in *Scritti in onore di L. Sturzo.* Bologne: N. Zanichelli, 1953.

DE LUCA, G., «Il fascismo e la filosofia gentiliana», *Vita Italiana* (Rome), 1928.

LICITRA, C., «Giovanni Gentile e il fascismo», in his *Dal Liberalismo al fascismo.* Rome: De Alberti, 1925.

POZZO, G. M., «La filosofia politica dell' ultimo Gentile», in *Humanitas* (Brescia, Italy), 1952, pp. 254-261.

(gg) POSITIVISM

See above, Ch. I, 2, p. 35; Law above, Ch. III, 3, p. 139.

COMTE, Auguste (1798-1857), — see above, pp. 35, 139.

——, *Calendrier positiviste, ou système général de commémoration publique destiné surtout à la transition finale de la grande république occidentale composée des cinq populations avancées, française, italinne, germanique, brittannique et espagnole.* 4th ed. Paris: L. Mathias, 1852. Pp. 43. First published in 1849.

——, *Catechisme positiviste, ou sommaire exposition de la religion universelle.* Édition apostolique. Paris: Apostolat positiviste, 1891. Pp. XIV, 420. First published in 1852.

——, *Système de politique positive, ou traité de sociologie.* 4 vols. Paris: L. Mathias, 1851-1854.

Cavillier, A., «Auguste Comte y la economia politica de su tiempo», *Revista mexicana de Sociologia* (Mexico), 1957, pp. 777-786.

Vidal, E., *Saint-Simon e la scienza politica*. In appendice: Il sistema di politica positiva di Auguste Comte. Milan: A. Giuffrè, 1959. Pp. 234.

Spencer, Herbert (1820-1903), — see Ethics, above, Ch. I, 2, p. 35; Sociology, below, Ch. V, 3, p. 242.

——, *Prophecy Come True: Some Thought on Political and Social Questions from the Writings of Herbert Spencer*. Edited by E. H. Blakeney. London: Society for Individual Freedom, 1949. Pp. 11.

Parsons, Frank, *Government and the Law of Equal Freedom: An Examination of Herbert Spencer's Theories of Government and Individual Liberty*. Boston: New Nation Publishing Co., 1892. Pp. 29.

Ward, Lester Frank, «The Political Ethics of Herbert Spencer», *The Annals of the American Academy of Political and Social Science* (Philadelphia), 1894, pp. 582-619.

Roberty de, Eugène, *Auguste Comte et Herbert Spencer*. Paris: F. Alcan, 1894. Pp. X, 201.

(hh) Anarchism: opposed to any centralized authority.

See Marxism, below, p. 205; Socialism, above, p. 86.

Gray, Alexander, *The Socialist Tradition*. London: Longmans, 1946. Pp. 523. Critique of Godwin, Proudhon, Bakunin.

Joll, James, *The Anarchists*. New York: J.J. Little and Ives Co., 1965. Pp. 303.

Tucker, Benjamin Richetson, *State Socialism and Anarchism*. New York: B. R. Tucker, 1899. Pp. 33.

——, *Individual Liberty: Selection*. Ed. by C.L.S. New York: Vanguard Press, 1926. Pp. 294.

Woodcock, George, *Anarchism: A History of Libertarian Ideas and Movements*. Cleveland, Ohio: Meridian Books, 1962. Pp. 504.

——, «Anarchism», in *The Encyclopedia of Philosophy* (8 vols. New York: The Macmillan Co., 1967), Vol. I, pp. 111-115.

Nettlau, Max, *Der Anarchismus von Proudhon zu Kropotkin*. Berlin: Asy-Verlag. 1927. Pp. 312. Covers years 1859-1880.

——, *Anarchisten und Social-Revolutionäre*. Berlin: Asy-Verlag, 1931. Pp. 409. Covers years 1880-1886.

——, *Der Vorfrühling der Anarchie*. Berlin: Verlag «Der Syndicalist», 1925. Pp. 235. Cover years from the beginning till 1864.

Représentatives

Bakunin, Mikhail Aleksantrovich ('814-1876), *Michail Bukanins sozial-politischer Briefwechsel mit Alexander I Herzen und Ogarjow*. Translated by B. Minzes. Stuttgart: Bibliothek russischer Denkwürdigkeiten, 1895. Pp. CX, 420.

——, *God and the State*. Translated by B. R. TUCKER. Boston, Massachusetts: B. R. Tucker, 1883. Pp. 52.

——, *La Révolution sociale ou la dictature militaire*. Paris: Portes de
France, 1946. Pp. 280.

——, *The Organization of the International, 1814-1876*. Translated by Fre-
da COHEN. London: Bakunin Press, 1919. Pp. 7.

——, *Marxism, Freedom, and the State*. Selections from Bakunin. Translated and edited by K. J. KANAFICK. London: Freedom Press, 1950.
Pp. 63.

——, *Political Philosophy of Bakunin: Sientific Anarchism*. New York:
The Macmillan Co., 1964. Pp. 434.

GODWIN, William (1756-1836), *An Enquiry concerning Political Justice and
Its Influence on General Virtue and Happiness*. 2 vols. New York:
A. A. Knopf, 1926. First published in 1793.

KROPOTKIN, Peter Aleksieevich (1842-1921), *Ethics, Origin and Development*.
Authorized translation from the Russian by Louis S. FRIEDLAND and
Joseph PIROSHNIKOFF. New York: The Dial Press, 1924. Pp. XVI, 349.

——, *The Great French Revolution, 1789-1793*. Translation. London: W.
Heinemann, 1909. Pp. XI, 610.

——, *Law and Authority — An Anarchist Essay*. London: International
Publishing Co., 1886. Pp. 23.

——, *The State, Its Part in History*. London: W. Heinemann, 1898.

——, *Mutual Aid, a Factor of Evolution*. London: W. Heinemann, 1904.
Pp. XIX, 348.

——, *Modern Science and Anarchism*. London: Freedom Press, 1912. Pp.
110.

PROUDHON, Pierre Joseph (1809-1865), *Qu'est-ce que la propriété ?* Paris:
J. F. Brocard, 1840. Pp. XII, 244. English translation by Benjamin R.
TUCKER, *What is Property: An Inquiry into the Principle of Right and
of Government*. New York: The Humboldt Publishing Co., 1890. Pp.
XII, 457.

——, *Système des contradictions économiques, ou Philosophie de la misère*. 2nd ed. Paris. A. Lacroix, 1850. First published in 1846.

——, *De la justice dans la Révolution et dans l'Église*. 3 vols. Paris: Garnier frères, 1858.

SOREL, Georges (1847-1922), *Réflexion sur la violence*. 3rd ed. Paris: M.
Rivière, 1912. Pp. 440. English translation by T. E. HULME and J. ROTH,
Reflexions on Violence. New York: P. Smith, 1941. Pp. X, 299. See
Fascism, below, p. 204.

——, *La décomposition du marxisme*. Paris: M. Rivière, 1908. Pp. 64.

THOREAU, Henry David (1817-1862), *On the Duty of Civil Disobedience*. London: The Simple Life Press, 1903.

——, *The Writings of Henry David Thoreau*. 11 vols. Boston: Houghton,
Mifflin and Co., 1894-1895.

(ii) MATERIALISM

See Ethics, above, Ch. I, 2 Contemporary, p. 38.

Marxism

See Economics, above Ch. II, 3 Modern, p. 98.

Studies

ALFANAS, Victor G., *Marxist Philosophy*. Translated by L. LEMPERT. New York: Universal Distributors Co., 1963. Pp. 393.

CROCE, Benedetto, *Materialismo storico ed economia marxistica*. 3rd ed. Bari: G. Laterza, 1918. Pp. XVI, 298. Translated by C.M. MEREDITH, *Historical Materialism and the Economics of Karl Marx*. New York: Russell and Russell, 1966. Pp. XXIII, 188.

GRAMSCI, A., — see Representatives, below.

O'NEILL, John, «Alienation, Class Struggle and Marxian Anti-Politics», *Review of Metaphysics*, 1963-1964, pp. 462-471.

TALMON, J. L., *The Origins of Totalitarian Democracy*. 3 vols. London: Secker and Warburg, 1952.

Representatives

MARX, Karl (1818-1883) and ENGELS, Friedrich (1820-1895): struggle of classes, necessity of violent revolution for classless state.

MARX, Karl and ENGELS, Friedrich, *Basic Writings on Politics and Philosophy*. Ed. by Lewis FEUER. Garden City, New York: Doubleday, 1949.

——, *Russian Meanace to Europe*. A collection of articles, speeches of K. Marx and F. Engels. Ed. by Paul W. BLACKSTOCK and Bert F. HOSELITZ. London: Allen and Unwin, 1953. Pp. 288.

MARX, Karl, *Selected Writings in Sociology and Social* Philosophy. Ed. by T. B. Bottomore and M. RUBEL. London: F. F. Watts, 1956. Pp. 268.

ENGELS, Friedrich, *Herr Eugen Dühring's Revolution in Science*. New York: International Publishers, 1939. Pp. 365.

——, *Landmarks of Scientific Socialism*. Translation by Austin LEWIS. Chicago: C. H. Kerr and Co., 1907. Pp. 266.

LENIN, Vladimir Ilich (1870-1924), *Imperialism, the Highest Stage of Capitalism*. New revised translation. New York: International Publishers, 1939. Pp. 128. First published in Petrograd, 1917.

——, *L'état et la révolution*. Moscow: Comité exécutif de l'Internationale Communiste, 1919. Pp. 92.

——, *Collected Works*. Revised edition. New York: International Publishers, 1927—.

CANTRIL, Hadley, *Soviet Leaders and Mastery over Man*. New Brunswick, New Jersey: Rutgers University Press, 1960. Pp. XX, 173.

DENNO, Theodore, *The Communist Millenium: The Soviet View*. The Hague: Martinus Nijhoff, 1964. Pp. XI, 166.

HOOVER, J. Edgar, *Masters of Deceit*. New York: Henry Holt and Co., 1958. Pp. 374. Communism in America.

KELSEN, Hans, *The Political Theory of Bolshevism*. Berkeley, California: University of California Press, 1948.

——, *Sozialismus und Staat. Eine Untersuchung der politischen Theorie des Marxismus*. 2nd ed. Leipzig: C. L. Hirschfeld, 1923. Pp. VIII, 208.

MEYER, Alfred George, *Leninism*. Cambridge, Massachustts: Harvard University Press, 1957. Pp. 324.

BARATONO, Adelchi, *Le due facce di Carlo Marx*. Geneva: Di Stefano, 1946. Pp. 220.

MONDOLFO, R., *Sulle arme di Marx*. 4th ed. Bologne: Cappelli, 1948. Pp. VIII, 163.

STALIN, Josif V. (1879-1953), *Dialectical and Historical Materialism*. New York: International Publishers, 1940. Pp. 48.

——, (ed.), *Leninism: Selected Writings*. New York: International Publishers, 1942. Pp. 479.

MAO, Tse-tung (1893-   ), — see Dialectical Materialism, above, Ch. I, 2, p. 38; *PQS*, No. 5.

——, *China's New Democracy*. New York: New Century Publishers, 1945. Pp. 72.

——, *The Fight for a New China*. New York: New Century Publishers, 1945. Pp. 80.

——, *Analysis of the Classes in Chinese Society*. Peking: Foreign Languages Press, 1956.

——, *The Dictatorship of the People's Democracy*. New Haven, Connecticut: Yale University, Oriental Studies, 1951. Pp. 21.

——, *On Contradiction*. New York: International Publishers, 1953. Pp. 61.

——, *On the Correct Handling of Contraditions among the People*. New York: New Century Publishers, 1957. Pp. 32.

——, *The Question of Agricultural Co-operation*. Peking: Foreign Languages Press, 1956. Pp. 39.

——, *New-democratic Constitutionalism*. Peking: Foreign Languages Press, 1960. Pp. 15.

——, *Chinese Communist Revolutionary Strategy, 1945-1949*. Extract from his *Selected Writings* (ed. by S.M. CHIU at Princeton, N. J.). Princeton, New Jersey: Center of International Studies, 1961. Pp. 49.

——, *Selected Works*. 5 vols. New York: International Publishers, 1954-1956. Covers period 1926-1949.

Mao Tse-tung: An Anthology of His Writings. Ed. by Anne FREMANTLE. New York: New American Library, 1962. Pp. 300.

The Political Thought of Mao Tse-tung. Anthology edited by Stuart R. SCHRAM. New York: Praeger, 1963. Pp. IX, 319.

MAO, Tse-tung, *Selected Works*. 2 vols. Peking: Foreign Languages Press, 1965.

——, *Collection of Pamphlets*. Peking: Foreign Languages Press, 1966. 12 pamphlets.

Mao-Tse-Tung, Emperor of the Blue Ants. Garden City, New York: Doubleday and Company, Inc., 1963. Pp. 393. Bibliography. See also China, below, p. 210.

PALOCZI-HORVATH, George, *The Road to Power*. London: Secker and Warburg, 1960. Pp. 304.

PAYNE, Robert, *Portrait of a Revolutionary: Mao-Tse-Tung*. London: Abelard-Schuman, 1950. Pp. 311.

GRAMSCI, Antonio (1891-1937), *The Modern Prince and Other Writings*. Translated by Louis MARKS. London: Lawrence and Wishart, 1957. Pp. 192.

——, *Opere*. 6 vols. Turin: 1947-1954.

Communism, — see above, p. 98; below, p. 215.

Fascism, — see below, p. 217.

Russia, — see below, p. 261.

Socialism, — see above, p. 89; Hitlerism, below, p. 211.

(jj) TRADITIONALISM: the principles of political and intellectual order transcend human reason; thus they must be revealed by God and handed down to men.

Studies

MATCZAK, S. A., «Traditionalism», in *The New Catholic Encyclopedia* (15 vols. New York: McGraw-Hill, 1967), Vol. XIV, pp. 228-230. Cf. «Fideism», *ibid.*, Vol. V, pp. 908-910.

MENCZER, Béla (ed.), *Catholic Political Thought (1789-1848)*. Westminster, Maryland: Newman Press, 1952. Pp. VIII, 205.

FERRAZ, Martin *et al.*, *Histoire de la philosophie en France au 19ème siècle*. 3rd ed. Paris: Didier, 1882. Pp. XXXV, 501.

HENRY, J., *Le traditionalisme et l'ontologisme à l'Université de Louvain* (1835-1865). Louvain, 1922.

LUPUS, J., *Le traditionalisme et le rationalisme*. 3 vols. Liège, 1858.

MÉDINE, Henry, *Esquisse d'un traditionalisme catholique*. Paris: Nouvelles éditions latines, 1956. Pp. 125.

Representatives

BONALD DE, Louis (1754-1840), *Législation primitive considérée dans les derniers temps par les seules lumières de la raison*. 2 vols. Paris: Le Clère, 1802.

——, *Recherches philosophiques sur les premiers objects de nos connaissances morales*. Paris: A. Le Clère, 1818. Pp. 360.

LAMENNAIS DE, Félicité R. (1782-1854), *Essai sur l'indifférence en matière de religion*. 4 vols. Paris: Tournachon — Molin, Librairie classique élémentaire, 1817-1823.

MAISTRE DE, Joseph (1753-1821), *Essai sur le principe générateur des consti-
tutions politiques.* Paris: Société typographique, 1814. Pp. X, 104.
First published in Petrograd, 1809.
——, *Du pape.* 2 vols. Lyons: Rusand, 1819.
——, *Les soirées de Saint-Péterbourg.* 2 vols. Paris: Russand, 1822. Vol. I
only published in 1821 at Paris: Librairie grecque, latine et française.

CONTEMPORARY

See Modern, above.

(a) Comprehensive Studies

BRECHT, Arnold, *Political Theory.* Princeton, New Jersey: Princeton Uni-
versity Press, 1959. Pp. 612. An examination of a foremost issue
of 20th century political science.
KARIEL, Henry S., *In Search of Authority: Twentieth Century Political
Thought.* New York: Free Press of Glencoe, 1964. Pp. XII, 258.
—— (ed.), *Sources in Twentieth Century Political Thought.* New York:
Free Press of Glencoe, 1964. Pp. XI, 308.
LASLETT, Peter, RUNCIMAN, W. G. *et al.* (eds.), *Philosophy, Politics and So-
ciety.* New York: Oxford University Press, 1962. Pp. 310.
OAKESHOTT, Michael (ed.), *Social and Economic Doctrines of Contempora-
ry Europe.* 2nd ed. New York: The Macmillan Co., 1942. Pp. XXIII,
243.
——, *Rationalism in Politics.* London: Methuen, 1962. Pp. 333.
POPPER, Karl Raimund, *The Open Society and Its Enemies.* 4th ed. 2 vols.
London: Routledge and Kegan Paul, 1962.
——, *The Poverty of Historicism.* London: Routledge and Kegan Paul,
1957. Pp. 166.
STANKIEWICZ, W. J., *Political Thought since World War II.* New York: Free
Press of Glencoe, 1964. Pp. XVII, 462.

(b) Specific Studies

Analytic Philosophy

See Neo-positivistic School, Ch. III, 3, 149.

WELDON, T. D., *The Vocabulary of Politics.* London: Penguin Books, 1953.
Pp. 119. See also above, 1 c.

Marxism, — see above, p. 205.
Idealism, — see above, p. 200.
Federalism, — see above, p. 194.

Other Trends

See Particular Countries, below, 4; Sociology, below, Ch. V
3, p. 243; Special Questions, below, p. 213.

4. PARTICULAR COUNTRIES

NORTHROP, F. S. C., *The Meeting of East and West: An Inquiry Concerning World Understanding.* New York: Free Press of Glencoe, 1963. Pp. XVI, 304.

WALZER, Michael, *History and Sources of Continental Political Thought.* New York: The Macmillan Co., 1966.

AFRICA

RIVKIN, Arnold, *The African Presence in World Affairs: National Development and Its Role in Foreign Policy.* New York: The Macmillan Co., 1963.

AMERICA

See Federalism, above, p. 194.

ADAMS, Henry, *History of the United States during the second Administration of Jefferson and Madison.* 2 vols. New York: Charles Scribner's Sons, 1890.

——, *History of the United States during the second Administration of James Madison.* 3 vols. New York: Charles Scribner's Sons, 1891.

——, *History of the United States during the Administration of James Madison.* 2 vols. New York: A. and B. Boni, 1930.

——, *Characters and Events: Popular Essays in Social and Political Philosophy.* 2 vols. Ed. by Joseph RATNER. New York: H. Holt and Co., 1929. See also China, Russia, below.

DEWEY, John, *German Philosophy and Politics.* New York: H. Holt and Co., 1915. Pp. 134.

GEIGER, George R., «Dewey's Social and Political Philosophy», in Paul A. Schilpp (ed.), *The Philosophy of John Dewey* (New York: Tudor, 1951), Chapter XI.

GINZBERG, Eli and EICHNER, Alfred S., *The Troublesome Presence: American Democracy and the Negro.* New York: Free Press of Glencoe, 1964. Pp. XIII, 339.

JEFFERSON, Thomas, *The Writings.* 20 vols. Washington, D. C.: Thomas Jefferson Memorial Association, 1903-1904.

BOWERS, Claude Bernard, *Jefferson and Hamilton.* Boston: Houghton Mifflin Co., 1933. Pp. XVIII, 531. See above, p. 195.

JENKIN, Thomas P., *History and Sources of American Political Doctrines.* New York: The Macmillan Co., 1966.

LANE, Robert E., *Political Ideology: Why the American Common Man Believes What He Does.* New York: Free Press of Glencoe, 1962. Pp. XI, 509.

——, *Political Life: Why People Get Involved in Politics.* New York: Free Press of Glencoe, 1959. Pp. 374.

LASKI, Harold J., *The American Democracy: A Commentary and an Interpretation.* London: George Allen and Unwin, 1949. Pp. X. 785.

ROYCE, Josiah, *Race Questions, Provincialism and Other American Problems.* New York: The Macmillan Co., 1908. Pp. XIII, 287.

Latin America

See Fascism, below, p. 220.

CHINA

See Communism, below, p. 215.

ALLEN, A. Stewart, *China under Communist Control.* Toronto: Canadian Institute of International Affairs, 1954. Pp. 16.

DEWEY, John, «The International Duel in China», *New Republic* (Washington, D. C.,) August 27, 1919, Pp. 16-18.

——, «Transforming the Mind of China», *Asia* (New York), November 1919, pp. 1103-1108.

——, «Chinese National Sentiment», *Asia* (New York), December 1919, pp. 1237-1242.

——, «The Consortium in China», *New Republic* (Washington, D. C.), April 13, 1921.

——, «Federalism in China», *New Republic* (Washington, D. C.), October 12, 1921, pp. 176-178.

——, «Is China a Nation or a Market», *New Republic* (Washington, D. C.), November 11, 1925, pp. 298-299.

——, «We Should Deal with China as Nation to Nation», *Chinese Students' Monthly,* May 1926, pp. 52-54.

TANG, Sheng-hao, *Communist China Today: Domestic and Foreign Policies.* 2 vols. New York: Praeger, 1957-1958.

THOMAS, Elbert Duncan, *Chinese Political Thought.* New York: Prentice-Hall, 1927. Pp. XVI, 317.

ENGLAND

See Modern, above.

BARKER, Ernest, *Political Thought in England from Spencer to the Present Day.* New York: Henry Holt and Co., 1915. Pp 256.

GOOCH, George Peabody, *English Democratic Ideas in the Seventeenth Century.* 2nd ed. New York: The Macmillan Co., 1927. Pp. X, 315.

WHITE, Albert Beebe, *Self-Government at the King's Command: A Study in the Beginnings of English Democracy.* Minneapolis: University of Minneapolis Press, 1933. Pp. 130.

FRANCE

See Modern, above, p. 185.

Comte, Auguste, see p. 202.

Racism, — see above, p. 30, cf. 218.

GERMANY

Hitlerism: favors totalitarian state, authority centered at the top; Führer's will has to be people's will, and the Aryan race enjoys absolute supremacy. It is also called Nazism; abbreviaton of *National sozialistische* (Partei).

See Autonomous Ethics, above, Ch. I, 2, p. 28.

DARRÉ, R. W., *Neu Adel aus Blut und Boden.* Munich: J. F. Lehmann, 1939. Pp. 248.

FEDER, Gottfried, *Das Programm der N.S.D.A.P. und seine weltanschaulichen Grundgedanken.* Munich: Eher, 1932. Pp. 64. English translation by E. T. S. OUGDALE. London: Allen and Unwin, 1934.

ZIMMERMANN, Karl, *Deutsche Geschichte als Rassenschicksal.* 6th ed. Leipzig: Quelle und Meyer, 1936. Pp. XI, 186.

GÖBBELS, Joseph (1897-1945),*Das Wesen und Gestalt des Nationalsozialismus.* Berlin: Junker und Dünnhaupt, 1934. Pp. 22.

——, *Signale der neuen Zeit.* Munich: Zentralverlag der NSDAP, 1934. Pp. 362.

——, *Der Angriff.* Munich: Zentralverlag der NSDAP, 1936. Pp. 340.

——, *My Part in Germany's Fight.* London: Hurst and Blackett, 1940. Pp. 253.

——, *Tagebücher.* Ed. by Louis LOCHNER. Zurich: 1948.

HIMMLER, Heinrich (1900-1945), *Die Schutzstaffel als antibolschevitische Kampforganisation.* Munich: Eher, 1936. Pp. 31.

HITLER, Adolph (1889-1945), *Mein Kampf. Eine Abrechnung.* 2 vols. Munich: F. Eher Nachfolger, 1925-1927. English translation by James MURPHY, London: Hurst and Balckett, 1939.

Adolf Hitlers Reden. Ed. by Otto von KURSELL. Munich: E. Boepple, 1925. Pp. 159. Other edition, *loc. cit.,* 1933, pp. 127.

——, *Liberty, Art, Nationhood.* Three addresses, delivered at the Seventh National Socialist Congress in Nüremberg, 1935. Berlin: M. Müller and John, 1935. Pp. 79.

——, *Sozialismus wie ihn der Führer sieht.* Worte des Führers zu sozialen Frage. Ed. by F. Meystre. Munich: Heerschild-Verlag, 1935. Pp. XII, 128.

——, *Der grossdeutsche Freiheitskampf.* Reden. Adolf Hitlers vom 1. September 1939 bis 10. Marz 1940. Munich: Zentral-Verlag der NSDAP, 1940. Pp. 198.

——, *The Speeches of Adolf Hitler, April 1922 — August 1939.* Ed. by Norman H. BAYNES. 2 vols. Oxford: Oxford University Press, 1942.

Hitler's Secret Conversations, 1941-1944. Ed. by H. R. TREVOR-ROPER. Translated by Norman CAMERON and R. H. STEVENS. New York: Farrar, Strauss and Cudahy, 1953. Pp. XXX, 597.

Hitler's Table Talk, 1941-1944. Translation by Norman CAMERON and R. H. STEVENS, with an essay on Hitler's mind by H. R. TREVOR-ROPER. London: G. Weidenfield and Nicholson, 1953. Pp. 746.

BULLOCK, Alon, *Hitler: A Study in Tyranny.* Revised edition. New York: Bentam Books, 1961. Pp. 780. First published in 1953.

HANFSTAENGL, Ernst F. S., *Hitler: The Missing Years.* Ed. by Brian CONNELL. London: Eyre and Spottiswood, 1957. Pp. 299.

HEIDEN, Konrad, *Adolf Hitler. Eine Biographie.* Zürich: Europa-Verlag, 1936. Pp. 447. English translation by Winifred RAY, *Hitler: A Bibliographie.* New York: A Knopf, 1936. Pp. 390.

Hitler a Menace to World Peace. Addresses and Messages delivered at the Peace and Democracy Rally at Madison Square Garden, March 15, 1937. Ed. by The Council of the American Jews. New York: Joint Boycott Council, 151 West 40th Street, 1937. Pp. 120.

Hitler Doomed to Madness. Smuggled manuscripts reveals secrets of new Nazi horrors. Greenwich, Connecticut: Country Press, 1940. Pp. 66.

JETZINGER, Franz, *Hitler's Youth.* Translated from the German by Alan Lawrence WILSON. London: Hutchinson and Co., 1958. Pp. 200.

ROSENBERG, Alfred, *Wesen, Grundsätze und Ziele der Nationalsozialistischen Deutschen Arbeiterpartei.* Munich: Deutscher Volksverlag Dr. E. Boepple, 1930. Pp. 48.

——, *Der Mythus des 20. Jahrhunderts.* Munich: Hoheneichen Verlag, 1930. Pp. 670.

——, *Die Protokolle der Weisen von Zion und die judische Weltpolitik.* Munich: S. A. Nilus, 1933. Pp. 143. First published in 1923.

LASKI, Harold Joseph, *The Germans-Are They Human? A Reply to Sir Robert Vansittart.* London: Victor Gollancz, 1941. Pp. 8.

SHIRER, William L., *The Rise and Fall of the Third Reich: A History of Nazi Germany.* New York: Simon and Schuster, 1960. Pp. 1245.

WHEELER-BENNETT, John W., *The Nemesis of Power: The German Army in Politics, 1918-1945.* London: Macmillan and Co., 1953. Pp. 829.

Hitler et Rosenberg, ou le vrai visage du national-socialism. Paris: Maison de la Bonne Presse, 1936. Pp. 161.

ITALY

See Particular Periods, above, 3.

Cicero, M.T. — see above, 3, p. 182, cf. 80, 126.
St. Thomas Aquinas, — see 3, p. 184.

MACHIAVELLI, N., — see above, 3, p. 186.

VICO, G., — see, 3, p. 189.

CROCE, B., see above, Ch. III, 3, p. 141, cf. 201.

GENTILE, G., — see Fascism, below, p. 219.

POLAND

BRZEZINSKI, Z. K., *The Soviet Block: Unity and Conflict.* Revised and enlarged edition. Cambridge, Massachusetts: Harvard Universtiy Press, 1967. Pp. XVIII, 599. First published in 1960.

KOMARNICKI, Titus, *Rebirth of the Polish Republic.* London: W. Heinemann, 1957.

ROZEK, Edward J., *Allied Wartime Diplomacy: A Pattern in Poland.* New York: John Wiley and Sons, 1958.

JARRA, Eugeniusz. *Historia polskiej filozofii politycznej.* London: Ksiegarnia Polska Orbis, 1968. Pp. XV, 288.

POBÓG - MALINOWSKI, Wladyslaw, *Najnowsza historia polityczna Polski.* 2 vols. London: Ksiegarnia Polska Orbis, 1969.

RUSSIA

See Marxism, above, 3, p. 205.

CARR, Edward Hallett, *History of Soviet Russia.* 5 vols. New York: The Macmillan Co., 1951-1958.

MARCUSE, Herbert, *Soviet Marxism: A Critical Analysis.* New York: Columbia University Press, 1958. Pp. 271.

TROTSKY, Leon, *History of the Russian Revolution.* Translated from the Russian by Max Eastman. 3 vols. New York: Simon and Schuster, 1936. below, Ch. V, 6, p. 277.

5. SPECIAL QUESTIONS

AUTHORITY

See State, below, p. 223; Responsability, above, p. 167.

ADORNO, Theodor *et al., The Authoritarian Personality.* New York: Harper, 1950. Pp. XXXIII, 990.

COHEN, Hymen Ezra, *Recent Theories of Sovereignty.* Chicago: University of Chicago Press, 1937. Pp. IX, 169.

COHEN, Julius, ROBSON, R. A. H. and BATES, Alan, *Parental Authority: The Community of Law.* New Brunswick, New Jersey: Rutgers University Press, 1958.

COMMONS, John Rogers, *A Sociological View of Sovereignty, 1899-1900.* New York: Augustus M. Kelley, 1965. Pp. XIV, 109.

FIGGIS, John, *The Divine Right of Kings.* Cambridge: University Press, 1914. Pp. XI, 406.

FORD, Guy Stanton (ed.), *Dictatorship in the Modern World.* 2nd ed. Minneapolis, Minnesota: The University of Minnesota Press, 1939. Pp. XIV, 362.

FRIEDRICH, Carl J. (ed.), *Revolution*. New York: Atherton Press, 1966. Pp. 256.

—— and BRZEZINSKI, Zbigniew K., *Totalitarian Dictatorship and Autocracy*, Cambridge, Massachusetts: Harvard University Press, 1956. Pp. 346.

GREEN, Thomas Hill, *Principles of Political Obligation*. Ed. by R. L. NETTIE-SHIP. London: Longmans, 1895.

IGGERS, Georg G., *The Cult of Authority: The Political Philosophy of the Saint-Simonians*. The Hague: Martinus Nijhoff, 1958. Pp. VIII, 210.

KARIEL, Henry S., *In Search of Authority: Twentieth Century Political Thought*. New York: The Free Press (Macmillan) 1964. Pp. 258.

KELSEN, Hans, *Das Problem der Souveränität und die Theorie des Völkerrechts*. 2nd ed. Tübingen: J. C. B. Mohr, 1928. Pp. XII, 320.

LASKI, Harold J., *Authority in the Modern State*. New Haven, Connecticut: Yale University Press, 1919. Pp. 398.

——, *The Foundation of Sovereignty and Other Essays*. London: G. Allen and Unwin, 1922. Pp. XI, 317.

SANFORD, F. H., *Authoritarianism and Leadership*. Philadelphia: Stephenson Brothers, 1950. Pp. IV, 189.

CHRISTIANITY

See Christianity and Economics, above, Ch. II, 5, p. 99.

CARRIER, Hervé, S. J. and PIN, Emile, S. J., *Sociology of Christianity: International Bibliography*. Rome: Gregorian University Press, 1964. Pp. 313.

Index to the American Sociological Review. New York: New York University (Washington Square), 1961—. See Periodicals to Sociology, below, Ch. V, 6, p. 278.

BAKER, Ernest, *Christianity and Nationality*. Oxford: At the Clarendon Press, 1927. Pp. 32.

——, *Church, State and Study*. London: Methuen, 1930. Pp. VII, 280.

FIGGIS, John N., *Churches in the Modern State*. London: Longmans, 1913.

HEARNSHAW, Fossey John Cobb, *Some Great Political Idealists of the Christian Era*. London: G.G. Harrap and Co., 1937. Pp. 273. See also Historie, above 2, p. 174.

HOOKER, Richard, *The Laws of Ecclesiastical Polity*. Written c. 1590, published partly in 1594, completely in 1662.

RYAN, John A. and BOLAND, F. J., *Catholic Principles of Politics*. New York: The Macmillan Co., 1940. Pp. VIII, 366.

WEBER, Max, *The Protestant Ethic and the Spirit of Capitalism*. Translated by Talcott PARSONS. London: G. Allen and Unwin, 1930. Pp. 292.

WILLS, Garry, *Politics and Catholic Freedom*. Chicago, Illinois: Henry Regnery Co., 1964. Pp. 302.

COLONIES

BENTHAM, Jeremy, *Emancipate Your Colonies! Addressed to the National Convention of France*. London: R. Howard, 1830. Pp. 48.

CAREY, Henry Charles, *The Slave Trade, Domestic and Foreign: Why It Exists and How It May Be Extinguished.* Philadelphia: A. Hart, 1853. Pp. 426.

FRANKLIN, John Hope, *From Slavery to Freedom: A History of American Negroes.* 2nd ed. New York: Alfred A. Knopf, 1966. Pp. XV, 639, XLII.

MACKENZIE-GRIEVE, Averil, *The Last Years of the English Slave Trade.* London: Putman and Co., 1941. Pp. XII, 331. Reprint in New York: Augustus M. Kelley, 1966.

BALLU DE, E. Belin, *L'histoire des colonies grecques du littoral nord de la Mer Noire: Bibliographie annotée des ouvrages et articles publiés en U.R.S.S. de 1940 à 1962.* Leiden, Holland: E. J. Brill, 1965. Pp. XXVI, 208.

DEL VECCHIO, Giorgio, «Giurisprudenza e colonie», in *Atti della Società Italiana per il Progresso delle Scienze*, 1937.

KELSEN, Hans, *Das Problem der Souveränität und die Theorie des Volkerrechts.* 2nd ed. Tübingen: J. C. B. Mohr, 1928. Pp. XII, 320. See also Authority, above.

ZIMMERMANN, Alfred, *Geschichte der deutschen Kolonialpolitik.* Berlin: E. S. Mittler und Sohn, 1914. Pp. XVI, 336.

——, *Die Kolonialreiche der Grossmächte, 1871-1916.* Berlin: Ullstein und Co., 1916. Pp. 250.

COMMUNISM

See Materialism, above, 3, p. 204; Democracy, below; Dialectical Materialism, above, p. 38.

BARNETTE, Henlee H., *An Introduction to Communism.* Grand Rapids, Michigan: Baker Book House, 1964. Pp. 117.

DANIELS, Robert Vincent, *Understanding Communism.* New York: The L. S. Singer Company, 1964. Pp. 201.

FEDOSEEV, P. N., «The Dialectics of the Growth of Socialism into Communism», *Soviet Studies in Philosophy* (New York), 1962-1963. No. 2, pp. 25-35. See also *Voprosy filosofii*, 1961, no. 10.

O'BRIEN, Frank, *Crisis in World Communism: Marxism in Search of Efficiency.* New York: Free Press of Glencoe, 1965. Pp. 191.

DELLA VOLPE, Galvano, *La Libertà comunista.* Milan: Avanti, 1963. Pp. 183.

MOSCA, Gaetano, «L'utopia di Tommaso Moro e il pensiero comunista moderno», in *Scritti in onore di Antonio Scialoia.* Milan: Vallardi, 1928.

PHILIP, André, *La gauche, mythes et réalité.* Paris: Aubier-Montaigne, 1964. Pp. 224.

SARTRE, Jean P., *Situations, VII: Problèmes du marxisme.* Paris: Gallimard, 1965. Pp. 352.

——, *Critique de la raison dialectique.* Paris: Librairie Gallimard, 1960. Pp. 755.

China, — see above, p. 210, cf. 206.

Russia, — see above, p. 105.

Der Sowjetkommunismus Dokumente. Ed. by Hans J. Lieber and Karl H.
    Ruffmann. 2 vols. Köln: Kiepenheuer und Witsch, 1963-1964.
Garthoff, Raymond L., *Soviet Military Doctrine.* Glencoe, Illinois: Free
    Press, 1953. Pp. XVIII, 587.
Leites, Nathan, *A Study of Bolshevism.* Glencoe, Illinois: Free Press, 1953.
    Pp. 639.
Selznick, Philip, *The Organizational Weapon: A Study of Bolshevik Stra-
    tegy and Tactics.* Glencoe, Illinois: Free Press, 1960. Pp. 350.

DEMOCRACY

See Autority, above; Communism, above.

In English

Benn, Stanley I., «Democracy», in *The Encyclopedia of Philosophy* (8 vols.
    New York: The Macmillan Co., 1967), Vol. II, pp. 338-341.
—— and Peters, R. S., *Social Principles and the Democratic State.* London:
    George Allen and Unwin, 1959. Pp. 404. Reissued, *Principles of Po-
    litical Thought.* New York: Collier Books, 1964. Pp. 478.
Girvetz, Harry K., *Democracy and Elitism: Two Essays with Selected Read-
    ings.* New York: Charles Scribner's Sons, 1967. Pp. 368.
Glover, Terrot Reaveley, *Democracy in the Ancient World.* London: Mac-
    millan Co., 1927. Pp. VIII, 263.
Gooch, George Peabody, *English Democratic Ideas in the Seventeenth
    Century.* 2nd ed. by H. J. Laski. Cambridge: Cambridge University
    Press, 1927. Pp. X, 315.
Grazia de, Alfred, *Public and Republic: Political Representation in Ame-
    rica.* New York: A Knopf, 1951. Pp. XIII, 262. Annotated bibliography.
Jászi, Oscar and Lewis, John D., *Against the Tyrant.* Glencoe, Illinois:
    Free Press, 1957. Pp. 288.
Kornhauser, William, *The Politics of Mass Society.* New York: The Mac-
    millan Co., 1959. Pp. 256.
Laski, Harold Joseph, *The American Democracy: A Commentary and an
    Interpretation.* London: George Allen und Unwin, 1949. Pp. X, 785.
Lindblom, Charles E., *The Intelligence of Democracy: Decision Making
    Through Mutual Adjustment.* New York: The Macmillan Co., 1965.
    Pp. VII, 352.
Lipset, Seymour Martin and Bendix, Reinhard, *Idiological Equalitarianism
    and Social Mobility in the United States.* Los Angeles, California:
    University of California Institute of Independent Relations, 1955. Pp.
    20. Reprint.
——, *Union Democracy.* Chicago: Free Press, 1956. Pp. XXVII, 455.
Mayo, Henry Bertram, *An Introduction to Democratic Theory.* New York:
    Oxford University Press, 1960. Pp. 316.
McKeon, Richard Peter (ed.), *Democracy in a World of Tensions, A Sympo-
    sium.* Chicago: University of Chicago Press, 1951. Pp. XVIII, 540.
Michels, Robert, *Political Parties: A Sociological Study of the Oligarchical
    Tendencies of Modern Democracy.* Translated by Eden and Cedar
    Paul. Chicago: Free Press, 1949. Pp. 416.

Naess, Arne et al., Democracy, Ideology and Objectivity. Oslo: Oslo University Press, 1956. Pp. 355. Study of McKeon's Symposium.

Pennock, James Roland, Liberal Democracy: Its Merits and Prospects. New York: Rinehart and Co., 1950. Pp. XII, 403.

Pound, Roscoe et al., Federalism as a Democratic Process. New Brunswick, New Jersey: Rutgers University Press, 1942. Pp. 90.

Sartori, Giovanni, Democratic Theory. Detroit: Wayne State University Press, 1962. Pp. 479.

Schweinitz de, Karl, Jr., Industrialization and Democracy: Economic Necessities and Political Possibilities. New York: The Macmillan Co., 1964. Pp. VII, 309.

Spitz, David, Patterns of Antidemocratic Thought. New York: The Macmillan Co., 1949. Pp. XIII, 304.

Talmon, J. L., Rise of Totalitarian Democracy. Boston: Beacon Press, 1952. Pp. XI, 366.

Tocqueville de, Alexis Charles H., De la démocratie en Amérique. 2 vols. Paris: C. Gosselin, 1835-1840. English translation by H. Reeve, Democracy in America. 2 vols. New York: A. Knopf, 1945.

In Other Languages

Brunello, Bruno, «La concezione democratica di Francesco Suarez», Humanitas (Brescia), No. 2, 1949.

Crosa, Emanuele, Il principio della sovranità popolare dal medievo alla Revoluzione francese. Turin: Bocca, 1915. Pp. VIII, 269.

Kelsen, Hans, Vom Wesen und Wert der Demokratie. New edition. Aalen: Scientia Verlag, 1963. Pp. VII, 119. First published in 1920.

Lacharrière, René, Études sur la théorie démocratique: Spinoza, Rousseau, Hegel, Marx. Paris: Payot, 1963. Pp. 218.

Pareto, Vilfredo, «Il crepuscolo della libertà», Rivista d'Italia, No. 2, 1904.

——, «L'économie et la sociologie au point de vue scientifique», Scientia (Cono, Italy), No. 2, 1907.

——, Trasformazione della democrazia. Ed. by M. Missiroli. Modena: Guanda, 1946. Pp. 151.

Reiner, Hans, «Selbstbestimmungsrecht und Demokratie», Archiv für Rechts-Sozialphilosophie (Bern), 1961, pp. 477-502.

Spirito, Ugo, Critica della democrazia. Florence: Sansoni, 1963. Pp. 224.

Talmon, J. L., Die Ursprünge der totalitären Demokratie. Köln: Westdeutscher Verlag, 1961. Pp. 318.

Walter, Wilhelm, Die sozialethische Definition der Demokratie. Fribourg, Switzerland: The University Press, 1964. Pp. 24, 167.

FASCISM

Fascism: good is that which provides for the interest of the state, nation, race; the individual and his right are subordinated to them.

France

L'ACTION FRANÇAISE: restoration of the monarchy in France; subordination of morality and law to the exalted national interest.

Les pièces d'un procès: L'A.F. et le Vatican. Paris, 1927.

Pourquoi Rome à parlé ? Paris. 1927. See also the magazines: Civiltà Cattolica (Rome), 1927; Études (Paris), 1927.

MAURRAS, Charles, Libéralisme et libertés: démocratie et peuple. Paris: Aux bureaux de «l'Action française,» 1906. Pp. 14.

——, Enquête sur la monarchie, 1900-1909. Paris: Nouvelle librairie nationale, 1909. Pp. LVI, 565.

——, La politique-religieuse. Paris: Nouvelle librairie nationale, 1912. Pp. LXI, 428.

——, «L'Action française» et la religion catholique. 2nd ed. Paris: Nouvelle librairie nationale, 1913. Pp. III, 354.

——, Kiel et Tanger, 1895-1905: La République française devant l'Europe. New edition. Paris: Nouvelle librairie nationale, 1914. Pp. LXVIII, 433.

——, Le Pape, la guerre et la paix. Paris: Nouvelle librairie nationale, 1917. Pp. XVI, 272.

——, Les idées royalistes sur les partis, l'état, la nation. New edition. Paris: Service des publications de «L'Action Française», 1919. Pp. 32.

——, Le chemin de Paradis, contes philosophiques. Paris: E. de Boccard, 1921. Pp. XCL, 275.

——, L'œuvre. 7 vols. Paris: Nouvelle librairie nationale, 1905-1926.

SOREL, Georges E., De l'Église et de l'état, fragments. Paris: 8, rue de la Sorbonne, 1901. Pp. 72.

——, La crise de la pensée catholique. Paris: G. Jacques, 1903. Pp. 47.

——, Insegnamenti sociali della economia contemporanea: degenerazione capitalista e degenerazione socialista. Milan: R. Sandron, 1907. Pp. XXXII, 398.

——, Les illusions du progrès. Paris: M. Rivière, 1908. Pp. 283.

——, L'Europa sotto la tormenta. Ed. by Mario MISSIROLI. Milan: Corbaccio, 1932. Pp. LXIV, 292.

Racism, — see above, p. 30.

Germany.

See Hitlerism, above, pp. 30, 211.

Italy

Italian fascism favors corporative state, with a tendency toward totalitarian political control, glorification of the leader and an attempt to revive the glory of the Roman Empire.

SANTANGELO, Giulio and BRACALE, Carlo, *Guida Bibliografica del fascismo.* Rome: Libreria del Littorio, 1928. Pp. XI, 320.

ASHTON, E. B., *The Fascist, His State and His Mind.* New York: Putnam, 1937. Pp. XV, 320.

BINCHY, David A., *Church and State in Fascist Italy.* Oxford: Oxford University Press, 1941. Pp. IX, 774.

EBENSTEIN, William, *Fascist Italy.* New York: American Book Company, 1939. Pp. X, 310.

ELLIOTT, William Yandell, *The Pragmatic Revolt in Politics: Syndicalism, Fascism and the Constitutional State.* New York: The Macmillan Co., 1928. Pp. XVII, 540.

MATTEOTTI, Giacomo, *The Fascisti Exposed: A Year of Fascist Domination.* Translated by E. W. DICKES. London: Labour Party Publication, 1924. Pp. XI, 128.

PREZZOLINI, Giuseppe, *Fascism.* Translated by Kathleen MACMILLAN. London: Methuen and Co., 1928. Pp. XIII, 201.

SALVEMINI, Gaetano, *Under the Axe of Fascism.* New York: Viking Press, 1936. Pp. XIV, 402.

SCHNEIDER, Herbert Wallace, *The Meaning of the Fascist State.* New York: Oxford University Press, 1928. Pp. XI, 392.

——, *The Fascist Government of Italy.* New York: D. van Nostrand Co., 1936. Pp. XII, 173.

STURZO, Luigi, *Italy and Fascismo.* Translated by B. CARTER. London: Faber and Gwyer, 1926. Pp. XII, 305.

DI CARLO, Eugenio, «Sociologia e dottrina politica nel pensiero di L. Sturzo», *Il diritto publico della regione siciliana* (Palermo), 1951, No. 5-6.

VILLARI, Luigi, *The Fascist Experiment.* London: Faber and Gwyer, 1926. Pp. XI, 253.

WELK, William G., *Fascist Economic Policy: An Analysis of Italy's Economic Experiment.* Cambridge, Massachusetts: Harvard University Press, 1938. Pp. XX, 365.

BAGALA, G., *Fascismo e corporativismo, essenza e definizione: lineamenti di filosofia politica.* Bologne: Cantelli, 1942.

BRUNELLO, Bruno, «L'elemento dogmatico nello stato fascista», *Vita nuova* (Bologne), No. 4, 1930.

C. M. R., *Histoire du fascisme italien, 1919-1937.* Paris: Rieder, 1938. Pp. 294.

PERTICONE, Giacomo, «Gli studi di filosofia del diritto in Italia nel ventennio fascista», *Il pensiero giuridico italiano* (Rome, 1941), Vol. I.

ROSSI, Angelo, *La naissance du fascisme, l'Italie de 1918 à 1922.* 4th ed. Paris: Nouvelle Revue française, 1938. English translation by Peter and Dorothy WAIT, *The Rise of Italian Fascism.* London: Methuen Co., 1938. Pp. XVI, 376.

Representatives

GENTILE, Giovanni (1875-1944), — see Idealistic School, above, Ch. III, 3 p. 142; *PQS*, No. 5; below, Index.

——, *Che cosa è il fascismo.* Florence: Vallecchi, 1925.

——, *Origini e dottrine del fascismo*. Rome: Libreria del Littorio, 1929.

BERTELÉ, A., «La dottrina fascista di Giovanni Gentile», *Critica fascista* (Rome), No. 7, 1930.

HARRIS, Henry S., *Social Philosophy of Giovanni Gentile*. Urbana, Illinois: University of Illinois Press, 1960. Pp. XII, 87.

SMITH, William A., *Twentieth Century Fascism*. New York: Monarch Press 1965. Pp. 79.

STELLA, Vittorio, «Il pensiero sociale del Gentile negli studi sociali del dopoguerra», *Giornale critico della filosofia italiana* (Florence), 1962, pp. 87-119.

MUSSOLINI, Benito (1883-1945), il Duce.

——, *Scritti e discorsi*. From November 1914 till 1943. 13 vols. Milan: Hoepli, 1934-1940.

——, *La dottrina del Fascismo*. Commento filosofico di Pietro EUSEBIETTI. 2nd ed. Turin. Società editrice internazionale, 1940. Pp. X. 113. English translation by E. COPE, *The Doctrine of Fascism*. 2nd ed. Florence: Vallecchi, 1937. Pp. 65.

——, *Fascism: Doctrine and Institutions*. Rome: Ardita, 1935. Pp. 313.

——, *Four Speeches on the Corporate State*. Rome: Stato, 1935. Pp. 35.

——, *Programma di governo*. Rome: Berlutti, 1923. Pp. 50.

——, *Il nuovo stato unitario italiano*. Milan: A. Mondadori, 1927. Pp. 116.

——, *Discorsi politici*. Milan: Popolo d'Italia, 1921. Pp. 203.

——, *Scritti politici, 1914-1922*. Ed. by Arnaldo MUSSOLINI and Dino GRANDINI. Milan: Casa editrice Imperia, 1924. Pp. XXII, 472.

——, *Il Fascismo e l'Italia*. Rome: Littorio, 1929. Pp. XIV, 309.

——, *Educazione nazionale*. Selected writings edited by P. ORANO. Rome: Pinciana, 1937. Pp. 152.

——, *Dottrina politica e sociale del fascismo*. Rome: Società aeronautica italiana, 1938. Pp. 23.

——, *Dizionario Mussoliniano*. 2nd ed. Milan: Hoepli, 1940. Pp. VIII, 1940.

——, *Opera omnia*. Ed. by Edoardo and Duilio SUSMEL. 36 vols. Florence: La Fenice, 1951-1963.

BORGESE, Giuseppe Antonio, *Goliath: The March of Fascism*. New York: Viking Press, 1937. Pp. IX, 483.

LUDWIG, Emil, *Talks with Mussolini*. Translated from the German by E. and C. PAUL. London: G. Allen and Unwin, 1932. Pp. 223.

MEGARO, Gaudens, *Mussolini in the Making*. London: Houghton Mifflin Co., 1938. Pp. 347.

MONELLI, Paolo, *Mussolini: the Intimate Life of a Demagogue*. Translated by Brigid MAXWELL. New York: Vanguard, 1954. Pp. 304. First published in 1953.

SARFATTI, Margherita, *The Life of Benito Mussolini*. Translated by Frederic WHYTE. London. Thornton Buuerworth, 1925. Pp. 352.

CARLINI, A., *Filosofia e religione nel pensiero di Mussolini*. Rome: Istituto Nazionale Fascista di Cultura, 1934. Pp. 74.

FERRARA, Mario, *Machiavelli, Nietzsche e Mussolini*. Florence: Vallecchi, 1939. Pp. 179.

RATTO, L., «Caratteri della regola di Mussolini», *Secolo fascista*, Nos. 3-4, 1934.

Latin America

ALEXANDER, Robert Jackson, *The Perón Era*. New York: Columbia University Press, 1951. Pp. X, 239.

BLANKSTEN, George I., *Perón's Argentina*. Chicago: University of Chicago Press, 1953. Pp. 478.

Russia

See Communism, above.

DEWEY, John, *Impressions of Soviet Russia and the Revolutionary World: Mexico, China, Turkey*. New York: New Republic, Inc., 1932. Pp. 270.

Spain

Falangist.

MATTHEWS, Herbert L., *The Yoke and the Arrows: A Report on Spain*. New York: George Braziller, Inc., 1957. Pp. 203.

INTERNATIONALISM — NATIONALISM

See above, Ch. III, p. 160; War, above, Ch. I, p. 67; Sociology, below, Ch. V, p. 275.

A Code of International Ethics, and the Foundations of International Order. Pamphlets published by the Catholic Social Guild. Oxford: Catholic Social Guild, 1940.

DAWSON, Christopher, *The Judgment of the Nations*. New York: Sheed & Ward, 1942. Pp. 222.

MACLEAN, Donald, *Dynamic World Order*. Milwaukee: Bruce, 1945. Pp. XII, 235.

MAGRUDER, Frank Abbot, *National Governements and International Relations*. Revised edition. Boston: Allyn and Bacon, 1942. Pp. VIII, 634. First published in 1929.

MATHEWS, Jackson (ed.), *History of Politics*. Translated by Denise Folliot and Jackson Mathews. Princeton, New Jersey: Princeton University Press, 1962. Pp. 686. From *The Collected Works of Paul Valéry*; his concern with international affaires, the essays spanning from 1895 to 1945.

PLATER, Charles, *A Primer of Peace and War*. New York: Kenedy, 1915. Pp. XI, 282.

STURZO, Luigi, *Nationalism and Internationalism*. New York: Roy Publishers, 1946. Pp. VIII, 308.

WRIGHT, John J., *National Patriotism in Papal Teaching*. Westminster, Maryland: Newman Bookshop, 1943.

Communism, — see above, p. 215.

Fascism, — see above, p. 217.

Hitlerism, — see above, p. 211, cf. p. 30.

Messianism, — see *PQS*, No. 5.

Racism, — see above, p. 30.

METHOD

See General Studies, above 2 c, p. 178; Law, above, Ch. III, 5, p. 163; Sociology, below, Ch. V, 5, p. 263.

CATLIN, George E. G., *The Science and Method of Politics.* New York: A. A. Knopf, 1927. Pp. XII, 360.

——, *A Study of the Principles of Politics, Being an Essay toward Political Rationalization.* New York: The Macmillan Co., 1930. Pp. 469.

OAKESHOTT, Michael, *Rationalism in Politics, and Other Essays.* London: Methuen, 1962. Pp. 334.

POPPER, Karl Raimund, *The Open Society and Its Enemies.* 4th ed. 2 vols. London: Routledge and Kegan Paul, 1962.

BADURA, Peter, *Die Methoden der neueren allgemeinen Staatslehre.* Erlangen: Palm und Enke, 1959. Pp. 248.

BATTAGLIA, Felice, Bertolino, A., *Problemi metodologici nella storia delle dottrine politiche ed economiche.* Rome: Il Foro Italiano, 1939. Pp. 206.

MILITARY FORCE

See War, above, p. 67.

GARTHOFF, Raymond L., *Soviet Military Doctrine.* Glencoe, Illinois: Free Press, 1953. Pp. XVIII, 587. See Communism, above.

HUNTINGTON, Samuel P. (ed.), *Changing Patterns of Military Politics.* New York: Free Press of Glencoe, 1962. Pp. 272.

VAGTS, Alfred, *A History of Militarism.* New York: 1937.

NAZI

See Hitlerism, above, p. 211.

PEACE AND WAR

See War, above, p. 67.

SLAVERY

See Colonies, above, p. 214; State, below.

CAREY, Henry Charles, *The Slave Trade, Domestic and Foreign: Why It Exists and How It May Be Extinguished.* Philadelphia: A. Hart, 1853. Pp. 426.

STATE

See Colonies, above, p. 214; Modern, above, p. 185.

In English

BENN, Stanley I., «State», in *The Encyclopedia of Philosophy* (8 vols. New York: The Macmillan Co., 1967), Vol. VIII, pp. 6-11.

—— and PETERS, R. S., *Social Principles and the Democratic State*. London: Allen and Unwin, 1959. Pp. 404. Reissued as *Principles of Political Thoght*. New York: Collier Books, 1964. See Philosophy, above, 178.

BOSANQUET, Bernard, *The Philosophical Theory of the State*. 4th ed. London: Macmillan and Co., 1923. Pp. XVIII, 342. First published in 1899. See also English Idealism, p. 200.

PFANNESTILL, Bertil, *Bernard Bosanquet's Philosophy of the State*. Translated by Bert HOOD. Lund, Sweden: Gleerup, 1936. Pp. 324.

CAREY, Henry Charles, *The Slave Trade, Domestic and Foreign: Why It Exists and How It May Be Extinguished*. Philadelphia: A. Hart, 1853. Pp. 426.

CHANG, Sherman Hsiao-Ming, *The Marxian Theory of the State*. Philadelphia: University of Pennsylvania, 1931. Pp. XV, 230.

COLLINGWOOD, Robin Georg, *The New Leviathan*. New York: Oxford University Press, 1942. Pp. VIII, 387.

——, *Three Laws of Politics*. New York: Oxford University Press, 1941. Pp. 26.

GIERKE VON, Otto F., *Johannes Althusius und die Entwicklung de natürrechtlichen Staatstheorien*. 4th ed. Berlin: G. Schade, 1929. Pp. XVIII, 322. English translation by Bernard FREYD, *The Development of Political Theory*. London: G. Allen and Unwin, 1939. Pp. 364.

HOBHOUSE, Leonard Trelawney, *Metaphysical Theory of the State*. London Allen and Unwin, 1918. Pp. 156.

KRABBE, Hugo, *Die moderne Staats-Idee*. The Hague: Martin Nijhoff, 1915. English translation by G. H. Sabine and W. J. SHEPARD, *The Modern Idea of the State*. New York: Appleton, 1922.

LINDSAY, Alexander Dunlop, *The Modern Democratic State*. New York: Oxford University Press, 1943. Pp. 286.

MABBOTT, John David, *The State and the Citizen: An Introduction to Political Philosophy*. London: Hutchinson and Co., 1948. Pp. 192.

MARITAIN, Jacques, *Man and the State*. Chicago: University of Chicago Press, 1951. Pp. 219.

NEUMANN, Franz, *The Democratic and the Authoritarian State*. Glencoe, Illinois: Free Press, 1957. Pp. X, 303.

ROMMEN, Heinrich, *The State in Catholic Thought*. St. Louis, Missouri: Herder, 1945. Pp. VIII, 747.

In Other Languages

DEL VECCHIO, Giorgio, *L'état et le droit; essais de philosophie politique*. Paris: Dalloz, 1964. Pp. 184.

Die Geschichte der europäischen Staaten. 6 vols. Ed. by A. H. L. Heeren and F. A. Ilkehrt. Gotha: F. A. Perthes, 1853-1858.

Entrèves d', A. P., *La dottrina dello stato: elementi di analisi e di interpretazione.* Turin: 1962.

Groppali, Alessandro, *Dottrina dello Stato.* 7th ed. Milan: Hoepli, 1945. Pp. 287.

Hippel von, Ernst, *Bacon und das Staatsdenken des Materialismus.* Halle (Saale): M. Niemeyer, 1939. Pp. 164.

——, *Geschichte der Staatsphilosophie in Hauptkapiteln.* 2 vols. Meisenheim am Glan: A. Hain, 1955-1957.

——, *Allgemeine Staatslehre.* Berlin: F. Vahlen, 1963. Pp. XII, 414.

Kelsen, Hans, *Hauptprobleme der Staatsrechtslehre.* Tübingen: J. C. B. Mohr, 1923. Pp. XXXVI, 709. First published in 1911.

——, *Sozialismus und Staat.* 2nd ed. Leipzig: C. L. Hirschfeld, 1923. First published in 1920. See also Socialism, above, Chapter II, 3, p. 89, cf. p. 206.

——, *Der Staat als Übermensch. Eine Erwiderung.* Vienna: Julius Springer, 1926. Pp. 24.

——, *Der soziologische und juristische Staatsbegriff.* 2nd ed. Tübingen: J. C. B. Mohr, 1928. Pp. VIII, 253. First published in 1922.

Legaz y Lacmbra, Luis, *Filosofia del derecho.* Barcelona: Bosch, 1953. Pp. 687. First published in 1943 under the title: *Introducción a la ciencia del derecho.*

Leo XIII, *Immortale Dei.* Rome: Vatican, 1885. See also Christianity, p. 214.

La «Immortale Dei»: la constituzione cristiana degli stati. Ed. by R. Vuillermin. Turin: S. E. I., 1929.

Ravà, Adolfo, *Le teorie filosofische sullo Stato.* Appunti da alcune lezioni di filosofia del diritto compilati da V. Lonigo et al., *Padua:* Università di Padova, 1933. Pp. 88.

Meinecke, F., *Die Idee der Staatsräson in der neueren Geschichte.* Munich, Berlin: Oldenbourg, 1924. Pp. 545.

Perticone, Giacomo, *La teoria del diritto e dello Stato.* Milan: Bompiani, 1937. Pp. 275.

Polacci, Giuseppe, *Lo Stato e l'individuo in Aristotele: raffronti con gli indirizzi moderni.* Palermo: Priulla, 1929. Pp. 192.

Polak, Karl, *Zur Dialektik in der Staatslehre.* 3rd ed. Berlin: Akademie-Verlag, 1963. Pp. XVIII, 571.

Rommen, Heinrich A., *Der Staat in der katholischen Gedankenwelt.* Paderborn: Bonifacius-Druckerei, 1935. English translation, *The State in the Catholic Thought: A Treatise in Political Philosophy.* London: B. Herder Book Co., 1955. Pp. VIII, 747.

Staat, Recht, Kultur. Festgabe für Ernst von Hippel zu seineur 70. Geburtstag, 28. September 1965. Bonn: Röhrscheid, 1965. Pp. 360.

Waldecker, Ludwig, *Allgemeine Staatslehre.* Berlin: W. Rotschild, 1927. Pp. XIV, 788.

VALUE

See above, Ch. I, 3, p. 64, also pp. 111, 277.

6. PERIODICALS

See Ethics, above, Ch. I, 4, p. 71; Law, above, Ch. III, 6, p. 169; Sociology, below, Ch. V, 6, 278.

(a) General

In English

American Political Science Review. Ed. by American Political Science Association. Washington, D. C.: 1726 Massachusetts Ave., N. W., 1906—.
Background of World Politics. A Digest of military, scientific, economic and social developments bearing on world politics. Waco, Texas: Baylor University Center for Foreign Service Studies, 1957—.
Columbia University Forum: A Journal of Fact and Opinion. New York: Columbia University, 1957—.
Ethics: An International Journal of Social, Political and Legal Philosophy. Chicago: University of Chicago Press, 1890—.
International Political Science Abstracts. Ed. by International Political Science Association. 5 Oxford: 15 Basil Blackwell, 49 Broad St., 1951—.
Midwest Journal of Political Science. Detroit, Michigan: Wayne State University Press, 1957—.
Orbis: A Journal of World Affairs. Philadelphia, Pennsylvania: Foreign Policy Research Institute, 1957—.
Political Science. Wellington, N. Z.: School of Political Science, Victoria University of Wellington, 1948—.
Political Science Quarterly. New York: Academy of Political Science, Columbia University, 1886—.
Political Studies. Ed. by Political Studies Association of the United Kingdom. London: Oxford University Press, Warwick Square, 1953—.
The Review of Politics. Notre Dame, Indiana: University of Notre Dame Press, 1939—.

In Other Languages

Année politique et économique. Paris: 19 Quai de Bourbon, 1924—.
Aussenpolitik. Zeitschrift für internationale Fragen. Stuttgart, Germany: Neckarstrasse 121, 1950—.
Démocratie nouvelle: revue de politique mondiale. Paris: S. A. R. L. Démocratie Nouvelle, 1947—.
Politique: revue internationale des doctrines et des institutions. Paris: 3, rue du Faubourg St-Honoré, 1958—.
Rassegna Italiana di politica e di cultura. Rome, Italy: Centro Italiano di Studi per la Riconciliazione Internazionale, 1918—.
Rivista internazionale di filosofia politica e sociale. Padua, next Genoa, 1935-1943, 1964—.

(b) Special

(aa) COUNTRIES

East

Eastern World: The Asia Monthly. London: Foreign Correspondents Ltd., 1947—.

China

Chinese Social and Political Science Review. Peiping: Chinese Science and Political Association, 1916—.

Japan

Contemporary Japan: A Review of Far Eastern Affaires. Ed. by Foreign Affaires Association of Japan. Tokyo, Japan: Togyo Kaikan 7 (1 - chome, Yurakucho, Chiyoda-Ku), 1932—.

East Europe

East Europe: A Review of East European Affairs. New York: Free Europe Committee, 1950—.

West

Free World Forum: A Journal on Foreign Affaires. Washington, D. C.: Free World Forum, Inc., 1959—.

America

— See above, a.

Hispanic American Report: An Analysis of Developments in Spain, Portugal and Latin-America. Stanford, California: Bolivar House, Stanford University, 1948.

England

— See above, a.

France

— See above, a.

Germany

German Foreign Policy. Berlin: Rutten und Loening, 1962.
Neue Politische Literature. Villingen, Schwarzwald, Germany: Klosterring
    1, 1956—.
Staat. Zeitschrift für Staatslehre, öffentliches Recht und Verfassungsge-
    schichte. Berlin, Germany: Duncker und Humblot, 1962—.

Italy

Civitas: rivista di studi politici. Rome: Piazza del Jesin, 1919.
Rassegna Europea: Rivista per la Federazione Europea. Trieste, Italy: Via
    Giuha 35, 1961—.

Poland

Cahiers Pologne-Allemagne. Paris: Editions Sarmatia (9, Place de la Made-
    laine), 1959—.
Państwo i Prawo. Warsaw, Poland: Institut Nauk Prawnych, Wiejska 12,
    1946—. Summaries in English, French and Russian.
Polish Western Affairs. To scholars interested in present day economic,
    social and political problems of Central Europe. Poznan, Poland:
    Stary Rynek 2, 1960—. Text in English, French and German.

Russia

Anglo-Soviet Journal. Ed. by Society for Cultural Relations with the USSR.
    London: 14 Kensington Square, 1940—.
Cahiers du monde russe et soviétique. The Hague, Netherlands: Mouton
    et Co., 1960—. Text in English and French.
Marxist Quarterly. Toronto, Canada: 44 Stafford St., 1962—.
Sowjetstudien. Ed. by the Institute for the Study of the USSR. Munich,
    Germany: Mannhardtstrasse 6, 1958—. Also English text, *Studies on*
    the Soviet Union.

(bb) QUESTIONS

Communism

See Russia, above, b.

Christianity.

Christian Statesman. Devoted to Christian and political and social science.
    Pittsburgh, Pennsylvania: 109 Monitor Ave., 1867—.

Philosophy

See General, above, a.

CHAPTER V

SOCIOLOGY

Sociology is the science of human society and societal relations. The term was coined by Auguste Comte (1798-1857). The main objects of sociological studies are the psychological phenomena of social interrelations. Prior to our own times, the methods used in the physical sciences were applied to social phenomena (for example, by A. Comte, A. L. J. Quetelet, and H. Th. Buckle); this has been done to some extent in the contemporary mechanistic schools. Therefore, sociology was originally called social physics. This approach was displaced by a biological or organic consideration of society, presented basically by P. Lilienfeld and A. E. F. Schäffle. Today a psychological concept of society prevails; social law and methodology in the social sciences are among the major concerns of current sociologist.

The perennial problem of social philosophy arise from the interrelationship of society and the individual. These include the nature, justification, principles, and duties of social relationships. The various schools listed below give an idea of the scope and the endeavor to solve these problems.

Some specific questions treated in detail by individual thinkers are listed below under the headings: Particular Countries, and Special Questions.

Bibliography

1. INTRODUCTORY BIBLIOGRAPHIES

See also Encyclopedias (Sociology), in *PQS*, No. 4; Periodicals, below, 6, p. 278.

BARBANO, F. and VITERBI, M., *Bibliografia della sociologia italiana, 1948-1958*. Turin: Ramella, 1959. Pp. 168.

Bibliographie der Sozialethik, Grundsatzfragen des öffentlichen Lebens, Recht, Geselschaft, Wirtschaft, Staat. Freiburg i. B.: Herder, 1964. Pp. 530.

Bibliographie française établie à l'intention des lecteurs étrangers: sociologie et psychologie sociale en France 1945-1958. Paris: Association pour la diffusion de la pensée française, 1960. Pp. 92.

CARRIER, Hervé and PIN Émile, *Sociology of Christianity: International Bibliography*. Rome: Pontificia Universitas Gregoriana. 1965. Pp. 316.

UTZ, Arthur, *Bases for Social Living: A Critical Bibliography Embracing Law, Society, Economics and Politics*. New York: Herder, 1961. Pp. 446.

——, *Bibliographie der Sozialethik, 1956-1963*. 3 vols. Freiburg: Herder, 1957-1964.

WHITE, Carl M. *et al.*, *Sources of Information in the Social Sciences: A Guide to the Literature*. Totowa, New Jersey: The Bedminister Press, 1964. Pp. 498. The Literature of Social Sciences, History, Economics.

GOULD, Julius and KOLB, William L., *A Dictionary of the Social Sciences*. New York: The Free Press of Glencoe, 1964. Pp. 761.

WILLEMS, E., *Dictionnaire de sociologie*. Ed. by Armand CUVILLIER. Paris: Marcel Rivière, 1961. Pp. 272.

2. GENERAL STUDIES

See Excerpts from Selected Writings, below, p. 238.

(a) Histories

In English

ARON, Raymond, *Main Currents in Sociological Thought*. 2 vols. Translated by Richard HOWARD and Helen WEAVER. New York: Basic Books, 1965-1967. Vol. I: Montesquieu, Comte, Marx, Tocqueville, the Sociologists and the Revolution of 1848. Vol. II: Durkheim, Pareto, Weber.

BARNES, Harry E. (ed.), *An Introduction to the History of Sociology*. Chicago: University of Chicago Press, 1948. Pp. XVI, 960.

——, *Historical Sociology: Theories of Social Evolution from Cave Life to Atomic Bombing*. New York: Philosophical Library, 1948. Pp. X, 186.

——, and Becker, Howard, *Social Thought from Folklore to Science.* 2 vols. London: Harrap, 1938.

BOGARDUS, Emory S., *The Development of Social Thought.* 3rd ed. New York: Longmans, Green and Co., 1955. Pp. 660.

CHAMBLISS, Rollin, *Social Thought from Hammurabi to Comte.* New York: Dryden Press, 1954. Pp. 500.

GOUGH, John W., *The Social Contract: A Critical Study of Its Developments.* Oxford: Clarendon Press, 1936. Pp. VI, 234. See also Contracts, above, Chapter III, 5, p. 156.

KILZER, E. and Ross, E. J., *Western Thought.* Milwaukee: Bruce Publishing Co., 1954. Pp. 525.

LICHTENBERGER, James P., *Development of Social Theory.* New York: Appleton-Century Co., 1938. Pp. XIII, 482.

MATHEWS, Jackson (ed.), *History of Politics.* From *The Collected Works of Paul Valéry.* Translated by Denise Folliot and Jackson Mathews. Princeton, New Jersey: Princeton University Press, 1962. Pp. 686. Valéry's concern with international affaires; his essays spanning from 1895 to 1945.

NESBIT, Robert, *The Sociological Tradition:* New York: Basic Books, 1966. Pp. 349.

PLAMENATZ, John, *Man and Society.* New York: McGraw-Hill Co., 1963. Vol. I: Machiavelli through Rousseau. Vol. II: Bentham through Marx.

VALÉRY, Paul, *Œuvres complètes.* Ed. by Jean Hytier. 2nd ed. Paris: Gallimard, 1959—. First edition in 1957. English translation edited by Jackson Mathews. New York: Pantheon Books, 1956.

In Other Languages

BOUTHOUL, Gaston, *Histoire de la sociologie.* Paris: Presses Universitaires de France, 1950. Pp. 128.

DOLLÉANS, Édouard, *Histoire du mouvement ouvrier.* 3 vols. Paris: A. Colin, 1953.

Gründer der Soziologie. Ed. by Fritz Karl MANN. Jena: G. Fischer, 1928-.

GURVITCH, G. D., *L'idée du droit social, notion et système du droit social: Histoire doctrinale depuis le XVIIe siècle jusqu'à la fin du XIXe siècle.* Paris: Librairie du Recueil Sirey, 1932. Pp. IX, 713.

PARETO, Vilfredo (ed.), *Biblioteca di storia economica.* 6 vols. Milan: Società editrice libraria, 1903-1929.

SCHOECK, H., *Soziologie: Geschichte ihrer Probleme.* Freiburg: Alber, 1952. Pp. IX, 430.

WIESE VON, Leopold, *Soziologie: Geschichte und Hauptprobleme.* Berlin: W. de Gruyter, 1926. Pp. 98.

(b) Systematic Studies

In English

BAILEY, Robert B, *Sociology Faces Pessimism: A Study of European Sociological Thought Amidst a Fading Optimism.* The Hague: Martinus Nijhoff, 1958. Pp. 173.

BARBER, Bernard, *Social Stratification: A Comparative Analysis of Structure and Process.* Ed. by Robert K. MERTON. New York: Harcourt, Brace, 1957. Pp. 540.

BELL, Earl Hoyt. *Social Foundations of Human Behavior: Introduction to the Study of Sociology.* New York: Harper, 1961. Pp. 612.

BENN, S. I. and PETERS, R. S., *Social Principles and the Democratic State.* London: Allen and Unwin, 1959. Pp. 404. Reissued as *Principles of Political Thought.* New York: Collier Books, 1964. See also Politics (State), above, Chapter IV, 5, p. 223.

BERGEL, Egon Earnest, *Social Stratification.* New York: McGraw-Hill Book Company, 1962. Pp. 480.

BERGER, Peter L., *Invitation to Sociology: A Humanistic Perspective.* Garden City, New York: Doubleday Anchor, 1963. Pp. 191.

BERTRAND, Alvin L., *Basic Sociology: An Introduction to Theory and Method.* New York: Appleton-Century-Crofts, 1967. Pp. X, 452.

BROWN, Robert, *Explanation in Social Science.* London: Routledge and Kegan Paul, 1963. Pp. 198.

CAREY, Henry Charles, *Principles of Social Science.* 3 vols. Philadelphia: J. B. Lippincott and Co., 1858-1859. Reprint in New York: Augustus M. Kelley, 1963.

CATLIN, George Edward Gordon, *Political and Sociological Theory and Its Applications.* Ann Arbor, Michigan: University of Michigan Press, 1964. Pp. 118.

——, *The Science and Method of Politics.* Hamden, Connecticut: Shoe String, 1964. Pp. 360.

DURKHEIM, Emile, — see Method, below, 5, p. 263.

GINSBERG, Morris, *Sociology.* London: Thornton Butterworth, 1934. Pp. 255.

HOBHOUSE, Leonard T., *Principle of Sociology.* 4 vols. London: G. Allen and Unwin, 1918-1924.

INKELES, Alexander, *What is Sociology? An Introduction to the Discipline and Profession.* Englewood Cliffs, New Jersey: Prentice Hall, 1964. Pp. 120.

KETTELER, Wilhelm Emmanuel, — see Christianity, above, p. 248.

KUHN, Alfred, *The Study of Society, a Unified Approach.* Hamewood, Illinois: Richard D. Irwin, 1963. Pp. 812.

LANDIS, Paul Henry, *Sociology.* Boston: Ginn and Co., 1964. Pp. 531.

LAZARSFELD, Paul F., SEWELL, William and WILENSKY, Harold L. (eds.), *The Uses of Sociology.* New York: Basic Books, 1967. Pp. XXXIX, 902.

LE PLAY, Frédéric, — see below, pp. 248, 264.

LUNDBERG, George A., *Foundations of Sociology.* New York: The Macmillan Co., 1939. Pp. XX, 556.

——, *Social Research: A Study in Methods of Gathering Data.* New York: Longman, Green and Co., 1942. Pp. XX, 426.

——, *Can Science Save Us?* New York: Longmans, Green and Co., 1947. Pp. 122.

MADGE, Charles, *Society in the Mind: Elements of Social Eidos.* London: Faber and Faber, 1964. Pp. 158.

MERTON, Robert K., *Social Theory and Social Structure.* Revised edition, 9th printing. London: Collier-Macmillan, Ltd., 1964. Pp. XVIII, 645.

PARETO, Vilfredo, *Compendio di sociologia generale.* Ed. by G. FARINA. 3 vols. 2nd ed. Florence: Barbera, 1923. First published in 1920. English translation by Arthur LIVINGSTON and Andrew BONGIORNO, *Mind and Society.* 4 vols. New York: Harcourt, Brace and Co., 1935.

PARK, Robert Ezra, and BURGESS, Ernest W., *Introduction to the Science of Sociology.* 2nd. Chicago: The University of Chicago Press, 1924. Pp. XXIII, 1040. First published in 1921.

REX, J., *Key Problems of Sociological Theory.* London: Routledge and Kegan Paul, 1961. Pp. IX, 194.

RILEY, Matilda W. *et al., Sociological Studies in Scale Analyses.* New Brunswick, New Jersey: Rutgers University Press, 1954. Pp. 433.

SMALL, Albion Woodbury, *The Meaning of Social Science.* Chicago; The University of Chicago Press, 1910. Pp. VII, 309.

—— and Vincent, E. George, *Introduction to the Study of Society.* New York: American Book Co., 1894. Pp. 384.

SOROKIN, Pitirim A., *System Source Book in Rural Sociology.* 3 vols. London: Russell and Russell, 1965.

——, *Social and Cultural Dynamics.* 4 vols. American Book, 1937-1941.

STARK, Werner, *The Sociology of Knowledge.* Chicago: The Free Press of Glencoe. 1958. Pp. 356. See also, Sociology and Science, below, p. 276.

——, *The Fundamental Forms of Social Thought.* New York: Fordham University Press, 1963. Pp. 270.

TAYLOR, John F. A., *The Masks of Society.* New York: Appleton-Century-Crofts, 1966. Pp. 288.

TÖNNIES, Ferdinand, *Gemeinschaft und Gesellschaft.* Leipzig: R.Reisland, 1887. Pp. XXX, 294. English translation by Charles P. Loomis, *Fundamental Concepts of Sociology.* New York: American Book Company, 1940. Pp. XXXiv, 293. Reedited as *Community and Association.* London: Routledge and Kegan Paul, 1955. Pp. XXXIV, 293.

VINE, Margaret Wilson, *An Introduction to Sociological Theory.* New York: Longmans, Green and Co., 1959. Pp. XVII, 350.

WELFORD, Michael A., GLASS, D. V. and MORIS, J. N., *Society: Problems and Methods of Study.* New York: Philosophical Library, 1962. Pp. VI, 586.

WIESE VON, Leopold M. W. and BECKER, Howard, *Systematic Sociology.* New York: John Wiley, 1932. Pp. XXI, 772.

In Other Languages

BATTAGLIA, F., «*Um eine neue Soziologie*», *Archiv für Recht- und Sozialphilosophie* (Berlin), 1949, pp. 25-49.

CUVILLIER, Armand, *Manuel de Sociologie avec notice bibliographiques.* 5th ed. Paris: Presses Universitaires de France, 1963. Pp. XC, 340.

FRODL, F., S. J., *Geselschaftslehre.* 2nd ed. Paderborn Schöningh, 1962. Pp. 419.

GURVITCH, G. (ed.), *Traité de sociologie.* 2nd ed. Paris: Presses Universitaires de France, 1963. Pp. VIII, 520.

LAMBRECHT, Stefan, *Die Soziologie.* Stuttgart: H. Seewald, 1958. Pp. 487.

LAMOUCHE, André, *D'une morale de l'amore a une sociologie de la raison.* 2 vols. Paris: Dunod, 1962-1963.

Pareto, Vilfredo, *Trattato di sociologia generale*. 2nd ed. 3 vols. Florence: Barbera, 1923. See above, In English.

Tönnies, Ferdinand, — see above, In English.

(c) Philosophy

See Special Questions, below, 5; Method, *ibid.*; Excerpts, below, d.

In English

Bart, Landheer, *Mind and Society: Epistemological Essays on Sociology*. The Hague: Martinus Nijhoff, 1952. Pp. XII, 112.

——, *Pause for Transition: An Analysis of the Relation of Man, Mind and Society*. The Hague: Martinus Nijhoff, 1957. Pp. V, 284.

Beck, Robert, *Perspectives in Social Philosophy: Readings in Philosophic Sources of Social Thought*. New York: Holt, Rinehart and Winston, 1967. Pp. 480. See also Excerpts, below, d.

Benn, Stanley I., «Society», in the *Encyclopedia of Philosophy* (8 vols. New York: The Macmillan Co., 1967), Vol VII, pp. 470-474.

Bonald de, Louis (1754-1840), — see Traditionalism, above, Chapter IV, 2, p. 207.

Braybrooke, David (ed.), *Philosophical Problems of the Social Sciences*. New York: The Macmillan, Co., 1965. Pp. 120. See Selections, below, d.

Buckle, Henry Thomas (1821-1862), — see England, below, 4, p. 259.

Cohen, Carl (ed.), *Communism, Fascism and Democracy*. New York: Random House, 1962. Pp. 704.

Diesing, Paul, *Reason in Society: Five Types of Decisions and Their Social Conditions*. Urbana, Illinois, University of Illinois Press, 1962. Pp. 262.

Fyvel, T. R., *The Frontiers of Sociology*. London: Cohen and West, 1964. Pp. VIII, 107.

Gerth, Hans Heinrich and Mills, Charles Wright, *Character and Social Structure: The Psychology of Social Institutions*. London: Routledge and Kegan Paul, 1954. Pp. XXV, 490.

Ginsberg, Morris, *Essays in Sociology and Social Philosophy*. 3 vols. London: Heinemann, 1956-1961.

Gré de, Gerad L., *Society and Ideology*. New York: Columbia University Bookstore, 1943. Pp. 114.

Isajiw, Wsevolod W., *Causation and Functionalism in Sociology*. Ed. by W. J. H. Sprott. London: Routledge and Kegan Paul, 1968. Pp. VII, 158.

Ketteler, Wilhelm Emmanuel, — see Christianity, below, 3 Contemporary, p. 248.

Laszlo, Ervin, *Essential Society: An Ontological Reconstruction*. The Hague: Martinus Nijhoff, 1963. Pp. X, 169.

——, *Individualism, Collectivism and Political Power: A Relational Analysis of Ideological Conflict*. The Hague: Martinus Nijhoff, 1963. Pp. VII, 172.

Lazarsfeld, Paul F. and Rosenberg, Morris (eds.), *The Language of Social Research*. Chicago: Free Press, 1955. Pp. 500. See also Selections, below, d.

La Tour du Pin, — see Christianity, below, 3, p. 248.

Lilienfeld von, Paul, — see In Foreing Languages, below.

Lundberg, George Andrew, *Foundations of Sociology*. New York: McKay Co., 1964. Pp. 179.

Mannheim, Karl (1893-   ), *Ideologie und Utopie*. Bonn: F. Cohen, 1929. Pp. X, 250. English translation by Louis Wirth and E. Shils, *Ideology and Utopie: An Introduction to the Sociology of Knowledge*. New York: Harcourt, Brace and Co., 1936. Pp. XXXI, 318.

Lieber, Hans, Joachim, *Wissen und Geselschaft*. Tübingen: Niemeyer, 1952. Pp. 166. On Scheler and Mannheim.

Martindale, Don, *The Nature and Types of Sociological Theory*. Boston: Houghton Mifflin, 1961. Pp. XIV, 560.

McEwen, William P., *The Problem of Social Scientific Knowledge*. Englewood Cliffs, New Jersey: Bedminster Press, 1963. Pp. XXIX, 590.

Mukeriee, Radha K., *The Philosophy of Social Science*. London: Macmillan Co., 1960. Pp. IX, 187.

Natanson, Maurice, *Philosophy of the Social Sciences*. New York: Random House, 1963. Pp. 570.

Pareto, Vilfredo (1848-1923), see above, pp. 231, 233; Economics (Mathematical School), above, Chapter II, pp. 76, 99.

Parsons, Talcott, *The Structure of Social Action: A Study in Social Theory with Special Reference to a Group of Recent European Writers*. Glencoe, Illinois: Free Press, 1949. Pp. XII, 817. Evaluation of theories of Alfred Marshall, Vilfredo Pareto, Emile Durkheim, Max Weber.

——, *Essays in Sociological Theory Pure and Applied*. Glencoe, Illinois: Free Press, 1949. Pp. 379.

——, *The Social System*. Glencoe, Iillinois: Free Press, 1951. Pp. 575. See Contemporary, below.

Quételet, Adolphe L. J. (1796-1874), *Sur l'homme et le développement de ses facultés, ou essai de physique sociale*. 2 vols. Brussels: L. Hauman, 1936.

——, *Du système social et des lois qui le régissent*. Paris: Guillaumin, 1848. Pp. XVI, 360.

——, *Physique sociale, ou essai sur le développement des facultés de l'homme*. 2 vols. Brussels: C. Muguardt, 1869. Comprising *Sur l'homme* and new material.

——, *Anthropométrie ou mesure des differentes facultés de l'homme*. Brussels: C. Muquardt, 1870. Pp. 479.

Hankins, Frank H., «Adolphe Quetelet as Statistician», in *Studies in History, Economics and Public Law*. New York: Columbia University Press, No 84 (1908).

Halbwachs, Maurice, *La théorie de l'homme moyen: Essai sur Quételet et la statistique morale*. Paris: F. Alcan, 1913. Pp. 180.

Lottin, Joseph, *Quételet statisticien et sociologue*. Louvain: Institut Supérieur de Philosophie, 1912. Pp. XXX, 564.

RUDNER, Richard, *Philosophy of Social Science*. Englewood Cliffs, New Jersey: Prentice-Hall, 1965. Pp. 128.

RUNCIMAN, W. G., *Social Science and Political Theory*. London: Cambridge University Press, 1963. Pp. 200. See also Politics, p. 310.

SCHÄFFLE, Albert E. F. (1831-1903), *Bau und Leben des sozialen Korpers*. 4 vols. Tübingen, 1875-1878.

——, *Die Quintessenz des Sozialisme*. 16th ed. Gotha: F. A. Perthes, 1919. First published in 1875. English translation by Bernard BOSANQUET, *The Quintessence of Socialism*. 7th ed. London: Swan Sonnenschein and Co., 1902. Pp. VIII, 127.

——, *Die Aussichtlosigkeit der Socialdemokratie*. 4th ed. Tübingen: J. C. B. MOHR, 1891. First published in 1885. English translation by A. C. MORANT, *The Impossibility of Social Democracy*. London: Swan Sonnenschein and Co., 1892. Pp. XX, 419.

SCHUTZ, Alfred, *Collected Papers*. 2 vols. The Hague: Martinus Nijhoff, 1962-1964. Vol. I: the Problem of Social Reality; Vol. II: Studies in Social Theory.

SEELY, Charles S., *Philosophy and the Ideological Conflict: An Analysis of Idealism and Materialism and the Influence of These Philosophies on the Over-all World Struggle between Capitalism and Socialism*. New York: Philosophical Library, 1953. Pp. 319.

SHILS, Edward, NAEGELE, K. D. and PITTS, J. R. (eds.), *Theories of Society: Foundations of Modern Sociological Theory*. 2 vols. New York: The Free Press of Glencoe, 1961.

BLACK, Max (ed.), *The Social Theories of Talcott Parsons*. Englewood Cliffs, New Jersey: Prentice-Hall, 1961. Pp. 363.

SIMMEL, Georg, *The Sociology of Georg Simmel*. Translated and edited by K. H. WOLFF. Glencoe, Illinois: The Free Press, 1950. Pp. 445. An Anthology of Simmel's works.

SINHA, Ajit K., *Principle of Sociology*. Agra, India: Lakshmi Narain Agarwal, 1963. Pp. 293.

SOROKIN, Pitirim A., *Social and Cultural Dynamics*. 4 vols. New York: American Book Co., 1937-1941.

——, *Social Philosophies of an Age of Crisis*. London: Adam and Charles Black, 1952. Pp. 345.

Studies in Social Philosophy. New Orleans: Tulane University, 1962. Pp. 115.

WEBER, Max, — see above, p. 75.

In Other Languages

BARLET, F. Ch., *L'évolution sociale, étude historique et philosophique de sociologie synthétique*. Paris: Librairie Hermétique, 1910. Pp. 206.

BARTH, Paul, *Die Philosophie der Geschichte als Sociologie*. Leipzig: O. R. Reisland, 1897. Pp. XVI, 396.

BOUGLÉ, C., *Qu'est-ce que la sociologie ?* 5th ed. Paris: F. Alcan, 1925. Pp. XXIII, 161. First published in 1907.

DUNKMANN, Karl (ed.), *Lehrbuch der Soziologie und Sozialphilosophie*. Berlin: Junker und Dunnhaupt, 1931.

DURKHEIM, Émile, *Sociologie et philosophie*. Paris: Presses Universitaires de France, 1951. Pp. 159. See also Contemporary, below.

FREYER, Hans, *Soziologie als Wirklichkeitwissenschaft. Logische Grundlegung des Systems der Soziologie.* 2nd ed. Stuttgart: Teubner, 1964. Pp. IV, 310. First published in 1930.

GEIGER, Theodor, *Ideologie und Wahrheit.* Stuttgart: Humboldt, 1953. Pp. 193.

GURVITCH, Georges, *La vocation actuelle de la sociologie.* 3rd. ed. Paris: Presses Universitaires de France, 1963. Pp. 512.

JONAS, Friedrich, *Sozialphilosophie der industriellen Arbeitswelt.* Stuttgart: F. Enke, 1960. Pp. 218.

KELSEN, Hans, *Aufsätze zur Ideologiekritik.* Ed. by Ernst TOPITSCH (Soziologische Texte, 16). Neuwied a. R.: Luchterhand, 1964. Pp. 369.

KINNEN, Eduardo, *Etica social.* Santiago, Chile: Universidad Católica de Chile, 1963. Pp. 384.

LILIENFELD VON, Paul (1829-1903), *Gedanken über die Socialwissenschaft der Zukunft.* 5 vols. Milan: E. Behre, 1875-1881.

——, *La Pathologie Sociale.* Paris: V. Giard et E. Brière, 1896. Pp. XLVII, 335.

——, *Zur Vertheidigung der organischen Methode in der Sociologie.* Berlin: G. Reimer, 1898. Pp. 76.

LUCINI, G., *Elementi di filosofia sociale.* Pavia: Renzo Cortina, 1960. Pp. 264.

MENDOZA SÁNCHEZ, Manuel, «Para una metafisica de lo social», *Memorias del XIII Congreso Internacional de Filosofia, Mexico, D. F., 7-14 de Septembre de 1963* (Mexico: Universidad Nacional Autonoma de Mexico, 1964), pp. 325-334.

PAGANO, S., «Principios filosoficos da ordem social», *Revista da Universidade de São Paulo,* Brasil, 1961-1962, pp. 75-112.

QUÉTELET, A., — see In English, above.

SCHÄFFLE, A. E. F.,— see In English, above.

SCHELER, Max F., *Schriften zur Soziologie und Weltanschauungslehre.* 3 vols. Leipzig: Der neue Geist, 1923-1924. See also Phenomenology, p. 50.

——, *Die Stellung des Menschen im Kosmos.* Darmstadt: O. Reichl, 1928. Pp. 114.

PEDROLI, Guido, *Max Scheler dalla fenomenologia alla sociologia.* Turin: Editioni di Filosofia, 1952. Pp. 132.

THIEL, Rainer, «Zur Anwendung mathematischer Begriffe in Geselschaftswissenschaften», *Deutse Zeitschrift für Philosophie* (Berlin), 1963, pp. 19-44.

TOPITSCH, Ernst, *Sozialphilosophie zwischen Ideologie und Wissenschaft.* Neuwied a. R.: Luchterhand, 1961. Pp. 302.

WENDLAND, H. D., *Einführung in die Sozialethik.* Berlin: De Gruyter, 1963, Pp. 144.

WORMS, René (1869-1926), *Organisme et société.* Paris: V. Giard et E. Brière, 1896. Pp. 412.

——, *Philosophie des sciences sociales.* 3 vols. Paris: V. Giard et E. Brière, 1903-1907.

——, *Les Principes biologiques de l'évolution sociale.* Paris: V. Giard et E. Brière, 1910.

——, *La sociologie, sa nature, son contenu, ses attaches.* Paris: M. Giard. 1921. Pp. 164.

(d) Excerpts from Selected Writings

BAIN, Read (ed.), *Sociology: Introductory Readings.* Philadelphia: J. B. Lippincott, 1962. Pp. 483.

BECK, Robert, *Perspectives in Social Philosophy: Readings in Philosophic Sources of Social Thought.* New York: Holt, Rinehart and Winston, 1967. Pp. 480.

BRANDT, Richard (ed.), *Social Justice.* Englewood Cliffs, New Jersey: Prentice-Hall, 1962.

BRAYBROOKE, David (ed.), *Philosophical Problems of the Social Sciences.* Sources in Philosophy. New York: The Macmillan Company, 1965. Pp. 120.

BRODBECK, May (ed.), *Readings in the Social Sciences.* New York: The Macmillan and Co., 1967. Pp. 640.

CASTELL, Alburey and KUYPERS, M. J. S. (eds.), *Selected Readings in Social Criticism from Adam Smith to Karl Marx.* St. Paul, Minnesota: Webb Publishing Co., 1946. Pp. X, 83.

GURVITCH, Georges and MOORE, Wilbert E. (eds.), *Twentieth Century Sociology.* New York: Philosophical Library, 1945. Pp. 754.

LAZARSFELD, Paul F. and ROSENBERG, Morris (eds.), *The Language of Social Research.* Chicago: Free Press, 1955. Pp. 590.

LOOMIS, Charles Price, and LOOMIS, Z. K., *Modern Social Theories: Selected American Writers.* Princeton, New Jersey: Van Nostrand, 1961. Pp. XXIV, 720.

MERTON, Robert K, GRAY, Ailsa P, HOCKEY, Barbara and SELVIN, Hannan C. (eds.), *Reader in Bureaucracy.* Chicago: Free Press, 1953.

MIHANOVICH, Clemont Simon (ed.), *Social Theorists.* Milwaukee, Wisconsin: Bruce Publishing Co., 1953. Pp. 521.

MILLS, C. W. (ed.), *Images of Man: The Classic Tradition in Sociological Thinking.* New York: George Braziller, 1960. Pp. 534.

NATANSON, Maurice (ed.), *Philosophy of the Social Sciences.* New York: Random House, 1963. Pp. 560.

OLAFSON, Frederick A. (ed.), *Society, Law and Morality: Readings in Social Philosophy from Classical and Contemporary Sources.* Englewood Cliffs, New Jersey: Prentice-Hall, 1961. Pp. IX, 518.

—— (ed.), *Justice and Social Policy.* Englewood Cliffs, New Jersey: Prentice-Hall, 1961.

PARSONS, Talcott, SKILS, Edward, NAEGEL, Vespar D. and PITTS, Jesse R. (eds.), *Theories of Society: Foundations of Modern Sociological Theory.* 2 vols. New York: The Free Press of Glencoe, 1961.

SOROKIN, Pitirim A. (ed.), *Modern Historical and Social Philosophies.* New York: Dover, 1963. Pp. XI, 345.

3. PARTICULAR PERIODS

ANTIQUITY

(a) Comprehensive Studies

See Histories of General and Ancient Philosophy, in *PQS*, No. 5.

GITTLER, Joseph, *Social Thought among the Early Greeks*. Athens: The University of Georgia Press, 1941. Pp. XII, 272.

POHLMANN VON, Robert, *Geschichte der sozialen Frage und des Sozialismus in der antiken Welt*. 2 vols. 3rd ed. Munich: Ch. H. Beck, 1925. See also Economics, above, Chapter II, 3, p. 80.

(b) Specific Studies

PLATO (427-437), *The Republic*. Translated by B. JOWETT. New York: The Modern Library, 1941.

VINE, Margaret Wilson, «Plato», in her *An Introduction to Sociological Theory* (New York: Longmans, Green and Co., 1959), pp. 2-5.

ARISTOTE (384-322), *Politics*. Translated by B. JOWETT. Oxford: Clarendon Press, 1908.

ELLWOOD, Charles Abram, «Aristotle as a Sociologist», *The Annals of the American Academy of Political and Social Science* (Philadelphia), 1902, pp. 227-238.

VINE, Margaret Wilson, «Aristotle», in her *An Introduction to Sociological Theory* (New York: Longmans, Green and Co., 1959), pp. 5-10.

DEFOURNY, Maurice, *Aristote et l'évolution sociale*. Louvain: Institut supérieur de philosophie, 1924.

——, *Aristote: études sur la «Politique»*. Paris: G. Beauchesne et ses fils, 1932. Pp. XX, 559.

MIDDLE AGES

(a) Comprehensive Studies

JARRETT, Bede, *Social Theories of the Middle Ages*. Westminster, Maryland: Newman Bookshop, 1942. Pp. IX, 280.

(b) Specific Studies

THOMAS Saint, Aquinas, — see above, Ch. I, 2, p. 15.

> DE LA VEGA, F. J., *Social Progress and Happiness in the Philosophy of St. Thomas Aquinas and Contemporary American Sociology.* Washington, D. C.: The Catholic University of America Press, 1949. Pp. 101.

> RZADKIEWICZ, A. I., *The Philosophical Bases of Human Liberty according to St. Thomas Aquinas: A Study in Social Philosophy.* Washington, D. C.: The Catholic University of America Press, 1949. Pp. 185.

> SMITH, I., *St. Thomas Aquinas and Human Social Life.* Washington, D. C.: The Catholic University of America Press, 1947.

MODERN

(a) Comprehensive Studies

ARON, Raymond, *Montesquieu, Comte, Marx, Tocqueville: The Sociologists and the Revolution of 1848.* New York: Basic Books, 1965. Pp. 272. Vol. I, — see Histories, above, 2 a.

PARSON, Talcott, *The Social System.* Glencoe, Illinois: The Free Press, 1951.
——— *et al.* (eds.), *Theories of Society. Foundations of Modern Sociological Theory.* 2 vols .New York: The Free Press of Glencoe, 1961. See Selections, above, d.

SOROKIN, Pitirim A., *Modern Historical and Social Philosophies.* New York: Dover Publications, 1964. Pp. 345. First published in 1950 with title, *Social Philosophies of An Age of Crisis.*

DURKHEIM, Émile, *Montesquieu et Rousseau, précurseurs de la sociologie.* Paris: M. Rivière, 1953. Pp. 200.

ESPINAS, Alfred, *La philosophie sociale du XVIIe siècle et la Revolution.* Paris: F. Alcan, 1898. Pp. 412.

(b) Specific Studies

(aa) ENLIGHTENMENT: rationalistic and empirical explanation of social events.

See above, Ch. IV, 2, 3, p. 192.

Biological Approach, — see Biological School, below, p. 244.

Christianity, — see Christian School, below, p. 247.

Geographical Approach, — see Geographical School, below, p. 249.

(bb) IDEALISM: social phenomena are spontanious development of an ideal (living) reality.

See above, Ch. I, 2, pp. 32, 48.

HEGEL, G. W. F. (1770-1831), — see Idealism, above, p. 32.

MARCUSE, Herbert, *Reason and Revolution: Hegel and the Rise of Social Theory*. London: Oxford University Press, 1941. Pp. XII, 431.

GENTILE, G., — see Fascism in Italy, above, p. 219.

(cc) INDIVIDUALISM: insists on the role and the importance of each individual; the individual is of primary concern.

See Contemporary, below, p. 257.

MACPHERSON, Crawford Brough, *The Political Theory of Possessive Individualism: Hobbes to Locke*. New York: Oxford University Press, 1962. Pp. 310.

HOBBES, Thomas, *Leviation or The Matter, Form and Power of a Commonwealth Ecclesiastical and Civil*. London: Andrew Crooke, 1651. Pp. 396. See below, p. 21.

ROUSSEAU, Jean Jacques, *Social Contract or Principles of Political Law*. Translated by Willmoore KENDALL. Chicago: Henry Regnery, 1954. Pp. 171. See Politics, above, chapter IV, 3, p. 194.

SUMNER, William Graham, *What Social Classes Owe to Each Other*. New York: Harper and Brothers, 1883. Pp. 169.

——, *Folkways*. Boston: Ginn and Co., 1907. Pp. 692.

—— and Keller, Albert Galloway, *The Science of Society*. 4 vols. New Haven, Connecticut: Yale University Press, 1927.

DAVIE, Maurice R. (ed.), *Sumner Today*. New Haven: Yale University Press, 1940. Pp. XXVI, 194.

(dd) SOCIAL PHYSICS: social processes are visualized mechanically as in physics.

See Contemporary, Mechanistic School, below, p. 250.

DURKHEIM, Émile, *Leçons de sociologie: physique des mœurs et du droit*. Paris: Presses Universitaires de France, 1953. Pp. XLVIII, 264. See below, Pp. 243, 252.

COMTE, Auguste (1798-1857), — see Postivism, above, Chapter I, 2, p. 35.

——, *The System of Positive Polity*. Translated by John BRIDGES *et al.* 4 vols. London: Longmans, Green and Co., 1875-1877.

CAIRD, Edward, *The Social Philosophy and Religion of Comte*. New York: Russell and Russell, 1965. Pp. XX, 216. First published in 1936.

GREENE, J. C., «Biology and social theory in the nineteenth century: Auguste Comte and Henry Spencer», *Critical Problems*, pp. 419-446.

MARVIN, F. S., *Comte: The Founder of Sociology*. London: Chapman, 1936. Pp. 216.

Vine, Margaret Wilson, «Auguste Comte», in her, *An Introduction to Sociological Theory* (New York: Longmans, Green and Co., 1959), pp. 21-43.

Defourny, Maurice, *La Sociologie positiviste: A. Comte.* Paris: F. Alcan, 1939. First published in 1902. Pp. 370.

Quételet, Adolphe L. J. (1796-1874), — see Philosophy, above, 1 c, p. 235.

Riezu, Jorge, O.P., «La moral social en el positivismo de Comte», *Estudios Filosoficos* (Las Caldas de Besaya, Santander), 1963, pp. 233-275.

(ee) Racial Theory : race value overemphasized.

Gobineau de, Arthur (1816-1882), — see Ethics, Politics, above, I, 2, p. 31.

(ff) Social Evolution Theory: persistence of gradual social changes.

See below, p. 251; Politics, above, Ch. IV, 3, p. 203.

Spencer, Herbert (1820-1903), *The Principles of Sociology.* 3 vols. London: Williams and Norgate, 1876-1896.
——, *The Study of Sociology.* 9th ed. London: Williams and Norgate, 1880. Pp. VIII, 438.

> Asirvatham, E., *Herbert Spencer's Theory of Social Justice.* New York: Stechert, 1936.
>
> Lacy, George, *Liberty and Law: Being an Attempt at the Refutation of the Individualism of Mr. Herbert Spencer.* London: Sonnenschein and Co., 1888. Pp. 377.
>
> Rumney, Jay, *Herbert Spencer's Sociology.* London: Williams and Norgate, 1934. Pp. XVI, 357. New ed. New York: Atherton Press, 1966. Pp. 376.
>
> Vine, Margaret Wilson, «Herbert Spencer, Social Evolution», in her, *An Introduction to Sociological Theory* (New York: Longmans, Green and Co., 1959), pp. 44-62.

> Roberty de, Eugène (1843-1915), *Nouveau programme de sociologie.* Paris: F. Alcan, 1904. Pp. 268.
>
> ——, *Auguste Comte et Herbert Spencer.* Paris: F. Alcan, 1894. Pp. X, 201.
>
> ——, *Sociologie de l'action: la genèse sociale de la raison et les origines rationelles de l'action.* Paris: F. Alcan, 1908. Pp. XI, 355.
>
> Salvadore, Guglielmo, *La scienza economica e la teoria dell' evoluzione: Saggio sulle teorie economico-sociali di Herbert Spencer.* Florence: Lumachi, 1901. Pp. 168.

Traditionalism, — see Politics, above, Ch. IV, 3, p. 207.

CONTEMPORARY

See Modern, above.

(a) Comprehensive Study

In English

ARON, Raymond, *Main Currents in Sociological Thought: Durkheim, Pareto, Weber.* New York: Basic Books, 1967. Pp. IX, 274. Vol. II, — see Histories, above, 2 a, p. 230.

BARNES, Harry E., BECKER, Howard and BECKER, F. B. (eds.), *Contemporary Social Theory.* New York: Appleton-Century, 1940. Pp. XX, 947.

GERTH, Hans and MILLS, Wright (eds.), *From Max Weber: Essays in Sociology.* London: Routledge and Kegan Paul, 1948. Pp. 490.

GINSBERG, Morris and FARQUARSON, A. (eds.), *Modern Sociologists.* 5 vols. London: Chapman and Hall, 1936.

GURVITCH, Georges and MOORE, Wilbert E. (eds.), *Twentieth Century Sociology.* New York: Philosophical library, 1945. Pp. 754.

LASLETT, Peter, RUNCIMAN, W. G. *et al* (eds.), *Philosophy, Politics and Society.* New York: Barnes and Co., 1963. Pp. 229.

MERTON, Robert K., BROOM, Leonard and COTTRELL, Leonard S., Jr., *Sociology Today: Problems and Prospects.* New York: Basic Books, Inc., 1959. Pp. XXXIV, 623.

MOUZELIS, Nicos P., *Organization and Bureaucracy: An Analysis of Modern Theories.* Ed. by W. J. H. Sprott. London: Routledge and Kegan Paul, 1967. Pp. IX, 230.

PA, J., *Sociological Theories of Today.* New York: Harper and Row, 1966. Pp. XI, 676.

PAKESHOTT Michael Joseph (ed.), *Social and Political Doctrines of Contemporary Europe.* 2nd ed. New York: The Macmillan Co., 1942. Pp. XXIII, 243.

SMALL, Albion W., *General Sociology: An Exposition of the Main Development in Sociological Theory from Spencer to Ratzenhofer.* Chicago: The University of Chicago Press, 1905. Pp. XII, 739.

SOROKIN, Pitirim A., *Contemporary Sociological Theories.* New York: Harper and Brothers, 1928. Pp. XXIII, 785.

—— (ed.), *A Systematic Source-Book on Rural Sociology.* 3 vols. Minneapolis, Minnesota: University of Minnesota Press, 1930-1932.

In Other Languages

DURKHEIM, Émile, *Pragmatisme et sociologie.* Cours inédit restitué d'après des notes d'étudiants. Ed. by Armand CUVILLIER. Paris: J. Vrin, 1955. Pp. 212.

GEHLEN, A. and SCHELSKY, H. (eds.), *Soziologie. Ein Lehr- und Handbuch zur modernen Geselschaftskunde.* Düsseldorf, Köln: Eugen Diederichs Verlag, 1955. Pp. 351.

GURVITCH, G. D. *et al.* (eds.), *La sociologie en XXᵉ siècle.* 2 vols. Paris: Presses Universitaires de France, 1947.

SPECHT, Karl Gustav (ed.), *Soziologische Forschung in unserer Zeit.* Cologne: Westdeutscher Verlag, 1951. Pp. 352.

(b) Specific Study

(aa) BIOLOGICAL SCHOOL: interprets social phenomena as various life phenomena bound by biological laws.

α) *Organismic Interpretations:* society conceived as one organism.

Studies

See also State, above, Ch. IV, 5, p. 223.

BATESON, William, *Biological Fact and the Structure of Society.* London: Clarendon Press, 1912. Pp. 34.

COKER, F. W., *Organismic Theories of the State: Nineteenth Century Interpretation of the State as Organism or as a Person.* New York: Columbia University, 1910. Pp. 209.

ROBERTS, Morley (1857-1942), *Bio-politics: An Essay in the Physiology, Pathology and Politics of the Social and Somatic Organism.* London: Dent, 1942. Pp. XV, 240.

——, *The Behaviour of Nations: An Essay in the Conduct of National Organisms in the Nutritional Field.* London: J. M. Dent and Sons, 1941. Pp. X, 130.

SOROKIN, Pitirim A., «Biological Interpretation of Social Phenomena», in his *Contemporary Sociological Theories* (New York: Harper and Brothers, 1928), pp. 194-218.

HERTWIG, Oskar, *Die Lehre vom Organismus und ihre Beziehung zur Sozialwissenschaft.* Jena: G. Fischer, 1899. Pp. 36.

——, *Lehrbuch der Entwicklungsgeschichte des Menschen und der Wirbeltiere.* 8th ed. Jena: G. Fischer, 1909. Pp. XIX, 706.

——, *Allgemeine Biologie.* 2nd ed. Jena: G. Fischer, 1906. Pp. XVI, 649.

KJELLÉN, Rudolf, *Der Staat als Lebensform.* Leipzig: S. Hirzel, 1917. Pp. VIII, 235.

KRIEKEN, Albert Th., *Über die sogennante organische Staatstheorie.* Leipzig: Duncker und Humblot, 1873. Pp. VII, 163.

TOWNE, E. T., *Die Auffassung der Gesellschaft als Organismus.* Halle: Hofbuch — Drückerei, 1903. Pp. 136.

Representatives

LILIENFELD, P. (1829-1903), — see Philosophy, above, p. 237.
SCHÄFFLE, A. (1831-1903), — see Philosophy, above, p. 236.
WORMS, R. (1869-1926), — see Philosophy, above, p. 237.

ß) *Anthropological Interpretations:* Social phenomena are solely determined by race heredity. This trend includes: αα) racism; ββ) nazism; γγ) hereditary theories; δδ) theories of survival.

Dixon, Roland Burrage, *The Racial History of Man.* New York: C. Scribner's Sons, 1923. Pp. XVI, 583.

Dixon, Russell A., *Economic Institutions and Cultural Change.* New York: McGraw-Hill, 1941. Pp. XIV, 529.

——, *Economic Institutions and Capitalism.* Ann Arbor, Mich.: Edwards Brothers, 1939. Pp. III, 242.

Hankins, Frank H., *The Racial Basis of Civilization.* Revised edition. New York: A. A. Knopf, 1931. Pp. X, 389.

——, *An Introduction to the Study of Society: An Outline of Primary Factors and Fundamental Institutions.* Revised edition. New York: The Macmillan Co., 1935. Pp. XI, 808.

Holmes, Samuel Jackson, *The Trend of Races: A Study of Present Tendencies in the Biological Development of Civilized Mankind.* New York: Harcourt, Brace and Co., 1921. Pp. V, 396.

Humphrey, Seth King, *Mankind: Racial Values and the Racial Prospect.* New York: C. Scribner's Sons, 1917. Pp. XVI, 223.

——, *The Racial Prospect.* New York: C. Scribner's Sons, 1920, Pp. XXI, 261.

Huntington, Ellsworth, *The Character of Races as Influenced by Physical Environment, Natural Selection and Historical Development.* New York: C. Scribner's Sons, 1927. Pp. XVI, 393.

Sorokin, Pittirim A., «Antropo-Racial, Selectionist and Hereditarist School», in his *Contemporary Sociological Theories* (New York: Harper and Brothers, 1928), pp. 219-308.

——, *Social Mobility.* New York: Harper and Brothers, 1927. Pp. XVII, 559.

Basler, Adolf, *Einführung in die Rassen und Gesellschafts Physiologie.* Stuttgart: Francke, 1925. Pp. 154.

Baur, Erwin Fischer Eugen and Lenz Fritz, *Grundriss der menschlichen Erblichkeitslehre und Rassenhygiene.* 2 vols. Munich: J. E. Lehmann, 1923.

Gini, Corrado, *I fattori demografici dell' evoluzione delle nazioni.* Turin: Bocca, 1912. Pp. 142.

Jacoby, Paul, *Études sur la sélection chez l'homme.* 2nd ed. Paris: F. Alcan, 1904. Pp. XVII, 620.

Sergi, Giuseppe, *Le origini umane.* Turin: Bocca, 1913. Pp. XI, 202.

——, *L'uomo secondo le origini, l'antichità, le varazioni e la distribuzione geografica: sistema naturale di classificatione.* Turin: Bocca, 1911. Pp. XXVII, 424.

Simar, Th., *Étude critique sur la formation de la doctrine des races au XVIIe siècle et son expansion au XIXe siècle.* Brussels. M. Lamertin, 1922. Pp. 403.

αα) *Racism*

GOBINEAU DE, Arthur (1816-1882), — see above, p. 31.

ββ) *Nazism*

HITLER, Adolf 1889-1945), — see above, p. 211.

γγ) *Hereditary Theories*

LAIRD, Donald Anderson, *The Psychology of Selecting Men.* 2nd ed. New York: McCraw-Hill, 1927. Pp. XIII, 345.

MACDONALD, Arthur, *Man and Abnormal Man.* Washington: Government Printing Office, 1905. Pp. 780.

RIPLEY, William Zebina, *The Races of Europe: A Sociological Study.* London: K. Paul, Trench Trübner and Co., 1913. Pp. XXXII, 624.

TERMAN, Lewis Madison (ed.), *Genetic Studies of Genius.* 2 vols. London: V. Front, 1925.

WOODS, Frederick Adams (1873-1939), *Mental and Moral Heredity in Royalty.* New York: H. Holt and Co., 1906. Pp. 85.

——, *The Influence of Monarchs: Steps in the New Science of History.* New York: The Macmillan Co., 1913. Pp. XIII, 422.

ODIN, Alfred, *Genèse des grands hommes.* 2 vols. Lausanne: H. Mignot, 1895.

Representatives

GALTON Sir, Francis (1822-1911), *Hereditary Genius: An Enquiry into Its Laws and Consequences.* A reissue. London: Watts and Co., 1950. Pp. XXVII, 379. First published in 1869.

——, *Inquiries into Human Faculty and Its Development.* London: Macmillan Co., 1883. Pp. XII, 380.

——, *Natural Inheritance.* London: Macmillan and Co., 1889. Pp. IX, 259.

PEARSON, Karl (1857-1936), *The Scope and Importance to the State of the Science of National Eugenics.* 2nd ed. London: Dulan and Co., 1909. Pp. 45.

——, *The Function of Science in the Modern State.* 2nd ed. Cambridge: The University Press, 1919. Pp. VII, 97.

——, *National Life from the Standpoint of Science.* 2nd ed. London: Adam and Charles Black, 1905. Pp. 106.

——, *Social Problems: Their Treatment, Past, Present and Future.* London: Dulan and Co., 1912. Pp. 40.

——, *Eugenics and Public Health.* London: Dulan and Co., 1912. Pp. 34.

——, *Darwinism, Medical Progress and Eugenics.* London: Dulan and Co., 1912. Pp. 29.

δδ) *Theories of survival from struggle for existence.*

BECKNER, Morton O., «Darwinism», in *The Encyclopedia of Philosophy* (8 vols. New York: The Macmillan Co., 1967), Vol II, pp. 296-306.

HAYCRAFT, John Berry, *Darwinism and Race Progress*. London: Swan Sonnenschein, 1895. Pp. XII, 180.

KELLOG, Vernon Lyman (1867-1937), *Darwinism To-day: A Discussion of Present-day Scientific Criticism of the Darwinian Selection Theories*. New York: H. Holt and Co., 1907. Pp. XII, 403.

——, *Human Life as the Biologist Sees it*. New York: H. Holt and Co., 1922. Pp. VII, 140.

——, *Mind and Heredity*. Princeton, New Jersey: Princeton University Press. Pp. 108.

——, *Evolution*. New York: D. Appleton and Co., 1924. Pp. X, 291.

MITCHELL, Peter Chalmers, *Evolution and the War*. London: J. Murray, 1915. Pp. XXVI, 114.

NASMITH, George William, *Social Progress and the Darwin Theory: A Study of Force as a Factor in Human Relations*. New York: G. P. Putnam's Sons, 1916. Pp. XXIII, 417.

SOROKIN, Pitirim A., «Sociological Interpretation of the 'Struggle for Existence», in his *Contemporary Sociological Theories* (New York: Harper and Brothers, 1928), pp. 309-356.

THOMPSON, J. A., *Darwinism and Human Life*. London: Andrew Melrose, 1946. Pp. 144.

NICOLAI, Georg F., *Die Biologie des Krieges*. 2 vols. Zürich: Orell Fussli, 1919.

NOVICOW, Jacques, *La critique du Darwinisme social*. Paris: F. Alcan, 1970. Pp. 407.

——, *Les luttes entre les sociétés humaines et leur phases successives*. 2nd ed. Paris: F. Alcan, 1896. Pp. 763.

STEINMETZ, S. Rudolf, *Die Philosophie des Krieges*. Leipzig: J. A. Barth, 1907. Pp. XVI, 352.

TARDE DE, Jean Gabriel, *Les lois de l'imitation, étude sociologique*. Paris: F. Alcan, 1890. Pp. VIII, 432.

——, *Les lois sociales, esquisse d'une sociologie*. Paris: F. Alcan, 1898. Pp. 172.

——, *L'opposition universelle*. Paris: F. Alcan, 1897. Pp. VIII, 451.

(bb) *Christian School*: developed on the basis of Christian principles.

See Scholastic Philosophy (Ethics), in *PQS*, No. 5.

McCORMACK, Arthur (ed.), *Christian Responsibility and World Poverty*. Montreal: Palm Publishers, 1963. Pp. 314.

TROELTSCH, Ernst (1865-1923), *Die Soziallehren der christlichen Kirchen und Gruppen*. Tübingen: Mohr, 1911. English translation by Olive WYON, *The Social Teaching of the Christian Churches*. 2 vols. New York. The Macmillan Co., 1931.

Welty, Eberhard, *Herders Sozialkatechismus. Ein Werkbuch der Katholischen Sozialethik in Frage und Antwort*. 4 vols. Freiburg: Herder, 1961-1966. English translation by Gregor Kirstein, O. P. and John Fitzsimons, *A Handbook of Christian Social Ethics*. 2 vols. Freiburg, New York: Herder and Herder, 1960-1963.

Cathrein, Viktor, *Die katholische Weltanschauung in ihren Grundlinien mit besonderer Verücksichtkeit der Moral*. 2nd ed. Freiburg i. B.: Herder, 1909. Pp. XVI, 578.
——, *Die Grundlage des Völkerrechts*. Freiburg i. B.: Herder, 1918. Pp. 108.
——, *Der Sozialismus*. 8th ed. Freiburg i B.: Herder, 1903. Pp. XVI, 1908.
——, *Die Aufgabe der Staatsgewalt und ihre Grenzen*. Freiburg i. B.: Herder, 1882. Pp. IV, 147.
——, *Socialism: Its Theoretical Basis and Practical Application*. Autorized translation with reference to the United States by Victor F. Gettelmann, S. J. New York: Benzinger Brothers, 1904. Pp. 424.

Representatives

Ketteler, Wilhelm Emmanuel (1811-1877), *Die Arbeitsfrage und das Christenthum*. 3rd ed. Mainz: F. Kirchheim, 1864. Pp. 212.
——, *Liberalismus, Socialismus und Christenthum. Rede*. 3rd ed. Mainz: F. Kirchheim, 1871. Pp. 20.
——, *Die grossen socialen Fragen der Gegenwart*. Mainz: F. Kirchheim, 1878. Pp. 117.
La Tour du Chambly de La Charge (1834-1924), *Aphorismes de politique sociale*. Paris: Nouvelle librairie nationale, 1909. Pp. 104.
——, *Vers un ordre social chrétien*. Paris: Beauchesne et ses fils, 1942. Pp. XI, 514. Beaussan, C., La Tour du Pin. Paris, 1951.
Le Play, Pierre Frédéric (1806-1882), *Les ouvriers européens*. 6 vols. 2nd ed. Tours: A. Mame et fils, 1877-1879. First published in one volume, 1855.
——, *Les ouvriers des deux mondes*. 5 vols. Paris: E .Le Plon, 1857-1885.
——, *La réforme sociale en France*. 4th ed. 3 vols. Tours: A. Mame et fils, 1872. First published in Paris: Le Plon, 1864.
——, *L'organisation de la famille*. 3rd. ed. Tours: A. Mame et fils 1884. Pp. XXVI, 520. First published in Paris: Téqui, 1871.
——, *La méthode sociale*. Tours: A. Mame et fils, 1879. PP. 648.

Herbertson, Fanny L. D. Richardson, *Life of Frederic Le Play*. Ledbury (Herefordshire, England: Le Play House Press, 1951. Pp. 120.

Sorokin, Pitirim, «Frédéric Le Play's School», in his *Contemporary Sociological Theories* (New York: Harper and Brothers, 1928), pp. 63-98.

Vignes, J. B. Maurice, *La science sociale d'après les principe de Le Play et de ses continuateurs*. 2 vols. Paris: Giard et Brière, 1897.

Traditionalism, — see above, Ch. IV, 3, p. 207.

(cc) DEMOGRAPHIC SCHOOL: insists on decrease or increase of the population as being a primary factor of social phenomena.

See Population, above, Ch. I, 3, p. 62.

KELLER, Albert Galloway (1874-1956), *Societal Evolution: A Study of the Evolutionary Basis of the Science of Society*. Revised edition. New York: The Macmillan Co., 1931. Pp. IX, 419. First published in 1915.

——, *Starting-points in Social Science*. Boston: Ginn and Co., 1925. Pp. V, 183.

PEARL, Raymond (1879-   ), *The Biology of Population Growth*. New York: A. A. Knopf, 1930. Pp. XIV, 260. First published in 1925.

——, *The Natural History of Population*. New York: Oxford University Press, 1939. Pp. XII, 416.

ROPER, A. G., *Ancient Eugenics*. Oxford: B. H. Blackwell, 1913. Pp. 75.

STANGELAND, Charles Emil, *Pre-Malthusian Doctrines of Population: A Study in the History of Economic Theory*. New York: The Columbia University Press, 1908. Pp. 356.

THOMPSON, Warren Simpson, *Population: A Study in Malthusianism*. New York: Longmans, Green and Co., 1915. Pp. 216.

GINI, Corrado, *I fattori demografici dell' evoluzione delle nazioni*. Turin: Bocca, 1912. Pp. 142.

Representatives

BERTILLON, Jacques, *De la dépopulation de la France*. Nancy: Berger-Levrault, 1896. Pp. 32.

REYNAUD, Pierre, *La théorie de la population en Italie du XVIe au XVIIIe siècle*. Lyon: A. Rey, 1904. Pp. 200.

WOLF, Julius, *Die Volkswirtschaft der Gegenwart und Zukunft. Die wichtigsten Wahrheiten der Allgemeinen Nationalökonomie*. Leipzig: A. Deichertsche Nachfolger, 1912. Pp. XIX, 335.

(dd) GEOGRAPHICAL SCHOOL: insists on the influence of the geographical environment on the social phenomena.

KOLLER, Armin Haiman (1878-   ), *The Theory of Environment: An Outline of the History of the Idea of Milieu, and Its Present Status*. Menasha, Wisconsin: George Banta, 1918. Pp. 104.

RATZEL, Friedrich, *Anthropo—Geographie*. Stuttgart: J. Engelhorn, 1882. Pp. XVIII, 506.

SOROKIN, Pitirim A., (1889-   ), «Geographical School», in his *Contemporary Sociological Theories* (New York: Harper and Brothers, 1928), pp. 99-101, cf. also 101-193.

THOMAS, Franklin (1878-   ), *The Environmental Basis of Society: A Study in the History of Sociological Theory*. New York: The Century Co., 1925. Pp. VII, 336.

Representatives

BEVERIDGE, William Henry (1879-   ), «British Exports and the Barometer», *The Economic Journal* (London), March 1920.
——, «Weather and Harvest Cycles», *The Economic Journal* (London), 1921, pp. 429-449.
CLAYTON, H. H. (1861-1946), «The Influence of Rainfall on Commerce and Politics», *Popular Science Monthly* (New York), December 1901.
HUNTINGTON, Ellsworth (1876-1947), *World Power and Evolution*. New Haven: Yale University Press, 1919. Pp. 287.
MITCHELL, Wesley Clair (1874-1948), *Business Cycles, the Problem and Its Setting*. New York: National Bureau of Economic Research, 1928. Pp. XXII, 489.
MOORE, Henry Ludwell (1869-   ), *Economic Cycles: Their Law and Cause*. New York: The Macmillan Co., 1914. Pp. VIII, 149.
——, *Generating Economic Cycles*. New York: The Macmillan Co., 1923. Pp. XI, 141.
SEMPLE, Ellen Churchill (1863-1932), *Influence of Geographic Environment*. New York: H. Holt and Co., 1927. Pp. XVI, 683.

(ee) MECHANISTIC SCHOOL: interprets social events more or less mechanistically, notably by way of physics, dynamics and mathematics.

DURKHEIM, Émile, *Leçons de sociologie: physique des mœurs et du droit*. Paris: Presses Universitaires de France, 1953. Pp. XLVIII, 264. English translation by Cornelia BROOKFIELD, *Professional Ethics and Civic Morals*. London: Routledge and Kegan Paul, 1957. Pp. XLIV, 228.
KNIBBS Sir, George Handley, *The Mathematical Theory of Population*. Melbourne: McCarron, Bird and Co., 1917. Pp. XVI, 466.
——, *The Shadow of the World's Future, or the Earth's Population Possibilities and the Consequences of the Present Rate of Increase of the Earth's Inhabitants*. London: E. Benn, 1928. Pp. 131.
SOROKIN, Pitirim A., «The Mechanistic School», in his *Contemporary Sociological Theories* (New York: Harper and Brothers, 1928), pp. 3-13, cf. also 13-62.
STARK, Werner, *The Fundamental Forms of Social Thought*. New York: Fordham University Press, 1963. Pp. 270. See Holism, below, p. 256.

SPEKTORSKY, Eugeny V., *Problema socialnoi physiki in XVII stoletia* [The Problems of Social Physics in the Seventeenth Century]. Warsaw, 1910. Pp. VII, 563, XIII.

Predecessors

QUÉTELET, Adolphe L. J., — see Philosophy of Sociology, above, p. 235.
COMTE, Auguste (1798-1857), — see Modern, above, p. 241.

Representatives

BARCELO, Antonio, *Essais de mécanique sociale*. Paris: M. Giard, 1925, Pp. XXVIII, 256.

CAREY, H. C. (1793-1879), *Principles of Social Science*. 3 vols. Philadelphia: Lippincott Co., 1877. Social physics developed.

CARVER, T. N. (1865-1961), *The Economy of Human Energy*. New York: The Macmillan Co., 1924. Pp. XIII, 287.

——, *Principles of National Economy*. Boston: Ginn and Company, 1921. Pp. VI, 773.

HARET, Spiru C., *Mécanique sociale*. Bucarest: C. Cöbl, 1910. Pp. V, 256.

LOTKA, Alfred James (1880-   ), *Elements of Physical Biology*. Baltimore: William and Wilkins Co., 1925. Pp. XXX, 460.

——, *Théorie analytique des associations biologiques*. Paris: Hermann et Cié, 1934.

OSTWALD, Wilhelm (1853-1932), *Energetische Grundlagen der Kulturwissenschaften*. Leipzig: W. Klinkhardt, 1909. Pp. 184.

PARETO, Vilfredo (1848-1923), — see above, p. 235.

——, *Trattato di sociologia generale*. 2 vols. Florence: Barbera, 1915-1916. French translation published in 1917-1919.

——, *Mind and Society*. 4 vols. Translated by Andrew BONGIORNO and Arthur LIVINGSTON. New York: Harcourt, Brace and Co., 1935.

BORKENAU, Franz, *Pareto*. New York: John Wiley and Sons, 1936. Pp. 219.

HENDERSON, Lawrence, *Pareto's Sociology: A Physiologists Interpretation*. Cambridge: Harvard University Press, 1925. Pp. VII, 119.

HOMANS, G. C. and CURTIS, C. P., *An Introduction to Pareto: His Sociology*. New York: Alfred A. Knopf, 1934. Pp. XIII, 299.

VINE, Margaret Wilson, «Vilfredo Pareto», in her, *An Introduction to Sociological Theory* (New York: Longmans, Green and Co., 1959), pp. 249-267.

(ff) SOCIOLOGISTIC SCHOOL: attempts to interpret social phenomena by psychological factors (derived from the activity of individuals) rather than by biological means.

α) *Theories of Social Conditions:* psychical phenomena are explained through social conditions.

BALDWIN, James Mark (1861-1934), *The Individual and Society or Psychology and Sociology*. Boston: R. G. Badger, 1911. Pp. 210.

GIDDINGS, Franklin Henry (1855-1931), *The Scientific Study of Human Society*. Chapel Hill: The University of North Coralina Press, 1924. Pp. VI, 247.

DRAGICESCU, D., *Du rôle de l'individu dans le déterminisme social*. Paris: F. R. de Rudeval, 1904. Pp. 366.

PALANTE, Georges, *Combat pour l'individu*. Paris: F. Alcan, 1904. Pp. 231.

——, *Antinomies entre l'individu et société*. Paris: F. Alcan, 1913. Pp. 292.

Predecessors

Sᴏʀᴏᴋɪɴ, Pitirim A., *The Sociology of Revolution*. Philadelphia: J. B. Lippincott Co., 1925. Pp. XII, 428.

——, *Social Mobility*. New York: Harper and Brothers, 1927. Pp. VII, 559.

——, «Sociologists School — Predecessors», in his *Contemporary Sociological Theories* (New York: Harper and Brothers, 1928), pp. 435-438.

——, *Man and Society in Calamity*. New York: E. P. Dutton and Co., 1942. Pp. 852.

——, *Sociocultural Causality, Time and Space*. Durham, North Carolina: Duke University Press, 1943. Pp. IX, 246.

——, *Society, Culture and Personality*. New York: Harper and Brothers, 1947. Pp. XIV, 742.

——, *The Reconstruction of Humanity*. Boston: Beacon Press, 1948. Pp. 223.

——, *Altruistic Love*. Boston: Beacon Press, 1950. Pp. VII, 253.

——, *SOS: The Meaning of Our Crisis*. Boston: Beacon Press, 1951. Pp. VI, 177.

——, *The Ways and Power of Love*. Boston: Beacon Press, 1954. Pp. XIV, 552.

——, *Fads and Foibles in Modern Sociology*. Chicago: Henry Regnery Co., 1956. Pp. 357.

Representatives

Cᴏᴏʟᴇʏ, Charles Horton (1864-1929), *Social Process*. New York: Charles Scribner's Sons, 1918. Pp. VI, 430.

——, *Sociological Theory and Social Research*. New York: Henry Holt and Co., 1930. Pp. XIII, 345.

——, *Social Organization, and Human Nature and the Social Order*. 2 vols. Glencoe, Illinois: Free Press, 1956.

Vɪɴᴇ, Margaret Wilson, «Charles Horton Cooley», in her *An Introduction to Sociological Theory* (New York: Longmans, Green and Co., 1959), pp. 147-163.

Dᴜʀᴋʜᴇɪᴍ, Émile (1858-1917), *De la division du travail social*. Paris: F. Alcan, 1893. Pp. X, 471. English translation by George Sɪᴍᴘsᴏɴ, *The Division of Labor in Society*. Glencoe, Illinois: Free Press, 1947.

——, *Les règles de la méthode sociologique*. Paris: F. Alcan, 1895. Pp. VIII, 186. English translation by Sarah A. Sᴏʟᴏᴠᴀʏ and John H. Mᴜᴇʟʟᴇʀ, *The Rules of Sociological Method*. Chicago: University of Chicago Press, 1938.

——, *Le suicide, étude de sociologie*. Paris: F. Alcan. 1897. Pp. XII, 462. English translation by John A. Sᴘᴀᴜʟᴅɪɴɢ and George Sɪᴍᴘsᴏɴ, *Suicide*. Glencoe, Iillinois: Free Press, 1951.

——, *Les formes élémentaires de la vie religieuse*. Paris: F. Alcan, 1912. Pp. 647. English translation by Joseph W. Sᴡᴀɪɴ, *The Elementary Forms of Religious Life*. London: George Allen and Unwin, 1915.

——, *Sociologie et philosophie: physique des mœurs et du droit.* Alcan, 1924. Pp. XV, 142. English translation by D. F. Pocock, *Sociology and Philosophy.* Glencoe, Illinois: Free Press, 1953.

Alpert, Harry, *Emile Durkheim and His Sociology.* New York: Columbia University Press, 1939. Pp. 233.

Gehlke, Ch. E., *Emile Durkheim's Contributions to Sociological Theory.* New York: Columbia University Press, 1915. Pp. 189.

Vine, Margaret Wilson, «Emile Durkheim», in her, *An Introduction to Sociological Theory* (New York: Longmans, Green and Co., 1959), pp. 125-146.

Winch, Peter, «Durkheim, Émile», in *The Encyclopedia of Philosophy* (8 vols. New York: The Macmillan Co., 1967), Vol. II, pp. 437-440.

Gumplowicz, Ludwig (1838-1909), *Rasse und Staat.* Vienna: Manz, 1875. Pp. 58.
——, *Der Rassenkampf.* Insbruck: Wagner, 1883. Pp. VIII, 376.
——, *Grundriss der Soziologie.* Vienna: Manz, 1885. Pp. VI, 246.
——, *Die Soziologische Staatsidee.* Graz: Leuschner und Lubensky, 1892. Pp. III, 134.

β) *Marxism:* struggle of classes.

See Economics, above, Ch. II, 3 Modern, Germany, p. 95.

Marx, Karl, *Selected Writings in Sociology and Social Philosophy.* London: Sainders, 1956. Pp. 268.
Adoratsky, V. (ed.), *Selected Works of Karl Marx.* Moscow: Cooperative Publishing Society of Foreign Workers in the USSR, 1935.
Stouffer, Samuel A., *Communism, Conformity, and Civil Liberties.* Garden City, New York: Doubleday, 1955. Pp. 278.

Lukács, Georg, *Geschichte und Klassenbewusstsein.* Berlin: Malik, 1923.

γ) *Theories of Individual Conditions:* social phenomena are explained through individual psychical conditions. The theories include: (αα) freudism, (ββ) behaviorism, (γγ) voluntarism.

Bernard, Luther Lee, *Instinct: A Study in Social Psychology.* New York: H. Holt and Co., 1924. Pp. IX, 550.
——, *An Introduction to Social Psychology.* New York: H. Holt and Co., 1926. Pp. X, 651.
——, *An Introduction to Sociology, a Naturalistic Account of Man's Adjustment to his World.* New York: Thomas Y. Crowell Co., 1942. Pp. XIII, 1041.
Davis, Michael M., Jr., *Psychological Interpretations of Society.* New York: Columbia University Press, 1909. Pp. 260.
Ellwood, Charles Abram (1873-1946), *Sociology in Its Psychological Aspects.* New York: D. Appleton and Co., 1912. Pp. XIII, 416.

——, *The Psychology of Human Society: An Introduction to Sociological Theory.* New York: D. Appleton and Co., 1925. Pp. XVI, 495.

Josey, Charles Conant (1893-), *The Social Philosophy of Instinct.* New York: C. Scribner's Sons, 1922. Pp. 274.

McDougall, William, *An Introduction to Social Psychology.* 14th ed. Boston: J. W. Luce and Co., 1921. Pp. 418.

——, *Psycho-analysis and Social Psychology.* London: Methuen and Co., 1936. Pp. IX, 207.

Sorokin, Pitirim A., (1889-), «The Psychological School», in his *Contemporary Sociological Theories.* (New York: Harper and Brothers, 1928), pp. 600-659.

Woodworth, Robert Sessions (1869-), *Dynamic Psychology.* New York: Columbia University Press, 1918. Pp. 210.

αα) *Freudism:* Instinctivist interpretation.

See Psychoanalysis, above, Ch. I, 2, p. 41.

Ellis, Havelock (1859-1939), *Man and Woman: A Study of Secondary and Tertiary Sexual Characters.* 8th ed. London: W. Heinemann, 1934. Pp. VII, 469. First Published in 1894.

Ellwood, Charles A. (1873-1946), *The Psychology of Human Society.* New York: D. Appleton and Co., 1925. Pp. XVI, 495.

Freud, Sigmund (1865-1939), *Group Psychology and the Analysis of the Ego.* Authorized translation by James Strachey. London: The International Psychoanalytical Press, 1922. Pp. 134.

——, *Totem and Taboo: Resemblances between the Psychic Lives of Savages and Neurotics.* Authorized translation by A. A. Brill. London: G. Routledge and Sons, 1919. Pp. XII, 268.

——, *Sex and Religion: A Study of Their Relationship and Its Bearing Upon Civilization.* London: Williams and Norgate, 1925. Pp. XI, 201.

Moll, Albert (ed.), *Handbuch der Sexualwissenschaften.* 2 vols. Leipzig: F. C. W. Vogel, 1926.

——, *Behandlung der Homosexualität: biochemisch oder psychisch ?* Bonn: A. Marcus und E. Weber, 1921. Pp. 71.

Patrick, George Thomas White (1857-), *The Psychology of Social Reconstruction.* Boston: Houghton Mifflin Co., 1920. Pp. IX, 273.

Sutherland, Alexander (1852-1902), *The Origin and Growth of the Moral Instinct.* 2 vols. London: Longmans, Green and Co., 1898.

Thomas, William Isaac (1863-), *Society: Studies in the Social Psychology of Sex.* Chicago: The University of Chicago Press, 1907. Pp. VII, 325.

Thompson, H. B., *Psychological Norms in Men and Women.*

Westermarck, Edward, (1862-1939), *The History of Human Marriage,* 5th ed. 3 vols. New York: The Allerton Book Co., 1922. First published in 1889.

Blüher, Hans, *Die Rolle der Erotik in der männlichen Gesellschaft, eine Theorie der menschlichen Staatsbildung nach Wesen und Wert.* 2 vols. Jena: E. Diederichs, 1924.

Larguier des Bancels, Jacques, *Introduction à la psychologie: l'instinct et l'émotion.* Paris: Payot, 1921. Pp. 286.

ββ) *Behaviorism:* muscular interpretations.

See above, Ch. I, 2, p. 55.

CANNON, Walter Bradford (1871-1945), *Bodily Changes in Pain, Hunger, Fear, and Rage.* 2nd ed. New York: D. Appleton Co., 1929. Pp. XVI, 404.

KAUFMAN, Arnold S. «Behaviorism», in *The Encyclopedia of Philosophy* (8 vols. New York: The Macmillan Co., 1967), Vol. I, pp. 268-273.

KOFFKA, Kurt, *The Growth of the Mind: An Introduction to Child Psychology.* Translated by Robert M. OGDEN. 2nd ed. London: K. Paul, Trench, Trübner and Co., 1928. Pp. XIX, 426.

LASHLEY, K. S., «The Behavioristic Interpretation of Consciousness», *Psychological Review* (Washington, D. C.), 1923.

PARK, Robert Ezra (1864-   ), *Human Behavior.* Chicago: The Zalaz Corporation, 1915. Pp. 62.

——, *Introduction to the Science of Sociology.* 2nd ed. Chicago: The University of Chicago Press, 1924. Pp. XIII, 1040.

—— (ed.), *An Outline of the Principles of Sociology.* New York: Barnes and Noble, 1939. Pp. VI, 353.

PARMELEE, Maurice Farr (1882-   ), *Science of Human Behavior: Biological and Psychological Foundation.* New York: The Macmillan Co., 1913. Pp. XVII, 443.

PAVLOV, Ivan, — see below.

ROBACK, Abraham Aaron, *Behaviorism and Psychology.* Cambridge; Massachusetts: University Bookstore, 1923.

——, Behaviorism at Twenty-Five. Cambridge, Massachusets: Sci-art Publishers, 1937. Pp. 256.

THOMAS, William Isaac (1863-   ), *Sex and Society.* Chicago: University of Chicago Press, 1907.

——, *Source Book for Social Origins.* Chicago: University of Chicago Press, 1909. Pp. XVI, 932.

——, «The Persistance of Primary — Group Norms in Present-Day Society and Their Influence on Our Educational System», in Herbert S. JENNINGS *et al., Suggestions of Modern Science Concerning Education* (New York: The Macmillan Co., 1917), pp. 159-197.

——, «The Behavior Pattern and the Situation», *Publications of the American Sociological Society: Papers and Proceedings*, 1927, pp. 1-13.

——, *Primitive Behavior.* New York: McGraw-Hill Book Co., 1937. Pp. IX, 847.

VINE, Margaret Wilson, «William Isaac Thomas», in her *An Introduction to Sociological Theory* (New York: Longmans, Green and Co., 1959), pp. 229-248.

VOLKART, Edmund (ed.), *Social Behavior and Personality: Contributions of W. I. Thomas to Theory and Social Research.* New York: Social Science Research Council, 1951, Pp. IV, 338.

WATSON, John Broadus (1878-   ), *Behavior: An Introduction to Comparative Psychology.* New York: H. Holt, 1914. Pp. XII, 439.

WEISS, Albert Paul (1879-1931), *A Theoretical Basis of Human Behavior.* 2nd ed. Columbus, Ohio: R. G. Adams and Co., 1929. Pp. XVII, 479.

γγ) *Voluntarism*: conditioned reflexes.

PARK, R. E. (1864-   ), — see Behaviorism, above.

PAVLOV, Ivan P. (1849-1936), *Lectures on Conditioned Reflexes*. Translated from the Russian by W. Horsley GANTT. 2 vols. New York: International Publishers, 1928-1941.

SHERRINGTON Sir, Charles Scott (1861-1952), *The Brain and Its Mechanism*. Cambridge: The University Press, 1933. Pp. 35.

——, *The Integrative Action of the Nervous System*. New York: C. Scribner's Sons, 1906. Pp. XVI, 411.

——, *Man on His Nature*. Cambridge: The University Press, 1941. Pp. 413.

TARDE, Gabriel (1843-1904), *Social Laws*. Translated by H. C. WARREN. New York: The Macmillan Co., 1899. Pp. XI, 213.

——, *The Laws of Imitation*. Translated by Elsie C. PARSONS. New York: Henry Holt and Co., 1903. Pp. XXIX, 604.

——, *Penal Philosophy*. Translated by R. HOWELL. Boston: Little, Brown and Co., 1912. Pp. XXXII, 581.

WARD, Lester Frank (1841-1913), *Dynamic Sociology, or Applied Social Science as Based upon Statical Sociology and the Less Complex Sciences*. 2 vols. New York: D. Appleton and Co., 1883.

——, *Outlines of Sociology*. New York: The Macmillan Co., 1898. Pp. XII, 301.

——, *The Psychic Factors of Civilization*. 2nd ed. Boston, Massachusetts: Ginn and Company, 1906. Pp. XXI, 369.

——, *Pure Sociology: A Treatise on the Origin and Spontaneous Development of Society*. 2nd ed. New York: The Macmillan Co., 1925. Pp. XIV, 607.

——, *Static and Dynamic Psychology*. Boston, Massachusetts: Ginn and Company, 1895. Pp. 220.

δ) *Holism*: social facts are not reducible to individual facts.

See Individualism, below, p. 257; above, p. 241.

BENN, Stanley I., «Society», in *The Encyclopedia of Philosophy* (8 vols. New York: The Macmillan Co., 1967), Vol. VII, pp. 471-474.

DRAY, W. H., «Holism and Individualism in History and Social Sciences», in *The Encyclopedia of Philosophy* (8 vols. New York: The Macmillan Co., 1967), Vol. IV, pp. 53-58.

MacIVER, Robert Morisson and PAGE, C. H., *Society: An Introductory Analysis*. New York: Rinehart and Co., 1949. Pp. XVII, 697.

STARK, Werner, *The Fundamental Forms of Social Thought*. New York: Fordham University Press, 1962. Pp. 270. See Systematic, above, 2 b.

TÖNNIES, Ferdinand, *Community and Association*. Translated by Ch. P. LOOMIS. London: Routledge and Kegan Paul, 1955. Pp. XXXIV, 293. See Systematic, above, 2 b, p. 234.

WEBER, Max, *Theory of Social and Economic Organization*. Translated by A. M. HENDERSON and Talcott PARSONS. New York: Oxford University Press, 1947. Pp. X, 436. See Economics (Philosophy), above, 2 c, p. 75.

Representatives

GELLNER, Ernest, «Holism versus Individualism in History and Sociology», in Patric GARDINER (ed.), *Theories of History* (Glencoe, Illinois: Free Press, 1959), pp. 489-503.

HEGEL, G. W. F., *Grundlinien der Philosophie des Rechts*. Berlin: Duncker und Humblot, 1821. English translation by T. M. KNOX, *Hegel's Philosophy of Right*. Oxford: At the Clarendon Press, 1942. See Law, above, p. 138.

MANDELBAUM, Maurice, «Societal Facts», *British Journal of Sociology*, Vol. VI (1955), No. 4, pp. 305-317.

——, «Societal Laws», *British Journal for the Philosophy of Science*, Vol. VIII (1957), No. 31, pp. 211-224.

PARSONS, Talcott, — see Philosophy, above, p. 235.

ε) *Individualism*: Properties and actions of collective community can be reduced to reaction and actions of individuals.

See Holism, above, δ.

See Holism, above, p. 256; Individualism, above, p. 241, cf. 253.

BRODBECK, May, «Methodological Individualisms: Definition and Reduction», *Philosophy of Science*, Vol. XXV (1958), No. 1, pp. 1-22.

DANTO, A. C., «Methodological Individualism and Methodological Socialism», *Filosofia*, Vol. XIII (1962), No. 1, pp. 3-24.

Representatives

BOSANQUET, Bernard, *The Philosophical Theory of the State*. 4th ed. London: Macmillan and Co., 1923. Pp. XVIII, 342. See also State, p. 223.

GOLDSTEIN, Leon J., «The Two Theses of Methodological Individualism», *British Journal for the Philosophy of Science*, Vol. IX (1958), No. 33, pp. 1-11.

HAYEK VON, Friedrich August, *The Counter-Revolution of Science*. Glencoe, Illinois: Free Press, 1952.

HOBBES, Thomas, *Leviathan*. New York: Oxford University Press, 1946. First published in 1651. See index, below.

POPPER, Karl Raimund, *The Poverty of Historicism*. 2nd ed. London: Routledge and Kegan Paul, 1961. Pp. 166.

——, *The Open Society and Its Enemies*. 2 vols. 4th ed. London: Routledge and Kegan Paul, 1962.

——, *Conjectures and Refutation: The Growth of Scientific Knowledge*. New York: Basic Books, 1963. Pp. 412.

WATKINS, J. W. N., «Ideal Types and Historical Explanations», in Herbert FEIGL and May BRODBECK (eds.), *Readings in the Philosophy of Science* (New York: 1953), pp. 723-743.

——, «Historical Explanation in the Social Sciences», *British Journal for the Philosophy of Science*, Vol. VIII (1957), No. 30, pp. 104-117.

4. PARTICULAR COUNTRIES

AFRICA

HOBHOUSE, L., WHEELER, G. and GINSBERG, M., *The Material Culture and Social Institutions of the Simpler Peoples*. London: Chapman and Hall, 1915. Pp. 299.

ODUM, Howard Washington (1884-   ), *Social and Mental Traits of the Negro: Research into the Conditions of the Negro Race in Southern Towns*. New York: Columbia University Press, 1910. Pp. 303.

——, *Southern Regions of the United States*. Chapel Hill: The University of North Carolina Press, 1936. Pp. XI, 664.

AMERICA

See above pp. 209, 230-238.

BARBOUR, Floyd B. (ed.), *The Black Power Revolt*. Boston, Massachusetts: Porter Sargent Publisher, 1968. Pp. 288.

BRIGHAM, Carl Campbell (1890-   ), *A Study of American Intelligence*. Princeton, New Jersey: Princeton University Press, 1923. Pp. XXV, 210.

BURR, Clinton Stoddard, *America's Race Heritage: An Account of the Diffusion of Ancestral Stocks in the United States during Three Centuries of National Expansion and a Discussion of Its Significance*. New York: The National Historical Society, 1922. Pp. VII, 337.

CATTELL, James McKeen and CATTELL, Jacques, *American Men of Science: A Biographical Directory*. New York: The Science Press, 1938. Pp. VIII, 1608.

CLARKE, Edwin Leavitt (1888-   ), *American Men of Letters: Their Nature and Nurture*. New York: Columbia University Press, 1916. Pp. 169.

HINKLE, Roscoe and Gisela, *The Development of Modern Sociology: Its Nature and Growth in the United States*. Garden City, New York: Doubleday and Co., 1954. Pp. X, 15.

KORNHAUSER, Arthur (ed.), *Problems of Power in American Democracy*. Detroit, Michigan: Wayne State University Press, 1957. Pp. IX, 239.

LOWENTHAL, Leo and GUTERMAN, Norman, *Prophets of Deceit: A Study of the Techniques of the American Agitator*. New York: Harper, 1949. Pp. XVII, 164.

LUNDBERG, George A., *Trends in American Sociology*. New York: Harper and Brothers, 1929. Pp. XII, 443.

MERTON, Robert, «Summary of the Development of American Sociology during the First Half of the Twentieth Century», *American Journal of Sociology* (Chicago), 1945, pp. 462-473.

ODUM, Howard W., *American Sociology: The Story of Sociology in the United States to 1950*. New York Longmans, Green and Co., 1951. Pp. VI, 501.

PAGE, Charles Hunt, *Class and American Sociology: From Ward to Ross*. New York: Dial Press, 1940. Pp. XIV, 319.

PETERSON, William (ed), *American Social Patterns*. Garden City, New York: Doubleday Anchor, 1956.

TOCQUEVILLE DE, Alexis, *Democracy in America*. 2 vols. New York: Vintage Books, 1954.

VINE, Margaret W., «American Sociological Theory», in her *An Introduction to Sociological Theory* (New York: Longmans, Green and Co., 1959), pp. 314-336.

WARD, Lester Frank, *Applied Sociology*. Boston: Ginn and Co., 1906. Pp. XVIII, 884.

——, *Dynamic Sociology*. 2 vols. 2nd ed. New York: Appleton and Co., 1911.

——, *Pure Sociology* New York: The Macmillan Co., 1925. Pp. XIV, 607.

CHUGERMAN, Samuel, Lester F. Ward, *The American Aristotle*. Durham, North Carolina: Duke University Press, 1939. Pp. XIII, 591.

WILLIAMS, Robin M., Jr., *American Society*. 2nd ed. New York: Alfred A. Knopf, 1963.

ZETTERBERG, Hans (ed.), *Sociology in the United States of America*. 2nd ed. Paris: UNESCO, 1964.

SHILS, E., «Lo stato attuale della sociologia americana», *Quaderni di sociologia* (Turin, Italy), 1953, No. 4, pp. 179-190; No. 5, pp. 3-10; No. 6, pp. 90-108; 1953, No. 7, pp. 155-167; No. 8, pp. 201-213.

CHINA

See Communism, above, pp. 103, 206, 215.

CHAI, Ch'u and Winberg, Chai (eds.), *The Sacred Books of Confucius and other Confucian Classics*. New York: University Books, 1965: Pp. 384.

YUNG-TEH CHOW, *Social Mobility in China: Status Careers among the Gentry in a Chinese Community*. New York: Atherton Press, 1966.

ENGLAND

BUCKLE, Henry Thomas, *History of Civilization in England*. 2 vols. London: J. W. Parker and Son, 1857-1861. Reprint in 3 vols. New York: Oxford University Press, 1925-1931.

——, *Miscellaneous and Posthumous Works of Henry Thomas Buckle*. Ed. by Helen TAYLOR. 3 vols. London: Longmans, Green and Co., 1872.

HUTH, Alfred Henry (1850-1910), *The Life and Writings of Henry Thomas Buckle*. New York: D. Appleton and Co., 1880. Pp. 502.

ROBERTSON, John Mackinnon (1856-1933), *Buckle and His Critics*. London: Swan Sonnenschein und Co., 1895. Pp. XV, 565.

FRÄNKEL, F., *Buckle und seine Geschichtsphilosophie*. Bern: Scheitlein und Co., 1906. Pp. 113.

CRAMB, John Adam (1862-1913), *The Origins and Destiny of Imperial Britain and Nineteenth Century Europe*. New York: E. P. Dutton and Co., 1915. Pp. 276.

——, *Germany and England: 130 thousand*. New York: E. P. Dutton and Co., 1915. Pp. XIV, 152.

ELLIS, Havelock (1859-1939), *A Study of British Genius*. Boston: Houghton Mifflin Co., 1926. Pp. XVI, 396. First published in London: Hurst and Blackett, 1904.

GALTON Sir, Francis (1822-1911), *English Men of Science: Their Nature and Nurture*. London: Macmillan and Co., 1874. Pp. XIII, 270.

MILNE, Alan John Mitchell, *The Social Philosophy of English Idealism*. London: Allen, 1962. Pp. 320.

FRANCE

Bibliographie française établie à l'intention des lecteurs étrangers: Sociologie et psychologie sociale en France 1945-1958. Paris: Association pour la diffusion de la pensée française, 1960, Pp. 92.

BOUGLE, C., *Bilan de la sociologie française contemporaine*. Paris: F. Alcan, 1935. Pp. 172.

LEROY, Maxime, *Histoire des idées sociales en France*. 3 vols. Paris: Gallimard, 1946-1954.

VILLEGARDELLE, François, *Histoire des idées sociales avant la Révolution française, ou les Socialistes modernes, devancés et dépassés par les anciens penseurs et philosophes*. Paris: Guarin, 1846.

WEILL, Georges, *Histoire du mouvement social en France, 1852-1924*. 3rd ed. Paris: F. Alcan, 1924. Pp. VIII, 512.

Christianity, — see above, p. 214.

Postivism, — see above, p. 202, cf. 241.

Racism, — see above, p. 30.

Traditionalism, — see above, p. 207.

GERMANY

Hitlerism, — see Politics, above, Ch. IV, 4, p. 211.

KORKHEIMER, M., *Survey of the Social Science in Western Germany*. Washington, D.C., 1952.

ARON, Raymond, *La sociologie allemande contemporaine*. Paris: F. Alcan, 1935. Pp. 176.

BOUGLE, C., *Les sciences sociales en Allemagne*. Paris: F. Alcan, 1938. First published in 1896. Pp. 172.

GÜNTHER, Hans F. K., *Rassenkunde des Deutschen Volkes*. 9th ed. Munich: J. F. Lehmanns Verlag, 1926. Pp. VIII, 504.

IRAN

ARASTEH, A. R., *Education and Social Awakening in Iran*. Leiden, Holland: E. J. Brill, 1962. Pp. X, 145.
——, and ARASTEH, Josephine, *Man and Society in Iran*. Leiden, Holland: E. J. Brill, 1964. Pp. XII, 193.

ITALY

Bibliograafia italiana delle scienze sociali: Scienze economiche, scienze politiche. Milan, Italy: Sacred Heart University, 1960-. *Rassegna annuale, ibid.*, 1959-.
BARBANO, F., «La sociologie in Italia, oggi: Saggio bibliografico», *Il politico*, 1954, No. 3. Reprint Paris, 1954.
BARBANO, F. and VITERBI, M., *Bibliografia della sociologia italiana, 1948-1958*. Turin: Ramella, 1959. Pp. 168. See Bibliography above, 1 a, p. 230.
FERRAROTTI, F., «La situazione degli studii sociologici in Italia», *Quaderni di sociologia* (Turin, Italy), 1954. No. 16, pp. 55-61.
ROMANO, Aldo, *Storia del movimento socialista in Italia*. 3 vols. Milan: Fratelli Bocca, 1954-1956.

Fascism, — see above, p. 217.

JAPAN

MORIOKA, KIYOMI and NEWELL, William H., *The Sociology of Japanese Religion*. Leiden: E. J. Brill, 1968. Pp. VI, 145.

POLAND

THOMAS, William I. and ZNANIECKI, Florian, *The Polish Peasant in Europe and America*. 5 vols. Boston: Richard G. Badger, 1918-1920.
SUCHODOLSKI, Bogdan, *Narodziny nowozytnej filozofii cztowieka*. Warszawa: Panstwowe Wydawnictwo Nankowe, 1968. Pp. 619.
——, *Rozwoj nowozytnej filozofii cztowieka*. Warszawa: Panstwowe Wydawnictwo Naukowe, 1967. Pp. 849.

RUSSIA

See above, pp. 98, 205.

KOHN, Hans, *The Mind of Modern Russia*. New Brunswick, New Jersey: Rutgers University Press, 1955. Pp. 298.
Woprosy naugovo ateisma. 2 nd ed. Moscow: Mysl, 1967. Pp. 462.

5. SPECIAL QUESTIONS

ART

See Sociology and Art, below, p. 270.

CHRISTIANITY

See above, p. 214.

GUERRY, Emile, *The Social Doctrine of the Catholic Church.* New York: Alba House, 1962. Pp. 200.

COMMUNISM

See above, pp. 98, 205.

ETHICS

See Philosophy, above, p. 3, cf. 234; Social Ethics, below, p. 266.

FAMILY

See Population, Sex, above, pp. 62, 64.

In English

BASSETT, Marion P., *A New Sex Ethics and Marriage Structure: Discussed by Adam and Eve.* New York: Philosophical Library, 1961. Pp. 332.

ELLIS, Albert, «1953 Classified Bibliography on Marriage and Family Relations», *Marriage and Family Living,* 1954, pp. 254-263.

GOLDSTEIN, Joseph and KATZ, Jay, *The Family and the Law.* New York: The Macmillan Co., 1965.

GOODE, William J., «The Sociology of the Family: Horizons in Family Theory», in Robert K. MERTON *et al.* (eds.), *Sociology Today: Problems and Prospects* (New York: Basic Books, 1959), pp. 178-196.

HANDEL, Gerald (ed.), *The Psychosocial Interior of the Family: A Sourcebook for the Study of Whole Families.* Chicago, Illinois: Aldine Publishing Co., 1967 (?). Pp. 544.

HOMANS, George Caspar and SCHNEIDER, David M., *Marriage, Authority and Final Causes: A Study of Unilateral Cross-Cousin Marriage.* Glencoe, Illinois: Free Press, 1955. Pp. 64.

MALINOWSKI, Bronislaw, *The Family among the Australian Aborigines.* London: University of London Press, 1913. Pp. XV, 326.

PARSONS, Talcott and BALES, Robert F., *Family Socialization and Interaction Process.* Glencoe, Illinois: Free Press, 1955. Pp. XVII, 422.

RUSSELL, Bertrand, *Marriage and Morals.* London: G. Allen, 1961. Pp. 158.

TILLICH, Paul J., *Love, Power and Justice.* Gloucester, Massachusetts: P. Smith, 1960. Pp. 127.

ZIMMERMAN, Carle C., *Family and Civilization.* New York: Harper, 1947. Pp. X, 829.

In Other Languages

LECLERCQ, Jacques, *Vers une famille nouvelle ?* Paris: Editions universitaires, 1962. Pp. 186.

LEVI-STRAUSS, Claude, *Les structures élémentaires de la parenté.* Paris: Presses universitaires de France, 1949. Pp. XIV, 639.

MEHL, R., *Société et amour: problèmes éthiques de la vie familiale.* Geneva: Labor et Fides, 1961. Pp. 231.

SAHUC, Louis J. M., *Homme et femme.* Paris: Bloud and Gay, 1960. Pp. 254.

METHOD

In English

BARTLETT Sir, Frederic Charles (ed.), *The Study of Society: Methods and Problems.* London: K. Paul, Trench, Trubner and Co., 1939. Pp. XII, 498.

DURKHEIM, Émile, *Les règles de la méthode sociologique.* 5th ed. Paris: F. Alcán, 1910. Pp. VIII, 186. First published in 1895. English translation by Sarah A. SOLOVAY and John H. MUELLER, *The Rules of Sociological Method.* New York: The Free Press of Glencoe, 1964. See Sociologistic School, above, p. 251.

——, *Sociologie et philosophie.* Paris: F. Alcan, 1924. Pp. XV, 142. English translation by D. F. POCOCK, *Sociology and Philosophy.* Glencoe, Illinois: The Free Press, 1953.

——, *Education et sociologie.* 3rd. ed. Paris: F. Alcan, 1934. Pp. 158.

——, *L'éducation morale.* Paris: F. Alcan, 1925. Pp. III, 326.

——, *De la division du travail social.* Paris: F. Alcan, 1893. Pp. X, 471. English translation by G. SIMPSON, *Division of Labor in Society.* New York: The Macmillan Co., 1933.

ALBERT, Harry, *Émile Durkheim and His Sociology.* New York: Columbia University Press, 1939. Pp. 233.

ELLWOOD, Charles Abraham, *Methods in Sociology, A Critical Study.* Durham, North Carolina: Duke University Press, 1933. Pp. XXXIV, 214.

FURFEY, P. H., *Scope and Method of Sociology: A Metasociological Treatise.* New York: Harper, 1953. Pp. 556.

GEE, Wilson, *Social Science Research Methods.* New York: Appleton-Century-Crofts, Inc., 1950. Pp. VII, 390.

GIBSON, Quentin, *The Logic of Social Inquiry.* New York: Humanities Press, 1960. Pp. X, 214.

GOODE, William J. and HATT, Paul K., *Methods in Social Research.* New York: McGraw-Hill, 1952. Pp. VII, 386.

GURVITCH, Georges D., *Dialectique et sociologie.* Paris: Flammarion, 1962. Pp. 242.

HOROWITZ, Irving Louis, *Philosophy, Science, and the Sociology of Knowledge.* Springfield, Illinois: Charles C. Thomas, 1961. Pp. 192.

JAHODA, Marie; Deutsch, M., and Cook, S. W., *Research Methods in Social Relations.* New York: Dryden, 1951. Pp. X, 759.

KAUFMANN, Felix, *Methodology of the Social Sciences.* New York: Oxford University Press, 1944. Pp. VIII, 272.

LARRABEE, Harold A., *Reliable Knowledge: Scientific Methods in the Social Studies*. Boston. Massachusetts: Houghton Mifflin Company, 1964. Pp. 440.

LAZARSFELD, P. (ed.), *Mathematical Thinking in the Social Sciences*. Glencoe, Illinois: The Free Press, 1954. Pp. 444.

——, «Problems in Methodology», in Robert K. MERTON (ed.), *Sociology Today* (New York: Basic Books, Inc., 1959), pp. 39-78.

LAZARSFELD, P. and ROSENBURG, M. (eds.), *The Language of Social Research*. Glencoe, Illinois: The Free Press, 1955. Pp. 590.

MADGE, John, *The Tools of Social Science: An Analytical Description of Social Science Techniques*. Garden City, New York: Doubleday and Co., 1965. Pp. XXXV, 362.

MERTON, R. K. and LAZARSFELD, P. F., *Continuities in Social Research*. Glencoe, Illinois: The Free Press, 1950. Pp. 255.

NIEUWENHUYZE, Christoffel A. O., *Society as Process: Essays in Social Sciences Method*. New York: Humanities Press, 1962. Pp. 281.

OGG, Frederic A., *Research in the Humanistic and Social Sciences*. New York: Appleton-Century-Crofts, Inc., 1928. Pp. VIII, 454.

RICE, S. A. (ed.), *Methods in Social Sciences*. Chicago: University of Chicago Press, 1931. Pp. XIII, 822.

SMALL, Albion Woodbury, *Adam Smith and Modern Sociology: A Study in the Methodology of the Social Sciences*. Chicago: The University of Chicago Press, 1907. Pp. IX, 247.

WEBER, Max, *The Methodology of the Social Sciences*. Translated and edited by E. A. SHILS and H. A. FINCH. Glencoe, Illinois: Free Press, 1949.

WOOLF, Harry (ed.), *Quantification: A History of the Meaning of Measurement in the Natural and Social Sciences*. New York: Bobbs-Merrill, 1961. Pp. 228.

YOUNG, Pauline V., *Scientific Social Surveys and Research* 3rd ed. Englewood CLIFFS, New Jersey: Prentice-Hall, 1958. Pp. XX, 540.

ZNANIECKI, Florian, *The Method of Sociology*. New York: Farrar and Rinehart, 1934. Pp. XII, 338. See also Method of History, in *PQS*, No. 4, Ch. II.

In Other Languages

DUVERGER, Maurice, *Méthodes des sciences sociales*. Paris: Presses Universitaires de France, 1961. Pp. VIII, 504.

FESTINGER, Léon and KATZ, Daniel, *Les méthodes de recherche dans les sciences sociales*. 2 vols. Paris: Presses Universitaires de France, 1963. Pp. 384.

LE PLAY, Frédéric, *La méthode sociale*. Tours: A Mame et fils, 1879. Pp. 648.

LILIENFELD VON, Paul, *Zur Vertheidigung der organischen Methode in der Sociologie*. Berlin: G. Reimer, 1898. Pp. 76.

STURZO, L., *Del metodo sociologico: risposta ai critici*. Bergamo, 1950. Pp. XIII, 305.

PEACE AND WAR

See War, above, p. 67.

PERSON AND SOCIETY

See Individualism, above, p. 257.

In English

BALES, Robert F., «Small-Group Theory and Research», in Robert K. MERTON, *et al.* (eds.), *Sociology Today: Problems and Prospects* (New York: Basic Books, 1959), pp. 293-305.

DANTO, Arthur C., «Persons», in *The Encyclopedia of Philosophy* (8 vols. New York: The Macmillan Co., 1967), Vol. VII, pp. 110-114.

INKELES, Alex, «Personality and Social Sturcture», in Robert K. MERTON *et al.* (eds.), *Sociology Today: Problems and Prospects* (New York: Basic Books, 1959), pp. 249-276.

LAVELY, John H., «Personalism», in *The Encyclopedia of Philosophy* (8 vols. New York: The Macmillan Co., 1967), Vol. VI, pp. 107-110.

LEFEVRE, Robert, *This Bread is Mine. Philosophy of Individualism*. Milwaukee: American Liberty Press, 1960. Pp. 397.

MACMURRAY, John, *Persons in Relation*. New York: Harper and Brothers, 1961. Pp. 235.

MANNHEIM, Karl, *Ideology and Utopia: An Introduction to the Sociology of Knowledge*. New York: Harcourt, Brace, 1936. Pp. XXXI, 318. See also Philosophy, above, p. 235.

MILLS, Charles Wright, *The Power Elite*. New York: Oxford University Press, 1956. Pp. 423.

——, *Images of Man: The Classic Tradition in Sociological Thinking*. New York: Braziller, 1960. Pp. 584.

——, *Power, Politics and People, Collected Essays*. Ed. by Irving Louis HOROWITZ. New York: Oxford University Press, 1963. Pp. 657.

NEWCOMB, Theodore M., «The Study of Consensus», in Robert K. MERTON *et al.* (eds.), *Sociology Today: Problems and Prospects* (New York: Basic Books, 1959), pp. 277-292.

TIRYAKIAN, Edward A., *Sociologism and Existentialism: Two Perspectives on the Individual and Society*. Englewood Cliffs, New Jersey: Prentice Hall, 1962. Pp. 176.

In other languages

BLOCH, Ernst, *Naturrecht und menschliche Würde*. Frankfurt a. Am.: Suhrkamp, 1961. Pp. 367.

DE KONINCK, Charles, *Tout homme est mon prochain*. Québec: les Presses de l'Université Laval, 1964. Pp. 152.

FOLLIET, Joseph, *L'homme social*. Paris: A. Fayard, 1961. Pp. 144.

LA PIRA, Giorgio, *Valeur de la personne humaine*. Paris: Mame, 1962. Pp. 224. *L'homme et les groupes sociaux*. Paris: Spes, 1960. Pp. 240.

MAUSS, Marcel, *Sociologie et anthropologie*. Paris: Presses Universitaires de France, 1960. Pp. 391.

MELONI, Angelo, *Persona, società e sociologismo: Appunti di filosofia sociale*. Pescara: Tipografia Artigianelli, 1961. Pp. 218.

Millan, Puelles A., *Persona humana y justicia social*. Madrid: Rialp, 1962. Pp. 166.

Plattel, M. G., *Sozialphilosophie. Der Mensch und das Mitmenschliche*. Köln: Bachem, 1962. Pp. 153.

Tabbah, Bichara, *De la personne humaine à la communauté humaine*. Paris: Librairie générale de droit et de jurisprudence, 1959. Pp. 270.

SLAVERY

See Colonies, above, Ch. IV, 5, p. 214.

SOCIAL CONTRACTS

See Contracts, above, Ch. III, 5, p. 156.

SOCIAL ETHICS

See Ethics, above, Ch. I; Christianity, above, Ch. IV, 5, p. 214.

In English

Buckley, M. J., *Morality and Homosexual: A Catholic Approach to a Moral Problem*. Westminster, Indiana: Newman Press, 1960. Pp. 214.

Deploige, Simon, *The Conflict between Etihcs and Sociology*. Translated by Ch. C. Miliner. St. Louis, Missouri: Herder, 1938. Pp. VI, 386.

Harris, Robert T., *Social Ethics*. Philadelphia: J. B. Lippincott Co., 1962. Pp. X, 320.

Messner, Johannes, *Social Ethics, Natural Law in the Modern World*. Translated by J. J. Donerty. St. Louis, Missouri: Herder, 1949. Pp. XIII, 1018.

Myrdal, Gunnar, *Value in Social Theory*. London: Routledge, 1958. Pp. 269.

Rader, Melvin Miller, *Ethics and the Human Community*. New York: Holt, 1964. Pp. 468.

Small, Albion Woodbury, *The Significance of Sociology for Ethics*. Chicago: The University of Chicago Press, 1902. Pp. 39.

Thielicke, Helmut, *The Ethics of Sex*. Translated by John W. Doberstein. New York: Harper and Brothers, 1964. Pp. 338.

Trevelt, R. F., *Sex and the Christian*. London: Burns and Oates, 1960. Pp. 126.

Welty, Eberhard, *Handbook of Christian Social Ethics*. Translated by Georg Kirstein and John Fitzsimons. New York: Herder and Co., 1960. Pp. 394.

In Other Languages

Albert, Hans, «Das Wertproblem in den Sozialwissenschaften», *Schweizerische Zeitschrift für Volkswirtschaft und Statistik*, 1958, pp. 335-340.

«Wertfreiheit als methodisches Prinzip», *Schriften des Vereins für Sozialpolitik*, 1963, pp. 32-63.

Giordani, I., *Le encicliche sociali dei Papa de Pio IX à Pio XII*. Rome: Studium, 1950. Pp. XXIII, 1192.

JARLOT, P. G. (ed.), *De principiis ethicae socialis, documenta ultimorum Romanorum Pontificum Leonis XIII, Pii X, Benedicti XV.* Rome: Universitas Gregoriana, 1932.

MESSNER, Johannes, *Kulturethik mit Grundlegung durch Prinzipienethik und Persönlichkeitsethik.* 2nd ed. Vienna: Tyrolia-Verlag, 1954. Pp. 681.

UTZ, Arthur Fridelin, *Etica social.* 5 vols. Biblioteca Herder, Vol. XLIV-XLVIII. Barcelona: Herder, 1965-. Vol. III and following in preparation.

WELTY, Eberhard, *Herders Sozialkatechismus. Ein Werkbuch der katholischen Sozialethik in Frage und Antwort.* 2 vols. 3rd. ed. Freiburg: Herder, 1961. Pp. XIV, 411.

SOCIALISM

See above, p. 86; below.

SOCIAL PSYCHOLOGY

See Psychology, in *PQS,* No. 6.

CANTRIL, Hadley (ed.), *The Psychology of Social Movements.* New York: John Wiley, 1941. Pp. XV, 274.

DEUTSCH, Morton and KRAUSS, Robert M., *Theories of Social Psychology.* New York: Basic Books, 1965. Pp. X, 144.

DEWEY, John, *Human Nature and Conduct: An Introduction to Social Psychology.* New York: Henry Holt and Co., 1922. Pp. VII, 336.

EVANS-PRITCHARD, E. E., *Social Anthropology.* London: Cohen, 1951. Pp. VII, 134.

HOMANS, George C., *Social Behavior: Its Elementary Forms.* New York: Harcourt, 1961. Pp. 404.

KLUCKHOHN, Clyde, *Mirror for Man.* New York: Whittlesey House, 1949. Pp. XI, 3313.

LINDZEY, Gardner (ed.), *Handbuch of Social Psychology.* 2 vols. Reading, Massachusetts: Addison-Wesley, 1954.

MILLS, C. Wright (ed.), *Images of Man: The Classic Tradition in Sociological Thinking.* New York: Braziller, 1960. Pp. 534.

TOCH, Hans, *The Social Psychology of Social Movements.* New York: Bobbs-Merrill, 1965. Pp. 272.

SOCIALISM AND COMMUNISM

Socialism, — See Economics, above, Ch. II, 3, p. 86.

In English

COLE, G. D. H., «What is Socialism», *Political Studies* (London), February 1953; June 1953.

——, *A History of Socialist Thought.* 7 vols. London: Macmillan and Co., 1953-1960.

GRIFFITHS, Dan, *What is Socialism?* London: Grant Richards, 1924. Pp. 102.

QUINT, Howard Henry, *The Forging of American Socialism: Origins of the Modern Movement.* Columbia, South Carolina: University of South Carolina Press, 1953. Pp. 409.

SCHUMPETER, Joseph A., *Capitalism, Socialism and Democracy.* London: G. Allen and Unwin, 1954. Pp. 381.

In Other Languages

DOLLÉANS, Edouard, *Histoire du mouvement ouvrier.* 3 vols. Paris: A. Colin, 1953.

DOLLÉANS, Édouard and CROZIER, M., *Mouvements ouvriers et socialistes; chronologie et bibliographie: Angleterre, France, Allemagne, États-Unis (1750-1918).* Paris: Les Éditions Ouvrières, 1949-1950. Pp. 380.

FETSCHER, Irving, *Vom Marx zur Sowjetideologie.* 9th ed. Frankfurt a. M.: Diesterweg, 1963. Pp. 224.

GURVITCH, Georges, *Dialectique et sociologie.* Paris: Flammarion, 1962. Pp. 248.

HALÉVY, Élie, *Histoire du socialisme européen.* Paris: Gallimard, 1948. Pp. 368.

KOLAKOWSKI, Leszek, *Der Mensch ohne Alternative. Von der Möglichkeit und Unmöglichkeit Marxist zu sein.* Munich: Piper, 1960. Pp. 282.

LOMBARDI, F., *Socialismo e comunismo.* Rome, 1945.

PIVERT, M., «Les bases doctrinales du socialisme», *Revue socialiste* (Paris), November, 1942.

SCHAFF, Adam, *Marx oder Sartre? Versuch einer Philosophie des Menschen.* Translated from the Polish by Erna REIFER. Vienna: Europa Verlag, 1964. Pp. 176.

THONISSEN, Jean Joseph, *Le socialisme dans le passé.* Bruxelles: A. Jamar, 1850. Pp. 292.

VALIANI, Leo, *Le socialisme et ses promesses.* 2 vols. Bruxelles, s.d. (1848-1876).

——, *Histoire du socialisme au XXe siècle.* Paris: Nagel, 1948. Pp. 288.

Communism, — see Socialism, above, p. 86, cf. 98.

In English

ACTON, Harry Burrows, *The Illusion of the Epoch: Marxism-Leninism as a Philosophical Creed.* London: Cohen and West, 1955. Pp. 278.

BOCHENSKI, I. M. and NIEMEYER, G. (eds.), *Handbook on Communism.* New York: Praeger, 1962. Pp. 686.

COHEN, Carl (ed.), *Communism, Fascism and Democracy: The Theoretical Foundations.* New York: Random House, 1962. Pp. 704.

DANIELS, Robert V., *The Nature of Communism.* New York: Random House, 1962. Pp. 398.

DELAYE, Emile, *What is Communism?* Translated by Bernard F. SCHUMACHER. St. Louis, Missouri: Herder, 1938. Pp. 191. Critical.

GAY, Peter, *The Dilemma of Democratic Socialism: Eduard Bernstein's Challenge to Marx.* New York: Columbia University Press, 1952. Pp. 334.

GREFTHEN, E. A., *Communism and Christianity: Their Differences and Their Relation to Socialism*. Washington, D. C.: Public Affairs Press, 1952. Pp. 16.

HUNT, Robert Nigel Carew, *Marxism Past and Present*. New York: The Macmillan Co., 1955. Pp. 180.

LEWIS, John, *Marxism and Irrationalists*. London: Lawrence, 1955. Pp. 142.

MAURIAC and others (symposium), *Communism and Christians*. Westminster, Maryland: Newman Press, 1949. Pp. 293. Critical.

MONNEROT, Jules, *The Sociology of Communism*. Translated by Jane DEGRAS and Richard REES. London: G. Allen and Unwin, 1953. Pp. 339.

——, *Sociology and Psychology of Communism*. Translated by Jane DEGRAS and Richard REES. Boston, Massachusetts: Beacon Press, 1953. Pp. 339.

TREADGOLD, Donald Warren, *Lenin and His Rivals: The Struggle for Russia's Future, 1898-1906*. New York: Praeger, 1955. Pp. 291.

WOLFE, Bertram David, *What Is Communist Opposition ?* 2nd ed. New York: Communist Party U.S.A., 1933. Pp. 52.

——, *Civil War in Spain*. New York: Workers Age Publishers, 1937. Pp. 112.

——, *Three Who Made the Revolution: A Biographical History*. New York: Dial Press, 1948. Pp. 661.

——, *Krushchev and Stalin's Ghost*. New York: Praeger, 1957. Pp. 322.

——, *Communist Totalitarianism: Keys to the Soviet System*. Revised edition. Boston, Massachusetts: Beacon Press, 1961. Pp. 328. First published in 1956.

In Other Languages

AZIZJAN, Ateik K., *Über das Werk J. W. Stalins* «Marxismus und Nazionale Frage». Berlin: Dietz, 1952. Pp. 79.

BIGO, Pierre, *Marxisme et humanisme: Introduction à l'œuvre économique de Karl Marx*. Paris: Presses universitaires de France, 1953. Pp. XXXII, 269.

BONNEL, P., «Signification du socialisme democratique», *Revue socialiste* (Paris), October, 1953, pp. 204 ff.

FALK, Heinrich, *Die ideologischen Grundlagen der Kommunismus*. Munich: Olzog, 1961. Pp. 154.

INGENSAND, Harald, *Die Ideologie des Sowjetkommunismus. Philosophische Lehren*. Hannover: Verlag für Literatur und Zeitgeschehen, 1962. Pp. 96.

MANCINI, Arturo, *Il collettivisimo nella storia e nella dottrina*. Milan: G. Intelisano, 1954. Pp. 242.

SAGER, Peter, *Die theoretischen Grundlagen des Stalinismus, ihre Auswirkungen auf die Wirtschaftspolitik der Sowjetunion*. Bern: Haupt, 1953. Pp. 99.

SOLERI, Giacomo, «Sulla morale del communismo marxista», *Sapienza* (Buenos Aires), 1961, pp. 213-246.

SOCIAL STRUCTURE AND DEMOGRAPHY

ANDERSON, C. Arnold, «Trends in Rural Sociology», in Robert K. MERTON et al. (eds.), *Sociology Today: Problems and Prospects* (New York): Basic Books, 1959), pp. 360-375.

BROOM, Leonard, «Social Differentiation and Stratification», in Robert
    K. MERTON et al. (eds.), Sociology Today: Problems and Prospects
    (New York: Basic Books, 1959), pp. 429-441.
DAVIS, Kingsley, «The Sociology of Demographic Behavior», in Robert
    K. MERTON et al. (eds), Sociology Today: Problems and Prospects
    (New York: Basic Books, 1959), pp. 309-333.
GOULDNER, Alvin W., «Organizational Analysis», in Robert K. MERTON et al.
    (eds.), Sociology Today: Problems and Prospects (New York: Basic
    Books, 1959), pp. 400-428.
HUGHES, Everett Ch., «The Study of Occupations», in Robert K. MERTON et al.
    (eds.), Sociology Today: Problems and Prospects (New York: Basic
    Books, 1959), pp. 442-458.
SIMPSON, George E. and YINGER, J. Milton, «The Sociology and Race and
    Ethnic Relations», in Robert K. MERTON et al. (eds.), Sociology Today:
    Problems and Prospects (New York: Basic Books, 1959), pp. 376-399.
SJOBERG, Gideon, «Comparative Urban Sociology», in Robert K. MERTON et
    al. (eds.), Sociology Today: Problems and Prospects (New York:
    Basic Books, 1959), pp. 334-359.

SOCIOLOGY AND ART

In English

BARNETT, James H., «The Sociology of Art», in Robert K. MERTON et al. (eds.),
    Sociology Today: Preblems and Prospects (New York: Basic Books,
    1959), pp. 197-214.
DUNCAN, Hugh Dalziel, Language and Literature in Society. Chicago: Uni-
    versity of Chicago Press, 1953. Pp. XV, 262.
EDMAN, Irwin, Arts and the Man. New York: New American Library, 1949.
    Pp. 246.
GOTTSCHALK, D. W., Art and the Social Order. Chicago: University of Chi-
    cago Press, 1947.
GROSSE, Ernst, The Beginnings of Art. New York: D. Appleton, 1914.
HARAP, Louis, Social Roots of the Arts. New York: International Publishers,
    1949. Pp. 192.
HAUSER, Arnold, The Social History of Art. 2 vols. New York: Vintage
    Books, 1957.
KALLEN, Horace Meyer, Art and Freedom: A Historical and Bibliographical
    Interpretation of the Relations between the Ideas of Beauty, Use and
    Freedom in Western Civilization from the Greeks to the Present Day.
    2 vols. New York: Duell, Sloane and Pearce, 1942.
LOWENTHAL, Leo, Literature and the Image of Man: Sociological Studies of
    the European Drama and Novel, 1600-1900. Boston, Massachusetts:
    Beacon Press, 1957. Pp. 242.
MUELLER, John H., The American Symphony Orchestra: A Social History of
    Musical Taste. Bloomington, Indiana: Indiana University Press, 1951.
    Pp. XII, 437.

Mukerjee, Radhakamal, *The Social Function of Art.* New York: Philosophical Library, 1954. Pp. XXII, 289.

Plekhanov, G. V., *Art and Social Life.* Ed. by A. Rothstein. London: Lawrence and Wishert, 1953. Pp. 235.

Read, Herbert, *Art and Society.* New York: The Macmillan Co., 1937. Pp. XIX, 282.

Schücking, Levin, *The Sociology of Literary Taste.* Routledge and Kegan Paul, 1944. Pp. V, 78.

Weber, Max, *The Rational and Social Foundations of Music.* Translated and edited by D. Martindali and J. Riedel. Carbondale, Illinois: Southern Illinois University Press, 1958. Pp. 148.

In Other Languages

Lalo, Charles, *L'art et la vie sociale.* Paris: Doin, 1921. Pp. 378.

Needham, H. A., *Le développement de l'esthétique sociologique en France et en Angleterre au XIXe siècle.* Paris: Champion, 1926. Pp. 331.

Silbermann, Alphonse, *Introduction à une sociologie de la musique.* Translated by Pierre Billard. Paris: Presses Universitaires de France, 1955. Pp. 225.

Staël-Holstein, Anne L. G., *De la litterature considérée dans ses rapports avec les institutions sociales.* Paris: Charpentier, 1842. Pp. IV, 533.

SOCIOLOGY AND EDUCATION

Brim, Orville G., Jr., *Sociology and the Field of Education.* New York: Russell Sage, 1958. Pp. 93.

Brookover, Wilbur A., *A Sociology of Education.* New York: American Book Co., 1955. Pp. 435.

Elsbree, Willard S., *The American Teacher.* New York: American Book Co., 1939. Pp. IX, 566.

Gordon, C. Wayne, *The Social System of the High School.* New York: The Macmillan Co., 1957. Pp. 184.

Greenhoe, Florence, *Community Contracts and Participation of Teachers.* Washington, D. C.: American Council of Public Affairs, 1941. Pp. 91.

Gross, Neal, «The Sociology of Education», in Robert K. Merton et al. (eds.), *Sociology Today: Problems and Prospects* (New York: Basic Books, 1959), pp. 128-152.

Havighurst, Robert J. and Neugarten, Bernice L., *Society and Education.* Englewood Cliffs, New Jersey: Allyn and Bacon, 1957. Pp. 465.

Huggett, Albert J. and Stinnett, T. M., *Professional Problems of Teachers.* New York: The Macmillan Co., 1956. Pp. 468.

Jenkins, David H. and Lippitt, Ronald, *Interpersonal Perceptions of Teachers, Students and Parents.* Washington, D. C.: National Education Association, 1951. Pp. 119.

Robbins, Florence G., *Educational Sociology.* New York: Henry Holt, 1953. Pp. 529.

SHERIFF, Mazafer and Sheriff, Carolyn W., *Problems of Youth: Transition to Adulthood in a Changing World.* Chicago, Illinois: Aldine Publishing Co., 1965. Pp. 352.

STILES, Lindley J. (ed.), *The Teacher's Role in American Society.* New York: Harper, 1957. Pp. XXI, 298.

WALLER, Willard, *The Sociology of Teaching.* New York: John Wiley, 1932. Pp. XIV, 467.

SOCIOLOGY AND KNOWLEDGE

See Sociology and Science, below, p. 276.

ADLER, Franz, «A Quantitative Study in Sociology of Knowledge», *American Sociological Review,* 1954, pp. 42-48. Logical positivism.

CHILD, Arthur, «The Theoretical Possibility of the Sociology of Knowledge», *Ethics,* 1940-1941, pp. 392-418.

——, «The Problems of Imputation Resolved», *Ethics,* 1934-1944, pp. 96-109.

COSER, Lewis A., *Men of Ideas: A Sociologist's View.* New York: The Free Press (Macmillan), 1965. Pp. XVIII, 374.

DURKHEIM, Emile, — see Method, above, p. 263.

FICHTE, J. G., «The Vocation of the Scholar», in *The Popular Works of Johann Gottlieb Fichte,* translated by William SMITH (2 vols. London: J. Chapman, 1848-1849), Vol. I.

——, *The Destination of Man.* Translated by Percy SINNETT. London: Chapman, 1846. Pp. 128.

FYVEL, T. R., *Intellectuals Today: Problems in a Changing Society.* New York: Schocken Books, 1968.

HOROWITZ, Irving Louis, *Philosophy, Science, and the Sociology of Knowledge.* Springfield, Illinois: Charles C. Thomas, 1961. Pp. 192. See methods, above, p. 263.

MANNHEIM, Karl, *Essays on the Sociology of Knowledge.* Ed. by Paul Kecskemeti. New York: Oxford University Press, 1952. Pp. 327.

MAQUET, Jacques Jérôme Pierre, *Sociologie de la connaissance.* Louvain: É. Nauwelaerts, 1951. Pp. 360. Translated by John F. LOCKE, *The Sociology of Knowledge: Its Structure and Its Relation to the Philosophy of Knowledge.* Boston: Beacon Press, 1951. Pp. XIX, 318. Critical analysis of the views of K. Mannheim and P. A. Sorokin.

MONTESQUIEU DE, Ch., — see Law, above, Chapter, III, 3 Modern, p. 193.

PARETO, Vilfredo, — see Systematic Studies, above, p. 233.

EISERMANN, Gottfried, «Vilfredo Pareto als Wissenssoziologe», *Kyklos* (Bern), 1962, pp. 427-464.

STARK, Werner, *The Sociology of Knowledge: An Essay in Aid of a Deeper Understanding of the History of Ideas.* Chicago: The Free Press of Glencoe, 1958. Pp. 356. See Systematic, above, 233; Montesquieu, above, p. 193.

——, «The Conservative Tradition in the Sociology of Knowledge», *Kyklos* (Bern), 1960, pp. 99-101.

——, «The Sociology of Knowledge and the Problem of Ethics», in *Transactions of the Fourth World Congress of Sociology*, Vol. IV. London, 1959.

——, «Die idealistische Geschichtauffassung und die Wissenssoziologie», *Archiv für Rechts- und Sozialphilosophie* (Berlin), 1961, pp. 355-374.

WEBER, Max, — see above, p. 75.

ZNANIECKI, Florian, *The Social Role of the Man of Knowledge*. New York: Columbia University Press, 1940. Pp. 212.

BARTH, Hans, *Wahrheit und Ideologie*. Zürich: Manesse Verlag Conzett und Huber, 1945. Pp. 350. See Nietzsche, above, p. 29.

GRÜNWALD, Ernst, *Das Problem der Soziologie des Wissens*. Vienna: Wilhelm Braumüller, 1934. Pp. VIII, 279.

LIEBER, Hans-Joachim, *Wissen und Gesellschaft. Die Probleme der Wissenssoziologie*. Tübingen: Niemeyer, 1952. Pp. 166.

LUKÁCS, Georg, *Geschichte und Klassenbewusstsein*. Berlin: Malik, 1923. Classic. See Index, below.

RÜSCHMEYER, Dietrich, *Probleme der Wissenssoziologie*. Cologne: 1958. Empirical approach.

SCHELER, Max Ferdinand (ed.), *Schriften zur Soziologie und Weltanschauungslehre*. 3 vols. Leipzig: Der Neue Geist Verlag, 1923-1924.

——, *Die Wissens Formen und die Gesellschaft. Probleme einer Soziologie des Wissens*. Leipzig: Der Neue Geist Verlag, 1926. Pp. XI, 565. Phenomenological approach; classic. See above, p. 237.

SOCIOLOGY AND LAW

See Law, above, Ch. III, 5, p. 162.

COHEN, Julius, ROBSON, R. A. H. and BATES Ollour, *Parental Authority: The Community and the Law*. New Brunswick, New Jersey: Rutgers University Press, 1958. Pp. 301. Empirical approach. See Authority, above Chapter IV, 5, p. 213.

DURKHEIM, Émile, *De la division du travail social*. Paris: A. Alcan, 1893. Pp. X, 471. English translation by G. SIMPSON, *The Division of Labor in Society*. Glencoe, Illinois: Free Press, 1952. See also Method, above.

ERLICH, Eugen, *Grundlegung der Soziologie des Rechts*. Munich: Duncker und Humblot, 1913. Pp. 409. English translation by Walter L. MOLL, *Fundamental Principles of the Sociology of Law*. Cambridge, Massachusetts: Harvard University Press, 1936. Pp. XXXVI, 541.

FRIEDMANN, Wolfgang Gaston, *Law in a Changing Society*. Berkeley, California: University of California Press, 1959. Pp. XXVI, 522.

GURVITCH, Georges D., *Sociology of Law*. New York: Philosophical Library, 1942. Pp. XX, 309.

LOUGHERY, Bernard Francis, *Parental Rights in American Educational Law*. 2nd ed. Washington, D. C.: Catholic University of America, 1957. Pp. 248.

POUND, Roscoe, «The Limits of Effective Legal Action», *International Journal of Ethics*, 1917, pp. 150-167.

——, *Jurisprudence*. 5 vols. St. Paul, Minnesota: West Publishing Company, 1959.

SAWER, Geoffrey, *Law in Society*. New York: Oxford University Press, 1965. Pp. 215.

SELZNICK, Philip, «The Sociology of Law», in Robert K. MERTON *et al.* (eds.), *Sociology Today: Problems and Prospects* (New York: Basic Books, 1959), pp. 115-127.

——, «Sociology of Law», in *The Encyclopedia of Philosophy* (8 vols. New York: The Macmillan and Co., 1967), Vol. VII, pp. 478-480.

STONE, Julius, *Human Law and Human Justice*. Stanford: Stanford University Press, 1965. Pp. XXIII, 415.

——, *Social Dimensions of Law and Justice*. Stanford: Stanford University Press, 1966.

——, *Law and the Social Science in the Second Half Century*. New York: Oxford University Press, 1966. Pp. 121.

TIMASHEFF, Nicholas, S., *An Introduction to the Sociology of Law*. Cambridge, Massachusetts: Harvard University Press, 1939. Pp. XIV, 418.

WEBER, Max, — see above, p. 75.

SOCIOLOGY AND MEDICINE

CASTIGLIONI, Arturo, *A History of Medicine*. Translated by E. B. KRUMBHAAR. New York: A. Knopf, 1941.

CLAUSEN, John A., *Sociology and the Field of Mental Health*. New York: Russell Sage Foundation, 1956. Pp. 62.

FREEMAN, Howard E. and REEDER, Leo G., «Medical Sociology: A Review of the Literature», *American Sociological Review* (Washington, D.C.), 1957, pp. 73-81.

GRINKER, Ray R., *Psychosomatic Research*. New York: W. W. Norton and Co., 1953. Pp. 208.

MERTON, R. K., READER, G. G. and KENDALL, P. L. (eds.), *The Student Physician*. Cambridge, Massachusetts: Harvard University Press, 1957. Pp. 360.

PAUL, Benjamin D. (ed.), *Health, Culture and Community*. New York: Russell Sage Foundation, 1955. Pp. VIII, 493.

READER, George G. and Goss, Mary E. W., «The Sociology of Medicine», in Robert K. Merton *et al.* (eds.), *Sociology Today: Problems and Prospects* (New York: Basic Books, 1959), pp. 229-246.

SAUNDERS, Lyle, *Cultural Differences and Medical Care*. New York: Russell Sage Foundation, 1954. Pp. 317.

SCHEFF, Thomas J., *Being Mentally Ill: A Sociological Theory*. Chicago, Illinois: Aldine Publishing Co., 1966. Pp. 192.

SHRYOCK, Richard H., *The Development of Modern Medicine*. New York: A. KNOPF, 1947. Pp. XV, 457. First published in 1936.

SIMMONS, Leo W. and WOLFF, Harold G., *Social Science in Medicine*. New York: Russell Sage Foundation, 1954. Pp. 254.

STERN, B. J., *Social Factors in Medical Progress*. New York: Columbia University Press, 1927. Pp. 136.

SOCIOLOGY AND POLITICS

See Law, above, Ch. III; State, above, Ch. IV, 5, p. 223.

BENDIX, R. and LIPSET, S. M., «Political Sociology — A Trend Report and Bibliography», *Current Sociology* (Oxford, England), 1957, pp. 79-169.

BLAU, Peter, *Bureaucracy in Modern Society*. New York: Random House, 1956. Pp. 127.

COSER, Lewis A., *Political Sociology: Selected Essays*. New York: Harper and Raw (Torchbooks), 1967. Pp. 274.

DRUCKER, Peter, *The New Society: The Anatomy of Industrial Order*. New York: Harper, 1950. Pp. IX, 356.

HEBERLE, R., *Social Movements: An Introduction to Political Sociology*. New York: Appleton-Century-Crofts, 1951. Pp. 478.

LIPSET, Seymour M., «Political Sociology», in Robert K. MERTON *et al.* (eds.), *Sociology Today* (New York: Basic Books, Inc., 1959), pp. 81-114.

NISBET, Robert, *The Quest for Community: A study in the Ethics of Order and Freedom*. New York: Oxford University Press, 1953. Pp. 303.

SOCIOLOGY OF RELIGION

See Christianity, above, Ch. IV, 5, p. 214.

BERKOWITZ, I. and JOHNSON, J. EDMUND, *Social Scientific Studies of Religion: A Bibliography*. Pittsburgh Press, 1967. Pp. 264.

BLANCHARD, Paul, *American Freedom and Catholic Power*. Boston, Massachusetts: Beacon Press, 1951.

DUNLAP, Knight, *Religion: Its Functions in Human Life*. New York: McGraw-Hill, 1946. Pp. XI, 262.

DURKHEIM, Émile, *The Elementary Forms of the Religious Life*. London: G. Allen and Unwin, 1915. Pp. XI, 456. See also Index, below.

FICHTER, Joseph, *Social Relations in the Urban Parish*. Chicago: University of Chicago Press, 1954. Pp. 263.

GLOCK, Charles Y., *Towards a Typology of Religious Orientation*. New York: Columbia University, Bureau of Applied Social Research, 1954.

——, «The Sociology of Religion», in Robert K. MERTON *et al.* (eds.), *Sociology Today: Problems and Prospects* (New York: Basic Books, 1959), pp. 153-177.

GUYAU, Jean Marie, *L'irreligion de l'avenir, étude sociologique*. Paris: F. Alcan, 1890. Pp. XXVIII, 480. English translation, *The Non-Religion of the Future, a Sociological Study*. New York: Schocken Books, 1962. Pp. 538.

HERBERG, Will, *Protestant, Catholic, Jew*. Garden City, New York: Doubleday, 1955. Pp. 320.

HOULT, Thomas F., *The Sociology of Religion*. New York: Dryden Press, 1958. Pp. 436.

JOLLAND, T. G., *The Origin and Evolution of the Christian Church*. London: Hutchinson's University Library, 1950.

KANE, John J., *Catholic-Protestant Conflict in America*. Chicago: Henry Regnery, 1955. Pp. 244.

KELLY, Robert L., *Theological Education in America*. George H. Doran, 1924. Pp. XIX, 456.

LING, Trevor, *Buddha, Marx and God*. New York: St. Martin's Press, 1967. Pp. 240.

MARSHALL, L. H., *The Challenge of New Testament Ethics*. New York: St. Martin's Press, 1967. Pp. 374. The New Testament and the needs of the 20th century.

MAY Mark A., *Institutions That Train Ministers*. New York: Institute of Social and Religious Research, 1923.

NIEBUHR, H. Richard, *The Social Sources of Denominationalism*. New York: Holt, 1929. Pp. VIII, 304.

NOTTINGHAM, Elizabeth K., *Religion and Society*. Garden City, New York: Doubleday, 1954. Pp. 84.

SKLARE, Marshall (ed.), *The Jews: Social Patterns of an American Group*. Chicago: Free Press of Glencoe, 1958. Pp. 1669.

TAWNEY, R. H., *Religion and the Rise of Capitalism*. New York: Penguin Books, 1947. Pp. 280.

TROELTSCH, E., *The Social Teaching of the Christian Churches*. 2 vols. New York: The Macmillan Co., 1932.

WACH, Joachim, *Sociology of Religion*. Chicago: University of Chicago Press, 1944. Pp. XII, 418.

——, *Religions-soziologie*. Ed. by H. SCHOECK. Tübingen: Mohr, 1951. Pp. X, 461.

WEBER, Max, *The Protestant Ethic and the Spirit of Capitalism*. New York: Charles Scribner's Sons, 1930. Pp. XI, 292.

YINGER, Milton J., *Religion, Society and the Individual*. New York: The Macmillan Co., 1957. Pp. 655.

——, *Religion in the Struggle for Power*. Durham, North Carolina: Duke University Press, 1946. Pp. XIX, 275.

SOCIOLOGY AND SCIENCE

See Sociology and Knowledge, above.

BARBER, Bernard, *Science and the Social Order*. Chicago: Free Press, 1952. Pp. 288.

——, «The Sociology of Science», in Robert K. MERTON *et al.* (eds.), *Sociology Today: Problems and Prospects* (New York: Basic Books, 1959), pp. 215-228.

BARBER, Bernard and HIRSCH, Walter, *The Sociology of Science*. New York: The Free Press of Glencoe, 1962. Pp. 662.

CROWTHER, J. G., *The Social Relations of Science*. New York: The Macmillan and Co., 1941. Pp. XXXII, 665.

GILFILLAN, S. C., *The Sociology of Invention*. Chicago: Follett Publishing Co., 1935. Pp. XIII, 185.

KNAPP, R. H. and GOODRICH, H. B., *Origins of American Scientists*. Chicago: University of Chicago Press, 1952. Pp. XIV, 450.

LILLEY, S., *Men, Machines and History*. London: Cobbett Press, 1948. Pp. 240.

LINDSAY, Robert B., *The Role of Science in Civilization*. New York: Harper and Row, 1963. Pp. 318.

MILLS, John, *The Engineer in Society*. Princeton, New Jersey: D. Van Nostrand, 1946. Pp. XIX, 196.

OBLER, Paul, and ESTRIN, Herman, (eds.), *The New Scientist*. Garden City, New York: Doubleday, 1962. Pp. 316.

OGBURN, W. F., *The Social Effects of Aviation*. Boston, Massachusetts: Houghton Mifflin, 1946. Pp. VI, 755.

VAVOLIS, Alexander and COLVER, A. Wayne, *Science and Society*. San Francisco, California: Holden-Day, 1966. Pp. 160.

WOLFLE, Deal, *Science and Public Policy*. Lincoln, Nebraska: University of Nebraska, 1959. Pp. 81.

WOOLF, Harry (ed.), *Science as a Cultural Force*. Baltimore: Johns Hopkins Press, 1964. Pp. VIII, 110. The Shell Companies Foundation Lectures.

ZNANIECKI, Florian, *The Social Role of the Man of Knowledge*. New York: Columbia University Press, 1941. Pp. 212.

SOCIOLOGISM

Sociologism is general intellectual tendency to consider social phenomena (law, ethics, religion, language, behavior) as a result of a social life of men.

A. Comte considered sociology as supreme science.
See above, p. 241.

BARTH, Paul, *Die Philosophie der Geschichte als Sociologie*. Leipzig: O. R. Reisland, 1897. Pp. XVI, 396. See above, 2 c, p. 236.

FREYER, Hans, *Soziologie als Wirklichkeitwissenschaft. Logische Grundlegung des Systems der Soziologie*. 2nd ed. Stuttgart: Teubner, 1964. Pp. IV, 310. First published in 1930. See Philosophy, above, 2 c, p. 237.

VALUE

See Philosophy, above, 2, p. 234.

ARROW, Kenneth J., *Social Choice and Individual Values*. 2nd ed. New York: Wiley, 1963. Pp. 125.

MYRDAL, Gunnar, *Value in Social Theory*. London: Longmans, 1958. Pp. 328.

ALBERT, Hans, «Das Wertproblem in den Sozialwissenschaften», *Schweizerische Zeitschrift für Volkswirtschaft und Statistik*, 1958, pp. 335-340.

CRONER, F., «Wissenschaftlogik und Wertproblematik», *Kölner Zeitschrift für Soziologie und Sozialpsychologie* (Cologne), 1964, pp. 327-341.

6. PERIODICALS

(a) General

In English

American Sociological Review. Ed. by the American Sociological Society. New York: New York University (Washington Square), 1936-. *Index* in 1961-.
Inquiry: An International Journal of Philosophy and the Social Sciences. Oslo, Norway: Universitetsforlaget (P. O. Box 307, Blindern), 1957-.
American Sociological Review. Ed. by American Sociological Society. New York: New York University (Washington Square), 1936-.
Current Sociology. Ed. by International Sociological Associations. Oxford: Basil Blackwell, 1952-.
Journal of Social Issues. Ed. by the Society for the Psychological Study of Social Issues. Ann Arbor, Michigan: University of Michigan, 1945-.
Journal of Social Philosophy: A Quarterly Devoted to a Philosophic Synthesis of the Social Sciences. New York: Hamilton Grange Station, 1935-1941. Title varies.
Sociological Review. Keele, Staffordshire: University College of North Staffordshire, 1908-.
Social Forces: A Scientific Medium of Social Study and Interpretation. Baltimore, Maryland: Williams and Wilkings (428 E. Preston St.), 1922-.

In Other Languages

L'année sociologique. Paris: F. Alcan, 1934-.
Archiv für Geschichte der Philosophie und Sociologie. Berlin: W. De Gruyter, 1888-.
Archiv für Rechts- und Sozialphilosophie. Berlin-Grunewald: W. Rothschild, 1907-.
Archiv für Sozialgeschichte. Hannover: Verlag fur Literatur und Zeitgeschehen, 1961-.
Cahiers internationaux de sociologie. Paris: École pratique des hautes études, 1951-.
Jahrbuch für Sozialwissenschaft und Sozialpolitik. Zürich, 1879-.
Kyklos. Internationale Zeitschrift für Sozialwissenschaft. Bern, 1947-.
Revue international de sociologie. Paris: V. Giard et E. Brière, 1893-1939.
Rivista di sociologia. Rome: Istituto di sociologia, 1963-.
Zeitschrift für Sozialwissenschaft. Berlin: J. Wolf, L. Pohle, 1910-.

(b) Special

In English

The American Journal of Sociology. Chicago: University of Chicago Press (5750 Ellis Ave.,) 1895-.
American Sociological Review. New York: New York University (Washington Square), 1936-.
British Journal of Sociology. London: Routledge and Kegan Paul, 1950-.
International Journal of Comparative Sociology. Dharwar, India: Karnatak University, 1959-.
International Journal of Sociology and Social Anthropology. Leiden, Holland: .E J. Brill, 1959-.
British Journal of Social Psychology. Provincetown, Massachusetts: The Journal Press, 1929-.
Journal of Social Psychology International. Ed. by The Association for Social Psychology. Washington, D. C.: Adams Mill Rd., N. W., 1961-.
Rural Sociology. Ed. by the Rural Sociological Society. Ithaca, New York: Cornell University, Department of Rural Sociology, 1936-.
Sociometry: A Journal of Research in Social Psychology. Ed. by the American Sociological Association. New York: Washington Square, 1937-.
The Eugenics Quarterly. New York: 230 Park Ave., 1954-.
The Eugenic Review. Oxford, England: Pergamon Press, 1909-.

In Other Languages

Archiv für Rassen und Gesellschafts-Biologie. Berlin: Verlag der Archive-Gesellschaft, 1904-.
Kölner, Vierteljahrshefte für Soziologie. Munich: Duncker und Humblot, 1921-.
Rivista italiana di Sociologia. Rome: Bocca, 1897-.

INDEX

Italics indicate more specific treatment of the author.

308   INDEX

D/1969/0081/4

Reprint in Belgium

par

Vander

rue de l'Eglise, 15
5998 — Beauvechain